The Politics of Heritage from Madras to Chennai

The Politics of Heritage from Madras to Chennai

Mary E. Hancock

Indiana University Press
BLOOMINGTON · INDIANAPOLIS

This book is a publication of

Indiana University Press
601 North Morton Street
Bloomington, IN 47404-3797 USA

http://iupress.indiana.edu

Telephone orders 800-842-6796
Fax orders 812-855-7931
Orders by e-mail iuporder@indiana.edu

The paper used in this publication meets the minimum requirements of American National Standard for Information Sciences—Permanence of Paper for Printed Library Materials, ANSI Z39.48-1984.

Manufactured in the United States of America

Library of Congress Cataloging-in-Publication Data

Hancock, Mary.
The politics of heritage from Madras to Chennai / Mary E. Hancock.
p. cm.
Includes bibliographical references and index.
ISBN 978-0-253-35223-1 (cloth : alk. paper) 1. Collective memory—India—Madras. 2. Cultural property—India—Madras. 3. Madras (India)—Cultural policy. I. Title.
DS486.M2H36 2008
306.0954'82—dc22

2008009116

1 2 3 4 5 13 12 11 10 09 08

Instead of condescending to heritage, or joining in the chorus of recrimination and complaint against it, it might be more profitable for historians to speculate on the sources of its energies and strength.

Raphael Samuel, *Theatres of Memory,* Volume 1: *Past and Present in Contemporary Culture*

I was neither born nor bred here.
But I know this city
    of casuarina and tart mango slices,
    gritty with salt and chilli:
    and the truant sands of the Marina
. . . and a language as intimate as the taste
of sarasaparilla pickle, the recipe lost,
the sour cadences as comforting
as home. . . .
City that creeps up on me
just when I'm about to affirm
world citizenship.

Arundhathi Subramaniam, "Madras"

Contents

Acknowledgments

More than two decades have passed since my first visit to India in 1985, and over that time the cultural, political, and economic stakes in "tradition"—its definition, ownership, mediation—have sharpened. The questions I explore in this book arose within this ferment, prodded as much by the reflectivity associated with India's fiftieth anniversary of independence as by the consumerist pleasures that heritage increasingly seemed to afford. While I, as author, bear the full responsibility for this book's content, I am indebted to the colleagues and friends in India and the United States who helped me appreciate Chennai's past, both its mutability and its sometimes vibrant presence, and thus helped shape my inquiry from its inception: S. Theodore Baskaran, V. R. Devika, Sara Dickey, Vincent D'Souza, John Harriss, Rani and Ranjith Henry, Rangaswamy Ilango, Gene Irschick, Aarthi Kawlra, P. T. Krishnan, Kalpana Kumar, Tara Murali, S. Muthiah, Janaki Nair, M. S. S. Pandian, Martha Selby, Deborah Thiagarajan, A. Srivathsan, and Joanne Waghorne. My colleagues in the history department at the University of California, Santa Barbara (UCSB), and especially the faculty, staff, and students affiliated with *The Public Historian*, which I had the privilege of editing from 2004 to 2006, were unfailingly encouraging and helped me think comparatively about Chennai's politics of heritage. Tamar Gordon was an engaged interlocutor, who also helped me see Chennai's stories in a global context. I must also mention the generosity of several kind friends in Chennai—Mr. and Mrs. S. V. Raman, along with their children and grandchildren, and Mrs. Chrystal Easdon and the late Rodney Easdon—who sustained me with conversations, shared meals, practical advice and assistance and humor.

This book is based on ethnographic and archival research conducted in Chennai from August to December 1996 and from September 1999 to May 2000. Follow-up interviews (in-person, telephone, and e-mail) were conducted between 2003 and 2007. Ethnographic research included interviews with leaders, employees, and volunteer members of private conservation associations, including the Chennai chapter of the Indian National Trust for Art and Cultural Heritage (INTACH), Exnora, the C. P. Ramaswamy Environmental Education Center, the Madras Craft Foundation, the Citizen, Consumer, and Civic Action Group, the Ramanujan Museum and Math Education Center, the National Folklore Support

Center, and the Roja Muthiah Research Library; I met, also, with representatives of organizations (the All-India Democratic Women's Association, the People's Union for Civil Liberties, the National Campaign for Dalit Rights and the International Dr. Ambedkar Centenary Movement) whose concerns encompassed public historical representation. I attended INTACH meetings, public and private, and interviewed state and municipal government officials associated with regional planning and development agencies. I visited all the museums, memorials, and public memory sites discussed in the book on multiple occasions, alone or in the company of staff or volunteer affiliates; I interviewed site directors, curators, volunteers, and employees, as well as persons residing near heritage sites and districts. Fifteen conservation or neo-traditionalist architects/builders (seven of whom were INTACH project consultants) were interviewed. My survey of Chennai's tourism industry included interviews with twenty-seven tour guides, six managers and owners, and three government officials. Additional archival research was undertaken at the Library of Congress, Washington, D.C., in May 1998 and from July 2004 through July 2005; at the University of Chicago's Regenstein Library in June 1998; and at the British Library in July 2000. My research and writing were supported by a Fulbright-Hays Faculty Research Abroad award from the U.S. Department of Education (1999–2000), a Residential Fellowship from the Woodrow Wilson International Center for Scholars (2004–2005), a Regents Humanities Fellowship from the University of California, Santa Barbara, and two Faculty Research Grants, also from UCSB. In India, I was privileged to be affiliated with the Madras Institute of Development Studies in Chennai. I gratefully acknowledge the generous support of all these agencies and institutions.

Portions of this book had an early life as conference presentations. For their enthusiasm and productive provocation, I am grateful to audiences at the Department of History at UCSB, the University of California–Berkeley, the University of Texas–Austin, the University of Neuchatel (Switzerland), the University of Applied Sciences, Schwaebisch Hall (Germany), the Free University, Berlin, and the Prakrit Foundation, Chennai.

I benefited from the insightful comments of Ann Hardgrove and Smriti Srinivas, both of whom read an early draft of the book—I thank them for their constructive criticism and helpful suggestions. I am indebted to my sponsoring editor, Rebecca Tolen, for her advice, guidance, and interest; I also thank James Brooks and Catherine Cocks, of SAR Press, who provided early encouragement and support for this project. I am grateful to Jim Craine, who found time, amid finishing a dissertation, to prepare the maps; I thank A. Srivathsan for the provision of INTACH reports and images. Finally, my partner, Toby Lazarowitz, deserves loving thanks for reading drafts of each chapter, always with a fresh eye and for sustaining my enthusiasm with his own over the long process of research and writing.

Portions of chapter 6 originally appeared in "Subjects of Heritage in Urban Southern India," *Environment and Planning D: Society and Space*, 20 (2002): 693–717, and have been reprinted here with the permission of Pion Limited, London. Portions of chapter 4 originally appeared in "Modernities Remade: Hindu Temples and Their Publics in Southern India," *City and Society,* 14 (2002): 5–35, and have been reprinted here with the permission of the American Anthropological Association. Three of the illustrations reproduced here are from the British Library collections: they are "Government House, Fort St. George," an aquatint by Thomas and William Daniell (London, 1798), BL Shelfmark P944; "Western Entrance, Fort St. George," an aquatint by Thomas and William Daniell (London, 1798), BL Shelfmark P947; and "Limits of Madras, as fixed on the 2nd of November, 1798 . . . Scale of 1800 feet to an inch" (Madras: Survey Office, 1904), BL Shelfmark Maps 5470.(23). All have been reproduced with permission of the British Library.

Note on Transliteration and Pseudonyms

Tamil terms have been transliterated following the University of Madras Tamil Lexicon system; I have used the Kriyāviṉ Taṟkālattamiḻ Akarāti [Dictionary of Contemporary Tamil] as a guide for the spelling of most Tamil words. When standard, Anglicized forms for words exist, those usages (without diacritics) have been adopted. For the sake of readability, I have not transliterated place names, individual and group names, and proper nouns, using instead conventional, Anglicized spellings for those terms.

Some respondents requested anonymity and I have used pseudonyms for them. The first usage of a pseudonym is enclosed within quotation marks.

Abbreviations

AIA-DMK	All-India Annadurai–Dravida Munnetra Kazhagam
BJP	Bharatiya Janata Party
CISR	Council of Industrial and Scientific Research
CMDA	Chennai Metropolitan Development Authority
DK	Dravida Kazhagam
DMK	Dravida Munnetra Kazhagam
EVR	E. V. Ramasamy
HUDCO	India's Housing and Urban Development Corporation
INC	Indian National Congress
INTACH	Indian National Trust for Art and Cultural Heritage
MAPS	Madras Atomic Power Station
MCF	Madras Craft Foundation
MGR	M. G. Ramachandran
MMDA	Madras Metropolitan Development Authority
PAC	People's Architectural Commonweal
PWD	Public Works Departments
SC	Scheduled Castes
TNSCB	Tamil Nadu Slum Clearance Board
TTDC	Tamil Nadu Tourism Development Corporation

The Politics of Heritage from Madras to Chennai

1
Making the Past in a Global Present: Chennai's New Heritage

Christmas, 2004

News of the Indian Ocean tsunami flashes on my computer screen. Almost real-time images of confusion and agony appear in short order. I see women searching for missing children and battered fishing boats run aground. Soon, bloated corpses will be nudged to shore. After trying unsuccessfully to telephone, I rely (again) on the promises of electronic immediacy and send frantic e-mail messages to friends in Chennai. Within a couple of days, replies have arrived. I am relieved to hear that all are okay if rather shaken. The same cannot be said for the city's beachfront, much of it occupied by fishing communities and hut colonies. The destruction in Chennai, including more than two hundred casualties, was concentrated along its twenty kilometer shoreline. Although Chennai fared better than areas farther south and in Sri Lanka, the tragedy was compounded by the loss of motorboats, catamarans, baskets, and nets—all of which portended disaster for the livelihoods of many in the city's fishing communities.[1]

The tsunami struck India's eastern coast when I had nearly completed a draft of this book, and although I do not deal with that event in any detail, it has shaped the book's direction and lent urgency to some of its questions. On a personal level, my concerns about its devastating effects were sharpened by the fact that it struck a city I had called home for several extended periods from the mid-eighties on. And there was painful irony in the coincidence of my having just completed a chapter on Chennai's Marina Beach memorials as the wave's force overtook those very sites. More important than any personal coincidences, however, is that the tsunami's impact is not explicable outside the transformations in statecraft, culture, and political economy that India, like other postcolonial nation-states, has experienced in recent decades. Natural disasters are rarely natural in their genesis or effects and Chennai's commercial and industrial development, especially with the impetus of privatization and deregulation, contributed to conditions that exacerbated the effects of the 2004 tsunami. Beachfront commercial developments from tourist resorts to shrimp farms have led to the removal of the buffers such as mangrove swamps and casuarina stands that would have mitigated the wave's intensity and its inland reach. And like the redevelopment that has occasioned the resettlement of inner-city slumdwellers in the city's hinterland, the tsunami added fuel to existing efforts to relocate fishing groups from beachfront sites that were being eyed for lucrative commercial use and high-end residential development. The instant destruction of the tsunami, like that of the bulldozers used for street clearing and demolition, wiped away the material fabric of everyday life and livelihood with its embedded forms of remembrance, both the implicit memory of bodily habitus and the explicit memory of semantic understanding, even as it brought forth new memories.[2]

The tsunami was an exceptional event, scarring indelibly the places it struck. The creative destruction of global capitalism, however, is remaking many of those same cities, towns, and villages in both catastrophic and routine ways.[3] These transformations, while exacerbating the destructive impact of the tsunami and other such disasters, also echo the globalizing force of capital during earlier centuries of European colonial expansion. Then, as now, the collisions and confluences of knowledge, goods, persons, and spaces have demanded reorientations to both shared pasts and futures. Like the outbreaks of nostalgia that, according to Svetlana Boym, followed episodes of revolutionary change in Europe, so also has the radical restructuring of neoliberal globalization called forth a "yearning for a different time," not only for a glorious past, but also "for unrealized dreams of the past and visions of the future that became obsolete."[4] Such yearnings are congealed in the imagery, narratives, built form, bodily practices, and artifacts by which shared pasts are represented and through which memories together with aspirations are engendered. It is the making of the past—the creation of both spaces of the past and the knowledges and sentiments glossed as past-consciousness—in the present conjuncture of neoliberal globalization that this book explores.

Several broad questions thread the chapters together. As a group, they hinge on the relation between cultural memory and postcolonial statecraft, in particular, their intersecting and diverging social spaces represented in the memorials, monuments, and commemorative place names authorized by the state, as well as the heritage sites, museums, and themed cultural environments sponsored by private organizations and individuals.[5] It is within these intersecting spatial fields that collective identities and political institutions are reified, acquire force, and incite resistance in the daily lives of citizens. Unpacking these processes, however, requires more than attention to the encoding of authority; as important are the ways in which state projects intersect with what Halbwachs termed "social memory," the common landmarks that constitute a shared framework for individual recollection.[6] In this book I am concerned, on the one hand, with the nature of the state's institutional investment in spaces of public memory and in the ways that those investments themselves mark transformations in statecraft from the planned, welfare state of the fifties, sixties, and seventies to the neoliberal designs of the nineties. What occasions the state's creation of public memoryscapes, and what do those sites "do" within statecraft? How is the phenomenology of remembrance implicated in the dynamics of postcolonial statecraft? How, for example, do technologies of memory "hail" or interpellate subjects as "citizens"? On the other hand, I attend also to the claims on the past made by non-state actors, with the forms of cultural citizenship negotiated with and through public spaces of cultural memory. How are competing forms of ethnic, sectarian, class, or gendered belonging mediated through the work of memory? What forms of countermemory are deployed against—and outside—the state?

In the chapters that follow I explore these questions through investigations of Chennai's historical geography and its sites of cultural memory. Like those anthropologically minded historians who have charted the richness and dynamism of popular historical consciousness in the United States, I, a historically minded anthropologist, am interested in the processes by which past-consciousness is generated and how the past, as history, myth, personal biography, and memory, animates and inscribes futurity within life as it is lived.[7] By framing my topic as "past-consciousness," I intend to move past the rather tired debate on the relative value and proper domains of "history" and "memory," a debate in which history's textuality, objectivity, and secular underpinnings are set in opposition to the subjectivity, religiosity, and orality of memory.[8] While attentive to the different evidentiary bases, media, and effects of various representations of the past, I propose to treat both history and memory, along with myth, genealogy, and life story as competing modalities by which individual and collective pasts are objectified and made representable.[9] These modalities encompass the various cultural landscapes, artifacts, and built environments that represent the past and evoke affective responses to it, as well as the statutory measures pertaining to the declaration and preservation of heritage sites, the governmental and nongovernmental bodies that concern themselves with retrieval and representation of the past, and the popular and educational media that communicate about the past.

My focus extends, therefore, to both the political economic and phenomenological matrices in which pasts are conjured, materialized, lived in, and denounced. I bring cultural phenomena to bear in analyses of globality, but, rather than relying on the abstract notions of culture informing the work of theorists of globalization such as Jameson and Miyoshi, and Hardt and Negri, my book privileges culture as lived and thus spatialized experience, negotiated within contradictory political and ethical terrains of postcoloniality.[10] In this book, I ask why, how, and by whom pasts are remembered, concentrating on the ways that the spatial dimensions of memory and its practice have become increasingly implicated in the creative destruction of the urban landscape, the cycles of construction and deconstruction tied to the growth and contraction of capital, and the formation of transnational imaginaries within the spaces of national statecraft.

The "Now" and "Then" of Statecraft

Public sites and practices of cultural memory are generally understood to be implicated in governance in at least two ways. Such representations may be treated as contingent outcomes of political decisions as well as the grounds on which political action and institutions are conceived. At the same time, they are also the material media with which the state, the nation, and other communities of imagination—territorial, ethnic, gendered, and sectarian—are represented, narrated, and inhabited. Put differently, the spaces and practices of public memory are not only *subject to* control by markets and governing bodies; they serve also as crucial *representations of* the principles that undergird specific systems of governance. Indeed, they may be critical media for communication between the state and its citizenry. This is a crucial point but one that is sometimes lost in analyses focusing solely on the political economy of heritage. I argue, however, that sites of public memory are among the principal landscapes on which such work is done.[11] Such an analysis allows reflection upon the cultural mediation of state sovereignty, while providing an opportunity to prise open the bureaucratic apparatus of governance in which pasts are solicited, represented, and managed.

The direction I take in this book follows previous efforts to enculture the state. The cultural emplotment of state power was considered in early work by Cassirer and explored more systematically by Corrigan and Sayer, in their analysis of English state formation, and by Abrams in an often-cited essay on the relations between ideological representations of the state and the exercise of power in modern statecraft.[12] The state, maintained Abrams, was the amalgamation of the state system—the institutions for rule making, policy formation and implementation, governance, and so forth—and the state idea, the repository of images and practices at the center of political life. The latter, comprising emblems, ceremonies, ritual discourses, architectural spaces, and so forth, represent "the state" as a unitary institution and, more crucial, mask the forms of domination it exercises. Abrams's intervention was twofold: he sought a more accurate and broadly applicable definition of the state as both idea and system, but he also intended to explain why the task of defining it was fraught with difficulties and inconsistencies. Rather than attributing this ambiguity to inadequacies in scholarship, he argued that it was strategic, that it was itself the means by which power was masked. He asserted:

> The state is . . . a triumph of concealment. It conceals the real history and relations of subjection behind an a-historical mask of legitimating illusion; contrives to deny the existence of connections and conflicts which would if recognized be incompatible with the claimed autonomy and integration of the state. The real official secret, however, is the secret of the non-existence of the state.[13]

The state, understood rhetorically, was not as much a unified entity that preceded discourse as an *effect* of political discourse, created semiotically and meant to mask the instrumentalities by which it dominated society.

For Abrams, semiosis was significant mainly insofar as it concealed the state's institutional power. For subsequent interpreters, however, his notion of the "state idea" has served as a ground for productive inquiry, prompting questions about its particular historical and cultural forms, the means by which it is produced, and the affective charge that it carries. Timothy Mitchell, using Abrams's argument as point of departure, identified the "state effect" as an object of inquiry:

> We should address the state as an effect of mundane processes of spatial organization, temporal arrangement, functional specification, supervision and surveillance and representation that create the appearance of a world fundamentally divided into state and society or state and economy. . . . These are processes that create the effect of the state not only as an entity set apart from economy or society, but as a distinct dimension of structure, framework, codification, expertise, information, planning and intentionality.[14]

As generated in the domain of monuments and public memory, the state effect can both mask the state's power as well as produce the state in the imaginations of its officials, political leaders, and subjects, and engender complex affective ties.[15] Visual culture, understood as both culturally salient visual representations as well as practices of looking, is a crucial medium for the state effect.[16] For example, state sovereignty can be represented as "natural" and thus inevitable and encompassing through monumental images that liken the state to a mythologized body—by borrowing figures from myths and folktales or by representing bodies of historical figures in mythic trappings.[17] In Hindu South Asia, the implication of visuality in spatial practice acquires added significance given the visual logic of *darśan*, the grace-laden exchange of gazes between deity and devotee that is a central part of Hindu praxis. Though *darśan* glosses a ritualized interaction, its logic pervades other arenas of popular visual practice, such as cinema, painting, and photography, and thus exerts influences in a wide range of visual and spatial fields including, as I show, spaces of public memory.[18]

I draw on the above cultural approaches to statecraft in calling, with Ferguson and Gupta, for an exploration of the metaphors and avenues of embodied practice by which states come to be understood and experienced as concrete, overarching, spatially encompassing, and invested with verticality and encompassment.[19] I extend Ferguson and Gupta's argument, however, in proposing that the spatialization of the state is also, and necessarily, a temporalization: that the state's qualities of verticality and encompassment are rooted in pasts—of the body, of landscape, of built form—and oriented toward futures; that its ontology is spatially inscribed. Memorials, in particular, may play significant roles in naturalizing the state because of the ways that they conflate the temporalities of the body and of the state.

Public memory sites are, in short, crucial embodiments of the state's spatiality and temporality; they emplot both logics of rule and modes of dissent within morally compelling stories and imagery. This dynamic becomes even more pronounced under conditions of neoliberal globalization, in which states cede some parts of sovereignty but still seek to retain the loyalties and affective attachments

Figure 1.1. Kanchi Kudil entry, Kanchipuram. *Photograph by author.*

of their citizens. How does the privatized, deregulated state retain or rewrite its myths of origin? How do spaces of public memory enact and challenge the state effect in these contexts? How is political voice mediated or silenced through the work of public memory? While remaining mindful of the calculated and exploitive political effects that state-sponsored sites of public memory are designed to have, I wish to take on, rather than dismiss, their visual culture and spatial practice in order to expose the role of technologies of memory in the "masking of practice and the practice of masking."[20]

Cultural Memory and Global Exchanges

Kanchi Kudil

On that overcast Sunday morning in February, I seemed to be the only visitor at Kanchipuram's newest "heritage" attraction, a century-old courtyard house named Kanchi Kudil. For a modest entry fee of Rs.20, visitors could "witness the lifestyle of a bygone period."[21] Kanchipuram, a temple town west of Chennai that had gained prominence in the seventh century CE as the center of the Pallava state, attracted scores of Hindu tourist-pilgrims each week, as well as a much smaller stream of international tourists, discouraged perhaps by the observation in the

Figure 1.2. Kanchi Kudil gift shop, Kanchipuram. *Photograph by author.*

Lonely Planet *Survival Kit* that, "other than the temples, Kanchipuram is a dusty and fairly nondescript town and there's precious little to see or do except when the temple cart festivals take place."[22] Kanchi Kudil's owner, the daughter of the original residents, had reclaimed the house from its tenants, and refurnished with her parents' and grandparents' original possessions. The house was indistinguishable from other courtyard houses in the town's center—indeed, the owner anticipated that its very typicality would be its selling point. Her reasoning served to demonstrate that it was not domestic travelers but foreigners who were the target audience, a fact borne out by the response of the Indian friend who declined my invitation to join me on this visit: "For you, it's okay. But for us, it's nothing special. I can see the same thing at my mother's place."

After taking up residence in one of Chennai's newer residential divisions a decade earlier, Kanchi Kudil's owner had hired Kannaki, a young woman from a nearby village as a hostess. "Kannaki," a warm and articulate young woman who held a bachelor's degree in commerce, was unmarried. Her family had struggled to achieve a middle-class status and welcomed the small salary provided by Kannaki's job. They also valued the limited demands the job made: Kannaki told me that her parents were in the midst of making marriage arrangements for her and she knew that, depending on how negotiations proceeded, she might have to leave the job at short notice. I spent almost three hours with her, as she told me about the home's original occupants (who, she was careful to point out, were non-Brahman like herself) and explained domestic life of the century past, making thoughtful and effective use of the material objects displayed in the house as illustrative props. Only gradually did I notice, however, that many of those objects bore price stickers. Although, like other museums and historic sites, this house had a small gift shop offering the usual postcards, guide books, and souvenirs, it seemed that the enterprising owner had transformed the entire space into a permanent estate sale.

The abandonment of family homes in villages and towns has been one of the consequences of the rural-urban migration that followed successive waves of urbanization and industrialization throughout the twentieth century. The re-signification of these former homes as sites of regional or national heritage and the reliance on the flexible labor pool of educated, underemployed women borrow on a template that has enjoyed success in Europe and North America during the past century, but yokes that model to possibilities and challenges specific to India and to other parts of the developing, postcolonial world. I return to this particular heritage house and to the issue of tourism's gendered labor in chapter 5. Here it can be read as an exemplar of the popular concerns with cultural memory—sites, practices, and discourses that represent collective pasts—that have proliferated and grown in contentiousness in India during the past two decades, a period during which the Indian state has become increasingly committed to neoliberal economic policies and institutions. The changing articulations of state and market have been inscribed in urban and rural spaces, as new metropolitan centers emerge and old ones are reconstituted around knowledge- and service-based economies. And it is on these new and remade landscapes that competing claims on the past are being staked and possible futures envisioned, for, as challenges to state sovereignty are lodged, the historicism of political modernity, its linear temporality and progressive telos, is questioned and the state's own myths of origin revisited and revised.[23] Demand-driven tourism, environmental activism, resurgent nationalisms, and sub-national quests for ethnic, linguistic, and sectarian autonomy draw inspiration from, and nurture, diverse public memory sites and practices.

These claims on the past and the spaces of cultural citizenship that they engender are not reducible to the structural conditions of economic liberalization or neoliberal state formation. They are, nonetheless, productively engaged in the processes of political and economic restructuring—sustaining, resisting, and mediating those forces. The proliferation of politically and affectively charged pasts is a symptom of what Andreas Huyssen has called the "globalization of memory," an expression meant to capture the global circulation of templates for representing the past as well as the global influences and interactions that all pasts disclose.[24] The political effects of memory's globalization are ambiguous. Those who participate in the work of memory, whether selling, conserving, recounting, or merely decorating themselves with the artifacts of heritage, do so in ways that are laden with contradictory desires and outcomes—whether arising from deeply felt needs for ethnic authenticity or from nostalgic yearnings, or to advance the critical perspective of counter-memory—and are always addressed to real or imagined others. Memory work, understood relationally, is suffused by what Michael Herzfeld has termed "cultural intimacy": the sharing of known and recognizable traits that define insiderhood but are also felt to be disapproved by powerful outsiders.[25]

Cultural intimacy may be apparent in the ironic or confrontational play of stereotypes insofar as it works through the

> recognition of those aspects of a cultural identity that are considered a source of external embarrassment but that nevertheless provide insiders with their assurance of common sociality . . . [and through the] familiarity with the bases of power that may at one moment assure the disenfranchised a degree of creative irreverence and at the next moment reinforce the effectiveness of intimidation.[26]

Again, consider Kannaki. She told me that she found satisfaction in a job with "no hurry up" and that she particularly enjoyed learning about the "traditional ways that people lived," describing in detail, and with apparent admiration, the lives of the non-Brahman women who had lived in the house during the early twentieth century: their management of household affairs, their dowry goods, their religiosity. Yet, in telling me about her own aspirations, she admitted that her own family's efforts to arrange a marriage were a source of tension. She herself recognized the importance of "adjusting" to her future in-laws' expectations, but since earning her B.A., she had continued to study computer programming and accounting through correspondence courses. If she were able to take up work outside the house, she said, she hoped for a government job. Did her account of traditional gender roles and expectations and her hesitation in assuming them anticipate a foreigner's stereotypes about India? I do not wish to speculate about her intentions, but it does seem fair to consider our interaction as a small instance of cultural intimacy. As the forces of globalization enable wider circulation of templates of mnemonic practice, for example, in the form and function of museums and in the labor of historical interpretation, they also expand and multiply the forums in which cultural intimacies are engendered and exchanged in self-fashioning and in the imagination of the Other.

Chennai

With a population now estimated at 4.5 million, Chennai, the capital of the South Indian state of Tamil Nadu, is one of India's mega-cities and one of the nodes through which forces of neoliberal globalization are transforming the country. A former colonial port, Chennai was known officially as "Madras," the name used by the East India Company, until 1996 when, like "Calcutta," "Bangalore," and "Bombay," the Anglicized moniker was abandoned in favor of its vernacular counterpart, "Chennai." Even as it is reclaiming a regional identity, however, the city is poised to follow other South Indian metropoles as a center for global software production, export processing, and back-office services. State and municipal authorities have launched new efforts to create a hospitable climate for investment and consumption by foreign nationals and Non-Resident Indians (NRIs), not only with regulatory changes in capital and financial markets but also by expanding its tourism industry.[27] Changes in land use have brought with them the "formalization" of the city: the creation of modernized, sanitized enclaves for formal

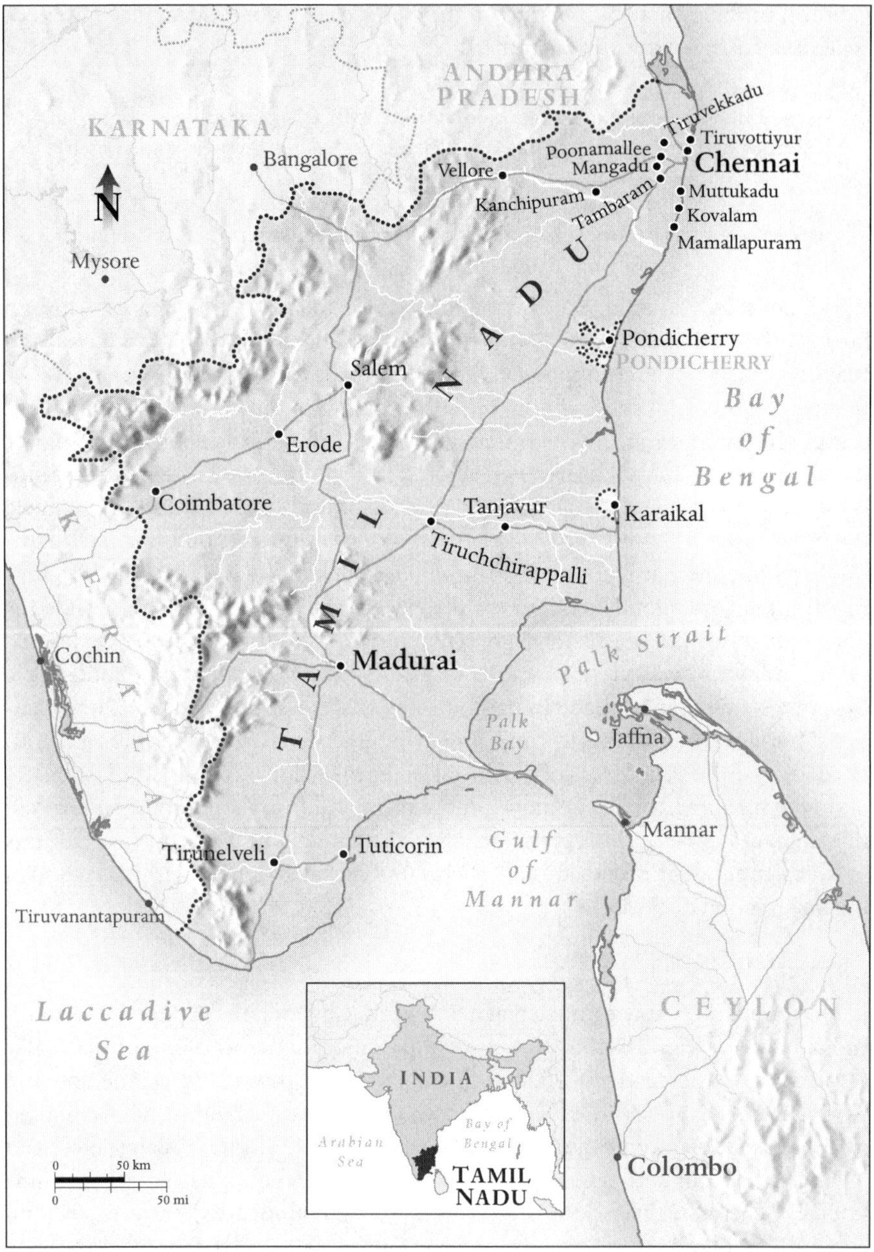

Map 1. Southern India. *Map prepared by James Craine.*

sector activities and the marginalization of informal sector spaces and activities. Changes have also included the creation of a "peri-urban fringe," as new industrial, export assembly, leisure, and residential sites have cropped up alongside the villages just outside Chennai's municipal boundary.[28] Villages in the urban

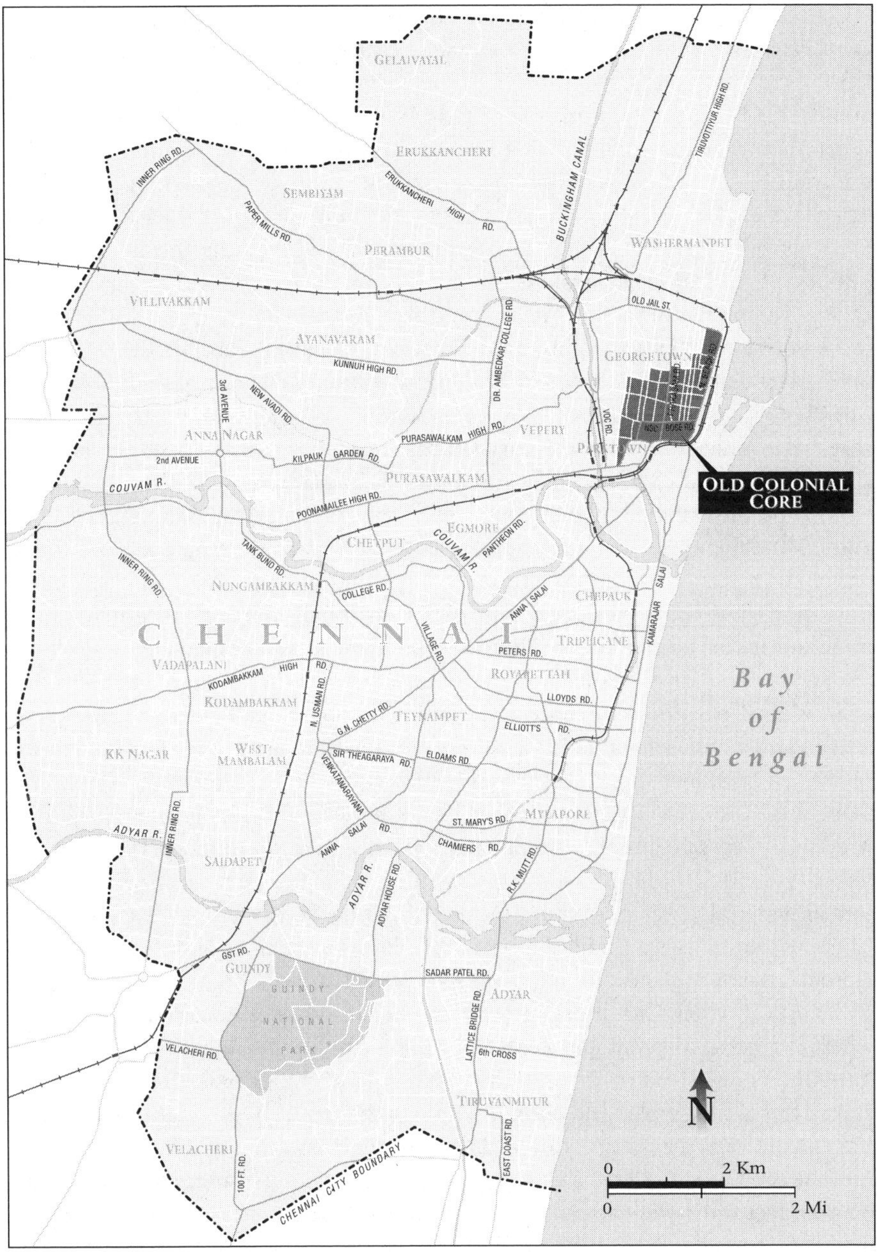

Map 2. Chennai. *Map prepared by James Craine.*

hinterlands have also been designated as resettlement sites for slum communities, who have been evicted from urban core areas to allow for redevelopment projects, such as the demolition of old building stock, expansion of transportation networks, and erection of high-rise office and residential structures.

Infrastructural and demographic changes have been accompanied by state, corporate, and voluntary efforts to fashion a heritage-conscious cityscape, one with historic precincts, museums, and memorials, portending (for some) the creation of Chennai as a recognizable "brand" among investment and travel destinations. In an updated take on what Renato Rosaldo called "imperialist nostalgia," the transition to a neoliberal political economy has invited mourning for what it has eliminated.[29] This dialectic is at the heart of new nostalgic formations, though their genealogy is deeper and can be linked to longstanding forms of identity politics. Historical consciousness, in the form of Tamil cultural nationalism, or Dravidianism, has been cultivated in southern India as a potent political force for more than a century and Tamil nationalist parties have controlled the state since 1967. Dravidianist public memory has included statues of political leaders and cultural heroes, commemorative sites such as Valluvar Kottam (honoring the Tamil sage, Tiruvalluvar), and the memorial parks created for two of the state's deceased chief ministers, M. G. Ramachandran and C. N. Annadurai.

While Dravidianist themes dominated urban memoryscapes during the 1970s and 1980s, the 1990s saw the appearance of new narratives on the past. Tamil nationalism has remained potent, but competing notions of the past, including Dalit history, colonial nostalgia, and Hindu nationalism, have made new claims on urban space and popular loyalties.[30] Among the sites that mediate these claims are parks, open-air museums, urban heritage districts, house museums, libraries, and cultural performance spaces. They can be monumental, like the modernist stelae marking the site of Rajiv Gandhi's assassination just outside Chennai or the re-created Buddhist stupa built to remember the Dalit legislator B. R. Ambedkar. Some are historicist: a new archive of Tamil periodicals and ephemera, the Roja Muthiah Research Library, commemorates the man whose collection was the library's nucleus while providing a carefully cataloged archive of primary historical materials. Many are more intimate, like the converted residence in north Chennai that houses a small museum and educational center honoring the Tamil mathematician Srinivasa Ramanujan. By contrast, a well-endowed craft museum and cultural center, DakshinaChitra, occupies a ten-acre campus south of the city, where it represents premodern southern India using the template of the outdoor museum, popularized in Europe, North America and East Asia. Others, like several of the city's temples and churches, follow the model of the registered historic site and are valued by conservationists not for their assertion of religious roots but because they bear the patina of time's passage. Still others—notably the vernacular architectural styles favored by some conservation architects for both community housing and upscale urban residences—are meant as embodied reminders of Gandhian values.[31] Reliant on globalized technologies of memory and fueled by state and market interests in heritage, these varied spaces retrieve and valorize the evanescent worlds of both plebian and elite pasts.

Chennai's growth and its formalization have meant that the boundaries between the city's urban core and its rural hinterland have become more permeable, re-creating what A. K. Ramanujan called the "rurban" landscape. The rurban, a recurrent topos within modern and classical Tamil literature, refers to urban centers that are "continuous with the countryside."[32] These changes in social space have engendered an anxious nostalgia among those elite city dwellers and their diasporic counterparts for whom "the village" is both a touchstone for familial and national pasts and a wellspring of national heritage. The built environment of rurban Chennai expresses both neoliberal futurity and its nostalgic longing, with heritage-themed resorts, house museums, and cultural centers that call forth the iconic past of the village even while transforming the villages of the hinterland with the introduction of new commercial and residential spaces.[33]

In terms that evoke Nora's argument about the transmutation of *milieux de memoire* into *lieux de memoire* that modernization precipitates, the production of public memory in the hinterland is encoded as a salvage operation, dedicated to the retrieval and preservation of almost lost traditions of oral narrative, performance, and plastic arts in workshops, performances, and exhibitions.[34] For city dwellers, these representations of the past in the form of folklore offer hedges against the anomie that the liberalizing economy has introduced. In the words of the director of one conservationist organization, they provide "cultural spaces for gathering, reflecting, creating and transforming our social life" in an urban environment made up of "broken families . . . partial families in diaspora communities, [a] widening gap between the classes . . . unaffordable consumables" and characterized by "the lack of community life and . . . basic amenities."[35] The folkloric past is treated as a trust that holds within it the nation-state's own authenticating traditions, even while constituted as remote, temporally, spatially, and experientially, from the worldly, metropolitan center of the nation-state.[36]

Lying in the shadows of these new leisure and industrial spaces are the actual villages where the majority of India's population continues to reside, though in conditions that have changed significantly over the past decade.[37] While "the village" as icon is an object of nostalgic longing, actual villages of rurban Chennai are complex mixes of rural and urban spaces, fears, and desires. As India's cities have expanded and industrialization accelerated, the rates of rural population growth have declined and rural poverty has increased. Many villages, especially those on the borders of major cities, have been transformed with the piecemeal introduction of industrial production and assembly facilities, urban services, and infrastructure. Although many villagers have migrated to urban centers, others—especially those in suburban Chennai—commute by bus to schools and jobs in Chennai and satellite towns. Others find work closer to home in chemical plants, automotive assembly sites, and export-processing zones.

In heritage venues and discourses, these rural settlements are cast in contradictory terms. They are both living examples of a past of virtuous rusticity as well as stagnant residues of a past that is soon to be abandoned. Within the lifeworlds of villages, however, cultural memory takes various forms.[38] The embodied pasts of caste difference and stigma persist in caste-segregated living spaces and in bodily performances (through dress, for example) of deference, avoidance, and defiance. Oral narratives and community shrines also engage difference though often to assert distinct genealogies, worldviews, and identities. Since the mid-1990s, an explicitly Dalit social space has been claimed with the erection of Ambedkar statues and busts. Cultural memory is also produced and disavowed in domestic space. Villages have long been sites of state surveillance and intervention, particularly through the succession of rural housing development programs inaugurated since the 1950s. Modernist in their implementation, goals, and architectural design, they were intended to erase the past (as known and embodied), though a few have made use of architectural praxis inspired by Gandhian nationalism's commitment to local self-sufficiency. These latter projects rely on vernacular materials and design to engender spaces of cultural intimacy in which new memories, to counter genealogies of stigma, could be produced and circulated. Just as urban and rural spaces are being rearticulated under neoliberal restructuring, so also are spaces of cultural intimacy with the past being reengaged to make claims on space and citizenship at Chennai's spatial and social margins.

About the Book

The book's chapters move from sites in Chennai's urban core (part 1) to its outskirts (part 2). The three chapters of part 1, "The Formal City and Its Pasts," deal with state-sponsored memory projects—the institutional contexts in which they function and the state effects that they mediate. I elaborate on the city's history and political economy in chapter 2, "Governing the Past: Chennai's Histories," organizing that narrative around the different ways that Chennai's past has been encoded and narrated over time and considering how those changing representations have articulated with patterns of land use and, more broadly, with successive phases in state formation. In chapter 3's exploration of the former chief minister M. G. Ramachandran's memorial, titled "Memory, Mourning, and Politics," I analyze the technologies of memory that encode the kingly models of sovereignty on which Dravidianist parties rely—noting the persistence, if not intensification, of rhetorics of kingship within statecraft as the state has ceded some areas of control to market forces with deregulation. Moreover, although efforts to enculture the state often retain an implicit focus on the nation-state, I use this case to argue for the heightened significance of sub-national units as mediators of the state effect, particularly as the state is reshaped under neoliberal globalization. Chapter 4, "Modernity Remembered: Temples, Publicity, and Heritage," investigates efforts by a private conservationist organization to designate a Hindu temple as a heritage site. I use the case as a spatialized frame on emergent debates—in this instance on secularism and statecraft—that I consider emblematic of the wave of "public-private" initiatives associated with neoliberalism.

Part 2, "Restructured Memories," moves from the urban core to the new, rurban hinterland that has expanded with the economic restructuring of the 1990s. Chapter 5, "Consuming the Past: Tourism's Cultural Economies," charts the development of regional tourist circuits. Working alternately from the macrostructural perspective of the tourist industry (managed, until recently, by the state) and from the more situated perspectives of tourist "hosts," I analyze tourism in terms of its mediation of changing national narratives and forms of cultural intimacy. Chapters 6 and 7 examine the technologies of cultural memory that have been entangled in the creation of Chennai's peri-urban fringe, noting their different engagements with the discourses and practices of Gandhian nationalism. The site dealt with in chapter 6, "Recollecting the Rural in Suburban Chennai," is the interactive museum and cultural center, DakshinaChitra, mentioned above. That site, I argue, engenders and sustains neoliberal nostalgia through its re-creation of a craft-centered rural world that invokes, without fully engaging, the artisanal commitments of Gandhian nationalism. Chapter 7, "The Village as Vernacular Cosmopolis," deals with a neo-traditionally styled village housing project that offers a new template for analyzing the politics of cultural memory. I explore the ways that its linkage of vernacular architecture with embodied historical consciousness draws upon Gandhian philosophy to propose that implicit memory—activated by changing the material lifeworld—can provide grounds for political voice. In this case, it is not the semantic memory of historical narrative that provides paradigms for present action but rather the embodied praxis and implicit memory associated with vernacular architecture, including participants' production of building materials and their acquisition of skills. Both cases consider the ways that pasts are deployed to make claims on space and citizenship at Chennai's spatial and social margins considering these in light of the various templates for heritage that have arisen with the restructuring of the urban landscape.

The book's chapters can be read as stand-alone essays. They work together, however, to argue that the diverse interests in the past and its material legacy are not contained by the goals of economic development but are embedded in other social, cultural, and political projects, new and longstanding, some of which are sharply critical of India's neoliberal turn. This polysemy, as it is mediated spatially and in narrative, is my point of departure. I consider how memory claims are both occasioned by and inscribed in the rapidly changing spaces of urban life—in the contexts of debates on development and planning, in memorialization and musealization, and in state-market couplings in the service of heritage. The result is an empirically grounded, but theoretically informed, anthropology of, rather than simply in, the city, which treats the metropole as subject of and stage for the evocation of the past as part of (and interruption in) the modern lifeworld.[39]

My goal is to capture the semiotic complexity and dynamic tension in the ways that public memory is created and used by interweaving informants' personal narratives and oral histories—their recollections, reinventions, and nostalgic laments—with accounts of the institutional and macrostructural conditions as they have evolved over time and with analysis of the visual culture and architectural space. Attention to these differently positioned narratives and narrators, moreover, is meant to underscore the agentive role that memory practices may fulfill, by enabling people to envision structural conditions as invented, unfinished, and malleable. Here I refer to the ways that discourses on the past were often punctuated by anxious assertions and queries about directionality—what does it mean to be Indian now? To be Tamil? I am interested, centrally, in the ways that acts of recalling and rewriting the past provide platforms for statecraft and governance, as well as for popular interventions in the cultural and political life of the present. Although territorialized Hindu nationalism has gained political strength and popular support over the past decade, the challenge for many is to imagine forms of collective belonging, citizenship, religiosity, and territorial identification that are less exclusionary, that incorporate the experiences and desires of de-territorialized groups, and that may provide a counterforce to the deleterious effects of neoliberal globalization even while working through global networks.

Engaging these issues has entailed that my project be conceived as an interdisciplinary one. Although the research has been rooted in ethnographic methods of inquiry and analysis, I have relied equally on historical sources (primary and secondary) and methods. Interdisciplinary work in history and anthropology, of course, has a deep and illustrious legacy. Attention to the historical record and to ethnohistory enabled anthropologists to interrupt the synchronic and presentist paradigms of structuralism and structural functionalism. Such work was particularly important in exposing the ways that relations of power associated with capitalist expansion engendered cultural forms and invented "traditions." Critical interventions such as these have been especially important in the scholarship on South Asia, notably in the contributions of Bernard Cohn and the Subaltern Studies Collective.[40] The history-anthropology interface is also exemplified in social history, in public and community history, in oral history, and in the path-breaking work of the Annales school and the social and cultural historiography that it influenced. In these settings, historians cultivated an ethnographic eye, as they attended to the minutiae of daily life and its material spaces, and excavated historically specific forms of "common sense" and everyday practice. My work recasts this interface in yet another way, by asking *how* people remember their pasts and what the effects of remembrance are. That is, while retaining the historical past as an object of inquiry, I have expanded the scope of my inquiry to the discursive, visual, and spatial practices, in the present, with which histories are made. This interdisciplinarity is meant to foster attention not merely to how historical events influence the present but to how histories are *made* and *made effective* in social and cultural life.

Part 1
The Formal City and Its Pasts

2
Governing the Past: Chennai's Histories

Madras to Chennai

Jet-lagged and diffident, I slumped in the seat of the "deluxe A-C coach" that carried me and thirty-odd other passengers from the government tourism office on Anna Salai, the main commercial thoroughfare of Madras.[1] It was October 7, 1985, and I had arrived only a few days earlier in the city still known officially as "Madras." It was my first visit to India, and friends in the city encouraged me to take some conducted tours, assuring me that they were good value for the money and that I would learn a great deal about local history. My fellow passengers, all Indian families, chatted quietly, though a vocal few had expressed disappointment that we were not traveling on one of the newly popular video-coaches, which screened popular Hindi and Tamil films during lengthy trips. Though admittedly curious about the films, I was absorbed in the countryside, with its rice paddies, palm trees, and small towns, whose clusters of open-air shops and temples punctuated our route.

Ours was an all-day tour, scheduled first to visit Kanchipuram, an ancient and still thriving temple town about fifty miles west of Madras.[2] Between the sixth and ninth centuries CE, Kanchipuram had been the seat of southern India's Pallava dynasty; still standing is the Sri Kailasanathar temple complex, dating from the seventh century. Mahaballipuram (now known as Mamallapuram), presently a coastal village but once a major Pallava port, was to be our second stop. Its chief attractions, the remains of rock-cut temples and bas-relief sculptures depicting scenes from the Mahabharata and the Panchatantra, earned it a designation as a UNESCO World Heritage site in 1984. Our day would conclude with a visit to the "Crocodile Bank," a small outdoor zoo, where local species of crocodile were maintained in their natural habitat.

That tour, like the nearly identical versions on offer now, some twenty-three years later, was meant to introduce visitors to the city's rural hinterland and, more important, to highlight the region's roots in an ancient civilization, roots that were barely acknowledged on the streets of Madras. Madras, of course, hosted its own share of tours, and the one I had taken during the same 1985 visit had been a briskly conducted, half-day affair. Visits to four sites were accompanied by brief and, to my ears, canned commentaries on their historical significance and character. The coach disgorged us—me and a couple dozen Indian tourists—first near the Victorian edifices of the state museum complex near the Egmore rail station and then at the Fort Museum, built near what remained of the seventeenth-century redoubt, Fort St. George, the nucleus of the original British settlement. The third stop was the Kapaleswarar Karpakampal Temple, dedicated to the god, Siva, in Mylapore. Its sanctum was open only to Hindus, but anyone could wander through the pavilions and courtyards that surrounded the shrines and, for a nominal fee, "save the moment" with photographs. The tour finished up on Marina Beach, a broad, sandy expanse, which stretched southward from the city's port facilities. I came away from that afternoon's activities with little more than a handful of visual clichés about the city's colonial roots, its Hindu sensibilities, and its modernist aspirations. Despite brief allusions to Mylapore's historical significance as a Pallava port, it seemed that the authentically Tamil lay elsewhere, in the places whose material remnants were encased behind the dusty glass barriers at the Government Museum.

I have more to say about these tour circuits in chapter 5. Of interest here is the way they encapsulated representations of the city that I had encountered in other popular discourses, which described Madras in terms of historical lack and contingency. A corresponding narrative emphasized its spatial incoherence: Madras was characterized as a "city of villages," an amalgamation of once dispersed settlements knitted together through the agency of colonial authority and the global capitalism that it served.[3] An accidental city, the product of decisions taken elsewhere, its growth by accretion was often contrasted with the spatial authenticity of Kanchipuram, Tanjavur, and Madurai, whose temple-centric plans preserved a premodern Hindu architectonic that was distinctive to peninsular South Asia.[4]

In 1996, with a stint of doctoral fieldwork (1987–88) behind me, I returned to Madras for a few months. Popular discourse, I discovered, had shifted and, not coincidentally, the stops on the city tour had multiplied. In the intervening years of industrial growth and urban expansion and redevelopment, Madras's own "heritage" had taken shape. It was the subject of local television programming and a new crop of periodicals, most of them weekly or biweekly community newspapers, many but not all of them English-language publications.[5] This was the outcome of efforts by government agencies (national, state, and municipal), eager to attract tourists, both foreign and domestic, and by an assortment of voluntary groups. All were determined to identify and conserve, even as they differed on what, exactly, was constituted by this heritage. The metropolitan development authority's Draft Master Plan recommended that the city be developed as a gateway for tourists and identified "conservation and development of heritage zones" within the city as places of tourist attraction.[6] Some nongovernmental groups focused on environmental degradation, linking efforts to clean the city's waterways and temple tanks, for example, to heritage conservation. Temples, churches, and historic homes, many lying in the shadows cast by new high-rises, were identified as heritage sites, as were a number of run-down, colonial-era public buildings. New commemorative spaces and museums had appeared and existing ones had been refurbished. And, during my visit, the city's name was changed officially, by order of the chief minister, from "Madras" to "Chennai," the Tamil name by which it had long been known locally.[7]

The name change, only one among various heritage-oriented efforts, was surprisingly controversial, particularly in light of the electoral clout of the regionalist party, the Dravida Munnetra Kazhagam (DMK), that controlled the state's government and the popularity of its brand of Tamil populism. Objections were made by representatives of the local chapter of INTACH, the Indian National Trust for Art and Cultural Heritage, and a lively and occasionally vitriolic debate ensued in which competing accounts of the city's history and its genesis *as* a city, were advanced.[8] These names, "Chennai" and "Madras," locked in uneasy twinship, signaled different territorial imaginaries and genealogies. "Madras," the name made official by India's colonial rulers, designated a meeting point where European merchants drew local artisans and merchants into uneven alliances that advanced global capitalism. "Chennai," the name used in Tamil print sources and colloquially, also referred to a meeting place, but it recalled the city's origin in a space where agents of peninsular India's crumbling Vijayanagara empire sought strategic advantage over Europeans through complex translations of words, money, and goods.

Between 1639, the year of the original grant, and 1858, when British India was declared a colony under the direct rule of the British crown, the settlement grew to a city made up of a spectrum of rural and urban spaces, each with its own sociospatial character.[9] It began as a compact unit formed by "White Town," the East India Company's fortified trading post, and neighboring "Black Town," a settlement of Telugu weavers and merchants, and became a city of twenty-seven square miles, with more than three hundred thousand inhabitants.[10] Although the racialized geography of the colonial city has disappeared, traces of the colonial state, whose growth was inextricably linked to Chennai, persist today in place names, in the style and syntax of the built environment, and in the very boundaries, set in 1798, that mark the city's geographic extent. Also embedded in these visual, architectural, and discursive residues are the historicist imaginaries—the linear and progressive temporalities of the modern—that have been critical parts of colonial and postcolonial statecraft.

This chapter places Chennai's history in the broader context of colonial and postcolonial state formation, charting its settlement history through maps, paintings, prints, official and popular narratives, and architecture. The spatial, visual, and discursive evidence reveals not only the physical appearance of some space at a moment in time, but also the pasts with which particular spaces have been endowed and the political, cultural, and social work that these pasts are made to do. I argue here that the state's territorial reach is made effective by the production and representation of its genealogy, through spatial strategies that include place names, architecture, and visual imagery.

This chapter proceeds through a series of moments—rendered by visual and discursive "snapshots" of the city from 1639, 1798, 1939, and 1996. Each represented and mediated the city for those who counted themselves among its residents and, through print capitalism, for audiences at greater remove. The first, the 1639 transaction that allowed British merchants to lease coastal land, depicts "Madras" as a borderland, an imperial frontier and commercial entrepôt that in the course of colonial expansion became a node for state formation. The second representation, the 1798 municipal map, was an artifact of "Company Raj," the military and economic domination exerted by the East India Company against rival imperial powers. In matters of style and syntax, the built environment and cultivated landscapes so meticulously recorded on the map encode the Greco-Roman imperial legacy with which the Company's agents outfitted their claims.

A third moment takes the form of an excerpt from the 1939 volume published to mark the city's three hundredth anniversary. The text anticipates the end of colonialism even as it reveals the persistence of colonial statecraft in the form of what I call the "curatorial state," with its well-developed apparatus for extracting, cataloging, and displaying the pasts of its territorial holdings. The fourth and final moment is captured in another brief text, a newspaper report on the Government Order mandating the city's name change. With this move, the postcolonial state, whose sovereignty rests on the futurity of rationalized, technocratic planning, also makes claims on the past, seizing those residues that anticipate the future that planning seeks to engineer. Together, these moments serve as accounts of settlement form and land use over time and as artifacts of the interweaving of history and memory that brought the pasts of city and territory into presence in the changing cityscape.

The Colonial City and Its Afterlife

1639: The Borderland

> Firman granted by Demala Vintatedro Nague unto Mr. Francis Day, Cheife for the English In Armagon, in behalfe of the Honble Company for their tradeing and fortifying at Medraspatam, to the effect as followeth:
>
> Whereas Mr. Francis Day, Captain of the English at Armagon, upon great hopes by reason of our promises often made unto him, hath repaired to our part of Medraspatam and had personall Conference with us in behalfe of the Company of that nation, Concerning their Trading in our territories and friendly Commerce with our subjects; wee, out of our spetiall Love and favour to the English, doe grant unto the said Captain, or whomsoever shall bee deputed to Idgitate the affaires of that Company, by virtue of this firman, Power to direct and order the building of a fort and Castle in or about Medraspatam, as they shall thinke most Convenient, the Chargees whereof, until fully and wholly finished,

> to bee defrayed by us, but then to bee repaied when the said English first make their enterance to take possession thereof. And to make more full Expression of our effection to the English nation, wee Doe Confirme unto the said Mr. Francis Day, or whatsoever other substitutes or Agents for that Company, full power and authority to governe and dispose of the Government of Madraspatam for the terme and space of two yeares Next Insueing after they shall be seated there and possest of the said fortifications; and for the future by our Equall Division to receive halfe the Custom and revenues of that port.
>
> Moreover, Whatsoever goods or Merchandize the English company shall either Import or Export, forasmuch as Concernes the dutyes and Customs of Medraspatam, they shall, not only for the Prementioned two years in which they Injoy the Government, but for ever after, be Custom free. Yett if they shall transport or bring any commodities up into, or through my countray, then shall they pay halfe the dutyes that other Merchants pay, whether they buy or sell the said Commodities either in my Dominions or in those of any other Nague whatsoever.
>
> Also that the said English Company shall perpetually Injoy the priviledges of minta[e] without paying any Dewes or dutyes whatsoever, more then the ordinary wages or hire unto those that shall Quoyne the moneyes.
>
> If the English shall Accquaint us before they deliver out any moneys to the Merchants, Painters, Weavers, &c., which are or shall hereafter reside in our prementioned part or territories, and take our word for their sufficcency and honest dealeing, then doe wee promise, in case those people faile in their performances, to make good to the English all such sumes of money as shall remaine on their Accounts, or Else deliver them their persons, if they shalbe found in any part of my territories.
>
> That whatsoever provisions the English shall buy in my countrey, either for their fort or ships, they shall not be liable to pay any Custom or Dutyes for the same.
>
> And if any ship or vessel belonging to the English (or to any other Countray whatsoever which tradeth or shall come to trade at that port) shall by misadventure suffer shippwrack and bee driven upon any part of my territories, they shall have restitution upon Demand of whatsoever can bee found remaining of the said wrack.
>
> Dated the 22th July 1639.[11]

It was in 1639 that a local governor or "nayak," Damarla Venkatapati, granted a plot of coastal land to servants of the British East India Company.[12] A fortified trading post, Fort St. George, was built on the site. The factory, in turn, attracted weavers and merchants, who established a settlement just north of the fort called "Gentu Town," and later "Black Town" by the Company. The grant was located in a region that had been known since Pallava times as Tondaimandalam. It was largely agrarian and extended about 160 miles along the coast, from Tirupati to Cuddalore, and about 50 miles inland, to Kanchipuram. It included textile-producing villages, the temple towns of Mylapore and Kanchipuram, as well as fishing and agricultural villages and hamlets.

The coastal stretch in which the grant was wedged had already attracted European mercantile interests. In 1522 Portuguese settlers had founded San Thome, just east of Mylapore; to the north, in Pulicat, a Dutch fort had been built in

1609.[13] Thriving commercial networks coordinated by indigenous merchant communities had existed along the coast from early in the first millennium CE and Europeans, like Roman and Arab traders before them, sought access to these networks and to the trade goods and precious metals that circulated through them.

This same space was a frontier of a different sort for indigenes. The territory the Company acquired lay in the eastern hinterland of the Vijayanagara empire, whose original capital lay in the southern reaches of India's Deccan plain. All but dissolved by 1639, what remained of the Vijayanagara empire were "little kingdoms" presided over by rajas and their vassals, each of whom sought to retain and expand their individual holdings.[14] The political instability of the seventeenth century, moreover, was exacerbated by military threat, including that posed by the southward advance of forces of the Delhi-based Mughal empire and the rival Marathas. Their southward advance, involving military engagements and shifting alliances among all the groups having territorial interests in peninsular South Asia, did not halt until 1799, when Tippu, Sultan of Mysore, was defeated by East India Company forces in the Battle of Seringapattinam. It was only then, with the annexation of Tippu's peninsular holdings, that the Company's territorial control over the region was secured.

"Madras," the name for the settlement that the British merchants favored, was a variant of "Medraspatam," listed in the original grant as the name of a fishing village north of the plot that had been leased to the traders. "Chinnapattinam," whose first use in English was recorded in 1644 in a grant relating to the endowment of the Chenna Kesava Perumal Temple in Black Town, was used by Tamil and Telugu speakers as an appellation for the settlement.[15] It was subsequently used interchangeably with "Chennapattinam," "Chenna," "Chenna Kesava Patna" and "Chennapuram," and is the source for the current "Chennai." Those names continue to appear in Tamil and Telugu sources as names for Black Town, and sometimes for the entire settlement. They were also affixed to local organizations claiming various constituencies and to institutions, especially temples, that served as central places in settlement form while commemorating the generosity and status of donors and patrons. The roots of "Chennai" and "Madras" thus came into existence as names for the same settlement nearly contemporaneously, albeit attached to different territorial imaginaries and ambitions.

1798: "Madras" Imagined

At the close of the eighteenth century, "Madras" was conjured into cartographic reality by the Company's municipal mapping exercise.[16] The 1798 map (Fig. 2.1) distinguished different land uses and revealed the boundaries of various categories of individual and corporate property—all laid out within the newly bounded municipality. Though lacking street names, it showed the radial network of roads that radiated from the Fort as well as the grid-pattern of residential streets.

This nominal claim on territory was accompanied by other visual and discursive claims on the settlement and its past. Neoclassical public buildings erected by the East India Company along the beachfront near the Fort in the final years of

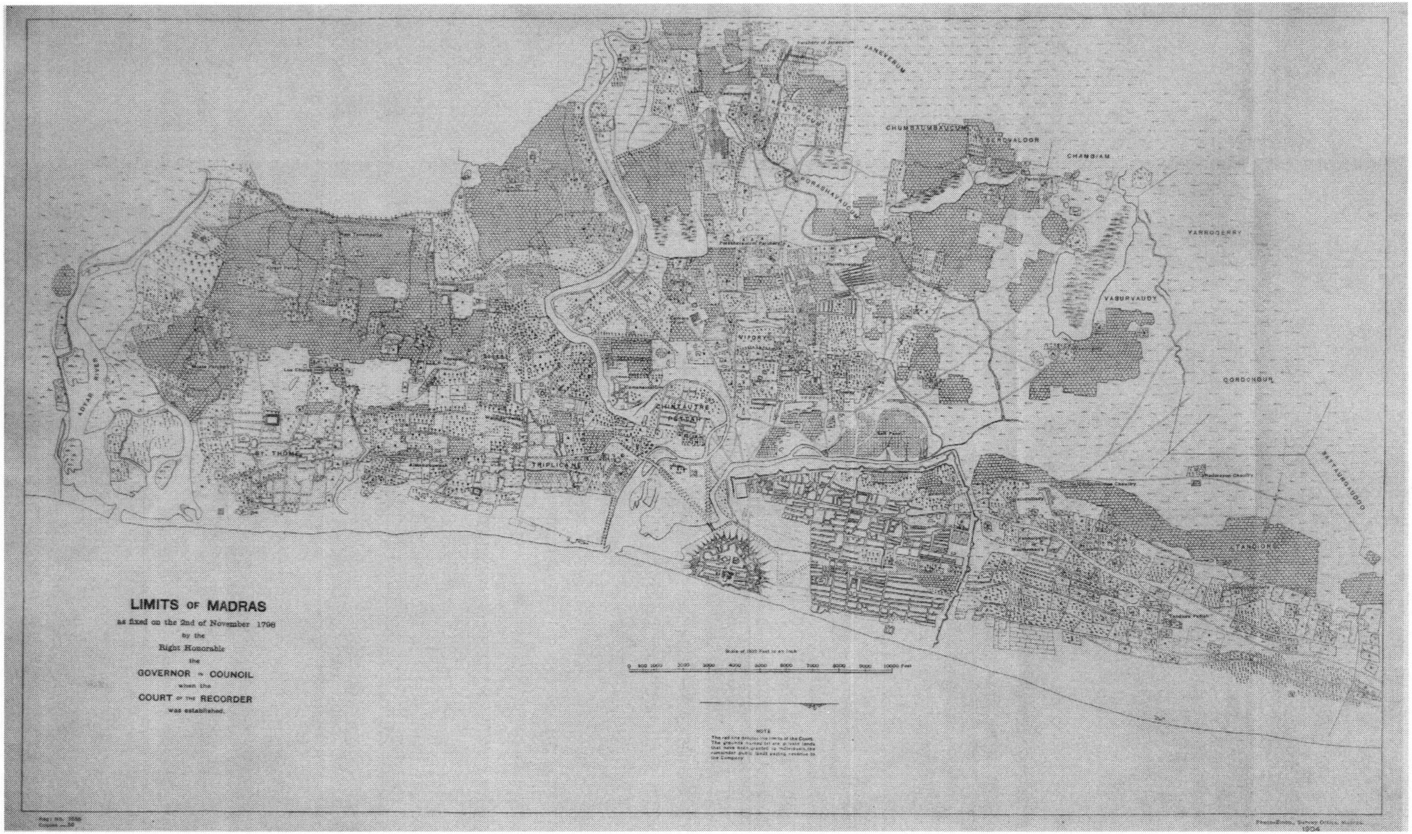

Figure 2.1. "Limits of Madras, as fixed on the 2nd of November, 1798." *Reproduced with permission of the British Library.*

the century endowed the emerging urban landscape with a Greco-Roman imperial legacy. A spate of European artists' renderings (paintings, drawings, prints, and aquatints) depicted these landscapes according to picturesque compositional norms, emphasizing their "Oriental" exoticism, often as illustrations for travelers' tales. During the same period, indigenous literary and architectural projects, commissioned by newly wealthy and mainly Hindu dubashes (translators and business brokers) and merchants, declared "Chennapattinam" to be a place of prosperity, artistic expression, and religious merit. The growth of the settlement was thus tied to competing claims by colonizers and indigenes not only on goods and resources but also on representation and meaning.[17]

The consolidation of the dispersed towns and villages into a bounded urban center began in the late seventeenth century, with the improvement and realignment of Mount Road. That roadway, described by Love as "ancient," extended in a southwest direction from the Fort for seven miles to St. Thomas Mount.[18] It was the corridor along which new residential space was created outside the Fort district and the adjoining Black Town.[19] The separation of work and residential space, adopted initially by Europeans and a smaller number of wealthy Indians, began with the erection of town houses in Triplicane in the 1670s but gathered momentum in the 1700s, as garden houses appeared in converted agricultural land west of the fort, on the Choultry Plain, in the villages identified as Nungumbaucum (Nungambakkam), Pudupakkam, and Egmore, and, later, in Vipory (Vepery), Tanampetta (Teynampet), Porashavaucam (Purasawakkam), Keelpaucam (Kilpauk), and the old Portuguese settlement of San Thome. The houses, called "bungalows," were popular throughout British India and were based loosely on Bengali vernacular architecture.[20] They were square, usually single-storeyed, with hipped roofs and wide verandahs. Most had adjacent gardens and were enclosed within walled compounds.

The Anglo-Indian bungalows of the Choultry Plain marked the western boundary of European settlement and evoked comparisons with the country homes of European aristocracy, even as they nodded toward the subcontinent's vernacular architecture. They were nodes from which their occupants gazed eastward, toward their offices and worksites in the Fort, all the while grounding themselves in an imagined aristocratic past. In a 1765 letter, one Mrs. Kindersley, the wife of a Company officer stationed in Bengal, described a brief visit to Madras:

> The English boast much of a delightful mount about ten miles distant where [they] have garden houses which, they say, are both cool and elegant. . . . They [the English] are expensive in horses, carriages, palenqueens and number of servants; are fond of entertainments, dress and pleasure; sociable with each other; hospitable and civil to strangers.[21]

For those Indian dubashes and merchants who resided in similarly styled homes in villages south and west of the Fort, the bungalows were indexes of a different but still hybrid imaginary.[22] Their spacious country homes were nodes from which they forged connections in two directions: eastward, to the mercantile wealth of the Fort, for example, by playing host to their European guests, and westward, to the agrarian wealth and ritual status of their ancestral lands and temples in Tondiamandalam.[23] In the latter instances, garden houses were social spaces in which mercantile wealth could be transmuted into status, by entertaining poets, musicians, dancers, and other retainers, according to medieval models of royal patronage.

Although the trafficking in signs and currency during the seventeenth and eighteenth centuries resulted in the formation of various kinds of dialogic relations between Europeans and Indians, the growth of the colonial settlement—"Madras"—was predicated on the Company's power to incorporate indigenous space and to create new settlements, as well as to defend its claim against other powers, European and indigenous. Central to this landscape of power was the Fort and its environs, located on the beachfront at the northeast terminus of Mount Road. It was the center of commerce, manufacture, and governance, as well as the settlement's military core, a function that remained essential as the Company wrested control of the surrounding territory from both Mughal governors and other European powers.

The development of the Fort district as a space of military, political, and economic power was under way by the late seventeenth century. By 1700 the Company had created the offices of governor, mayor, and councillors, formed a Corporation of Madras with the power to tax and provide public services, and established a court. Perhaps the most dramatic indicators of administrative developments were the public buildings that appeared both inside and outside the Fort's walls. By the first decade of the eighteenth century, the Fort contained within it a Town Hall, an arsenal, a mint, and a church, as well as assorted residences, including the Government House, where the governor resided. Within fifty years, public buildings had multiplied beyond the walls of the Fort. They were constructed in the neoclassical styles popular for European public buildings and signaled the governance role that the Company had assumed.[24] Among the new buildings that housed institutions of governance and sociality were the Assembly Rooms near St. Thomas Mount; the Pantheon, a space of social and cultural gatherings in Egmore; and the renovated Government House and Banqueting Hall, both located in the park-like setting of the Government Estate in Triplicane.

With such structures, Company architects re-created classicized landscapes that made the cityscape legible to its European residents and visitors, who welcomed their familiarity and voiced appreciation for their presence and execution.[25] The artist, William Hodges, described the city's neoclassical buildings as consisting "of long colonnades, with open porticoes, and flat roofs and offer to the eye an appearance similar to that of what we may conceive of a Grecian city in the age of Alexander."[26] The Rev. J. Hobart Caunter, writing fifty years later in *The Oriental Annual* (1834), described the Government House as a "superb building, fronted by a splendid colonnade, which leads down to the sea-gate."[27]

Visual images of these spaces fed the Orientalist historical imagination as they re-circulated beyond the subcontinent through illustrated traveler's accounts and in paintings, prints, and drawings. Artists were encouraged to tour India with visual aids, drawing equipment, and compositional guidelines in order to create "picturesque" images that took advantage of its "exotic" qualities: its vegetation, animals, and colorfully clad peoples. The scenes that they produced lent order to imperfect nature and deliberately recalled the classical landscapes of Claude Lorrain, Gaspar Poussin, and Salvator Rosa. Among the more productive landscape painters were George Chinnery and William Hodges. There were also numerous traveler-artists, whose prints and drawings were published as illustrations to accompany written accounts of their adventures.

Among the traveler-artists, Thomas and William Daniell were particularly prolific. Their illustrations accompanied the six-part *Oriental Scenery* (1795–1801) and *A Picturesque Voyage to India; by Way of China* (1810); they also prepared and exhibited scores of oil paintings of Indian subjects, based on drawings completed during their travels.[28] An aquatint, "The Government House, Fort St. George," dated March 1792, represented the Fort and the neoclassical public buildings it contained as a solid plane in the landscape's middle ground (Fig. 2.2).[29] The buildings, the landscape's lone, austere edifices, define and dominate the terrain, and its prospect is elevated, as if the viewer were approaching by sea. The Fort's flagpole and buildings are outsized, lending monumentality to the structure, in contrast to the tiny human figures in the foreground. The foreground figures are shown in the work of trade, with clothing that identifies most as Indians of various ranks and occupations.

Another view of Fort St. George, "Western Entrance of Fort St. George," dated January 1798, follows classical compositional norms even more closely (Fig. 2.3).[30] The Fort, with its clearly outlined buildings and massive, unfurled flag, is viewed from a submerged prospect, its outline forming the landscape's horizon. Dominating the middle ground is a bridge across which a line of human figures, in procession, extends. The procession is depicted moving toward the Fort and forms the landscape's obligatory serpentine. Signs of the exotic and picturesque are present in the procession—Europeans on horses, a mahout-mounted elephant, numerous laborers bearing palanquins and other loads—and in the bucolic scene on the river bank below the bridge. There, cattle graze in the company of Indian figures, grouped symmetrically along the lower plane of the landscape's middle ground. As in Figure 2.2, the colonial built environment offers the visual foci, with humans and landscape details added to complement the Fort's orderly classical proportions.

The Indian figures in these and other images, associated with natural features of the landscape and rendered with sufficient sartorial detail to encode occupation and status, were key signs of the exotic. They were also reminders that the Company's power rested on its control of a population whose numbers far exceeded its own. The population of Madras city at the end of the eighteenth century was estimated, probably too generously, at three hundred thousand of which no more than five hundred were European.[31] Madras was the seat from which the Company ruled; it was also the product of Company rule, having grown by the incorporation of surrounding villages through annexure, force, purchase and lease, and in-migration. The spaces that Madras comprised ranged from rural

Figure 2.2. "The Government House, Fort St. George" (aquatint), Thomas and William Daniell. *Reproduced with permission of the British Library.*

Figure 2.3. "Western Entrance of Fort St. George" (aquatint), Thomas and William Daniell. *Reproduced with permission of the British Library.*

villages and hamlets (including settlements of marine and inland fishing communities), to temple-centric settlements of traditional urban form (Mylapore, Triplicane), to hybrid forms characteristic of colonial borderlands with their multiple zones of ethnic, economic, sectarian, and linguistic contact (Black Town, Chintadripet).

The retention of original place names as well as the form of settlements and their geographic dispersal contributed to distinctions in their respective sociospatial characters. Half the city's indigenous population resided in Black Town, which grew from the original weavers' settlement to include temples, markets, schools, and mosques, in addition to homes and small-scale manufacturing sites.[32] It was Black Town that formed the core of what Tamil and Telugu speakers called "Chennapattinam."[33] Geographically it corresponded to vernacular settlement models in being a decentralized urban space, with partially autonomous, caste-based neighborhoods and mixed land-use patterns. Nonetheless, with its grid plan, the presence of a central market street that catered to Europeans (Popham's Broadway, opened in 1789) and the heterogeneity of its population, Black Town was an exceedingly complex and not particularly traditional urban space. The hybridity of Black Town was also encapsulated in the new, sometimes eclectically designed temples endowed by newly wealthy dubashes and merchants.[34] The merit and generosity of donors were commemorated by these temples, even as they anchored territorial claims within and beyond the new settlement.

While Black Town and its environs remained the commercial and population center of the settlement, Mylapore also became more populous during the eighteenth century. Its temples, markets, and cultural institutions attracted elites, as well as various laborers and service workers. Wealthier Indians and some Europeans began to construct bungalow-style garden houses on its open, agricultural land. In Mylapore, as in Black Town, however, vernacular architectural styles predominated, with row houses, many with central courtyards, and more modest mud-and-thatch huts.[35]

Another, distinct space of Indian habitation in the city was created by the migration in 1768 of the Nawab of the Carnatic, with his family and retainers, to the city, where they had been granted asylum by the Company. The Nawab, a Mughal governor, was awarded a plot of 117 acres, in the northern sections of Triplicane in return for allying with the British. Though officially protected by the Company, the settlement and its population remained under the Nawab's authority. By remaining outside the jurisdiction of the municipal government, residents were exempted from the various taxes and tariffs levied on other city inhabitants. By the early 1800s, the Nawab and family members had acquired additional lands and houses in Triplicane, as well as in Black Town, Pudupakkam, and Mylapore. The community remained self-contained, politically, socially, and economically, even after the original grant was subdivided and the Nawab divested of power later in the nineteenth century.[36]

In comparison with European residential areas, which were located near the city's major transportation networks, indigenous spaces of habitation (with the exception of Black Town) were more dispersed and lacked direct access to major roads. Further, the spatial separation of residential and work areas, made possible for Europeans by the improvement of Mount Road, was considerably more limited among its Indian population. Where separation of work and residence did appear, it was initially among wealthy dubashes and merchants who maintained both townhouse residences in Black Town and garden houses in Mylapore, Triplicane, and on the Choultry Plain. More common was the mixture of residential, commercial, and manufacturing uses within Indian habitation areas—a feature that contributed to their distinctive spatial organization. They were often arranged as caste-based neighborhoods spread among the quadrilateral streets that surrounded central structures such as temples and adjoining markets. Indigenous settlements were denser, with narrower streets and less mediating space between domestic interiors and exterior, public areas. Spaces of work and residence often overlapped, for example, with market stalls in the front of houses.

Over the seventeenth and eighteenth centuries, a single, albeit heterogeneously imagined, city was born that encompassed, without erasing, preexisting spaces of habitation and meaning and spawned new settlements. "Madras" was built into an administrative center, from which the East India Company and later the British Crown governed its territorial holdings in peninsular South Asia. Its name was made official by signage, cartography, and written records generated by the Company's municipal administration, the Madras Corporation, formed in 1688. "Chennai" occupied the same geographic space and over the same period remained the city's vernacular name, describing the new city that emerged as a center of commerce, industry, and education and, later, signaling new political aspirations and regional patriotisms.

1939: The Curatorial State

> The following pages describe in great detail the remarkable growth and development of the city of Madras and its varied activities during the past three hundred years. When Francis Day obtained a grant of land from the Naik of Poonamalee in August 1639, the English merchants were not very hopeful of the future of their settlement. They were convinced, however, that "this place may prove as good as the best; but all things must have its growth and time." The tercentenary of Madras is a fitting occasion for reviewing what "time and growth" have accomplished for the city.[37]

These words introduced *The Madras Tercentenary Commemoration Volume*, released in honor of the three hundredth anniversary of the city's founding. Articles on the city's political and commercial history, its geography, and the history of its religious and cultural institutions were contributed by eminent Tamil and Telugu scholars, professionals, and civil servants as well as several British scholars and colonial officers. Madras, once a stage for imperial imaginaries derived from both Europe and the subcontinent, had become a historical subject, its own past represented in images and detailed narratives.

The volume portrayed a city assuredly modern in appearance, governing institutions, and aspirations. It was a city penetrable by historicism, littered with remnants of the past that, retrieved, documented, and displayed by the colonial state's apparatus of conservation, could be plumbed for a utilitarian narrative in service of the nation-in-waiting. The "historical mindedness" of the 1939 portrait was influenced by the historicism of Europe's Romantic era.[38] Turned on India, it captured an urban landscape rich in what Pierre Nora has since called *lieux de memoire,* the museums, libraries, textual narratives, and monuments where the past could be encountered through sensory modalities, as memory, but which were nonetheless engendered and managed by the dictates of dispassionate, objective, and temporally driven history.

Between 1798 and 1939 the city's population increased in size and density, with major jumps between 1881 and 1901 and between 1921 and 1931.[39] Despite British hegemony in matters of name, territory, and law, these numbers included only a small number of Britons, and the city's residential areas remained a checkerboard on which spaces of European and indigenous occupation were interposed.[40] Both waves of population increase coincided with industrialization, which drew migrants seeking education and employment in the provincial capital.[41] With the 1923 annexation of the village of Mambalam, the city grew in area as well. Improvements in roads and the introduction in 1904 of an electric tramway, followed in 1931 with an electric rail connection between the beachfront and the town of Tambaram to the southwest, led to in-fill of the city's open lands.

The urban economy, still reliant on trade and commerce, became more dependent on the administrative and service sectors that expanded with the development of Madras as a provincial capital. Education and the possibility of employment in the colonial bureaucracy drew upper-caste migrants to the city, and the colonial administration absorbed Indian clerks, teachers, lawyers, judges, accountants, and eventually legislators. By the end of the nineteenth century the former suburbs to the west and south of the Fort had become home to a new elite, composed of high-caste, English-educated professionals. It was this group that formed the political base of the pan-Indian nationalist movement in the city.[42]

Black Town had been renamed "Georgetown" in 1906, to commemorate the tour of India by the Prince of Wales. It retained the spatial form and character that existed in 1798, by which point it had grown to include temples, markets, schools, and mosques, in addition to the homes and small-scale manufacturing sites it originally contained. It continued to be a cultural and residential center for the old mercantile elite, including members of the Nattukkottai Chettiar banking caste, a community that, since the seventeenth century, had maintained trade and migration networks between southern India and peninsular and insular Southeast Asia. With the colonial state's prohibitions on Indian capital accumulation and investment, however, their wealth and influence had declined. They nonetheless maintained forms of patronage evocative of earlier generations of merchants and dubashes, by endowing temples and cultural performances in the city and the countryside. In the late nineteenth century they funded temple renovations and constructed palatial homes in the areas south of Madras from which their ancestors hailed.[43] They also took direct political action to address entwined problems of economic decline and colonial governance. The "Non-Brahman Manifesto," issued in 1916 by prominent members of this community, borrowed on existing anti-Brahman sentiment and nascent Tamil nationalism to demand entitlements for non-Brahman communities in education and employment. Colonial authorities, attentive to what they identified as Brahman "nepotism" and to Brahman sympathies with pan-Indian nationalism, soon responded by initiating positive discrimination policies to benefit members of non-Brahman communities.[44] Though the agitation was launched for the benefit of non-Brahman elites, the mobilization of non-Brahman interests, in conjunction with other populist, rationalist, and anti-caste movements, laid a foundation for the Dravidianist ideology that, in the late 1940s, crystallized into an influential regionalist political party.

A few European-owned industrial ventures (textile mills, railway carriage works) were launched in the northern section of Perambur during the final quarter of the nineteenth century. The employment opportunities they offered, coupled with recurrent famines and agricultural market instability, attracted lower-caste rural migrants. Labor line housing was built, and squatter settlements multiplied. Migration rates increased sharply after 1920, and in 1933 the population of the city's 189 hut colonies was estimated to be 202,910.[45] Film production, one of the few indigenously owned industries and one for which Madras became known in the early twentieth century, was concentrated in a few studios in western and southwestern divisions.[46] The Tamil film industry, which grew quickly into India's second largest, communicated nationalist ideologies through its content and was an incubator for a number of Dravidianist propagandists who, in conjunction with screenwriting and acting careers, developed political careers.

Altogether, infrastructural developments, coupled with socio-demographic and economic change and the expansion of vernacular print and visual media, made for wider associational networks, especially among the city's indigenous residents, whose spatial dispersal during the seventeenth and eighteenth centuries had militated against such connections.[47] Improvements in communication and transportation enabled citywide subaltern and vernacular publics to take shape. Though catalyzed initially in response to specific issues and grievances including opposition to Christian missionization, networks were soon forged around reform, social welfare, and nationalism (Indian and Tamil), through educational, labor, and professional linkages, and through the caste associations that came into existence in the late nineteenth century. Spaces of sociality expanded from temples and mosques to include schools, performance venues, clubs, and philanthropies. And as opposition to the colonial regime gained mass support, in the 1920s and 1930s, these spaces extended to the colonial built environments, to streets, parks, and public buildings, as rallies, strikes, public fasts, and processions became common parts of nationalist repertoires.

SPACES OF CURATORIAL STATECRAFT

The built environment of Madras was crafted by colonial authorities as a stage to accommodate and mediate European modernity and the state institutions central to its functional, representational, and rhetorical projects. The city's business district was also the ceremonial core of the colonial state, its buildings, statues, fountains, gardens, and monuments dense with visual and architectural referents to the state's power, genealogy, and telos.[48] Stylistically and iconographically, these sites quoted imperial pasts and outfitted the colonial state with a legacy of imperial rule. The neoclassicism popularized during the eighteenth century, with its high pediments, columns, heavy entablature, monumental interiors, and commemorative battle murals and trophies, continued to furnish the visual vocabulary of empire in the nineteenth century.[49] It was supplemented in the century's final quarter with the new, hybrid lexicon of Indo-Saracenic style, an amalgamation of Hindu and Muslim imperial architecture featuring additional elements drawn from Gothic and Byzantine styles.[50] Indeed, the concentration of Indo-Saracenic buildings earned Madras a reputation as the birthplace of the style.

During the second half of the nineteenth century, Indo-Saracenic buildings multiplied in the Fort district, which was enlarged in 1855 when colonial authorities divested the Nawab of most of his holdings. Though this section of the city retained a marked Muslim character with the Amir Mahal, Wallajah Mosque, Muslim schools, and many Muslim-owned businesses, the Chepauk Palace was appropriated for the Presidency's Revenue Board and its Public Works Department and renovated in Indo-Saracenic style. Between 1870 and 1905 other buildings affecting an Indo-Saracenic style were erected: Madras Post and Telegraph (1875–85), Presidency College (1874–79), Senate House (1874–79), Government Museum (1899), Victoria Hall (1906), High Court (1889–92), Law College (1894), Egmore Rail Station (1905–8), and the Bank of Madras (1896–99). The same style was adopted for stores, hotels, theaters, and clubs, which multiplied in the last half of the nineteenth century along Mount Road and other arteries that connected European residential space with spaces of work and governance. These included the Spencer and Company Department Store, built in 1895, which remained a prominent landmark until 1985, when it was destroyed by a fire.

These new public structures were tied to the state's surveillance apparatus by their styles and functions. They were headquarters for agencies that enabled British rulers to "see" the territory and inhabitants of British India: census operations, mapping, property and taxation records, courts, and schools. And, together with the new parks and gardens that surrounded them, they created a single visual field in which colonial sociality, historicism, and statecraft were interwoven and infused with Victorian tastes and notions of civility.[51] Here, the colonial state and the empire of which it was a part could be "seen," that is, materially, acoustically, and visually encountered, by both its own agents and the subjects it sought to dominate.

TOWN PLANNING

As the nineteenth century advanced, decisions about infrastructure and about the management of public space in Madras and other colonial cities were informed by the precept, fundamental to Euro-Western modernity, that the cityscape was a spatial system, subject to state control, as well as a medium of governmentality. The city served and mediated the state; in turn, the design and function of the built environment contributed to the historicism on which state institutions relied and sought to impart among colonial subjects. These principles were codified in the new science of town planning, which in Europe and North America designated a liberal discourse on the spatial means and correlates of societal well-being.[52] Henry Lanchester, an early theorist of town planning, described it as the implementation of "civic hygiene" through the coordination of the knowledge and practice associated with architecture, engineering, and agriculture.[53] In Lanchester's view, town planning enabled urban centers to be more efficiently articulated with modern state operations, both its institutional fabric and surveillance functions. He proposed that a city's historically evolved spatial morphology be used as the template for achieving a functional articulation of statecraft and urban form.

In the early twentieth century, strenuous arguments were posed in favor of town planning in Madras, particularly because of the rapidity of its population growth.[54] Like other colonial cities, it was seen as a victim of the lack of systematic planning as well as a laboratory for developing and testing theories about societal organization and progress. Though the Madras Corporation had been charged with municipal administration since 1688, it had never functioned as a planning agency. The aforementioned Henry Lanchester was commissioned with the preparation of a civic survey meant to lay the groundwork for a systematic program of town planning. The resulting work, *Town Planning in Madras,* was published in 1918, and two years later a Town Planning Act was passed by the Presidency's Legislative Council.

Lanchester's proposal differed from those that came in its wake by advocating explicitly that "tradition" guide planning activities. He maintained that settlement planning principles of some sort existed in all societies and that an effective modern planning instrument, defined in terms of its goals of vibrant civic life, health, order, and economic prosperity, should take cognizance of those principles and selectively incorporate those most likely to contribute to progress. His presentation, copiously documented with comparative and historical examples, treated Madras as an assemblage of historically distinct landscapes, in which traditional mores and social arrangements were embedded in settlement pattern and spatial morphology. He likened the material embodiment of tradition in the cityscape to spaces of Europe's own past, medieval cities such as Antwerp.[55]

Town Planning in Madras was both a civic survey—an analytic description of the city's population, land use, and settlement patterns—and a prescriptive text. "Tradition," materialized in spatial form and distinct from the scientific, objective representation of the "historic" past, figured within both aims. It was, in Lanchester's words, "superfluous to discuss tradition in India," as tradition was "generally respected" there, despite having "lost ground" under the "abnormal condition" of colonial state formation.[56] Tradition, understood as lifeways and values that persisted over time, was engendered by religion and manifest in the built environment, notably for Lanchester with residential segregation by caste and occupation and by the mixing of spaces of work and habitation.[57] The erosion of tradition was most apparent in the city's lack of cohesion and centricity.[58] Among the correctives proposed was the retention of caste and occupational settlement patterns but also the recapture of tradition through conservation of places of historic significance within the fragmented cityscape. Fort St. George was principal among the sites whose preservation was recommended; also included were larger mosques, temples, and churches, the remains of Nawab's estate in Chepauk, and San Thome's homes and cathedral.[59]

Recommendations about conservation were based on principles of civic hygiene, which meant that Lanchester advised the discard or revision of some traditions. For example, he faulted traditional spatial norms for their lack of provision of open space, attributing Indians' underdeveloped individuality and "passivity" to inadequate recreation. Gardens, parks, and green belts were prescribed both at the city's outskirts and in proximity to living/working areas to enhance bodily health and improve civic consciousness.[60] One "defect of the city," he wrote, was the "dependence on spectacle for entertainment rather than exercises for people to develop [their] own faculties."[61] Another innovation proposed was zoning for use, along with the clustering of public buildings within those zones. The government/business zone was to be centered around Fort St. George and the public buildings of the Marina and Chepauk; Central Rail Station and clubs and hotels in the Southwest, near Adyar, were to provide dual social centers. These measures, along with the provision of scenic vistas through the use of axial planning, appropriate landscaping, and wider streets, would enable the city to be seen as a city, with a distinct identity and image.

Through town planning, Lanchester hoped to make the population conscious of the tradition in which, theretofore, they had been enveloped and to produce a modernist understanding of tradition. The latter was to be achieved among Indians through the cultivation of both individuality and historicist consciousness.[62] Astute planning could help objectify tradition, by extracting it from the built environment and re-presenting it in order to promote civic hygiene.

STAGING HISTORY: THE MUSEUM AND THE ARCHAEOLOGICAL SURVEY

The state that planned and that saw and was seen was, I have suggested, a curatorial state, whose production of space entailed the production and circulation of historical knowledge and the embedding of that knowledge in spaces of collective memory. In Madras Presidency and elsewhere in British India, these formations of the historical past rested on a network of institutions charged with reclaiming evidence about the past and producing knowledge about it, which appeared in the mid-nineteenth century. Prominent among them were the Archaeological Survey of India (ASI) and the allied network of museums, libraries, and monuments which the survey's operations

Figure 2.4. National Gallery of Art (formerly Victoria Hall), Chennai
Photograph by author.

helped inaugurate and sustain. Together, these agencies were responsible for excavating, inventorying, cataloging, and conserving residues of the past, reproducing them photographically, and exhibiting them. Their operations were headquartered in provincial capitals, like Madras, and the new public buildings in which these institutions were housed made up the landscape of imperial power. The pasts that these agencies discovered, cataloged, and displayed yielded emblems that the state used to craft new spaces of memory in which its own genealogy could be encoded.

The preeminent space in which the historicism of the imperialist aesthetic was married to its surveillance procedures was, of course, the museum.[63] In 1851 a collection of natural history specimens was presented to the provincial government for display in its museum, then located in the "suburban village" of Nungambakkam in a building that formerly had housed the Asiatic Society. The Government Museum remained on this site, gradually accumulating specimens of both natural and cultural history, until 1899, when a new museum was opened in Egmore, near the former site of the Pantheon, a cultural and literary club founded in 1778. The new Government Museum, housed in an Indo-Saracenic structure, was situated in a spacious park near the Connemara Library (built 1896). Similarly hybrid structures were soon added. Victoria Hall (later converted to the National Art Gallery) (Fig. 2.4) was completed in 1909; in that same year, a new building for the Presidency's Archives was erected near the museum complex.

This space of Victorian public culture mirrored the museums and exhibition halls in colonial metropole in its design and exhibition format, and in the embodied norms of civility that visitors were expected to adopt, as they quietly contemplated the order of the natural world and the glories of past civilizations. The Government Museum, through both pedagogy and bodily praxis, was expected to carry out the state's "civilizing mission"—particularly by introducing Indians to the civilizational roots that, like their spatial traditions, they were thought to have forgotten and to scientific methods for retrieving and organizing those pasts. The comments of one ASI superintendent, William Longhurst, portrayed these goals and the links between historicism and modern statecraft that underlay them:

> It is certainly a fact that the average educated Indian knows far more about the history and architecture of Greece and Rome than he does about that of his own country and this is surely not as it should be especially if, in the future, he desires to take a more active part in the administration of the country. Architecture has been described very truly as the printing press of all ages, and it is to be hoped that in these days of enlightenment the study of architectural history will soon take its proper place as part of a liberal education.[64]

The museum's collections and exhibitionary spaces asserted a common order in the unfolding of both nature and culture, particularly in the colonies, whose social worlds were regarded as close to the order of nature. The museum director, Edgar Thurston, expanded and modernized the museum with these principles in mind.[65] The 1908 *Imperial Gazetteer* commended Thurston's approach:

> The policy adopted has been to render it a popular illustrated guide to the natural history . . . arts, archaeology, ethnology, and economic resources of the Presidency; and that it is appreciated by the public is sufficiently shown by the fact that it is visited annually by more than 400,000 persons.[66]

Closely tied to the organization, operations, and holdings of this and other museums in British India was the Archaeological Survey of India, founded in 1861.[67] The ASI was an All-India agency with provincial offices in each of the regional "circles" into which British India was divided for the purpose of survey operations.[68] The agency was critical to knowledge production and to mapping of history onto the territorial space of the Raj. It was both the descendent of and functional counterpart to the territorial and social survey operations launched earlier in the nineteenth century, which collected and cartographically re-presented information about topography, biotic and mineral resources, population distribution, land ownership, and agriculture. The ASI was charged by the Government of India with the identification, recovery, and listing of antiquities and monuments, and its mission soon included the preparation of photographic records.[69]

In concert with the museum and backed by force of law, the ASI retrieved and organized the past, using the techniques, practices, and vision of science. In the early twentieth century, under the vice-regency of Lord Curzon, ASI functions were amended to include an emphasis on conservation. In a speech to the Asiatic

Society, Curzon transferred Britain's nationalist template for defining and preserving heritage to its colonial holdings. He declared: "it is . . . equally our duty to dig and discover, to classify, reproduce and describe, to copy and decipher and to cherish and conserve."[70] The Ancient Monuments Preservation Act of 1904 officially added conservation to the Survey's charge, placing it within the "civilizing mission" of imperialism and anticipating its contribution to nation building.

Early reports (1881, 1882, 1885) listed monuments, inscriptions, and other antiquities. In Madras Presidency, these included the Pallava-era temples and rock sculptures at Mahaballipuram, the Fort at Trichinopoly, the ruins of Vijayanagara capital at Hampi, and several large temples (Tanjore, Conjeevarum, Challambaram, Tiruvallur, Saidapet, and Tinnanur), a mosque (Poonamallee), churches (Little Mount, St Thomas Mount, Santhome), and St. Thomas's grave, near Mylapore.[71] The reports of the 1880s were faulted, however, as unsystematic, because of "untrustworthy information supplied by native subordinates."[72] A second All-India Survey (1891) was commissioned, with the requirement that its list include only monuments examined firsthand by British officers. In his contribution, the new superintendent for ASI's Madras circle, Alexander Rea, appealed to the taxonomic logic of natural history, revising the list of "buildings of historic interest" that had been prepared in 1885 to include "only such monuments as are unique or very ancient or possess exceptional merit as typical specimens of their style of architecture and the periods to which they belong."[73] Specific criteria for listing were offered and conservation was explicitly embraced and distinguished from "renewal." In another reference to Indians' shallow historical sensibilities, Rea advised that "buildings . . . not be modernized in course of repair" and cautioned that local workers be closely supervised to prevent them from applying "modern imitations of classic details . . . indiscriminately in place and out of it on all classes of buildings."[74]

ASI reports document some of the conflicts between European historicism and vernacular forms of historical consciousness engendered by the curatorial state. Hindu temples, because of their significance as artifacts of the subcontinent's architectural history, were particularly important flashpoints where different modes of spatial and commemorative practices collided. The Survey's assertion of rights to manage the use of temples' spaces—accomplished by official declaration of their antiquarian value—challenged the existing, delicately calibrated networks of persons (temple servants, priests, donors, worshipers, tenants) who regulated the space. Rea recounted one such dispute, at the "Tripurantakeswaraswami Temple," a Pallava-era temple in "Conjeevarum" (Kanchipuram). Despite Rea's instruction that certain carved surfaces were to be left exposed, temple authorities insisted on whitewashing those surfaces. They first obstructed the government conservator's access by "lock[ing] and seal[ing] the temple without giving notice to the contractor to remove his material and tools." In the contractor's absence, they completed their own restoration. Such actions, complained Rea, threatened to destroy "all archaeological interest the temple possesses [by] making it appear like a newly built one, which is apparently what they want."[75]

ASI's claim of jurisdiction, moreover, did not stop with architectural conservation but led to efforts to intervene in worship practices, on the grounds that they damaged the sites. In general, the ASI's recommendations for conservation conflicted with the embodied, sensory interactions between deity and devotee (e.g., anointing deity icons with solid and liquid substances and with the smoke of incense and camphor; whitewashing sculpted relief work) that formed the core of worship rituals. Coming in for criticism were food preparation, "offensive smells," residential use of temple compounds, the smoke generated from ritual offerings, and the liquids used to anoint deity images and other structural features in the course of worship. Similarly troubling to colonial authorities was the use of sections of temple compounds for markets and the related matter of the proximity of bazaar streets to temples. These earned pejorative comments because of the ways that they obscured the temples' artistic merits.[76] Perceiving worship itself as a danger to the temple architecture, ASI officials regularly attempted to remove objects they deemed to have antiquarian value, often the icons that, for Hindus, were material embodiments of deities.

Together, the ASI and the Government Museum advanced the state's curatorial operations with their shared missions and labors. Besides trading personnel, the organizations functioned in complementary ways, with ASI recovering the residues of the past and the museum providing spaces for storage and exhibition. The chronology developed in Rea's 1891 report was a case in point. It outlined the region's civilizational sequence, based on remains of temples, beginning with Buddhist remains and continuing through Pallava, Chola, Chalukyan, Jaina, and Dravidian periods. Of special import for its civilizational narrative were the sculpted marble remains of the railing of the Buddhist stupa at Amaravati, a monument of the second century CE. These objects typified what colonial scholars and government authorities considered the region's "golden age," the Buddhist legacy, which the subcontinent's current (largely Hindu) inhabitants had to be coaxed to remember and re-learn.[77] The museum's exhibition translated Rea's sequence into spaces of visual pedagogy. The Amaravati gallery was the museum's most imposing section and its costliest exhibition. Like the more famous Elgin marbles, the remains had been dismantled on-site and reassembled in a special gallery built for their display and meant to re-create the effect of monumentality. Their representation within the imperial memoryscape of the museum was meant to cure the amnesia that had stymied civilizational advance and, along with political reforms, to introduce the historicist consciousness on which modern nationhood depended.

MADRAS AS A HISTORICAL SUBJECT

As Lanchester's 1918 proposal for town planning suggested, the apparatus with which historicism was wedded to statecraft in Madras could be turned on Madras itself. During most of the nineteenth century, Madras's own past had not engaged the antiquarian imagination of the colonial state. Sewell's ASI Report for 1882 had confirmed the shallowness of Madras's history: as a "mere fishing village up to 1639 AD. . . it is not be expected that there is much of antiquarian interest in the place."[78] However, even as the curatorial state was documenting the subcontinent's ancient past, colonial officers and private citizens were beginning to assemble documentary histories of the city, starting with J. Talboys Wheeler's publication of extracts of Fort St. George Records in *Madras in the Olden Times* (1861–62).[79]

Following its own emphasis on conservation, the Archaeological Survey added more Madras sites to its lists of historic monuments and began to include photographic documentation. At the same time Lanchester assembled his aforementioned survey. With these measures, the city began to emerge as a historically formed subject, requiring documentation and conservation, rather than just a stage for display. Most sites listed as having historic significance were so designated by virtue of their colonial origins, with the exception of the city's larger Hindu temples. For example, the remnants of the town wall, built in the mid-1600s, was listed as an antiquity in the 1903–1904 report; with that, funds were budgeted for its conservation. Other colonial features, including additional boundary markers and European tombs, found their way into subsequent reports.[80]

The residues of the city's colonial past that surfaced in ASI reports reappeared in the narratives, popular and scholarly, of the city's history that were compiled in the early decades of the twentieth century. The most ambitious of these works was prepared by a colonial military officer, Col. Henry Davison Love, whose multivolume account of the city's history covered the period between 1639 and 1800. *Vestiges of Old Madras* combined chronologically based historiographical narratives with edited reproductions of primary-source (English-language) documents, most of which had been gathered from the records of Fort St. George and the India Office Library, as well as a number of manuscripts and secondary works.[81] Detailed appendices listed place names and their original referents.

Historicist knowledge was produced also in guidebooks, such as those published by John Murray, that catered to an emergent tourism industry.[82] *The Story of Madras* (1921) by Glyn Barlow took advantage of available documentation with an account geared to popular audiences.[83] The city's greatest charm, opined Barlow, was its history which he sought to excavate for his readers. The work, meant as a guide for touring the city, contained fifteen chapters. The chapters progressed chronologically, and each focused on specific landscapes, buildings, and districts considered emblematic of particular periods or events. He addressed English-speaking residents and visitors, inviting his readers to grasp the stories of the past that lay embedded in the built environment, to see the cityscape as residues of past lives and events of the area's European residents. Barlow assisted them with this task by closing many chapters with passages that re-created some episode associated with the sites described, employing visual language to create an enlarged, historicized sense of place, accompanied by a nostalgic experience of time's passage. Government House, he wrote, was

> suggestive of dinner parties within and garden parties without. . . . But to people who can look at Government House . . . with an historic glance it rouses other memories. Within its original walls more than two centuries ago a belaced Senhor kept Portuguese state. . . . It was here that Lally lived sumptuously in prison. . . . It was within these grounds that Tipu's horsemen were scampering

> about on a September morning, looking for houses where money or jewels could be commandeered. It was here that an ennobled Governor of Madras lived in gilded captivity till death set him free.[84]

The guide, in short, invited readers to participate imaginatively in a past that led, inexorably, to the colonial present.

In contrast to Barlow's celebratory narrative were the struggles between colonial authorities and subaltern subjects over the state's designation of historical sites and its prescribed conservation measures. State officials, for example, lamented the unevenness with which Indians absorbed the lessons they sought to impart with the museum's collections. Elites, whose service in the colonial state extended to work in the museum and affiliated agencies, both labored on the historicizing projects as catalogers, translators, and transcribers, and were among its more appreciative audiences. The majority were described as child-like spectators, visiting museum grounds as a form of recreation on festival days, like *Poṅkal,* which in 1895, attracted more than thirty-six thousand visitors.

Stories of colonial occupation and improvement such as Barlow's were absent or, at best, marginally noted in the vernacular caste histories that became more popular toward the end of the nineteenth century. These accounts interpolated Madras within Tondaimandalam, sometimes in an effort to staunch declining family fortunes with claims on property or status.[85] The 1911 caste history produced by a section of the Vellalar community, an important and influential landowning group, linked their organization to territorial claims that both predated and encompassed the European presence.[86] The site granted to English traders was described as part of a village under Vellalar jurisdiction. Despite their later migration to Madras, undertaken for commercial gain, they retained their rural, pre-British social order. Madras, they implied, had intruded into but not reorganized the political geography of their community.

Finally, different streams of nationalist discourses on the pasts of territory, language, and race engaged in complex ways with the historicist modes of narrating and representing the past that the colonial state authorized. The same subaltern civil servants whose labor was commandeered for state-sponsored history making as translators, excavators, exegetes, and curators often employed the same modes of knowledge production in anticolonial movements. Among the English-educated professional elite were early promulgators of pan-Indian nationalism and its historiography.[87] Contemporaneous with their efforts were the vernacular history-making projects of self-declared devotees of "Pure Tamil." Building on philological claims of Tamil's antiquity, advanced by Bishop Caldwell in the mid-1800s, they argued that Tamil speakers were the subcontinent's original inhabitants.[88] Sumathi Ramaswamy has argued that, for some, Madras and the Tamil country surrounding it were indexes of absence, imagined as the remnants of an ancient mega-continent, Kumarikkantam, home to the academies that were said to have produced the chief works of Tamil's classical literary corpus.[89] According to these accounts, although Kumarikkantam's submergence in a vast flood had caused Tamil speakers to scatter, it had been the cradle of the human race, a civilization that anticipated the achievements of modernity and that could be recalled, as a living memory, through the Tamil language. Nationalist projects, Tamil and pan-Indian, were limited in the ability to produce and control the urban built environment, and, in the case of Kumarikkantam, they worked through the potency of absence and loss. They produced spaces of memory nonetheless: temples and ancestral homes underwent conservation and renovation, and phantasmic spaces, such as vanished or hoped for homelands, were mediated in poetry, song, and images.

"MADRAS" IN/AND THE CURATORIAL STATE

In the nineteenth and early twentieth centuries architectural design and town planning both worked to create an urban landscape studded with places of memory. Specific state agencies were also charged with the production of historical knowledge, with the retrieval, documentation, and conservation of residues and with pedagogical functions capable of enrolling subjects within the histories it had "discovered." "Madras" emerged as a stage on which antiquities might be assembled, displayed, and performed, and as a home to organizations charged with the production of historical knowledge. And by the final years of the nineteenth century the city was increasingly considered a historical subject in its own right, with pasts, embedded in its built environment, worthy of documentation and conservation.

The Tercentenary Commemoration volume quoted above is an artifact of these impulses: it documented the manifold ways that the past had come to be understood as present in the city, in its homes, public buildings, and temples, and in its libraries, monuments, and place names. It also gestured, in veiled ways, to the vibrant historical imaginaries of pan-Indian and Tamil nationalisms. At least some of the contributors to the volume shared the convictions of a growing number of Madras residents that the city and the region surrounding it had been only superficially designed by colonial rule. Using historicist tools, they imagined pasts of language, land, and race that ran far deeper than the three hundred years that the volume celebrated. S. Krishnaswami Aiyangar observed that, "what we now-a-days call Madras goes in history at least down to the beginning of the Christian era," and he listed documentary evidence for the antiquity of several of the city's shrines and the cultural boundaries that they marked.[90] Another contributor, C. Achyuta Menon, dealt with the philological evidence for Tamil nationalism in his review of the status of Dravidian language studies in the city.[91]

These implicit references contrasted with the materiality of competing nationalisms on the city's streets. The year the volume was released, 1939, saw escalating conflict in Madras City between proponents of pan-Indian and Tamil nationalisms, much of it concerning vernacular language instruction in the Presidency's secondary schools.[92] Whereas advocates of Hindi saw it as an instrument of pan-Indian nationalism, Tamil's proponents argued both for the deeper antiquity of the Tamil language and its centrality to Tamil identity.[93] These imaginaries inserted themselves into the interstices of the built environment, with rallies, processions, and public fasts, and into mediated space, as images of the bodily and territorial sovereignty that the languages encoded proliferated in poems, essays, songs, maps, and other images. It was not until independence, however, that these imaginaries found their way into statecraft and were materialized in architecture and made official in names and maps.

1996: "Chennai" Returns

> Keeping the universal acceptance of the name, Chennai, in view and keeping also the historical, social, cultural and other details of the City of Madras in view, the Government has taken a policy decision that Madras would be hereafter called "Chennai" in all languages as against "Madras" and "Madharas" now.[94]

The proposal to change the city's name officially to Chennai was delivered with an avowedly nativist flourish by the state's ruling party, the Dravida Munnetra Kazhagam (DMK). It placed the city within the context of Tamil singularity, drawing on the spirit of Tamil devotionalism that had infused ethnic and linguistic nationalisms of the late nineteenth and early twentieth centuries. The 1996 action had been preceded by an earlier name change sponsored by the same party upon their gaining control of the state Legislative Assembly in 1967: this change was the adoption of "Tamil Nadu" to replace "Madras" as the state's name. It bears noting that the Dravidianist political parties that have dominated state government since 1967 have been uneven in their support for Tamil language and culture, and that their genesis as parties is linked only indirectly to Tamil-language revitalization movements. Nonetheless, Tamil devotionalism has been consistently employed as an emblem of party identity and has infused political oratory and visual culture. The 1996 adoption of "Chennai" followed in this direction with its bid to Dravidianize the city and thereby authenticate, even if post facto, the seat of government and the state apparatus with which they exercised political power. Even as it assured voters of the Tamil commitments of the party, it announced the city's identity—its "brand"—to the global investors that the state, since the deregulation initiatives of the early 1990s, had sought aggressively.

After gaining independence in 1947, India retained much of the colonial state's bureaucracy, including its civil service cadres, but realigned those institutions toward the developmentalist goals of a centrally planned, nationalized economy. With the New Industrial Policy of 1991, the name by which the first generation of structural adjustment policies was known, India's central government reversed direction and initiated privatization and deregulation of major state-run industries and the devolution of economic policy making to states. In 1993 India's constitution was amended to include provisions granting local governing bodies (urban and rural) more authority in creating policy. These amendments, the seventy-third and seventy-fourth, were crafted to create the political conditions to support deregulation and privatization. The combined effects of decentralization and deregulation led to greater competition among Indian cities and states to attract investment, especially in secondary and tertiary sectors. Since the mid-1990s, Tamil Nadu, already one of India's more industrialized and urbanized states, has attracted significant public and private investments in industry, services (tourism, information technology, and export processing), and infrastructure.[95]

Economic change after independence had profoundly transformed Chennai's social and geographic landscape.[96] The city's municipal boundary had remained unchanged but its population had increased, spiking in the 1940s and 1960s, as a result of industrial expansion during both periods. As occurred in other major cities, Chennai grew laterally, and the municipality, along with what had become its peri-urban fringe, was redefined as an Urban Agglomeration.[97] The city and its environs, now known as the Chennai Metropolitan Area, comprises a total area of 1,189 square kilometers. Rural in-migration has continued, and by 2001 the city's population had reached 4.2 million, with an additional 1.8 million in its outskirts. The city's slum population is now estimated at 1.6 million and is spread among 1,279 slums.[98] Chennai's poverty level of 38 percent is higher than the statewide average, and, despite having the state's highest per capita income and Human Development Index (.757), its levels of economic inequality are also the state's highest.[99]

Broad patterns of land use in Chennai have followed colonial precedents, with industrial sites in the north and northwest, and residential and commercial uses predominating in the districts to the west and south of the central business and financial districts. The temple towns incorporated in the seventeenth and eighteenth centuries retain their preindustrial footprints, with their bazaars, central courtyard houses, and open shop fronts, but old building stock has been replaced with flat complexes, high-rise offices, and shopping malls. The Fort district remains the locus of government activities, though the vistas of the city's colonial past are interrupted by the memorials, statues, and stylized facades with which Tamil Nadu's Dravidianist ruling parties reclaimed the Marina, beginning in the late 1960s. Marking the late-twentieth-century turn to the "new economy," driven by service and knowledge industries, are the gated communities, malls, and export processing and information technology campuses in the far south and southwest divisions. These, as well as new resorts, theme parks, and restaurants define the new "industrial corridor" that extends from the city's southern edge to the village of Mamallapuram, the new (Dravidianized) name for Mahaballipuram.

Changes to the cityscape can be summed up in the term "formalization," which glosses the expansion of the built-up portion used for formal sector economic ventures, with their deeper ties to global capitalism.[100] Formalization, in general, entails, for example, the elimination of informal sector actors and activities in public spaces, the creation of transportation and communications networks that allow for smooth flows of people, goods, and information, and stricter zoning of administrative, commercial, industrial, and residential areas. Chennai's infrastructural growth and refurbishment during the 1990s were geared to these ends. With international aid and private investment to augment expenditures by state and national agencies, the commuter rail system was extended, streets and major arteries were widened, more than twenty overpasses were constructed, the storm drain network was expanded, the river-canal system was de-silted, and more technologically sophisticated power generation facilities were constructed.[101]

Formalization has been led by state and municipal agencies. The Chennai Metropolitan Development Authority (CMDA), supported by Chennai's Corporation and City Council, has advocated growth in selected industries and in the services generally. Urban development control rules regarding pollutant levels, building heights and size, and water usage were relaxed to encourage more industrial ventures, including the aforementioned industrial estates and export processing zones in the city's southern and western suburban fringe and an updated power generation facility north of the Port.[102] These changes supported statewide industrial growth rates of 5.35 percent per annum in the 1990s, largely in secondary and tertiary sectors. Changing employment patterns, which include a sharp rise in informal sector employment, indicate retrenchment and decreased job security.[103]

Capitalism's creative destruction—its restless innovation—is captured as much in the images of the new as it is in the, by now, classic images of demolition. In Chennai, cycles of slum demolition and resettlement have accelerated, accompanied by repeated, usually fruitless efforts to eliminate street vendors, pavement dwellers, and encroachments. The city's western fringes, where chemical plants, car and car ancillary factories, and export-processing campuses are found, have been targeted as sites for slum relocation.

Inequalities in health, livelihood, and housing have deepened with the environmental degradation that accompanies industrialization. Problems that were already pressing have worsened. These include a rapidly dropping water table, inadequate sewage and solid waste disposal systems, increased water, soil, and air pollution, and higher incidences of insect-, air-, and water-borne diseases, such as malaria, filaria, and tuberculosis.[104] Exacerbating these negative impacts, much of the new residential, commercial, and industrial development in the city's southern divisions has taken place in a fragile estuarine zone, in contravention of national environmental regulations.[105] In addition to the effect on the estuarine ecosystem, these have drained groundwater from an increasingly larger catchment zone, accelerating the water table drop. The poor, again, are disproportionately affected because of the marginal locations of slums (often on river or canal banks) and their lack of civic amenities.

Environmentalists' efforts to halt or reverse the degradation of natural resources and loss of biodiversity in the region rely on litigation, public education, and various self-help and government-sponsored initiatives, such as tree planting, water harvesting, and composting. There has also been a tendency, on the part of the state and municipality, to cloak its development and relocation initiatives in environmentalist and "beautification" garb. In Chennai, numerous programs made their appearance in the mid-1990s, including solid waste collection and recycling and water harvesting. In these programs, discourses of ecological sustainability were paired with those of beautification; they were framed as efforts to enhance the city's attractiveness to tourists, transnational corporate actors, investors, and the diasporic community from whom many of the latter were recruited.[106] Members of India's far-flung Non-Resident Indian community are especially sought after as investors, property owners, and consumers with appeals that speak to their complex desires for "home." Some of the same local and multinational corporations whose expansion has hastened the degradation of regional ecosystems have "adopted" city parks, recreation areas, and historical sites, and assist in their maintenance. Slogans were coined to capture these orientations, and phrases such as "Singara (Beautiful) Chennai" and "Clean Chennai, Green Chennai" soon appeared on decorative banners and archways that framed the city's new thoroughfares.

THE PLANNING STATE

The city's formalization in the 1990s capped a process of urban development that, since independence, had been informed by technocratic, rationalized planning instruments. Postcolonial narratives on the city's history often allude to the failure of planning, meaning the failure to implement planning recommendations, as well as specific weaknesses of content. By contrast, the rhetoric of planning, in which the city's history is narrated as a process of modernization, has been quite successful. The rise of the formal city is understood as being infused by the spirit, if not the letter, of planning canons. Unlike the curatorial state, the planning state is much less concerned about claiming territory on historical grounds. Planning rhetoric casts the city as a space of possibility, the materiality of its pasts being, for the most part, unwelcome interruptions and sources of disorder. The planning state, however, retains the institutional capacity to objectify, excise, and re-present those traditions as ornamental *lieux de memoire;* indeed, landscapes of modernity demand signs of the pasts that they supersede. This is the condition in which heritage was reengaged in the 1990s for the purposes of branding the city.

Despite the reverence for traditional spatial norms voiced by Lanchester in 1918, the planning discourses that his work inaugurated were considerably more skeptical than he about the possibility of producing modernity within the spaces of traditional life. Town-planning activities of the early twentieth century were neither systematic nor consistent in their implementation. They did, however, attempt to make spatial sense of the city's population and economy, and identified the proliferation of squatter settlements as the central problem that planning should tackle.[107] Slums were taken to be the principal material signs of tradition and its pathological quality, its infectiousness, and its propensity to decay.[108] Ranson explained that the "habitually antisocial conduct of the community in matters of sanitation and hygiene may create new housing problems as quickly as builders solve old ones. . . . [A sense of] impermanence colors his outlook and behavior and [he lacks] housepride."[109] Social workers argued that both the physical improvements in housing and targeted social services would help impart an "enlightened civic and sanitary conscience."[110]

Despite the moral panic that precipitated town planning, its actual implementation was piecemeal during most of the colonial period. With independence, economic, social, and spatial planning were embraced in a forthright manner. The

Nehruvian development model, a modified state socialism that focused on central planning to achieve self-sufficiency, was emblematized by large-scale projects (dams, hydroelectric plants, mechanized agriculture, irrigation) undertaken to jump-start the national economy. Futurity was the central trope of the national narrative, and traditions were evaluated according to their contributions to national development and integration. The 1961 Census Report provided a systematic and insistently empirical account of those traditions, mainly in the form of its enumeration of religious sites and festivals. Numerous other committees and commissions were charged, in the 1950s and 1960s, with similar projects of cataloging and evaluation.[111] As chapter 5 details, domestic tourism was treated as a particularly rich possibility for conjoining the projects of national integration and domestic consumption.

The five-year plans authored by both central and state planning commissions set economic goals for states and local bodies, but there was little coordination between their operations and those of local town-planning agencies. In practice, it was state-level housing authorities that took on the work of planning. The Tamil Nadu Housing Board was formed in 1961 to coordinate public housing activities in the state; in 1970 the Tamil Nadu Slum Clearance Board was created to address housing problems of the urban poor. Declaring slums to be a "blot on any civilized society . . . a cancer in the heart of the city . . . cradle of disease, birthplace of crimes, nursery for perverted human bundle of complexes suffering from unbalanced social equilibrium and training ground for crooks," Tamil Nadu's Slum Clearance Board aimed to clear all of the city's twelve hundred slums and squatter settlements and re-house residents in modern tenements.[112] Like dams, these new housing projects were icons of modernist futurity—order inhered in functional efficiency (achieved through uniformity, rationalization of spatial form, mass production, economy of scale) and, with it, erasure of the residues of the past, which, like dirt, represented "matter out of place."[113]

Although the state's General Town Planning Scheme was drafted in 1957, it was not until India's third five-year plan, covering the period from 1961 to 1966, that metropolitan master plans were mandated.[114] The Madras Metropolitan Plan (1973) envisioned the city as a municipal core linked to satellite towns by radial corridors and identified a developable corridor south of the city.[115] Elements of the city's past were selectively reclaimed under the goal of "imageability," a quality described in terms of a "visually vivid and well structured" landscape, with "component parts [that could be] easily recognized and inter-related" and would attract local visitation and tourism.[116] Clustering of key public buildings and the development of parks and other spaces for leisure and recreation would contribute to imageability, as would the preservation of "special visual areas in their natural condition and development of historical and cultural sites."[117] Historical sites, like other beautification measures, were described as

> "frills" . . . necessary to give the City a character and dignity of its own and to act as a booster for civic morale to keep the environment clean and tidy. Many cities

> which have invested in such schemes have, apart from satisfying the aesthetic needs of citizens, earned more than they had spent through tourist earnings.[118]

The recommendations of the 1973 plan were not revisited until 1992, when MMDA convened a national seminar.[119] A draft version of the second master plan was circulated in 1995, and, as in earlier plans, a vexed relation with the city's past was evident. Residues of the past were both pathological invaders of the modern and necessary sources of "imageability." This was captured in its frontispiece, a photomontage evoking the rhetoric of earlier plans. The foreground of the image was dominated by a scooter, on which six or seven people were mounted. The downtown street scene was framed against the ornate horizon of Raja Annamalai Hall (built in 1953 to honor the Chettiar merchant banker), which rises in the background. The caption read: "too small for too many." The image, with its visual irony, encapsulated the report's modernist narrative: its identification of the city's problems as population growth; inadequate housing, infrastructure, and transport; low employment; inattention to environmental and cultural conservation; and high pollution levels. Its solution, however, departed from the tenets of central planning by offering recommendations in keeping with neoliberalism. These recommendations were encapsulated in a growth strategy known by its acronym, MIDOS, which stood for "minimally directed organic growth scheme." To facilitate the expansion of export processing, financial services, tourism, and electronics, the plan proposed "flexible zoning" and introduced, as a new category, the "urbanizable" zone in which minimum constraints were imposed on entrepreneurs as long as "environmental safeguards" were met.[120]

More important than the specific recommendations, however, was MMDA's advocacy of a more central role for itself—as a nodal agency responsible for the coordination of economic development through a permanent metropolitan economic monitoring and planning body. In its new role, MMDA was to be a "facilitator" of private-sector undertakings through the administration of new financing mechanisms, including tax incentives, to encourage private-sector investment in infrastructure and housing. Among these mechanisms were "Build–Operate–Transfer" projects, in which the private sector invests in public undertakings and eventually takes over their management. Other proposals included land sharing and readjustment, higher FSI incentives (Floor Space Index, referring to the ratio between the plot area and the total built area within it), and transfer of development rights. The growth anticipated by the 1995 plan hinged upon the city's attractiveness to investors. Madras, the plan stated, should be developed as a "gateway" for tourists, both international and domestic; in conjunction with that goal, heritage zones should be conserved and developed as tourist sites. Plan authors enthused that new, commercial uses for old buildings might make conservation self-supporting.[121]

Objections to specific provisions of the draft and to MMDA's limited public consultation were raised by consumer groups, heritage proponents, environmentalists, and advocates for the poor. As a result, the 1995 draft was not approved by the state government. A revised Master Plan, submitted for government review in

2005, was released for public comment in April 2007.[122] The 2007 Plan embraced a free-market growth model and emphasized the role that a "new economy," based in information technology (IT), would play in the city's development; the land-use changes it anticipated included decongestion of the urban core and urbanization of the periphery, with proposals for expanded transport networks, additional satellite towns, continued slum resettlement, and the enlargement of the IT-corridor.[123] Further, the privately funded "integrated townships," business and IT parks, and gated communities that appeared in the 1990s were expected to grow in number in the city's hinterland as well as in some of the older industrial centers in Chennai's northern and western divisions.

The metropolitan area's rapid development, therefore, has continued without explicit or approved planning guidelines, under the stimulus of an increasingly speculative real estate market.[124] As a consequence, the laissez-faire growth strategy advocated by the 1995 draft plan has prevailed, as urban development proceeds with case-by-case decisions made by the state and city government agencies that, by and large, are committed to liberalization. International bodies, most prominently the World Bank, have been tapped as sources of funds and expertise for urban development since the late 1990s. These lenders have funded the ambitious infrastructure projects, solid waste management, and power generation, which together have re-sculpted the urban landscape. As important is the government's courting of private investors who are responsible for the new townships, gated communities, and business parks that have multiplied in the city's hinterland and for the gentrification of old industrial zones within the city's northwestern sections.

LIVING MEMORY IN THE FORMAL CITY

Articulated with the desire for modernist spaces and amenities of the formal city that planning encodes are anxieties about the defamiliarization of the cityscape. Longtime residents describe experiences of disorientation, for example, as vernacular housing gives way to flat complexes. For the poor, cycles of demolition and resettlement threaten the social networks on which survival sometimes depends. Many reactions have been triggered by reorganization of streets. Until the past two decades, Chennai's streets, like those of many other Indian cities, were spaces defined by interactions with diverse others, existing as pedestrian-dominated spaces of work, religious and civic life, and commerce. Vendors, tailors, cobblers, and performers made their livings in the mediating spaces of footpaths and sidewalks; small food stalls, shrines, and kiosks were clustered at intersections; processions regularly transformed the street into a space of (sometimes oppressive) festivity (Fig. 2.5). Lately, to serve more effectively as arteries for automotive transport and storage, streets have been widened and overpasses, bridges, and ring roads constructed. Efforts to remove hawkers and other unlicensed users have accelerated with the city's formalization. Not only do these changes eliminate or attenuate the range of uses to which the street can be put, they also change the architectural relations between the street and the built forms at its edges. This is particularly

Figure 2.5. Busy street corner, Mylapore. *Photograph by author.*

acute in residential areas. New, multi-unit flat complexes are now oriented away from the street, in contrast to vernacular urban architecture, which often communicated directly with surrounding streets and lanes. Over a single generation, residents have experienced the loss of many of those interstitial sites that mediated the domestic interior and the street: the verandahs, threshold stoops, and footpaths that had been common places of conversation, commerce, and play.

The kinds of displacement that residents experience in the formal city are often expressed in terms of anxiety and loss. Discourses on losses of relational familiarity, of history, and of cultural distinctiveness have fed a range of conservationist endeavors, with concerns ranging from neo-traditionalist Hindu nationalism to architectural conservation, Dravidianist memory, and folklore documentation. Some but not all are enabled by privatization and deregulation, even as they criticize their means and effects. These projects engage local residents but connect them to networks of transnational support, including multinational corporations, philanthropic foundations, international nongovernmental organizations (NGOs), and Non-Resident Indians.

Combinations of corporate philanthropy and investment have underwritten elite conservationist projects, such as new museum and performance spaces, as well as the aestheticized representations of the past found in high-end hotels, galleries, and parks.[125] One site, DakshinaChitra, a new interactive museum and craft education center in Chennai's fast-developing southern suburbs is the subject of chapter 6. Concerned by the pace of demolition and redevelopment, activists affiliated with INTACH pressed the city to convene a "Heritage Committee" in 1999, for the purpose of generating a list of heritage sites and conservation recommendations, in which temples, churches, and colonial structures, as well as examples of natural heritage, were prominently included. The same group has repeatedly proposed that a statewide Heritage Act be passed. Allying themselves with other advocates for political decentralization, spokespersons take the seventy-fourth amendment as a point of departure, arguing that it provides the avenue for wider public participation in devising and implementing conservation policies. Chapter 4 charts the different and at times competing interests at work in this group's efforts to conserve a Hindu temple in one of the city's newer commercial and residential neighborhoods.

Rather different appropriations of heritage have been made by slumdwellers who, in the 1990s, increasingly argued against relocation using the language of heritage—maintaining that their rights to habitation were based on histories of continuous occupation and cultural identification. In other instances, as discussed in chapter 7, heritage has taken the form of conserving vernacular architecture and building techniques. Both efforts, which incorporate interests in heritage within housing rights activism, are complemented by other, more conventional forms of public memory work. For example, Dalit activists, whose transregional and transnational networks have become more effective in the past decade, include memorial building among their strategies for claiming social and geographic space in the city, specifically with networks of similarly styled memorials dedicated to B. R. Ambedkar, the architect of India's constitution and a Dalit leader.

Political parties and affiliated interest groups are, of course, vocal participants in the naming and claiming of diverse spaces of heritage. Besides the Dravidianist parties, to whom I return below, Hindu nationalists have mounted efforts to redefine spaces of public memory in Chennai. Whereas elite conservationists tend to voice concern about retaining vernacular and historic elements of the built environment and enlarging public access to such spaces, nationalists claim that they are recovering cultural spaces of Hindu identity by demolishing mosques and churches, and by colonizing existing public space with new temples.[126] Since the mid-1980s Hindu nationalists have laid claim to Chennai's public space by staging festival processions, installing street furniture, archways, and pavilions in conjunction with these events, and erecting sidewalk shrines.[127]

It is within these dense cross-currents that the city's Dravidianization, including its 1996 name change, should be understood. The process of Dravidianizing the city began in 1967, the year that the DMK party gained control of the state government, first under C. N. Annadurai and then M. Karunanidhi, both of whom used Tamil cinema to build political reputations and power bases. Unlike some examples of postcolonial remaking of cityscapes, party leaders did not demolish the colonial fabric or create a new urban center outside the original colonial core. Their actions took the form of commemorative architecture in honor of party leaders and culture heroes, some with neo-traditionalist stylistic statements. The Marina, the beachfront promenade facing the state government buildings, was the preferred site for many statues and memorials, including one dedicated to

Figure 2.6. C. N. Annadurai Memorial, Chennai Marina. *Photograph by author.*

Annadurai, who died less than a year after taking office (Fig. 2.6). In commissioning public architectural projects, DMK leaders used the medium of public memory to declare their own and their party's genealogy and legitimacy, as well as to cultivate loyalty and affective attachments among their non-Brahman electoral constituency. Leaders of the rival party, the All-India Annadurai–Dravida Munnetra Kazhagam (AIA-DMK), which has held power in alternation with the DMK since 1967, have pursued similar projects; one of these—a memorial to M. G. Ramachandran (MGR)—is discussed in the next chapter.

These measures, which colonized the seat of state government, made few direct references to the city's own history. They were offered, instead, as narratives of a history whose prime movers were elsewhere and whose apotheosis had been reached with the Dravidianist electoral victories in the 1960s.[128] The 1996 declaration that the city was "Chennai" brought this past home with its claim on the city's history. The name change was ordered by DMK Chief Minister M. Karunanidhi, who came to office after his party swept the 1996 elections, following nearly two decades of rival party rule. The adoption of the new name, like a triumphal arch, marked the victorious return of the DMK.[129] The history indexed by the name is recounted on the city's official Web site, and it traces city origins not to ambitions of European merchants but to the acumen, territorial reach, and commemorative sentiment of Damarla Venkatapathy Nayak.[130] The declaration of Chennai as the city's name is thus presented as the restoration of both the city's original name and the reputation of Venkatapathy. While his power was ultimately undone by the collapse of the empire and by the incursion of Europeans, through acts of commemorative naming, he could be made into an ancestor of the modern Dravidianist rulers of the state—his fall avenged by their political ascent and their own territorial claim on Chennai. This action and subsequent measures to promote Tamil-language education, IT initiatives and cultural memory sponsored by the DMK between 1996 and 2002 and, since its return to power in 2006, as well as by the AIA-DMK (2001–2006) are emblematic of both parties' strategies for retaining the loyalties and attachments of their Tamil-speaking, non-Brahman base as party leaders deepen Tamil Nadu's commitment to neoliberal economic policy.[131]

Critics of the name change favored the retention of "Madras" and took the incoherence of its spatial form and built environment as their point of departure. Instead of treating these qualities as signs of lack, however, they celebrated them as artifacts of the city's origins as a colonial port and its status as the ground zero of Indian modernity. S. Muthiah, the editor of *Madras Musings* and one of INTACH's conveners, was one of the more persistent critics of "Chennai," writing, "there is little doubt that [all of India's major cities] owe much to the beginnings of modern progress that Madras gave the rest of the subcontinent. . . . Madras, till the 1760s, lay the foundations on which modern India has grown."[132] It was precisely this history—unfolding in the restless expansion of capital—that was being brought into prominence as the city's role as an articulation point in the global economy expanded. Muthiah and other partisans of "Madras," making their points in English-language print media and presentations, offered histories that led from the city's origin as a colonial translocality to the city's present-day aspirations in global circuits of manufacture, export processing, services, and information technology.

Conclusion

This chapter ends, as it began, with a collision of names. This cross-talk marked the city as a borderland, a conjunctural space of imperial power; it made arguments, too, about its origins. Partisans of both "Madras" and "Chennai" used those names to assert that the city was, from its inception, a volatile borderland, a point of contact, mixing, hybridity. For its part, "Chennai" suggests the frontier of premodern empire, whereas "Madras" is a frontier of modern imperial expansion. Both names, however, assert that the city is a "glocality"—a global entrepôt in which diverse populations, exchange media, languages, and ideas were brought into intimate and enduring relationships, and, more recently, a product of and staging ground for globalizing capitalism.[133] In the 1990s neoliberal policies of deregulation and privatization, hastened by structural adjustment measures, fostered rates of urbanization and industrial growth in Tamil Nadu that were among the highest in the country. Chennai is at the epicenter of the creative destruction that this growth entails.

In revisiting the history of the city now known officially as Chennai, I have charted the major developments and turning points in its formation as an urban space, noting in particular how the work of history making and state formation have been inextricable parts of the city's development. The city's genesis as a city is owing to its service as a node for administering the territory claimed in colonial state formation. Just as important, it has been a node for the cultural work of statecraft, for the spatial rhetorics that naturalize and historicize territorial claims and inscribe them as memory. Chennai, seen at the moments captured in the four snapshots discussed in this chapter, is inscribed with *histories* of naming and claiming discernable both in changing patterns of land use and in the images, names, and narratives with which the urban landscape has been mediated. How these representations are used to create and sustain affective attachments to state institutions and projects is taken up in the next chapter.

3
Memory, Mourning, and Politics

A Death

Madras, December 24, 1987

The day is clear and unseasonably cool. Like the other women on my street, I am preparing the day's meal—*mōrkuḻampu, racam, poriyal,* and, of course, rice.[1] My own bodily clock and appetites have shifted over the months that I have been in India, and I have come to crave a mid-morning meal of this sort. That it is Christmas eve barely registers, certainly not in the solidly Hindu neighborhood where I live. There are no lights, ornaments, or decorated trees, and no store displays. The season is, rather, more austere. Since mid-December I have awakened on thickly gray mornings to the softness of women's songs in praise of the saintly Andal. Their *bhajans*, along with prayer and fasting, are part of a month-long vow made to that goddess-saint in hopes for good marriages, whether their own, their daughters', or their granddaughters'. Men's beards mark them as being in the midst of a vow that will culminate in a January pilgrimage to Sabarimalai, the abode of the god Aiyappa.

As I work, using a pressure cooker that only recently I had begun to consider a boon rather than a weapon of mass destruction (at least in my untrained hands), I mentally sort through the day's tasks. Just then, my neighbor, Lata, peers into my kitchen window. "Have you heard?" she asks anxiously. Before I can ask her what she means, she quickly resumes, "It's the chief minister, MGR. He is no more, he's passed away." Well, I hadn't heard—I had no television and had not listened to the morning's radio broadcast. I am not entirely surprised by this news. M. G. Ramachandran, known popularly as MGR, was a one-time film star who assumed the position of chief minister of Tamil Nadu in 1977. He had been in poor health for almost three years and his visits to his office in the Secretariat had dwindled to the point where the occasional half-hour spent at his desk was front-page news. "That's a sad—" I begin. She interrupts, seeing that I haven't grasped the import of her words: "Do you have provisions? The shops will be closing, so you should buy now. Who knows when they will open again? And try not to go out after that—don't take the bus." Having delivered her warning, she returns to the hissing "cooker" in her own kitchen.

December 25, 1987

Public disorder—looting, riots, assaults, even self-mutilation—follows the news of the popular leader's death, with incidents in the city limited, mostly, to its major commercial areas. Today members of MGR's political party, AIA-DMK, throng Rajaji Hall, where MGR's body has lain in state, and join the procession that bears him to the gravesite. All this is televised, and I have joined my neighbor's family to view the spectacle. To no one's surprise, the funeral has become a melodrama, in which MGR's lover, party propaganda secretary Jayalalithaa, is pitted against his widow, Janaki. Today this becomes a literal war of position, when Jayalalithaa, wearing a white sari trimmed with AIA-DMK party colors, tries to take a seat on the vehicle that will carry MGR's corpse to the gravesite. In the camera's eye, one of Janaki's relatives shoves her aside, and, red with shame, Jayalalithaa stalks away from the funeral cortege. These details are savored by Lata's husband, Subramanian, an affluent and well-traveled engineer who has never made a secret of his disdain for MGR. He cracks jokes and laughs at the displays of piety among party officials. The family's servant, Omana, however, is clearly grieved by the loss of MGR. She, like many rural Tamils, reveres MGR—indeed, love may not be too strong a term for her sentiment. She finally begs Subramanian to stop mocking the event and to let her grieve the loss of her beloved "Puraṭci Talaivar."[2]

Affect and Politics

MGR and the Embodiment of Sovereignty

In 1989 a memorial dedicated to MGR was built on the Marina funeral site and later enlarged. State-sponsored memorials, in India and elsewhere, are key political signifiers, and few, if any, sites of officialdom lack a commemorative statue, pavilion, or plaque. Scholars have argued that the attention to loss and the continuous invocation of loss are definitive features of modernity, and the ubiquity of memorialization in political spaces and discourses seems to confirm this view.[3] These spaces of public memory are not just decorative accessories of rule, and though they may serve as masks that conceal its workings, they are not only that. They are, I contend, key material signifiers of the state, material metaphors that, like other monuments, naturalize authority by conflating the body of the ruler with the state. With this, they invite a thickening of affective ties between the state and its subjects, capturing at once the liminal force and institutional form of the state.

Recent cultural analyses of state sovereignty can illuminate the roles that memorials play in constituting the state and its subjects. In a review of the literature,

Begoña Aretxaga observed, "The state as phenomenological reality is produced through discourses and practices of power, produced in local encounters at the everyday level, and produced through the discourses of public culture, rituals of mourning and celebration, and encounters with bureaucracies, monuments, organization of space."[4] While acknowledging the importance of rationalized technologies of control in statecraft, she stressed that these require and regenerate an embodied, affective substrate. This substrate emerges with "the continuous recreation of the body of national heroes, in corpses and funerals, as acts of possession and rebirth." In these acts, the corpse "mediates between the state and the people in a process that seems intrinsic to the materialization of the state."[5]

Memorials, I contend, are crystallizations of key moments in this process, for it is the body's death that occasions their existence and the absence of that body that they mark. The social space of the memorial, in turn, is constituted over time through the embodied practices of mourning and remembrance. As indexes of the absent body, memorials cultivate and redirect the affective energies of the "state of exception," or suspension of law, that a ruler's death may precipitate and, with that, serve to sustain the state itself.[6] A memorial's significance, moreover, does not arise solely from its spatial syntax, its architectural features, or the actions that occur on its grounds. These features and the meanings ascribed to them emerge in wider *inter*-textual and *inter*-spatial fields: the guidebooks that report on their styles, the films that mythicize them, the buildings that surround them.[7]

Like other memorials honoring deceased leaders and heroes, MGR's memorial, known in Tamil as a *camāti,* has served in the years since its construction as a stage for political ceremony that ritually recalls, re-mourns, and honors MGR as an instantiation of a Tamil polity, an embodiment of virtues and sentiments felt to be specifically Tamil.[8] AIA-DMK party leaders and would-be leaders regularly gather at the memorial on the anniversaries of MGR's birth and death for the day's events: to affirm their loyalty to the party, and reenact specific bonds of dependence and patronage that establish their and the party's Dravidianist lineage. The same spaces are animated, as well, by quotidian acts of remembrance by party cadres and sympathizers, who arrive throughout the year to pray and leave ritual offerings.

The site's key architectural elements—a massive entry arch, an altar-like platform marking the gravesite, a grassy esplanade, and detached pavilions known as *maṇṭapam*—are found on the grounds of other memorials in southern India. Their spatial syntax, together with visitors' practical repertoires, borrow on rituals of worship and point to the aesthetic and devotional logics that subtend their design and use. MGR's memorial is an emotive institution, in which emotions are embedded as elements integral to the constructions of identity, action, and sociality associated with its formation and use as social space.[9] The memorial is designed to extend the charismatic authority that MGR enjoyed during his lifetime, an authority cultivated in both cinematic and political fields, and modeled, morally and materially, on the logics of embodiment associated with Hindu kingship. The commemorative space of the *camāti* is meant to inspire nostalgia for his leadership and popular consent to the legacy that his political successors, Jayalalithaa, in particular, claim to uphold.[10] It is a space in which the work of embodying the state is carried out by recalling the trauma of MGR's death and ritually restaging acts of mourning. Quotidian practices of visitation incorporate the gestural grammars of mourning; mourning is also engaged, ostensibly on behalf of the polity, by party leaders in their own shows of worshipful remembrance. Of even greater significance is the sequence of acts that brought the memorial site into existence, beginning with the burial of MGR on the site and continuing through the construction of its monumental shell.

These same affective dynamics are present in the interspatial and intertextual relations that exist *between* the memorial's actual grounds and the texts that describe it, the built environment that surrounds it, and the virtual spaces that mediate it. Among the latter, virtual venues, the AIA-DMK party Web site, the "Dr. J. Jayalalithaa Led AIADMK Political Party Official Web site," mounted between 2001 and 2007, is especially pertinent to my argument.[11] As at the actual memorial, visitors to the Web site were invited to enter a space suffused with visual and discursive idioms of kingly sovereignty, where relations with the party and its leadership could be forged. The AIA-DMK Election Manifesto, for example, introduced the party's commitment to law and order with a quotation from the Tamil sage, Tiruvalluvar: "the king who performs his duty judiciously and safeguards his subjects will be held as a divine being by his people" (*muṟaic-eytu kāppāṟṟum maṉṉavaṉ makkaṭku iṟaiyeṉṟu vaikkappaṭum*).[12] This ideal, the Web site assured visitors, had been "put into action in letter and spirit" in Jayalalithaa's Chief Ministry. Elsewhere on the site the memorial was rendered as a material effect of the entwined histories of the party, MGR's rise and demise, and Jayalalithaa's succession.

Whether in the virtual space of the Web site or on the actual site of the memorial, images, discourses, and actions pertaining to MGR's rule are, like Omana's grief, suffused with idioms of love, mutuality, and dependence. They can engender relations of hierarchical intimacy that are at once familial, devotional, and erotic, and are organized by what Lynn Hunt, following Freud, described as a "family romance," the collective, unconscious images of the familial order underlying politics.[13] The bourgeois patriarchal family of Freud's model limits its direct applicability to other cultural and historical contexts, but the argument, embedded in Freud and developed by Hunt, that relations of power are enacted and objectified through familial paradigms, particularly the developmental dynamic of a child's attachment to and estrangement from his or her parents, has broader applicability. Enduring expressions of the family romance in Hindu South Asia are present in the two major epics, the Mahabharata and the Ramayana, that have circulated on the subcontinent for more than two and a half millennia as oral narratives, texts, dramatic performances, and, recently, in electronic and televisually mediated forms.[14] In both epics, political and familial orders intersect and infuse each other: the bonds and ethos of family threaten a state's order and its claim of sovereign rule; those same bonds and ethos are the keys to the recovery and persistence of the sovereign's authority. The manifold possibilities of how the familial and the political intersect and the always contested forms of those intersections are explored in each epic's many variations, but the family romance remains the generative idiom and narrative frame, its embodied representation of power enabling the naturalization of political authority.

At MGR's *camāti*, the affective energies, which circulate around MGR, the party he founded, and his political ancestors and descendents, have often been framed using the plot elements and characters of the Mahabharata (discussed below), a tale of warring families. They congeal in an image of the state that, on the one hand, is deliberately anti-state, insofar as it strains against the institutional model of state as a rationalized bureaucratic apparatus. This state is cast as the intermediary that separates leaders from the people and as the corruptible instrument of AIA-DMK's political rival, the DMK and its leader, M. Karunanidhi. At the same time, the memorial's architecture and the ritualized memory work it stages and of which it is, itself, a material effect, engender another vision of the state. This one, infused by idioms of kingly sovereignty drawn from the Mahabharata and cast in the specifically Hindu shape that kingship takes in Tamil South India, gains traction from the still potent notion of Tamil Nadu's territorial, linguistic, and ethnic autonomy that neoliberal globalization has helped to recuperate.[15]

Commemorative Praxis and the Neoliberal State

Political commemoration, by which I mean the public mourning associated with leaders' funerals as well as less charged activities like commemorative naming practices, instantiates a family romance in which party cadres and the population at large are invited to participate. Critics, such as M. S. S. Pandian, see this affect-laden exercise of power as a fascist bargain, in which leaders identify culturally with the poor as they enroll them in exploitative political and economic programs.[16] Certainly, in AIA-DMK political oratory, texts, and images, invoked more often than "rights" (*urimai*) or "democracy" (*jaṉanāyakam*) are terms such as "devotion" (*pakti*), "attachment" (*pācam*), "protection" (*pātukāppu*), and "love" (*aṉpu*).[17] These discourses and the spaces and practices in which they are embedded have not abated over the forty-plus years of Dravidianist rule in Tamil Nadu even, most recently, as both of the dominant parties have deepened the state's commitment to neoliberal economic policies.[18]

Pandian's analysis focused on MGR's screen image and the use of that image to craft a political persona and sell specific policies and programs during MGR's eleven-year rule. Since MGR's death, however, activities, spaces, and images associated with his commemoration have continued to serve as media of political practice, especially for his successor, Jayalalithaa, who has relied on these in crafting her own political persona. Indeed, commemorative practices and discourses pervade the entire political field, and AIA-DMK's rival, the DMK, also has been active in this arena. In 1968, for example, DMK party leaders erected statues along the Marina honoring Tamil leaders and culture heroes, and commissioned a lavish memorial park for the founder of the party C. N. Annadurai; to mark the new millennium, DMK Chief Minister Karunanidhi commissioned a massive statue of the Tamil sage Tiruvalluvar just off Tamil Nadu's southern tip.[19] And in 2006 Karunanidhi celebrated his return to power with the reinstallation of the statue of the Tamil literary heroine, Kannaki, that had been removed during AIA-DMK rule as well as a succession of gifting ceremonies, each scheduled to coincide with the birth date of a Tamil luminary.[20] Color televisions were given to poor rural households on September 15 and 17, the birth dates, respectively, of Annadurai and the founder of the Self-Respect Movement E. V. Ramasamy; additional eggs were allotted for the noon-meal program on July 15, the birth date of the former chief minister Kamaraj. On Karunanidhi's own birth date (June 3), the cost of a twenty-kilogram bag of rice—southern Indians' staple food—was lowered to Rs.2.

While the reliance on commemoration to cultivate charismatic authority and bind the loyalties of party cadres, officialdom, and the population has a deep genealogy and a broad geographic spread, such strategies have acquired particular significance in India's neoliberal order because of the conjoined effects of deregulation and decentralization. The Indian state, like other federal systems, comprises a nested hierarchy of administrative units that correspond to discrete territorial entities ("states," "municipalities," "villages," and so forth), some of which—states—are defined on the basis of language and ethnicity. With the deregulation and decentralization mandated by the New Industrial Policy of 1991, states have initiated and implemented various new projects and, because of their diverse resources and capacities, individual states have experienced different levels of market-led growth in production and consumption. Tamil Nadu, as noted in chapter 2, has courted private investment aggressively and has been among the more productive states.

Concurrent with decentralization have been changes in party politics, which have intensified the effects of regulatory shifts on state-level political culture.[21] On the one hand, the national profiles of single-state (or regional) parties have sharpened. Over the past two decades, regional parties, among whom Tamil Nadu's Dravidianist parties were early exemplars, have gained political power at the expense of national parties and now hold more than one-third of the seats in the lower house of India's parliament, the Lok Sabha. On the other hand, regional parties' electoral bases and styles of political rhetoric have shifted in response to neoliberal initiatives. For example, in her comparison of Andhra Pradesh and Tamil Nadu, the political scientist Lorraine Kennedy points out that both have sought to create an investor-friendly environment through incentives, regulatory reform, and the development of a specialized infrastructure.[22] They have diverged, however, in their modes of packaging these changes.[23] The Andhra government, while taking a more overt and active role in championing such changes, has highlighted governance reform and framed it as "transformational." Tamil Nadu relies on private initiatives and presents government as an enabler, rather than instigator, of change, and continues to frame state programs with paternalist idioms. Kennedy relates those differences to various signaling strategies, which, she suggests, arose because of the different capacities and resource bases of the two states.[24] Andhra's transformationalist rhetoric is directed to potential investors and designed to overcome its infrastructural gaps and weaknesses of capacity, whereas Tamil Nadu, with its stronger growth capacity, has retained its paternalist rhetoric to signal its populist credentials to its low-caste constituency and so forestall fragmentation of its political base.

Despite the ethological associations that Kennedy's analytic terms carry, her findings, which are consistent with Pandian's arguments about MGR's populist style, invite a more serious engagement with the visual, linguistic, and spatial rhetorics on which political practice relies. These rhetorical strategies may be particularly significant elements within political cultures as statecraft is reorganized under the force of neoliberal globalization. I argue that attachment to the state and consent to sovereignty under neoliberal globalization should be understood as mediated not just by nationalism(s) but also by the ethnic and linguistic identifications that connect people to individual states and regions, and by the affective energies that suffuse those identifications. This dynamic implies the need for a subnational analytic in parsing the cultural constitution of India's postcolonial state and invites questions about how "the state," as imagined by and enacted through the bureaucratic apparatus of individual states, compares and intersects with that which is engaged in the spaces of central administrative projects. It requires particular attention to the role of political parties in mediating the "state idea." Political parties, though crucial units within the formal apparatus of democratic polities, are also spaces of informal participation and of practices framed by tropes of kinship. To understand how the state is encultured, the "family romance" enacted in party membership, communications, and activity should be scrutinized.

Rather than dismissing the technologies of memory that suffuse Dravidian political culture as relics of the pre-, or incompletely, modern, then, my goal in this chapter is to expose the visual and spatial rhetorics that are enacted in spaces and practices of memory associated with state-level governance and to uncover the particular work that these rhetorics perform within the neoliberal order. While animating this specifically Tamil case, they also serve as evidence of the pervasiveness and necessity of the aesthetic within avowedly modern political institutions and practices. Thus, although I agree with the conclusions of both Pandian and Kennedy about the calculated and exploitive political effects of the AIA-DMK's use of devotional idioms, I wish to take on, rather than dismiss, these idioms and to unpack their workings in an effort to understand the means by which this bargain is struck.

The specific effectiveness of commemoration in reifying and producing consent to sovereignty is, therefore, the larger issue I grapple with in this chapter. Of most interest to me is the state effect that is constituted through devotional logics of commemoration and how, in this space of seduction, state sovereignty is imagined and enacted, even as it is being reorganized through neoliberal globalization. How the social space of the memorial has been constituted through this practical imaginary, and how, in turn, it comes to signify the state, are the subjects of the following pages.

Figure 3.1. MGR Memorial Arch, Chennai Marina. *Photograph by author.*

The *Camāti* in Sight

If you view MGR's *camāti* from Kamarajar Salai, your gaze will be swept inward, along its central east-west axial plane, toward the gravesite that forms its core. Even at this distance you can see the ring of curved, sculpted white columns surrounding the platform that covers the grave and the sword-shaped obelisk towering above it.

You enter through a threshold formed by a curved double arch, which straddles the memorial's landscaped grounds and the street. Like the entry to a home or a city gate, the arch faces outward, framing the memorial's grounds as an "interior," even as the memorial's location on Chennai's beachfront transforms that "interior" into a limitless, oceanic plane. The designer intended the curved, white archway as an abstract rendering of a human torso, with palms pressed together in a typical pose of reverential welcome. The outer, convex arch forms an oval outlining the upper body, and the inner, concave arch comprises two columns that rise, spire-like, suggesting a pair of folded hands.

You pass through the arch onto a stone-lined walkway. Just ahead, the walkway divides to encircle a small manicured lawn. Beyond that, a grassy maidan stretches eastward from the entry area to the memorial's core. At the western edge of this lawn is a sculpted bust of MGR, wearing his trademark sunglasses and fur

Figure 3.2. MGR Memorial grounds. *Photograph by author.*

hat. If you visit the memorial on the anniversary of his birth (January 17) or death (December 24), you will see leaders of the state's major political parties paying homage to MGR by garlanding his bust and offering prayers.

You continue eastward toward the gravesite, following one of the two stone walkways that line the approach path. Both these paths, which skirt the north and south borders of the central maidan, follow parallel courses through two sets of detached, open pavilions. The pavilions, known as *maṇṭapam,* were typical structures in medieval palace compounds and today are common in large temple complexes, where they function as assembly sites.[25] This approach path, with enfilade that evokes palaces and Hindu temples, takes you to the innermost space of intimate, sacralized action, the memorial core of the gravesite. With this, the deepest interior is differentiated from the mediating space of the approach path, just as the memorial grounds, as a whole, are differentiated from the mundane exterior of the streetscape. The nesting of these spaces and the two sets of relational interiors and exteriors it creates mimic the spatial organization of Hindu homes and temples.[26] The memorial grounds evoke both domestic and sacred space, and your passage, as a visitor, enacts the socio-spatial distance between yourself and the figure whose remains are entombed on the site.

A walk of several hundred feet brings you to the edge of the sculpted lotus. At its center you can see an elevated platform and, on its surface, a flame, which burns day and night. The platform is positioned at the center of a circular stone base on which the massive lotus sits, its open petals suggested by the curved white columns that encircle the platform. Surmounting the central platform is an obelisk.

The lotus, ubiquitous in Hindu iconography, is here a dense signifier. It is associated with the AIA-DMK party's own history, having been chosen as a party emblem by the MGR-led faction that, in 1972, broke with the DMK in order to form the new party (A-DMK) that later became the AIA-DMK. Its more pervasive cultural association, however, is with deities and royals, whose thrones are commonly depicted as lotuses. It connotes feminine beauty and auspiciousness, and forms an impervious and protective physico-moral barrier between deities and royals and the mundane world that surrounds them.

The memorial is also a gravesite. This is worth pausing over, for the burial of bodily remains departs from the Hindu funerary practice of cremation. This may mark the Dravidianist ideology of rationalism and anti-Brahmanism, but it has also invited questions about MGR's religious affiliation. Was he a Hindu? He was known to worship at Hindu shrines and to have inaugurated programs designed to support temple building, sometimes in alliance with Hindu nationalist interests. Like other political leaders, he employed the grammars of Hindu worship and deference in the context of political performance. Nonetheless, though his birth in Sri Lanka and early migration to Tamil Nadu are well known, his religious affiliation has never been a matter of public record. MGR, a consummate actor, never revealed this information, suggesting that these gaps operated rhetorically, enabling him to maintain a flexible and multivalent political persona, particularly in a state with a fairly substantial Christian minority, most of whom are poor and of low caste.

In spite of these ambiguities about MGR's own sectarian identity, those who visit the memorial often perform acts of deference and supplication drawn from the corpus of Hindu ritual. These you view as you come closer to the sculpted lotus. Near the north and south edges of the lotus, where the approach pathways terminate, you see chappals, sneakers, and leather shoes. Should you wish to set foot on the lotus's paved base, you must discard your footwear and approach the center as you would a temple sanctum. Visitors, with folded hands and bowed heads, move toward the flame. Drawing near, they open their palms and, with waving motions, draw the smoke toward their heads. Some circumambulate the flame multiple times by walking along the path that curls around the outer edge of the lotus. Both gestures are deferential actions and recognizable parts of *pūja,* a core ritual of Hindu worship. In the contexts of both domestic and temple worship, these actions supplicate and praise a deity; they protect vulnerability of the god's embodied form, even while seeking the deity's divine protection; they fulfill vows and demonstrate devotion.

The rituals that take place at the memorial core are accompanied by other more casual uses. The landscaped grounds surrounding the *maṇṭapams,* walkways, and sculpted lotus are crossed by serpentine paths, along which visitors can stroll and relax. Because the site is easily reached by bus, picnics and other outings are common here and in the adjoining memorial park dedicated to C. N. Annadurai, founder of the DMK and MGR's political mentor. Vendors stationed on the sidewalk just outside the entry arch do a good business selling soft drinks, snacks, and souvenirs, especially on weekends, when thousands descend on the Marina to enjoy a picnic, amble along the beach, and meet friends.

For many, popular visual and aural culture, especially as mediated by Tamil cinema, frames the experience of a visit to the memorial. Images, songs, and dialogue from MGR's films provide a corpus that, throughout his political career, was drawn upon to frame or supplement visual and textual accounts of his accomplishments as party leader and chief minister. MGR cultivated a "Robin Hood" persona, sometimes assuming roles of both elite and subaltern heroes in the same films. In these roles, he eschewed the opulence of kingship but traded on its moral authority by portraying characters marked by their dedication to the poor, their protection of women, and their willingness to sacrifice themselves for the community's welfare. As a politician, he highlighted these qualities with policies and cultural performances that emphasized his embodiment of the Tamil land and polity and his role as its chief protector, especially its women and children.[27] It is this MGR who is recalled on the grounds of the *camāti*. Its built form and the ritualized praxis of visitation are designed to call forth cinematically framed recollections that, like Freudian "screen memories," both reveal and conceal a benevolent MGR. This MGR was simultaneously a brother, father, and husband, whose acts as a political leader were indistinguishable from the kinds of moral bargains that his screen characters struck, as they sacrificed their own wealth for others, rescued women from dishonor, confronted injustice, and bested villains in swordfights and martial arts displays.

Before leaving the *camāti*, it may be worth mentioning what you have *not* seen. Although its features evoke a vaguely limned tradition of Hindu empire, conventional historical references are absent, apart from a plaque bearing MGR's name, the dates of his birth and death, and information about the site's dedication. This is in contrast to the nearby memorial dedicated to C. N. Annadurai, affectionately known as Anna (a term that also glosses as "elder brother"), the state's first Dravidianist chief minister. In addition to a similar array of pavilions, paved walkways, and gravesite, Anna's memorial hosts an exhibition gallery. There, using captioned photographs and documents, the conjoined stories of Anna's life and the rise of the DMK party are narrated. Devotional rituals take place on this site as well, but the gallery supplements those with civics pedagogy that emphasizes citizenship, rights, and the electoral process. During my own visits, on weekdays as well as weekends, the galleries were packed with families and I heard lively discussions about political scandals and governance principles. Also, the plentiful visual references to party affiliation, including the use of party colors and its rising sun symbol as details on the arch, which one sees at Annadurai's memorial, are nearly nonexistent at MGR's, which suggests, instead, the continuity of tradition and its embodied, familial locus.

Virtual Memory

Let us now move from actual memoryscape of party politics to its virtual counterpart, "The Dr Jayalalithaa Led AIADMK Political Party Official Web Site." Visitors were welcomed to the site by a splash page, which featured a series of photographic images of Jayalalithaa and a stationary banner containing the phrase, "*Amma eṉṟāl* . . ." ("If one says 'Amma' . . ."). That phrase exhibits a common grammatical structure—a noun followed by the verb, *eṉṟu*—used to designate some term or phrase as reported speech. In this instance, below the word "*Amma*" ("mother"), one of Jayalalithaa's preferred appellations, Tamil words flashed sequentially on the screen. Each was meant to gloss or modify "*Amma*"—to signify what is meant when the name, "*Amma*," is uttered. Those Tamil terms were "*aṉpu*" (love), "*amaiti*" (peace), "*ataravu*" (support, affectionate concern), "*āṭci*" (government), and finally "*nallāṭci*" (benevolent rule), all qualities meant to be associated with Jayalalithaa or "*Amma*." The lexical associations were reinforced by the montage of images of Jayalalithaa that flashed on the screen as backdrops for each term. With this, the page asserted Jayalalithaa's legitimacy as party leader and her emotive encompassment of its members.

This page served as the portal for both the Tamil and English versions of the Web site. The home page of each was identical and modeled on Dravidianist political posters: it was dominated, visually, by portraits of party leaders, which framed a brief text.[28] Stretching across the upper border of the page, like the decorative arches erected at rally sites, was a welcome message, flanked by flashing images. On the left, smiling cameos of MGR, Anna, and Jayalalithaa appeared in succession; on the right, the party's symbol of two leaves and its flag flashed in alternating sequence.[29] The center of the page held its focal elements: images of party headquarters, MGR, and Jayalalithaa, and, below them, the party's motto: "We will not live as slaves!/We will never seek separation!/We will unite as equals!" (*naṅkaḷ aṭimaiyāka vāḻa māṭṭōm!/naṅkaḷ eṉṟum piriviṉai kōrōm!/naṅkaḷ camamāṉ avarkaḷāka oṉṟupaṭuvōm!*). The use, in the site's Tamil version, of the exclusive first-person plural—*naṅkaḷ*—positions readers outside the circle of the "we" who make these declarations, the "we" of the party and its leadership.[30] This latter "we" was represented visually in the cameos of MGR and Jayalalithaa, who were shown as intimates. Each cupped their chin in a pensive manner and smiled beneficently. Their gazes were directed, obliquely, beyond the frame of the portrait and toward the image of AIA-DMK party headquarters that hovered between them. Their mirrored poses and exchange of gazes suggested a relation of reciprocal emotional attachment and hierarchical intimacy, a relation associated with *darśan,* the ritual exchange of glances at the center of many Hindu worship practices. Like the Marina memorial, the homepage evoked an intimate scene that was at once familial and devotional. We witnessed the party's progenitors at home, welcoming us, their visitors, as honored guests.

The Web site, like the Dravidianist political oratory that its texts, at times, incorporated, addressed its visitor as a potential supporter of the party. The

Election Manifesto, for example, led off with a formulaic address that presented the manifesto for the visitor's consideration and requested, in return, her support:

> Chiselled with the above objectives, the All India Anna Dravida Munnetra Kazhagam humbly presents its Manifesto for the forthcoming Legislative Assembly Elections, for your valuable consideration and requests your support for enabling it to render a clean and efficient administration to the public by implementing its ideology and goals.[31]

But what the Web site repeatedly sought to demonstrate was the affective bond between ruler and ruled that existed as the condition for such support. The scene of familial intimacy and mutuality that welcomed visitors on its splash page was extended, elsewhere on the site, to the polity, with textual references to the emotional ties that bound ruler and ruled. Sympathy toward the plight of the poor, workers, and women, and vigilant protection of the polity, were pledged. That legitimacy depended on the personalized quality of rule and its affective charge was repeatedly affirmed. This, the visitor was told, had roots in the popular sentiments toward MGR that brought forth the party: "The recent history of Tamil Nadu is entwined with the history of the AIADMK bounded as it is by mutual love, attachment and respect for the people."[32] The party, as already noted, was founded by MGR as a breakaway faction of the DMK, following his public chastisement of party leadership for corruption. It was a calculated gesture, done in defiance of party by-laws and intended to split the party. On the Web site, however, the party's birth was described as the upwelling of love: "MGR Fan Club members and DMK cadres with their overwhelming love for their Puratchi Thalaivar, of their own accord, improvised black and red flags, bearing the symbol of a Lotus and raised them aloft."[33]

In the virtual space of the Web site, MGR's memorial emerged within narratives framed as "history" (*varalāṟu*) and "epic history" (*kāviyattiṉ varalāṟu*), which recounted the party's origins and growth. Pages titled "History," "Achievements," "Historical Events," and "2001 Election Manifesto" featured overlapping narratives describing the *camāti* as a product of Jayalalithaa's devotion to MGR and underscored the significance of MGR's own devotion to his mentor, Annadurai.[34] They asserted that the memorial was concrete proof of Jayalalithaa's legitimacy as his successor, and references to the *camāti* construction and associated commemorative acts revealed and reiterated the hierarchical intimacy engendered by such devotion. The proximity of MGR's and Annadurai's memorials was the first and most obvious assertion of the legitimacy of the line of succession from Annadurai to MGR to Jayalalithaa: "On the sands of the Marine Beach, Dr. MGR's mortal body was interred in a Sandalwood coffin, close to the memorial of Perarignar Anna who had called him as his Idhayakani or Heart's Fruit."[35] This praise-name derived emotional power and salience through its mnemonic evocations. It calls to the visitor's mind visual representations of devotion, notably those of the Ramayana's paradigmatic devotee, Hanuman, the monkey-god who is Ram's chief devotee and most loyal servant. A popular devotional image of Hanuman depicts him opening his chest to reveal a small image of Ram and his wife, Sita, in a demonstration of the all-consuming attachment that makes this figure a cornerstone for Ram's righteous rule. It invited recollection, also, of MGR's cinematically mediated persona, for "Idhaya Kani" is also the title of a popular 1975 film that starred MGR.[36] The contiguity of the memorials paired with Annadurai's mode of addressing MGR were offered as evidence not only of devotional intimacy between MGR and his mentor but also of Annadurai's recognition and acceptance of MGR as his principal devotee and rightful successor.

Jayalalithaa's place in this chain of hierarchical intimacy was claimed, in part, through her own public acts of commemoration, including her sponsorship of MGR's memorial. In 1990, as part of her effort to restore the AIA-DMK to power, Jayalalithaa unveiled a gleaming statue of MGR on Chennai's main commercial street, Anna Salai (formerly Mount Road). She unveiled a portrait of MGR as soon as she became chief minister and quickly set to work enlarging the memorial to MGR that the state's previous chief minister, MGR's rival, M. Karunanidhi, had constructed, commissioning designs from "renowned architects."[37] The creation of memorial space was accompanied by commemorative nomenclature, including renaming the state transport corporation and several localities after MGR. Those gestures, like her own title, Puraṭci Talaivi (a feminized version of Puraṭci Talaivar, one of MGR's praise names), which MGR is said to have bestowed upon her, fused her political persona with his. This very public act of devotion symbolically consolidated the legitimacy that electoral success had granted her by confirming a relation of hierarchical intimacy with MGR and, through MGR, with Annadurai.[38] The heroic quality of that devotion was asserted repeatedly in the texts posted on the Web site and formed a melodramatic background story for the memorial. This story and its relation to the *camāti* are the subjects of the next section.

After MGR, Who?

Following MGR's death in December 1987, several members of his party vied to succeed him as chief minister. The party was quickly factionalized around two figures, MGR's widow, Janaki Ramachandran, and his erstwhile lover, the party propaganda secretary Jayalalithaa. The larger faction, headed by Janaki, initially retained control of the state's Legislative Assembly, but this was soon eroded by challenges from Jayalalithaa. In the end Jayalalithaa prevailed, though it was not until 1991 that she was named chief minister, an office she held until 1996.[39] The succession struggle following MGR's death was carried out in the halls of the legislature and on the streets. It produced memorial spaces (statuary, nomenclature, the refurbished *camāti*) and used nascent memorial sites as its stages. How the narrative of succession was entwined with and enacted through the social space of the memorial are the subjects of this section. I begin with a chronological account, compiled from contemporaneous newspaper reports, of Jayalalithaa's succession, including the role memorial building assumed during this process. I then turn to the AIA-DMK Web site, for an analysis of its narrative on succession, one that was melodramatic in tone and unfolded as an epic. I conclude by returning to MGR's memorial to reconsider the relations between the virtual and actual memoryscapes, showing how the Web site's epic narrative is encoded and decoded on the grounds of the *camāti.*

The Struggle in Print

Accounts in both English and Tamil print media describe challenges that began soon after MGR's death.[40] On January 1, 1988, Jayalalithaa assumed the General Secretaryship of the AIA-DMK party, a position whose occupant is frequently chosen for the Chief Ministership should the party hold an Assembly majority. A day later, a rival faction elected Janaki Ramachandran as General Secretary. Two days hence, Tamil Nadu's governor invited Janaki to form a cabinet. A confidence vote on Janaki's ministry was scheduled in the Legislative Assembly at the end of January. Jayalalithaa immediately challenged these moves. In a bid to assert her claim on the party's General Secretaryship, on January 13, she and her supporters arrived at party headquarters and demanded that the offices be turned over to them. Police blocked their entry and twenty-five persons, including Jayalalithaa, were arrested. On January 28 Jayalalithaa extended her political stage to MGR's gravesite. As the Legislative Assembly held an official condolence session in recognition of MGR's demise, Jayalalithaa and her followers staged a competing event at the funeral site, at which they tried to upstage the Assembly by passing their own resolution of condolence. The "assembly-in-exile" concluded its meeting with Jayalalithaa herself laying a commemorative wreath at the grave site.

The next day, January 29, was one of high drama. It began with the cancellation of the scheduled confidence vote because members of a minority party, who had previously agreed to vote in its favor, withdrew their support. The Legislative Assembly was adjourned, and Janaki's faction left the chamber; Jayalalithaa's faction remained there, reopened the session, elected a new speaker, and held the confidence vote. Not surprisingly, it was voted down. The Assembly was again adjourned, and Jayalalithaa, accompanied by her supporters, went to the governor's office to inform him of the vote and to demand that the Legislative Assembly be dissolved pending a new election. Meanwhile the members of the Legislative Assembly (MLAs) reconvened with members of both factions present. Two Speakers for the Assembly (the existing one and his newly "elected" successor) appeared on the dais and wrestled for control of the podium. Pandemonium ensued. The police entered the chamber in a lathi charge, and Jayalalithaa's supporters were removed. A second confidence vote was taken, and this time the measure passed. Two days later, however, the Legislative Assembly was dissolved on the grounds that the second confidence vote had lacked a quorum. The state's AIA-DMK government was dismissed by India's central government, which declared President's Rule and scheduled a new assembly election. That election, held in March 1989, returned the DMK to power. It was not until 1991 that the AIA-DMK, led by Jayalalithaa, regained control of the state legislature.

During the period between MGR's death and Jayalalithaa's 1991 appointment as chief minister, MGR's memorialization was itself a medium of contention as well as a context for political theater. With MGR's gravesite continuing as a site for party ceremony, a third faction within the party made a bid for control over MGR's residence. They challenged Janaki's right to reside there and brought a petition to the state's High Court to declare the residence as a memorial to MGR, a move that would have allowed them to establish an independent but still sacralized space for their own operations. The Court denied the petition, leaving Janaki with the house. By that point (March 1988), however, Janaki's control over the party had eroded. Her supporters had diminished in number and Tamil Nadu's government was under central control. But she was not ready to relinquish her effort to lead the AIA-DMK, so she did this by reasserting her patronage of MGR's gravesite on the Marina, which at that point was still undeveloped as a memorial site. At Janaki's behest, in April 1988, P. C. Alexander, Tamil Nadu's caretaker governor, announced a design competition and invited submissions. In December 1988, on the anniversary of MGR's death, work on the new memorial began. The original construction plans, however, were scaled down when the AIA-DMK lost to the DMK at the polls in 1989.

M. Karunanidhi, after being named the chief minister of the new DMK government, commissioned a garden and modest platform at MGR's burial site. During Karunanidhi's tenure, in 1990, another memorial began to take shape. This one, a temple, was part of a quest for visibility by an AIA-DMK splinter group. As its political fortune declined, the temple followed suit. During that same year, a statue of MGR was unveiled in Chennai's commercial center in a lavish ceremony, presided over by Jayalalithaa and marked by prayers and offerings typical of *pūja*. The Marina memorial reemerged as a stage for political action in 1992, when it was embellished and expanded by Jayalalithaa, after she was named the chief minister in 1991.

The Struggle Online: Mahabharata on the Marina

The AIA-DMK party Web site, mounted during the 2001 election campaign, presented a narrative of the party's founding and Jayalalithaa's rise to power that differed considerably from accounts found in the mainstream print media. It was, as already noted, a text-centered site, and in style, modes of address, and content, it adhered to the conventions of Dravidianist political oratory as those have been outlined by Bate.[41] The site's authorship was not disclosed, though its detailed and sympathetic account of Jayalalithaa's deeds and intentions suggest that the principal narrative voice was hers.

The Web site's historiography took the form of a chronicle of the party's founding, its leadership, and its achievements. This story was emplotted as romance and unfolded in the manner of a multigenerational epic of familial bonds and the betrayals that sever those bonds. This sort of melodramatic narrative, which frames social and political life in terms of familial relations, is a popular device in Tamil and Hindi cinema and resonates with the epics that have been retold over more than two millennia. The Mahabharata, consisting of multiple books or chapters, is a story of two warring branches of a royal family whose struggle for territorial mastery is also a fight to attain virtue and establish a morally ordered cosmos. Its central story line, as well as its many self-contained episodes and sub-genres, are refracted through specific regional literary and performance genres throughout south Asia, including court epics and praise poems, festivals and rituals. The epic history of the Web site unfolded in ways that invited visitors to make intertextual associations between its narrative and the grander and more compelling Mahabharata.

At the core of the virtual chronicle of the AIA-DMK history was a family romance that framed political action in ways similar to the family romance that Hunt uncovered in France's revolutionary political culture. In the Tamil case, the unit was a patrimonial triangle comprising the emotionally charged relations between four key figures who, together, spanned three dynastic generations. As in the Mahabharata, we encountered a clan divided: a patriarch (Annadurai), his two "sons" (MGR and Karunanidhi) and the figure (Jayalalithaa) who straddled roles of daughter and wife to one of those sons. The "family" headed by Annadurai was the DMK party, and it was this family that in the course of the epic was split into warring factions (DMK and AIA-DMK) by the actions of the sons. The epic's characters were bound by affection, envy, and dependence, and it was that unstable mix that moved the narrative forward to the fission and reconsolidation of the patriarch's "family."

Two principal crises punctuated this sequence. The first, Annadurai's death, pitted MGR and Karunanidhi as rival successors, with MGR eventually prevailing as head of the branch of the family/party (AIA-DMK) that represented the legitimate descendents of Annadurai. The second, MGR's death, reopened the original conflict and called forth Jayalalithaa, MGR's protégé, to avenge his name and the family's honor. With Jayalalithaa's emergence, the script deviated from the Mahabharata's gender politics. Though at times likened explicitly to Draupadi, the Pandavas' wife, whose very vulnerability was an indictment of the honor of the men around her, Jayalalithaa was cast as a heroine in her own right, one who was not only left unprotected but whose own body became the protective cover for her mentor and the party cadres. The events and spaces associated with MGR's memorialization—the funeral, the subsequent commemorations, and the memorial itself—entered the narrative as reported actions of the principal characters. They also stood as the material and pragmatic effects of the story's crises and its resolution.

Crisis I: In Which the Pandavas Prevail

The epic began with Annadurai's death, a crisis resolved with the birth of the AIA-DMK party. This story opened by recalling the Dravidian Eden of Annadurai's brief period of rule. The patriarch (Annadurai) had died less than a year after taking office in 1967, before his own vision of socio-moral order could be fully realized. The good son and hero (MGR) sought to carry out the patriarch's wishes. This son was the righteous heir, for it was his "dazzling popularity" that secured Annadurai's power.[42] The other son (Karunanidhi), corrupt and villainous, relied on trickery to subvert both the patriarch's moral vision and the hero's righteous action. This enabled Karunanidhi to displace MGR and succeed Annadurai, with disastrous results: "drunk with power and sunk in corruption," Karunanidhi "became a veritable dictator."[43] Karunanidhi's "wayward ways and unbridled corruption pained MGR."[44] For bringing charges of corruption against Karunanidhi, MGR was expelled from the DMK party but, with the "overwhelming love of the DMK cadres" behind him, founded a new party wholly dedicated to Annadurai's vision.[45]

Under MGR, this new party, the ADMK (later renamed AIA-DMK), gained electoral support, leading to Karunanidhi's ouster. MGR took his place in 1976 and carried out Annadurai's original intentions during an eleven-year period of "benevolent rule" (*nallāṭci*). Far from suggesting any element of calculation, the Web site framed MGR's actions as translations of popular will, assuring visitors that he was "welcomed as the hero of the people throughout Tamilnadu."[46] Even the envious Karunanidhi was cognizant of MGR's appeal: "His [Karunanidhi's] ascent was only possible by riding piggy-back on the all-encompassing popularity of MGR."[47]

Crisis 2: In Which Draupadi Turns the Tables

The first crisis and its resolution were narrated as the AIA-DMK's myth of origin and this same myth is called upon later, as party leaders struggled to resolve the second crisis, occasioned by MGR's death. This was recounted in the Web site's most detailed historical narrative, found on pages titled "Living Legend Dr. J. Jayalalithaa." With MGR's death, Karunanidhi (again) appeared and (again) reversed the moral order. This time, his undoing came at the hand of MGR's heir, Jayalalithaa, who sacrificed her own honor to restore the moral order of the patriarch's righteous rule. The narrative positioned Jayalalithaa as a critical mediating figure who conveyed MGR's intentions "down" to party cadres and to the people of Tamil Nadu, even as she received and translated the will of the people "upward" to their "Puratchi Thalaivar."

This narrative began with assertions of Jayalalithaa's unstinting devotion to MGR. It is this devotion that congealed in the memorial, a space that declared, publicly, Jayalalithaa's status as MGR's chief devotee and chosen heir. The relations that the memorial condenses are narrated on the Web site as evidence for the legitimacy of her succession. Making no mention of her own cinematic career or her romantic liaison with MGR, the Web site text reported that her political career debuted in 1982 at the AIA-DMK party conference, when MGR asked her to deliver a speech: "The Praiseworthy Qualities of Women."[48] This led to her appointment as the party's propaganda secretary. To show that her induction to the party hierarchy was not just a top-down decision, however, the Web site testified to the spontaneous emotion that bound her to the people, explaining that MGR entrusted her with party publicity, because "she endeared herself so much with the local people that they affectionately began calling her as Amma [mother]."[49]

All this was offered to substantiate the fusion between her and MGR, and to underscore her service as the bridge between MGR and the party cadres. The apotheosis of this fusion between Jayalalithaa and MGR, a bond at once erotic, filial, and devotional, came in 1985. In a dramatic gesture that employed the trappings of royal ritual, MGR designated Jayalalithaa as his successor. On this occasion MGR, already in poor health, was presented with a silver scepter by Jayalalithaa on behalf of the AIA-DMK party headquarters. He, in turn, presented it back to her to "resounding applause" from the audience, who both "welcomed this honor done to Puratchi Thalaivi" and cherished its memory.[50] This, it is stated, signified that MGR "considered none other than Puratchi Thalaivi as his political heir."[51] Less than two years later, MGR is said to have forced Jayalalithaa to take an oath, the style of which cloaks her ambition in a mantle of service to the party. Before a photograph of his own mother, MGR instructed Jayalalithaa as follows: "You are the protection to my cadres . . . in turn they will protect you. At no stage under any circumstance should you leave politics."[52] Thus MGR's devotion to his own mother (whose very name, Sathya, embodies truth) was the surety that guaranteed Jayalalithaa's "motherhood" of the party cadres.

Jayalalithaa's actions after MGR's death were framed in the Web site's narrative as acts of selfless devotion to avenge MGR's honor, even at the cost of her own. There is no hint that Jayalalithaa may have been ambitious, and scant reference is made to her confrontations with MGR's widow, Janaki. She was cast, instead, as a reluctant participant:

> Almost every day there was a confluence of people at Puratchi Thalaivi's house pleading with her: "Amma, you must lead us and show us the true path." . . . Though shattered by the death of her guru and mentor and marginalized by her jealous detractors within the party, Puratchi Talaivi, recalling her pledge to him, made a new resolve in her mind. She decided to swim against the tide, overcoming any impediment, to protect the Party founded by Puratchi Thalaivar Dr. MGR, and its Cadres.[53]

The narrative of the DMK's ascent in the turmoil that followed MGR's death played on Karunanidhi's earlier cunning. His party's reemergence was described as the "resurrection of the malevolent force called Karunanidhi, who returned to power after thirteen years in the wilderness."[54] Once in office, troubles were compounded when Karunanidhi insulted MGR by constructing only a modest commemorative platform at his gravesite. The inadequacy of such a memorial was sharpened by the proximity of the more elaborate memorial dedicated to Annadurai, a memorial commissioned earlier by Karunanidhi. MGR's memorial became the emblem of the moral turpitude of DMK rule, here represented as a dangerous interregnum, marked by efforts to shame both MGR and Jayalalithaa, the party's voice and its body. This period is crucial to the narrative—it is a period of self-abnegation and trial, during which the efforts to dishonor Jayalalithaa only enhance her heroism.

A 1989 incident in the legislative assembly, when Jayalalithaa was assaulted by a DMK minister, was emblematic of the tribulations of this period. During the 1991 electoral campaign that restored the AIA-DMK to power, the same story was recounted regularly and framed explicitly with the epic tale of Draupadi's disrobing.

The latter episode is found in an early book of the Mahabharata. In it, Draupadi, the wife of the five Pandava brothers, is dragged into court to be the stake in a game of dice between the Pandavas and their rivals, the Kauravas. The Pandavas lose the game and Draupadi is threatened with disrobing. In the epic, Krishna miraculously intervenes as Draupadi's protector when her human lords fail, clothing Draupadi in an endless sari that remains around her even as her tormentors continue to grasp at its edges. Draupadi herself presents a fearsome figure when, disheveled, she faces the cowering men of the court and begins to voice a curse. The curse is not completed, but she vows that she will keep her hair loose until she can wash it with blood from the rival clans' battlefield. On the Web site and on the campaign trail, Jayalalithaa's own vulnerability was likened implicitly to that of the dishonored and vengeful Draupadi:

> MLAs of the ruling DMK, disregarding the fact that Puratchi Thalaivi was a woman, started attacking her with murderous intent. A minister pulled at her saree and attempted to outrage her modesty, even as Karunanidhi and others looked passively on. . . . "There is no guarantee for life in Karunanidhi's regime," Puratchi Thalaivi exclaimed. "I will come again to the Assembly only if this Government is dismissed and that too only as Chief Minister!" Making this vow, Puratchi Thalaivi left the assembly.[55]

The epic framing of Jayalalithaa's vulnerability and dishonor at the hands of DMK party men, invited pity and sympathetic identification, even as it anticipated the transformation of Jayalalithaa herself into a powerful leader.[56]

Other incidents followed, including a road accident that she alleged was an attempt on her life. The Web site asserted that, even in the midst of these threats to her person, Jayalalithaa's devotion to MGR did not flag but instead grew. This period, like the forest exiles of epic heroes, was framed as a time of trial and austerity, during which Jayalalithaa's devotion to MGR was tested and her own power—coded as the divine, feminized energy of *cakti*—accumulated. Her dedication to her mentor was signaled in her continued service as a member of the Legislative Assembly and her enlistment of Congress party support to commission an MGR statue on one of the city's largest commercial streets (Anna Salai). The enlargement of the Marina memorial, however, had to wait until 1992, when Jayalalithaa was named chief minister, following the AIA-DMK's return to power in 1991, for what the Web site described as the reinstatement of MGR's "benevolent rule." Her vow in the Legislative Assembly, anticipated by her earlier vow to MGR, was thus fulfilled.

An Epic Memorial

How is this epic backstory told at MGR's memorial? This space, like most memorials, does not divulge the contingencies of its own making. There is no suggestion that it might not have existed. Its durability and monumentality suggest, instead, that it was inevitable, an effect of the moral order of the Dravidianist family romance. With its proximity to Anna's memorial and its plaques that bear witness to the filial piety of his successor, Jayalalithaa, the memorial stands as the material effect of this romance. It is also a space whose permeable monumentality invites visitors' sympathy and identification. In its sacred interior, familial intimacy and political praxis are collapsed, creating a space of intimate address, in which the encounter of state and citizen is framed as that between parent and child, husband and wife, deity and devotee.

The gendered logic of the memorial's design and visitation practices create spaces for participation in the Dravidianist family romance. Visitors are enveloped in a feminized and domesticated space that is, on the one hand, defined and delimited by MGR's (manly) protection and, on the other hand, constitutes a protective shelter for his now vulnerable body. The memorial's design accomplishes this with the folded hands of its entry arch as well as its lotus sanctum and flame. All evoke femininity as encoded in the popular iconography associated with the goddess, Lakshmi, and the rituals of hospitality and domestic life that Lakshmi-like wives are expected to perform. The flame is a multivalent sign, associated with the oil lamps and hearths that represent the feminine core of domestic life, as well as with the cremation fire that terminates the body's existence and serves as threshold to the afterlife. According to Hindu orthodoxy, the hearth defines the domestic sphere spatially and temporally. The hearth is lit to mark the beginning of married life but also furnishes the spark with which the householder's cremation pyre is ignited. Further, it is in the domestic interior that the deceased are made into ancestors and given a place in the afterlife through regular postmortem offerings of food, water, prayer, and deference.

The memorial draws on these root metaphors, representing MGR as deceased householder and inviting visitors to recall his personalized, charismatic, and paternalistic leadership. His status as head of both household and polity is represented iconically and spatially in the bust positioned midway on the axial plane that connects the entry arch and the sculpted lotus. Continuing inward, to the sacred core that evokes both temple sanctum and domestic interior, MGR's person is signified again, this time indexically, by the flame marking the burial site. However, his status here is ambiguous, both in sectarian and gendered terms. While the flame evokes the ritualized life cycle of the Hindu householder, the very presence of MGR's interred body violates Hindu norms. It is this same vulnerable body, indexed by the burial slab, that feminizes MGR by marking him as one in need of protection through care and through remembrance, even as the evocations of palace and temple render him a kingly protector and father to his "children." The phallic obelisk near the flame platform makes similarly transgendered assertions. It is a masculine signifier but its design, featuring four arm-like extensions from the base, has been described as a representation of the more feminized virtues of the "love and protecting care that MGR provided to the people."[57] The lotus is similarly encoded as signifier of both kingship and MGR's "purity of mind and soft-hearted nature," characteristics that Tamil speakers ordinarily and approvingly ascribe to women.[58]

The story about MGR that is condensed visually and spatially on the site is not a finished story, a past that remains past. Rather, it is a chapter of a still unfolding narrative, albeit one whose conflicts and resolutions are over-determined by the family romance at the heart of the epic. This narrative charts the struggles to claim Annadurai's legacy that have pitted Jayalalithaa and Karunanidhi, along with their respective parties, in continuous political combat, that have been played out in parliamentary alliances and electoral contests, mediated in the print, televisual, and electronic sources that each controls, and transmuted in the Tamil-inflected visions of state sovereignty that each seeks to translate institutionally and in the built environment. The memorial's relation to this story is metonymic (it is a part of the whole) and synecdochic (it is its condensed, material effect). The family romance, in turn, continues to frame action in the political field, giving narrative shape to both memory and futurity, transmuting states of the past into states of possibility.

With this story in mind, we might now return to and reread the memorial's architecture. The memorial officially extols the righteousness of MGR's rule and delivers him, in death, to the protection and care of his political descendents. The state, as imagined through MGR's body, stands above the people as an encompassing protector, a revered patriarch bound, nonetheless, to citizen-children by intimate ties of love and duty, ties demonstrated in acts of devotion and filial piety. The memorial invites piety and materializes it as patronage, as a demonstration of largesse and political legacy claimed by Jayalalithaa in her bid to succeed MGR as the new embodiment of the state. Thus, just as it commends MGR to popular memory, it also commemorates Jayalalithaa's acts of sacrifice on his behalf and her identification with him and his legacy. Reconsider the entry arch, with its reverential, feminized welcome. Is it not Jayalalithaa who welcomes visitors with modestly folded hands? Just as Jayalalithaa wrested control of the party and the state assembly from Janaki through a combination of political theater, parliamentary calculus, and sheer muscle, by welcoming visitors at the memorial's threshold she has used architectural semiotics to supplant MGR's legal wife from the role of caretaker/protector of his memory.

Jayalalithaa's path, from screen ingénue to political protégé to reigning, and occasionally sacralized, chief minister, can be discerned by shifting the focus from the memorial itself to the surrounding urban landscape.[59] Jayalalithaa is visually mediated within a dense, inter-ocular field that encompasses political posters, immense cutouts (exceeding in number those of other politicians), billboards, and her own, carefully staged appearances before supporters. Preminda Jacob finds that Jayalalithaa's political ascent was accompanied by an iconographic progression, with the authoritative monolithic cutouts of recent years having replaced earlier images in which a smaller, more sexualized Jayalalithaa was paired, deferentially, with larger figures of MGR.[60] The more recent cutouts, which tended to be raised at election times on major streets, at rally sites, and in neighborhoods controlled by the AIA-DMK, depicted Jayalalithaa face forward and standing, her upper body covered in a signature cape, reverentially clasping her hands together or extending her arm in a victorious greeting. The visual aspect of cutouts, posters, and performances capture and enthrall the spectator-devotee, deliberately miming gestures of worshipful deference and beneficent protection conveyed in the site's architecture and iconography, even as they cast their shadows of ominous protection over the city.

Memorial Rhetoric

On the memorial's grounds as well as in the virtual memoryscape of his party's Web site, the remembrance of MGR is structured by the practices and material idioms of Hindu ritual and kingship. This and the related entanglement of religious and political fields are neither coincidental nor merely decorative but derive from a deeper, historically salient fusion of kingship and divinity in Hindu India. Kings were chief worshipers and stood as temple patrons and protectors; like deities, they also were the objects of others' worshipful attention. And just as deities are represented and treated as royal protectors of individuals, families, and communities, Hindu kings were often understood as incarnation of or regent for the tutelary deity. Rulers, *with* deities and *as* deities, guaranteed the safety, prosperity, and well-being of their subjects and preserved social and cosmological order. The fusion of divinity and kingship was represented by and mediated through the body, and regent-as-deity and deity-as-regent were understood as entities whose bodies are coextensive with society and with the cosmos.[61]

Though most of India's dynasts were stripped of territorial and economic power under colonial rule and their kingdoms later absorbed into India's federal system, the principles of kingship and the Hindu worldview with which it is frequently conflated continue to surface in political discourses and practices, just as politically salient notions of order subtend ritual practice and discourse. To anticipate my argument in the next chapter, I simply note that these principles, reworked in colonial statecraft, laid the groundwork for the state's administration of Hindu institutions, creating a distinctive genealogy of India's secular state. The memorial space and practice discussed in this chapter can also be read within this genealogy. In commemorating a deceased political leader, the memorial furnishes a space for engaging imaginatively, through bodily habitus, with the model of sovereignty whose historical referent is medieval Hindu kingship but which nonetheless infuses the discourse, imagery, and practices of constitutional governance.

This rhetorical project is mediated by the stylistic and emblematic features of the memorial's architecture and by its spatial syntax. Like its linguistic counterpart, spatial syntax refers to the ordering of spatial elements and the information this order encodes about the actions that can take place in those environments.[62] Access can be regulated and surveillance exercised, for example, with specific architectural devices—Bentham's panopticon is the classic example—that both represent and enact disciplinary power. The memorial's spatial syntax offers several noteworthy features that suggest a different model of power. It is, first of all, open in ways that institutions based on disciplinary power are not. It is not a rigid container, with walls and roof, but relies, instead, on landscaping and sculptural elements to fashion permeable boundaries between its nested "interiors" and the "exteriors" that lie beyond those boundaries. Second, rounded, rather than rectilinear, forms are repeated throughout the memorial grounds. Its threshold is a curvilinear arch, paved walkways encircle lawns and platforms, and its sanctum is formed by a lotus-shaped pavilion. These, with the ritualized circumambulation that structures visitors' encounters, produce a spatial syntax evocative of a Hindu temple. Like a temple, it is accessed by multiple approach paths. This and the paucity of spatial control points encode power in ways that are quite different from those used in schools, prisons, or government offices, whose spatial syntax enables easy surveillance and regulation of users' movements. Power instead is experienced and encountered as a seductive center, using feminized cultural referents in some instances, into which people are drawn and to which they (willingly) defer.

The mirroring of Hindu spatial syntax is most apparent in those commemorative actions that incorporate worship forms associated with *pūja,* rituals that are ubiquitous, if not definitive, features of Hindu practice. These ritual repertoires, codified during the Pallava period, are formally identical with ritual forms adopted by kings to propitiate tutelary deities on behalf of their kingdoms and by which kings themselves were honored and their sovereignty renewed. In their more elaborated forms, they consist of serial acts and utterances that offer praise, deference, and allegiance, and that seek protection, favors, grace, and power. They are directed to the bodies of deities and rulers, to the supplicant bodies of worshipers, and the powerful bodies of deities/kings, understood to represent and encompass cosmos and polity. It is the body of the deity/king that is anointed and adorned with jewels and silk robes, it is that body to which food, incense, and camphor are offered, and it is worshipers' bodies to which offerings are returned, transvalued as grace-laden *prasadam.* Ritual praxis at the memorial is an abbreviated, metonymic reference to this complex, shares its aesthetic logic, and seeks to engender the same sort of hierarchical intimacy that is achieved in worship through the exchange of gazes and transfers of substance. This is the relation of authority that MGR strove for and to a large extent succeeded in establishing and which Jayalalithaa sought to replicate, in part through the cathexis of mourning that is engaged in commemorative practice, space, and discourse.

MGR's memorial, with its lotus throne and *maṇṭapam,* draw upon and extend the images of kingly protection that his films popularized. Another media space, the AIA-DMK Web site, draws upon the same pool of cinematic images in depicting the beneficence and power of MGR, supplementing and framing these with stylistic and rhetorical features of Tamil political oratory. Like the actual grounds of the memorial, the Web site virtually enacts commemoration and encodes sovereignty. And both the memorial and the Web site are projects sponsored by MGR's successor, Jayalalithaa. The righteousness of MGR's rule (and, not coincidentally, that of his successor) is architecturally condensed and devotionally engaged at the memorial site; it is narrated in epic fashion on the Web site. Although the memorial's architectural features receive cursory attention on the pages of the Web site, its texts supply an epic backstory that weaves the *camāti*'s creation and its use into an account of the party's emergence and growth, processes framed, explicitly, in terms of kingship.

Thus, besides its iconic and metonymic references to MGR and to the state as he claimed to embody it, the memorial also refers to its own patron and MGR's successor, Jayalalithaa. The *camāti*'s expansion and emergence as the principal and most opulent among the commemorative sites dedicated to MGR indexes Jayalalithaa's ascent in party hierarchy and her consolidation of political and policing power in the state. On the party Web site, the gravesite's construction and the commemorative practice that it hosts are woven into the epic narrative of the party's history: a narrative in which MGR's rise to the Chief Ministry and his founding of the AIA-DMK form an origin myth that foreshadows and legitimates Jayalalithaa's claim to be his successor. Indeed, some critics argue that over the 1990s, as she has consolidated her political power, Jayalalithaa has forged an iconography in which MGR has been gradually excised. This iconography is designed to convey her own sufficiency, authority, protective potency, and, at times, her sacrality. The ubiquity of such images is undeniable as is their association with a moral landscape shaped by Jayalalithaa's claim of kingly sovereignty.[63] At the same time MGR, as patron, father, and lover, remains a haunting supplement, a vulnerable body whose persistent need for and guarantee of protection are inscribed in the social space of the *camāti* and in the virtual epic to which Jayalalithaa must, finally, trace her own origin.

Conversely, while making an idealized version of MGR available to the public, the *camāti* is inscribed by the intentions of its sponsors who, extending the familial idioms of kingly sovereignty, engage in memorial practice as an act of filial piety. Just as the living honor their ancestors while grieving their absence, so also must living politicians honor, while mourning, their patrons and mentors. They enact a family romance that, in political oratory and on the Web site, is crafted as an epic of dynastic succession underlain by moral struggle. Citizens, as visitors to both virtual and actual spaces of party history, are addressed both as witnesses to the family romance that engenders the state, and as the infantile subjects of that romance. And in the corporeal spaces of ritual praxis, as spectator-devotees, they enact the relations of hierarchical intimacy with the state.

Conclusion

How, then, does MGR's memorial signify? And how is the state effected in this process? In one sense, the memorial can be decoded as simply an artifact of the instrumental power of its patron(s). Significance of this sort arises, contextually, within the contingent, historical field of political struggle. In another, more rhetorical sense, it is meant to communicate to ordinary citizens, party members, and elected officials, and to create a moral and affective substrate for the authority that MGR, his party, and his successor wield. Indeed, the rhetorical force of these spaces and images work to contain neoliberal transformation under the mantle of kingly authority—contributing to an environment that is more hospitable to autocratic power than to the sort of democratic participation anticipated by advocates of neoliberalism. In this chapter I have considered these issues through an interpretive analysis of the memorial, focusing on the affectively charged memory work—mourning—that generated and continues to transform it. As a social space, the memorial is understood not as a finished, inert artifact but as something that is continuously produced and reproduced through practice, such as routines by which MGR is ritually recalled and honored, through the conceptual apparatus of design and planning, and, phenomenologically, through the experiential and affective engagements that mediate human use.

The question of how the *camāti* means is not answered by appealing solely to its form and function, however. The communicative capacity of the *camāti*'s architecture depends on the interspatial and inter-textual fields of reference in which these architectural features and visitation practices exist. Their meanings—that is, their metaphoric, metonymic, and iconic relations to other spaces, images, practices, and words—arise within intersecting fields of signifiers, the films, Web site, billboards, cutouts, and ceremonies that recall MGR and reenact the hierarchical intimacies of rule.

The memory work of mourning—its affective charge, its longing for that which is lost—is also the work of politics. Memorial spaces may naturalize the state through embodied representational modes, making its claims of authority natural and inviting subjects' consent. More fundamentally, the same spaces materialize the state and invest it with agency and with temporal durability and directionality. Arguably such spaces become even more critical in enacting state sovereignty and naturalizing it as an ethnic, gendered body as the deregulated, decentralized state's authority becomes more circumscribed to accommodate market forces. Mourning and the memorial spaces and practices that mediate it are not just ways to embellish or mark political authority but are critical material media and emotive institutions that engender power and sovereignty, and, through the formation of structures of feeling, produce consent to it.

4

Modernity Remembered: Temples, Publicity, and Heritage

> Thiruvanmiyur traffic jams—at least those on the East Coast Road—seem to have their silver lining! Stuck in a particularly long one I was able to manoeuvre my car and park beside the wall of the Marundeswarar temple in Thiruvanmiyur. I had passed the temple many times knowing of its age but had never been inside. . . . What strikes one is the greenery and the quietness despite the throng of devotees. . . . On the way to the Thripurasundari Amman shrine, one is forced to pause and admire the pillars particularly those with warriors on prancing horses. . . . Nataraja has his own sannidhi here. The icon is large and very beautiful. That day, draped in white silk vastram He shimmered beautifully in the light. . . . The sound of the priests chanting the Vedas to the light coloured, slightly slanting main lingam comes across loud and clear. . . . The Thiruvanmiyur of the sages' times would have been a lot greener, but ours . . . a little away from the concrete tentacles of Chennai, doesn't seem to be much different from its ancient version![1]

Accounts like this one, celebrating serendipitous encounters between urban travelers and old temples, appear regularly in the "Heritage" column carried by the Chennai edition of *The Hindu,* an English-language daily founded in 1878. Written for *The Hindu*'s urban and transnational readership, these stories assert the presence of the ancient in the midst of the modern, and they index the persistence of Hinduism not only in India's built environment but in the knowledge and aesthetic sensibilities of its modern citizens. With this narrative of discovery, the author distinguishes his own contemplative style of engagement from the popular devotionalism favored by the temple's "throng of devotees," even as he confirms his attachment to and appreciation for Hinduism's richly sedimented praxis. Despite this being his first venture inside the temple complex, the encounter is framed in terms of recognition, of the remembrance of familiar pleasure. Just as important is the implication that the temple is a space on which multiple remembering publics may converge, a space to which co-religionists, city dwellers in search of green space, and heritage enthusiasts can lay equal claim. Indeed, the temple's visibility in Wikipedia contextualizes and underscores these convergences in light of globalization. There it is asserted that a "once unknown" area "is now an upcoming destination with the Tidel park being located nearby."[2]

This temple, like growing numbers of others, is currently the subject of a heritage conservation program spearheaded by private voluntary associations working in uneven collaboration with state agencies. Over the past two decades, propositions linking temple visitation and maintenance to nationalist sentiment have resurfaced in discourses and institutions concerned with heritage preservation, borrowing that rubric directly from European and North American contexts. Temples are likened to the monuments, memorials, and museums in which the nation's history is encoded and that can impart to visitors lessons in citizenship and national identification. But distinct from monuments and museums, temples are considered sites of productive nostalgia, guarantors of a still-present past.

The current reclamation of Hindu temples as *Indian* heritage and the English mediation of many of these activities have arisen within a broader set of discourses that aim to delineate the presence of the past in the rapidly changing built environment. Attention to temples' "pastness" and to their objectification of tradition is not new in itself, though state-led efforts to bind those interests to nationalist consciousness accelerated during the latter half of the twentieth century.[3] The most recent interests in heritage are tied to state institutions that themselves have been articulated with and reconfigured by neoliberal globalization, a congeries of forces that seem both to threaten and revitalize the material past. "Heritage" here glosses an array of objects, knowledges and practices that new legislative measures are designed to protect, committees and statutory bodies are convened to identify and list, and local and transnational NGOs aim to conserve. Colonial office buildings and churches, forested tracts, dilapidated rural mansions, ancient forts and palaces, temples, synagogues, and mosques—all are potential heritage sites. Nor have the commercial opportunities presented by heritage gone unnoticed, as private and state-sponsored bodies seek ever more aggressively to market its sites, commodities, and services. English-language and vernacular print media, televisual programming, Web sites and Web blogs all now serve to mediate and publicize heritage.

In some instances, proponents of heritage reiterate the alarmism with which supporters of Hindu nationalism, or Hindutva, regard Muslim and Christian "threats" to Hindu sites. Indeed, narratives on heritage, like those on Hindutva, often blur the boundaries between the secular and religious, a tendency that has been amplified by what Arvind Rajagopal describes as the advance of electronic capitalism in the context of the Nehruvian legacy of secularism.[4] In Rajagopal's words:

> Given the volume and velocity of image flows set in motion with electronic capitalism and the new conjuncture represented by liberalization, it is unlikely that the *cordon sanitaire* between "community" and "secular" life could have been

> maintained for long. . . . Resorting to religious and community culture draws not only from those spheres' own considerable affective power, but their status of semi-exclusion from the public realm affords a surplus charge, as a quasi-forbidden pleasure.[5]

Heritage discourses, I argue, may intersect with (and be used to legitimate) those of Hindutva; they are not reducible to, contained by, or isomorphic with Hindutva, however. As implied by this chapter's epigraph, heritage—its sites and artifacts, as well as the procedures by which their stories are discovered and composed—arises at conjunctures at which patriotisms, tourism, and consumption meet. This chapter examines these converging and competing streams of interest, their relations to Hindu sensibilities and practices, and their sociopolitical effects, taking the conservation of Chennai's Marundeswarar Temple as my case. Of special interest are the ways that heritage, as discourse, practice, and space, is deployed within statecraft to bridge the gap between bureaucracy and belonging. Whereas Tamil Nadu's Dravidianist leaders rely upon embodied metaphors of kingship to craft a legitimating past and produce affective attachment among the governed, Chennai's heritage enthusiasts envision subjects formed in articulation with modern, depersonalized institutions and ideologies of modern statecraft. It is a statecraft, however, in which Hindu discourses, spaces, and practices are always, albeit ambiguously, present as signifiers of national character and aspiration, as emblems of public space, and as markers of a shared past.

In the following pages I account for the ways that heritage came to frame the interventions of state and civil bodies in Hindu temples in Chennai during the 1990s, using as a lens a campaign to conserve and restore Marundeswarar's grounds.[6] Spread over nearly an acre in the heart of Tiruvanmiyur's commercial center, the temple's two tanks (stone-lined pools fed by underground acquifers and wells) had gone dry, and small shops abutted its compound walls. Conservationists aimed to recharge the tanks, improve the temple's natural landscaping, and clean and restore its grounds. Their efforts dovetailed with state interventions geared to enhancing the temple's visibility and the area's commercial development, and what successes they achieved cannot be disentangled from the combined forces of state and market.

I interpret the practices and discourses set in motion by the heritage campaign as moments in what Talal Asad called the "formation of the secular"—the sensibilities, attitudes, assumptions, behaviors, and discourses that precede and regulate the application (usually by the state) of the doctrine of "secularism." "Secularism," he wrote,

> builds on a particular conception of the world ("natural" and "social") and of the problems generated by that world. . . . In the discourse of modernity, "the secular" presents itself as the ground from which theological discourse was generated . . . and from which it gradually emancipated itself in its march to freedom. On that ground, humans appear as the self-conscious makers of history . . . and as the unshakable foundation of universally valid knowledge about nature and society.[7]

The conservation of the Marundeswarar Temple was an instance, like the prior development of a legal and bureaucratic apparatus for state oversight of Hindu temples, of an effort dedicated to producing the secular in, through, and finally beyond the terms, practices, and spaces of the religious.

I introduce these processes with a descriptive overview of the social space of the Hindu temple and the kinds of publicity it anchors, glossing publicity as both collective institutions and the "general social horizon of experience in which everything that is actually or ostensibly relevant for all members of society is integrated . . . a dimension of [people's] consciousness."[8] I then return to the case of the Marundeswarar Temple, to consider how recent concerns with cultural conservation have created new stages for contestation between state and nongovernmental agents, ritual actors and local citizens about the role of religious spaces, and practices and identities in civic life and political participation. A discussion then follows of the ways that the temples figured in colonial and postcolonial modernization projects and the different mappings of the secular with which these efforts were aligned. Threading these discussions together is attention to the relation between the historicism of "heritage" and the ways of knowing, narrating, and living in personal and collective pasts that Hindu praxis engenders. How do these two frames intersect in the ways that subjects engage, interrogate, and reframe modernity and their own modernist subject-positions as citizens?

The Hindu Temple as Social Space

Hindu temples (*kōvil*) were and continue to be ubiquitous parts of southern India's built environment.[9] Some seventy-five thousand temples are estimated to exist in Tamil Nadu, and, in Chennai, alone, temples may number in the thousands, ranging in size from small, open-air altars and sidewalk shrines (*naṭaippātai kōvil*) to complexes extending over several city blocks.[10] They are spaces of remunerative work, religiosity, expressive culture, sociality, and status production; they may be controlled by appointed committees, families, sub-sects, caste communities, or neighborhood groups. Temple wealth, acquired through donations of money, land, and valuables, and from rental income, can be considerable. Many have histories of close cultural, political, and economic ties with landowners, merchants, or regional dynasts, a pattern that extends to the present, with temples continuing to enjoy the patronage of businesspersons, industrialists, and elected officials.

As a consequence of their wealth and the competing interests among participants, temples have been flashpoints for conflict between managers, priests, tenants, and devotees. Since the latter part of the nineteenth century, a steady stream of legal and political measures, principally concerning rights in decision making and resource allocation, has enrolled temples within debates on publicity, citizenship, and nationhood. State oversight of Hindu religious institutions had been sought originally to manage internal disagreements and to limit Brahman influence in temple affairs and resources. Over time, the pattern of state intervention shifted from conflict adjudication to more routinized forms of administration

Figure 4.1. Sidewalk shrine, Chennai. *Photograph by author.*

designed to anticipate and prevent conflict and to introduce reforms in the service of nationalism and modernization.[11] The Hindu Religious Endowments Act of 1926 authorized the formation of a governmental agency whose members would be empowered to monitor (and, following later amendments, to redistribute) temple finances and organization. The Act, with some modifications, has remained in force ever since.[12] With few exceptions, large temples in Tamil Nadu are now managed by the state government's Hindu Religious and Charitable Endowments Department, which oversees the collection and distribution of temple revenues, the appointment of managers, priests, and temple servants, the physical upkeep of the temples, and the scheduling of renovation rituals.[13] At the national level, India's central government, while officially secular, has treated Hindu temples as icons of national memory and culture, sponsoring programs for preservation and restoration, and promoting them as destinations for domestic tourists.[14]

The state effects that temples produce are mediated in their material spaces, in their governance, and in forms of everyday sociality that they engender. At the heart of these social and material processes are the deities, saints, or preceptors who reside within temples, embodied usually as stone figures known as *mūrtti* or *mūlavar.* Each temple bears the name of its presiding deity or deities and is a site for worship, which includes prayer, the offering of foodstuffs and valuables to the deity, and the redistribution of food offerings. These commonalities notwithstanding, temples differ in architectural and iconographic features, and in wealth and popularity. Large complexes, like Tiruvanmiyur's Marundeswarar Temple, contain multiple shrines, dedicated to various gods, celestial bodies and saints, as well as assembly spaces, where recitations, musical performances, lectures, and devotional gatherings take place. They are enclosed by compound walls whose entry gates are framed by towering arches, *kōpuram,* on which characters and scenes from the Puranas are carved. Temple complexes also include tanks (*kuḷam*), stone-lined pools, fed by underground aquifers or wells. Like rivers and other water bodies, temple tanks are considered to have ritually purifying properties; devotees bathe in them, and they are centers for festival activities. Though many tanks in urban areas have become desiccated, they were integrated originally within the regional water storage and circulation systems, encompassing rivers, human-made and natural lakes, and irrigation works, established under the imperial dynasties that controlled peninsular south Asia during the millennium prior to British colonization.[15]

Lying in the shadows of the sometimes monumental temple complexes are thousands of small sidewalk shrines, Hindu and Christian.[16] Usually found at intersections and near bus and rail stops, shrines exist as street furniture, free-standing structures that occupy the mediating spaces between the street and surrounding buildings.[17] As land values have escalated, more shrines have cropped up as encroachments—illegal extensions of individual or corporate property—on footpaths, easements, and unoccupied government land.[18] Sidewalk shrines are home to the same deities who, in more opulent garb, preside in larger, wealthier temple complexes. Most common is Ganapati (known also as Vinayaka or Ganesa), the "Lord of Beginnings" whose protection enables devotees to overcome obstacles. He appears in endless variety, especially at intersections, where his presence is invoked as a hedge against the uncertainties represented, literally and figuratively, by crossroads. Ammans, such as Mariyamman, sometimes described as village goddesses and understood to be immanent within natural features of the landscape, particularly certain trees, are nearly as popular as Ganapati.[19]

In the past, large temples constituted the central places of urban settlements. Four *mada* (or *mata*) streets, oriented in each of the cardinal directions, enclosed the temple complex. Laid out along those streets were *agraharam,* residential blocks housing priests and temple servants.[20] Open-air markets were often adjacent, as were offices and shops, which typically occupied the front portion of a residence. *Agraharam* houses represent one of southern India's architectural vernaculars, the courtyard house; typical features include *tiṇṇai* (verandahs), over which tile roofs extend, and central and rear courtyards.[21] In those Chennai neighborhoods—Triplicane, Mylapore, and Tiruvanmiyur—that are located on the sites of precolonial temple towns, these settlement patterns remain discernable and examples of vernacular architecture still stand. Elsewhere, including in the city's suburban extensions, a new wave of temple construction adapted to recent land use and growth patterns has come with the emergence of a more prosperous and sizable middle class.[22]

Creating Social Space

Any Hindu temple, as social space, is predicated on the embodied agency of the divine. Regardless of size, wealth, or popularity, temples are spaces where divine power is understood—and felt—as immanent. As material manifestations of the deity's sovereignty, temples encapsulate the cosmos, itself. As Diana Eck has explained,

> In building a temple, the universe in microcosm is reconstructed. The divine ground-plan is called a *mandala,* a geometric map of the cosmos. At its center is the sanctum, where the image [is] installed. Its eight directions are guarded by the cosmic regents. . . . Various planetary deities, world guardians, and gods are set in their appropriate quadrants. . . . The particular *mandala* of the Hindu temple is called the *vastu-purusa mandala* . . . the cosmic "person," from the sacrifice of whose giant body the entire universe was created. . . . The body, as an organic whole diverse in the function of its parts and limbs, is here the image appropriated for the cosmos. . . . The temple is the condensed image of the cosmos.[23]

Divine power—creative, destructive, sustaining—lies at the heart of the complex, always evolving network of relations that connect human and nonhuman actors. Humans as well as deities in their embodied forms are regarded as having capacities to experience and be transformed by the transactions of ritual. Those who visit, work, and worship in temples experience those spaces interactively, as successions of the visual, olfactory, gustatory, auditory, and tactile relations that connect deities, priests, and devotees. These transactions, at once, produce and are situated within the social space of the temple.

LeFebvre's notion of social space provides an especially useful analytic entry into the temple life and helps to frame the temple's publicity, understood as the horizon formed by the temple's social organization of experience.[24] Using LeFebvre's vocabulary, a temple can be said to exist as a "perceived," practiced space, as a "conceived" representation of space, and as a "lived" representational space, its meaning and significance filtered through language and cultural media.[25] These three sets of terms, LeFebvre argued, denoted interpenetrating aspects of spatiality. As *representations* of space, temples offer schematic conceptions of cosmological wholes, for example, in the "ground plan" constituted by the *mandala*. More important, they are also iconic *representational* spaces. They may be treated by the state as embodiments of "Hindu culture," though for their communities of users, they are irruptions of divine energy, manifestations of the sacred taking material form "of its own accord," a capacity denoted by the use of the Sanskritic term, *swayambhu* (self-created).[26] Tiruvanmiyur's Marundeswarar Temple is renowned for the presence of such an icon. In its main shrine, Marundeswarar is embodied in the form of a *swayambhu lingam,* Siva in the form of a stone phallus, whose white color is ascribed to the milk that Kamadhenu, the divine, wish-fulfilling cow, showered on it to nullify a curse. That lingam, along with more than a hundred others, is housed within the temple's *mahāmaṇṭapam,* a stone canopy surrounding the shrine. The same space also contains images of the sixty-three Saivite saints, Ganapati, Muthukumaraswamy (also known as Kartikeya), and Nataraja. Another *maṇṭapam,* adorned by thirty-six carved stone pillars, holds the processional image of Siva, in the form of Tyagarajar.[27] Other, smaller *maṇṭapams* contain shrines for Marundeswarar's consort, Tirupurasundari, Vijayaganapati (Victorious Ganapati), and Subramanya (also known as Murukan).

Temples also exist as sensed or *perceived* spaces, that is, as ensembles of spatial practices associated both with temple building and ongoing use—processes that, in state-managed temples, are subject to regulation and oversight. A temple's construction is a deeply ritualized process. Hereditary builders, known as *stapati,* understand the structure to be a materialization of divine agency to which they, through the application of divinely revealed principles of design and construction, have lent form.[28] Such practices assure the community of believers that deity will live in the material name and form offered by the temple. A temple's ongoing sacrality depends as well on periodic reconsecration and renovation. The ideal interval for rituals of reconsecration—*kumpapiṣēkam*—is twelve years, but in practice these events are less frequent given the demands that they make on resources and personnel. Re-consecrations, as well as other activities associated with construction and maintenance, are scrutinized and managed in Tamil Nadu by the HR & CE Administration Department. Marundeswarar's reconsecrations in 1995, and again in 2004, were indicative of the patronage that the state lavished on temples under both the first (1991–1996) and second (2001–2006) Chief Ministerships of J. Jayalalithaa.

Also relevant to the spatial practice of the temple is the complex meshing of rituals of worship with more mundane routines of work (physical maintenance, repair, and cleaning), financial transactions, and administration, all of which entail greater or lesser degrees of state surveillance. Specific observances may mark transitions in the life cycles of temple deities and are performed at daily, lunar, seasonal, and annual intervals. Priests, singers, and other temple servants perform specific acts of worship that are directed to the deity in its embodied form; devotees may observe these rituals and participate by receiving shares of redistributed offerings, activities that require donations or the payment of specific fees, which are established and collected by the temple's trustees and the HR & CE department. Devotees may also sponsor rituals or engage in personal worship, for example, by circumambulating shrines or engaging in private prayer.

The core transactions of temple ritual occur within its interior shrines. It is there that deities receive priests' offerings of prayer, foods, and valuables, and that worshipers seek the deities' *darśan*. Ritual also involves circumambulatory processions by both temple deities and devotees. At the Marundeswarar Temple, as at other Siva temples, major annual events take place during the Tamil month of *Paṅkuṉi* (mid-March to mid-April). Then, during a twelve-day festival, the deity Siva, manifested as Tyagarajar, is taken out in procession and performs his eighteen sacred dances.[29] Ritualized spatial practices such as festivals and processions thus contribute as well to networks between temples and to the creation of streetscapes whose visual, spatial, and acoustic character is inflected by Hindu imagery and praxis.[30] Finally, also within the realm of spatial practice, are activities ancillary to worship but crucial to temple life. These include commercial transactions of surrounding shops, many of which furnish goods essential for worship and occupy space that has been rented from the temple.

Temples in and as Time

Technologies of memory are critical in the making of temples as social spaces. Temples are necessarily made over time. More important, they materialize cosmological, political, and societal pasts and present meta-narratives on those pasts. Some temples are erected on sites associated with a deity's earthly incarnation. Others are built to mark the spots at which deities' images or other embodied representations have appeared, actions interpreted as the deity's disclosure of her or his wish for a temple. Stories, oral and written, known as *sthalapurana*, recount temple origins.[31] The site of the Marundeswarar Temple is said to be where Siva restored health to the sage, Agastya, and to the divine celestials, the Sun and Moon. Siva's manifestation as a healer is alluded to in the name Marundeswarar, which translates as Lord of Medicine. Siva's actions are recalled and commemorated by devotees' worship of Marundeswarar and by the devotions of the Sun and Moon themselves, who are said to worship Marundeswarar each evening. And the garden of medicinal plants that the temple grounds once held formed a material mnemonic of Siva's foundational gesture.

The temple has been dated to the Pallava period (ca. 575–900 CE), and references to the temple's origin and opulence and to the piety of the village's inhabitants are found in hymns composed during the seventh century by the saints, Tirunavukkarasar and Tirugnanasambandar. Stone inscriptions on the temple grounds indicate its expansion and elaboration under Cola rule (950–1100 CE), during which time regents' gifts as well as the temple's tax obligations were noted. Carvings on one of the columns in the temple recall the austerities performed by Valmiki, the poet-saint reputed to be the author of the Ramayana epic.[32] In recognition of his devotion, the poet is said to have received a boon: *darśan* of Siva performing his cosmic dances, the same dances that are recalled and reenacted during the temple's annual *Paṅkuṉi* month festival.

Origin stories, poems, hymns, and other representations offer foundational narratives for the aesthetic praxis of worship and for the social communities, the publics, that are engendered by, sustained through, and instantiated as the temple. They capture the simultaneity of the temple's materiality and its sociality: the connections among plants, persons, deity, foodstuffs, currency, jewelry, cloth, and other valued objects that are formed through acts of divine disclosure, human communication, worship, and labor. The stories affirm the embodied and aesthetic (that is, the sensory) qualities of Hindu worship and reveal the ways it is threaded with the construction of temple and its ongoing social functions. The architecture and spatial syntax of any temple, new or old, large or small, arises from ritualized interactions such as those described in their origin stories. Put differently, ongoing ritual praxis commemorates and reenacts a temple's origin.

Thus, whether taking the form of a multi-block complex or a tiny shrine at the base of a tree, temples are complex socio-spatial worlds, shaped by ongoing interactions among deities, temple servants, administrators, and worshipers, overseen and, to varying degrees, regulated and appropriated by the state. These are the relations by which a temple is made as a social space and its sacrality constituted and regenerated. These spatial practices operate simultaneously as the means by which priests and other temple servants earn their livings, by which donors build their reputations, by which devotees seek blessings, jobs, children, and health, and in which state and non-state actors monitor and regulate flows of labor, knowledge, and resources. Temples, in short, form the anchor and dynamic hub of a "public" that includes laborers, administrators, worshipers, and deities themselves—a horizon of experience predicated on, but not limited to, Hindu praxis and that, with the participatory possibilities now offered by the Internet, overcomes geographic distance through the digital mediation of image and sound.

How do the publics that arise in relational networks of worship and work and divine presence relate to the deliberative publics to whose interests the state is (theoretically) accountable? How do heritage discourses mediate competing and colluding claims? The next section turns to the conservation of the Marundeswarar Temple, launched in the late 1990s, and considers various interests that intersected in the discourses and practices associated with heritage.

Places for People

In 2000 the Marundeswarar Temple became the subject of a conservation plan authored by a local voluntary association, the Chennai chapter of INTACH, the Indian National Trust for Art and Cultural Heritage. Over the next four years, the plan, in Power-Point format, was screened to local residents, business groups, state agencies, and fellow preservationists. Working with state agencies and other voluntary organizations, INTACH helped clean and restore sections of the temple. Additional maintenance and restoration projects were sponsored by the state, with the goal of promoting economic development and dispensing political patronage. Conservation was entwined with a productive nostalgia that unfolded in the shadow of, and in reaction to, Tiruvanmiyur's own commercial growth coupled with the greater visibility of and receptivity to Hindu nationalism among Chennai's residents.

INTACH

The first national organization dedicated to heritage preservation, INTACH was formed in 1984.[33] Its founding came in the wake of a broader state-led effort to develop an infrastructure for preserving, exhibiting, and marketing the crafts and performance styles of India's regions. It was an effort meant to promote a hegemonic national culture in the aftermath of the period of martial law known as the Emergency (1975–77) and to encourage greater production and consumption of cultural goods and services, domestically and abroad.[34]

INTACH draws its membership from India's English-speaking, cosmopolitan elites and was founded with close ties with the central government, at that point headed by the Congress Party under Rajiv Gandhi. It was administered by the central government's Department of Culture and received an initial budget allocation of Rs.5 crores.[35] With deregulation, INTACH lost most of its state funding and its chapters were decentralized. Local chapters now obtain funds from donations and occasional grants, seeking support from both domestic and international sources. The organization has also had an uneven alliance with Hindu nationalist interests, particularly during the period from 1998 to 2004, when a coalition led by the Bharatiya Janata Party (BJP) controlled India's parliament. A member of the Chennai chapter alluded to the difficulties posed by the presence of a "BJP man" at INTACH's national headquarters. Although chapters operated independently and did not receive operating funds from the center, they stood to lose influence and political allies if they took an overtly critical stance toward the leadership's nationalist orientation.

The group's charge is to provide guidance on the ways that the conservation of both cultural and natural resources might be incorporated into urban and regional planning.[36] In basic terms, this involves translating and implementing the notion of "heritage conservation" as defined in Europe and North America into terms compatible with Indian values and practices. As glossed by INTACH, "heritage" is not simply a generic reference to residues of the past but describes the conceptual and practical apparatus that define and organize these residues within historicist narratives. This apparatus encompasses techniques, spaces, and discursive regimes, including cataloging methods, photographic record keeping, museal architecture and practice, conservation techniques, and the ever expanding body of statutes and regulations by which the state manages its past.

The templates employed in managing and making pasts visible by INTACH are borrowed from the national trust models of heritage conservation used in Britain and North America. Although their roots lie in the colonial impulse to know, classify, and selectively conserve the remains of the subcontinent's premodern civilizations in the service of imperial rule, heritage templates are now sustained by English-mediated transnational flows of knowledge, funds, and technology, enabling their users to define and organize local pasts in ways that are legible to present-day global audiences of tourists, corporate investors, and development specialists.[37] Thus, although INTACH uses Euro-Western protocols, such as listing and grading, and partners with international bodies such as UNESCO, it distinguishes its aims. INTACH's 2004 Charter acknowledges that preservation involving minimal intervention and retention of patina has normative stature in the U.K. It maintains, however, that "India's indigenous traditions idealise the opposite"—including the regeneration of that which decays, for example, by periodic rituals of temple renovation and reconsecration.[38] The latter principles, they observed, mandate conservation of both architectural and "living" heritage (e.g., design and building techniques), as well as attention to the interdependence of natural and cultural resources.[39]

With this charge, INTACH situates its operations and policies within the network of organizations, regulations, and conservation practices that have arisen since the 1980s, a matrix comprising legislative and administrative measures such as state-level Heritage Acts and municipal development control rules, as well as state agencies, committees, and commissions that work in conjunction with voluntary bodies. The group's mission, however, is sufficiently broad that there are various competing interpretations about implementation, which I discuss later in the context of Marundeswarar project planning.

INTACH's Chennai chapter, founded in 1984, had achieved limited success, given its small membership base and funds.[40] The urban development of the 1990s, however, had sharpened local concern about the pace of change and the loss of the city's historic character. Following its 1994 success in blocking the demolition of a nineteenth-century building in the city's colonial core, the office of the Director-General of Police (DGP) (built originally as a Masonic Lodge in 1834), INTACH began to take a more proactive role in proposing conservation measures for other structures. The publicity gained from the DGP building action enhanced the group's visibility. Its operations were covered by the city's major daily newspapers, Tamil and English; several free, neighborhood weeklies also helped publicize INTACH's goals.[41] Buoyed by the public support it received, Chennai's chapter was reorganized in 1996, with architects interested in conservation playing more prominent roles.

In a related development, INTACH and affiliates increasingly sought institutional presence as expert interlocutors in the field of heritage. Working as private sector consultants, they proposed not just the development of specific procedures for conservation, such as protocols for inventorying, listing, and grading heritage sites and determining materials specifications for conservation architecture, but sought a role in decision making. For some, these activities dovetailed with commercial ventures. For example, one couple active in INTACH's Chennai chapter had obtained contracts for designing heritage-themed hotels and resorts for private developers; others found work meeting the small but growing demand for neo-traditionalist design in residential architecture. Thus, while fanning popular tastes in traditional styles of architecture, INTACH also hoped to participate in the planning process by drafting state-level heritage acts that would lend statutory authority to conservation efforts and ensure INTACH's ongoing participation in this arena.[42] It sought to create a legally secured space for regular participation in decision making about heritage conservation, especially in the context of the formalization of the cityscape.[43]

Spokespersons for INTACH often appropriated the normative language of civil society to frame their projects as "public-private partnerships" and themselves as "NGOs." These goals were expressed not only in specific mission statements but also in their own emphasis on transparency and deliberative modes of decision making. These orientations were also evident in the civil society networks in which INTACH members participated and in the public challenges, both in the courts and on the streets, members have mounted against some state and market-led development projects. INTACH's Pondicherry chapter carried out civil disobedience to protest the extension of East Coast Road without the mandated environmental impact assessment.[44] Members of the Chennai chapter have formed alliances with consumer-action and government transparency advocates. In the early 1990s one of INTACH's prominent members (Tara Murali) joined with environmentalists in successfully challenging the legality of a for-profit resort development scheme supported by the Tamil Nadu government and in which Chief Minister Jayalalithaa had invested personal funds.[45]

With these actions, INTACH sought to call attention to corruption within Tamil Nadu's Dravidianist ruling parties and to press for modes of decision making consistent with normative modern statecraft. Likewise, INTACH's historicist approach to conservation was conceived in contrast to the styles of public memory, for example, the Marina memorials that the state's ruling parties favored. INTACH members denigrated the latter as "myth" and regarded them as artifacts of the state's not-yet-modern style of rule. For their part, state authorities have been quick to suggest that INTACH's privileged membership was simply out of touch with the interests and sentiments of local people, who treat the memorials and monuments as popular spaces for leisure, education, and pilgrimage-style visitation.

In 1998 INTACH's Chennai chapter unveiled a new initiative, "Places for People," crafted to speak to popular concerns about the changing urban landscape and to enhance the group's visibility as a civil society actor. The plan for conserving Marundeswarar was to be the centerpiece of this new initiative.[46] "Places for People" represented INTACH's desire to distance its work from that of colonial-era museums and conservation projects. It hoped to replace musealization with conservation of the actual, often ritualized, processes by which architectural vernaculars and other culturally distinct components of the built environment were conceived, built, and renovated. INTACH, in other words, sought authenticity in the built environment through the preservation of what it identified as the traditional lifeways and social fabric associated with those spaces. At the same time "Places for People" was tied, inextricably, to a modernist vision of both the urban built environment and governance, particularly the attention to tradition that arises within modernist projects and discourses. The recuperation of tradition, in this instance reified in vernacular and historical architecture, was meant to engender ways of being and acting Indian that were compatible with consumerism, including tourism, and with the foundational categories and values of political modernity: citizenship, secularism, and democratic governance.[47]

INTACH's modernist vision was evident not only in the ways that the group objectified "tradition" but also in their attention to gentrification. In an interview I conducted in 1999, one of INTACH's convenors, "Venkatraman," justified the new initiative by pointing to the many areas in the city that had become "backyards," their original functions having been superseded by new structures elsewhere. He appealed explicitly to the "broken-window" theory of crime and disorder with the argument that further degradation would occur unless the sites were rehabilitated.[48] As an example, he pointed to the Elphinstone Bridge, which spanned the Adyar River and had been closed to vehicular traffic and replaced by a new bridge, Thiru-Vi-Ka, erected to accommodate the increasingly heavy traffic flowing between the city's core areas and the new industrial and residential developments of its southwestern quadrant. Upon its de-commissioning, Elphinstone Bridge became what Venkatraman likened to a "broken window": squatters took occupancy, and graffiti and hoardings appeared. Unwilling to evict the squatters, the city left the site in disrepair, resulting in a blighted "backyard."[49] Such incidents, he observed, had occurred with greater frequency with the city's expansion and its increasingly speculative real estate market. He opposed the demolition of these de-commissioned sites, hoping instead that they could be adapted for reuse. The bridge, he maintained, "could be made over into a pedestrian promenade, to watch birds, to stroll in the evening. What would it take to do it right now? We [INTACH] have even given them a plan to follow!" Conservation of this sort, he felt, both contributed in a positive way to gentrification and encouraged new ways of occupying and seeing the city that were compatible with modern citizenship.

INTACH's formal activities, though conducted in an anticipatory mode ("planning" sessions, "proposals"), were material and discursive effects of INTACH's intervention in heritage, particularly in their enactment of public/private institutional networks and their endorsement of modernist forms of cultural citizenship. Interactions such as the seminar on Places for People and the planning meetings for Marundeswarar's conservation, described below, demonstrate how INTACH has sought to constitute its exteriority vis-à-vis the state, while crafting an institutional space within the state apparatus, as a regular participant in both rule making and policy implementation.

Figure 4.2. Marundeswarar Temple tank, Tiruvanmiyur. *Photograph by author.*

A Plan to Conserve Marundeswarar

The proposal for Marundeswarar's conservation, drafted in 2000, was viewed by the group as a model for the Places for People initiative. Owned and administered by the state's Hindu Religious and Charitable Endowments Administration Department, its elaborate interior and antiquity, coupled with the mounting threats posed by the pace of urbanization led to INTACH's interest in its conservation. The group hoped to show that architectural history could be preserved in a way that accommodated the industrial and commercial growth ushered in by India's neoliberal economic policies.

By 1999, when INTACH began to explore possibilities for the temple's conservation, graffiti and poster advertisements covered the walls, its tanks were dry and filled with trash and sewage, and lean-tos and shop fronts abutted its exterior compound walls. The temple's grounds, and thus its sacred geography, had been fragmented by a north-south thoroughfare, West Tank Road, which separated the temple's core shrines from the larger of its two tanks.[50] Another roadway, formed by Kuppam Beach Road and its extension, Sannadi Street, had isolated a *maṇṭapam* at the southeast corner of the complex. Though the *maṇṭapam* had been built (and continued to be used) as a stopping point along the temple procession route, vegetable sellers used it regularly as an open-air market site. Within the area bounded by the *mada* streets, there had been significant residential in-fill; few courtyard houses remained, and the *mada* street that once had formed the west boundary of temple grounds had been replaced by the East Coast Road.

Figure 4.3. Marundeswarar Temple entry, Tiruvanmiyur. *Photograph by author.*

Figure 4.4. Courtyard house, Tiruvanmiyur. *Photograph by author.*

The despoliation of the temple's tanks, the loss of its garden and other greenery, and the fragmentation of its sacred geography were products of Tiruvanmiyur's urbanization. Until the 1960s the area had been a sparsely populated agrarian village. With the development of industrial and power generation facilities to the south in the late 1970s, as well as Chennai's own southward expansion, Tiruvanmiyur's population grew to 47,269, according to the 1981 Census of India. Commercial and infrastructural development followed, and high-rise flat complexes were built to house a fast-growing middle-class population, as recorded, in 1995, by the Madras Municipal Development Authority. The 1990s brought new information technology and industrial campuses to Chennai's southern and southwestern suburbs. Public transport services, including commuter rail, were extended and roadways widened to accommodate heavier automotive traffic. In 2006 both middle- and low-income flat complexes (built by the government in the late sixties) have been torn down to make way for luxury apartments. That growth strained the already inadequate sewage, storm drain, and transport systems; consequentially air and water pollution has increased, and the water table has dropped precipitously.

Following site visits by two members in late 1999 and early 2000, INTACH met to draft conservation and renovation measures. Members and invited consultants (engineers, architects, bureaucrats) participated in the meetings, which took place between February and May 2000.[51] The final version of the proposal took the form of a power-point slide show that was screened to residents, community groups, and representatives of those government agencies (the Public Works Department, the HR & CE Administration Department, and the Chennai Metropolitan Development Authority) whose cooperation was sought for the plan's implementation. In this project, as in previous efforts, INTACH aimed to partner with state and municipal agencies; indeed, they hoped that their services as consultants to planning and public works bodies might be regularized.[52] Despite friction stemming from the Tamil government authorities' view that INTACH represented the concerns of a Westernized elite, INTACH hoped to tap into a shared developmentalist vision and to demonstrate that preservation could be compatible with gentrification. An illustration of this may be seen in an exchange I recorded during an INTACH seminar convened jointly with the regional planning authority to publicize the Places for People initiative.[53]

S. Santhanam, a deputy planner in the Chennai Metropolitan Development Authority, delivered a pessimistic appraisal of INTACH's proposals, comparing them to European approaches: "It's not in synch with local attitudes. We don't go to parks like foreigners, we don't have Saturdays and Sundays free, as they do. We don't take walks for recreation, it's not part of our concept of health. For leisure, we spend time with our families." His comments elicited a sharp exchange among participants. "R. Jyoti," a member of INTACH, broke in: "We don't use our parks for recreation because of the condition they are in! Not because it is a foreign thing." She added, "Don't we have any self-esteem? Can't we look to a better future? You look at it as a contradiction between development and conservation. We set up this forum to show that heritage is not in contradiction with economic development. It is part of the quality of life, it is a quality of life issue."

Another CMDA planner, A. R. Doss, reacted impatiently to her comments. Referring to the memorials and monuments that the state's ruling parties had commissioned since the late 1960s, he asserted: "Historical awareness is present, yet it is not recognized by elite organizations like yours!" In an effort to mediate what had become a tense stand-off, a representative from INTACH's Hyderabad chapter encouraged those present to consider Hyderabad's success in balancing development and conservation:

> The Chief Minister took early morning walks from the time that he came into the office. Because people were aware that he would be seeing their streets close up, they tried to make the city cleaner. This has had the effect of improving people's habits. There's much less littering now. By educating people in this way, we garnered more support for heritage conservation measures, more compliance.

He alluded here to claims that are implicit in many INTACH proposals, including that prepared for Marundeswarar's preservation. Heritage conservation as practiced by INTACH was predicated on new repertoires of practice for using public space and on styles of civic consciousness that were couched in the awareness that individual use and occupancy of public space derived from constitutionally established rights. The need, members argued, was for an approach to conservation that could best be described as civic pedagogy, a reorientation of existing, commonsense notions about the use and value of public space. Such pedagogy, in combination with the state's adoption of "heritage" as a warrant for development and planning, they suggested, would wean people away from the tastes for the "myth" that ruling parties promoted in place of history (e.g., as represented in the Marina memorials) and would beget the postures, attitudes, and consciousness of modern citizenship.

The plan for Marundeswarar's conservation embodied these sentiments and aims. The goal was to make it a public space, a space open and accessible to a range of users, which would accommodate Hindu spatial practice as well as evening strolls and morning power walks. INTACH encouraged ways of occupying and seeing that were informed as much by historicism as by consumerism. The plan's core recommendations included repair of the temple tanks by cleaning and restoring their stone floors and walls. Members were less optimistic about restoration of water to the tanks, at least on a year-round basis. The well system that had once fed the tanks had gone dry, and engineers with whom they consulted were doubtful that it could be rehabilitated. Instead, they proposed to feed the tanks through storm drains laid on their north, east, and west sides, an ambitious goal that would require clearing and realigning the drainage channels. Such activities exceeded INTACH's capabilities and necessitated the involvement of the Public Works Department, the Municipal Corporation and other agencies. Allying with other civic groups, INTACH also encouraged the adoption of residential water harvesting technologies, anticipating that this technology would also contribute to the sustainability of the recharging system.

INTACH's conservation measures included recommendations for development control. The temple was conceived as the anchor of a heritage zone, whose spatial limits had been determined by mapping its festival procession routes. INTACH hoped to retain the locality's vernacular character within that zone. As it was, the vernacular was in short supply, given the recent building boom. It was only near the temple's east-facing entry gate that a few vernacular structures, courtyard houses, remained, and they were used as residences or offices (Fig. 4.4). To the immediate south, east, and north of the temple were multistoried flat complexes and commercial structures.

To retain what remained of the vernacular character of the area and to improve access to the temple, INTACH advised that the temple and environs be zoned as a mixed-use area, with the stipulation that natural assets be included as a defined use. Limits on paved coverage were proposed in order to facilitate groundwater recharging, as well as adaptive reuse of adjacent vernacular structures. INTACH members hoped to better delineate the temple grounds as sacred space with a plan for landscape design and restoration that included the reestablishment of an abandoned temple garden and the introduction of native species of trees to shade walkways and mark the boundaries of temple grounds. Other recommendations addressed problems related to encroachments and traffic. To reduce traffic congestion, allow for better access to the temple, and reintegrate its grounds, INTACH members proposed relocating the vegetable markets and shops that abutted the temple along its north and east compound walls. Accompanying these measures, they recommended converting Sannadhi Street into a pedestrian walkway and rerouting the traffic flow along East Mada Street to the east side of the *maṇṭapam*.

The proposal, finally, offered broad guidelines for development control with its suggestion that planning guidelines be extrapolated from the traditional stock, its style and the patterns of mixed use that existed. To preserve the existing streetscape, height limits and the retention of existing floor area ratios were proposed. To accommodate the various uses and users that they hoped the restored temple would attract, INTACH urged that public, pay-for-use toilets be installed and that space for automobile parking be reserved. After drafting the proposal, INTACH held slide shows to publicize it. Members also prepared press releases that appeared in *The Hindu*, and in *Madras Musings*, a free English-language biweekly. The implementation of the proposal's recommendations was left to other voluntary groups and government agencies, and required the commitment of public monies as well as private donations.

As of this writing (2007), only some of the project's recommendations have been implemented. Efforts to clean and restore the tanks, pitched to capture environmentalist interests, followed in the path of previous initiatives in attracting the patronage of local notables and civic groups. By 2003 the tanks beds had been cleared of debris, their steps repaired, and old water inlets cleaned. With encouragement from INTACH and from municipal agencies, a community group called Puduvellam came forward to maintain the tank area, with the support of the Corporation and private donors. Together, these measures ensured that Marundeswarar's tanks would be able to hold water at least on a seasonal basis.[54]

Like gentrification measures elsewhere in the city, the plan rested on the elimination of the encroachments that abutted the temple. INTACH had advised relocation of these shops and offices, but, in what has become a ritualized civic spectacle, the city's Corporation demolished the encroachments along East and North Mada streets in an early morning operation in 2003. The city's goals, however, diverged from INTACH's—rather than restoring temple grounds and retaining vernacular character, the aim was to increase traffic capacity in a section of the city that was becoming an important node between the financial core and new industrial sites to the south and southwest.

The outcomes can also be taken as indexes of the relations between INTACH and the state in the broader context of the state's obligation to administer and maintain Hindu temples. INTACH's ability to garner support from local business and community groups stemmed, in part, from the perception, commonly voiced among temple servants, devotees, and local residents, that the state's management of the temple was flawed. Many problems were attributed to party politics, with some claiming that the state's attention waxed and waned depending on the party in power; many believed that the neglect was greater during periods of DMK rule.

As noted earlier, under one AIA-DMK government (1991–1996), the temple had been reconsecrated, its 1995 *kumpapiṣēkam* funded through the Temple

Maintenance Fund.[55] In the late 1990s, however, the DMK government dismantled the fund and put further improvements on hold. In a conversation in early 2000, two of the five hereditary priests who served Marundeswarar complained to me about HR & CE "interference," and one pointedly remarked that he refused any salary, taking only a share of the monies donated by devotees, because of his disdain for the "rules and regulations" that the agency imposed.[56] Temple devotees maintained that managers and the Executive Officer were poorly remunerated at Marundeswarar in comparison with other large temples and attributed the temple's rundown condition to their lackadaisical attitudes.

Not until 2001, when the AIA-DMK party (still headed by J. Jayalalithaa) regained control of the Legislative Assembly, did the temple begin to enjoy state patronage again. It was among the first group of sites selected, in 2003, to participate in a special program, "Annadhanam," that combined meals distribution to poor children with religious education. That same year it was reconsecrated, less than a decade after the prior *kumpapiṣēkam*. In 2004 temple trustees proudly announced their plans for commissioning a new golden festival chariot. And with the growth of the IT industry and the influx of Web-savvy residents, the temple became more visible on travel and tourism Web sites, such as Chennai Online and occasionally effusive Web blogs.[57]

INTACH aimed to make the temple's environs an appealing space for religious and nonreligious public gatherings and to make conservation and the nostalgia it invited a cornerstone of the area's gentrification. To do this, INTACH took strategic advantage of both the existing dissatisfaction with HR & CE management prevalent among temple users and the temple's shifting fortune as a beneficiary of the state's largesse. From their perspective, the neglect of the HR & CE department was consistent with the preferences of ruling parties for mythicohistory. Mindful of the agency's uneven record of oversight, INTACH's initial survey and plan were completed in 2000 without its participation, though renewed state interest in the temple after 2001 dovetailed with the group's aims.

Central to the plan's ultimate sustainability was the local involvement. This was sought by appealing both to the nostalgia of long-term residents and to the aesthetic sensibilities of newly arrived urban professionals. These objectives were conjoined in the notions that the temple could be marketed as civic space, which accommodated religious and nonreligious uses and whose social space was organized through practices of consumption and the rights, desires, and expectations that flowed from consumption. This meant entangling memory and consumption, and melding consumer citizenship with the identifying practices of Hinduism.

Cultivating Local Tastes

It was to the civic sense of these new locals—software engineers, financial services managers, real estate developers, and retailers—that the proposal was pitched. INTACH project leaders, most of whom resided outside Tiruvanmiyur, repeatedly called for residents' participation. They hoped that residents might form voluntary associations for cleaning and maintaining temple tanks, harvesting rainwater, and planting trees. On one occasion, co-convenor Venkatraman recommended that the proposal specifically encourage people on the *mada* streets to form welfare associations for residents in order to better deal with municipal agencies and ward councilors. Using the new lexicon of development, namely, globalization, he and others hoped that locals would recognize that they were "stakeholders" in the improvements.

This was not just civic boosterism. Threaded through their proposals and observations was a concern with the relations between citizenship and public space. They hoped that residents and visitors would come to see the temple as they themselves did—not only as a space of Hindu worship but also as an artifact of the region's history, a space of performance and assembly, and an attractive tourist destination. They arrived at this only after discussion and debate, however. Despite shared social capital and cosmopolitan outlook, INTACH members were diverse in sectarian affiliation: some were Hindu by birth but characterized themselves as atheist or agnostic, others identified as devout Hindus, and still others were Christian or Muslim. Discussions during meetings reflected this diversity, echoing familiar modernist dilemmas concerning the relations between religiosity, citizenship, and public space. Did the value of the temple's landscape lay solely in its ritual usage? Or should the complex serve as a non-exclusionary public space, available for evening walks, performances, political speeches, and rallies? What were the norms of behavior in this sort of public space? What subjects were constituted in and through this sort of publicity? Their own plural sectarian identities were a microcosm of the pluralism that they hoped temple conservation would anchor.

These themes surfaced repeatedly. Consider the following discussion about the adaptive reuse of the temple's tanks during the summer months, a time when most went dry because of the region's depressed water table. The discussion took place in February 2000, during one of the INTACH meetings I attended. Venkatraman began, "We should define the sorts of activities that the dry tanks could be sites for—otherwise they will be misused, they will be dumps. If some defined and valued activity takes place, then this will prevent misuse." "Anjali," an Anglo-Indian architect, recalled that there were some social service agencies near the temple. "Perhaps they could be brought in to participate in dry-period uses?" Venkatraman mused. "Maybe use the area for cultural festivals? You know, like open-air theatres." "David," a Malayali Christian, interjected: "Well, kids are playing cricket in them now!" "Jaya," a devout Hindu, proposed, "We should suggest to the temple that they use the dry tank for [religious] discourses." She paused and then chuckled softly, "Maybe if it had something to do with Tiruvalluvar?"—a joking reference to the then chief minister Karunanidhi's lionization of the Tamil sage.

Friction emerged a few weeks later during a subsequent planning meeting after Anjali insisted: "The idea is to have a place that draws people for a variety of reasons, not only worship . . . [though] all activities should fit the temple function. . . . A better integration of spaces within the temple complex will lead to more temple-based usage." Objecting, David observed: "If there is open space for public activities, the first to exploit it will be politicians." "True," admitted Venkatraman, "but still it should be open, public, no mater which party wants to use it." Jaya interjected: "I think that all activities should be consistent with the temple's religious function." After several more minutes of heated discussion, Venkatraman, who was chairing the meeting, offered a resolution: "These activities on the temple grounds, well, they really can be anything in which people can be involved—we just want to keep it open and accessible, not a dump, not a backyard." Indicative of this flexibility and of the wider audience they hoped that the restored temple would attract, they agreed that public, pay-for-use toilets and a small parking lot were also essential features of the refurbished grounds.

The plan's authors eventually settled on the idea that the temple's grounds could fulfill a plurality of functions, from those associated with Hindu orthopraxy to those that were educational or simply recreational. Strategies for accommodating both religious and secular uses of the temple were offered; indeed, it was just such an amalgamation that defined both its modernity and its publicity. Notwithstanding their different assessments of the relative importance of secular versus religious uses of the space, the members hoped to make the temple part of a *modern* public realm. This included the expectation that embodied spatial practices accord with those observed in other spaces constitutive of modern publics. This matter touched on a more fundamental contradiction with which INTACH members grappled regularly. Despite their understandable disdain for the distanciating effects of musealization, INTACH members' representation of the heritage value of temples endowed them with some of the same modernizing capacities attributed to spaces of the bourgeois public, such as museums, parks, theaters, and assembly halls. They hoped that refurbished temple complexes might offer opportunities to stroll, to acknowledge but not encroach upon others, to gain an appreciation of the surroundings and the cultural and historical knowledge encoded therein, and, finally, to learn that the rights to control public space lay with the citizenry.[58]

The methods by which INTACH intervened in public discussion and the effects the organization sought to bring about by conservation revealed that public space and citizenship were both bound, implicitly, by class sensibilities and structured by class difference.[59] This surfaced in discussions about how to deal with those who currently occupied land along the perimeter of the temple grounds. Class difference here was expressed as a matter of taste and style, and the preferred style of habitation was that which conformed to sensibilities of urban elites, among whom upper-caste identity and class privilege were often conjoined. For example, meetings included lengthy and mostly unresolved discussions about the problems posed by persons who claimed these spaces for their livelihoods but lacked deeds, leases, or other official documentation of their rights to that property. These encroachments, as they are termed in English, are mostly small storefronts, temporary market sites, and offices used by local party operatives, businesses, and unions. They occupy lean-tos and, in some cases, more permanent structures that have been set against the temple's exterior compound walls; some have electrical connections, and all pay rent to temple authorities or local "big men."

These arrangements are not unusual in Indian cities. As Sudipta Kaviraj has observed, encroachment, as used by state actors and by propertied middle and upper classes, implies illegality.[60] For the poor and working classes whose settlements and worksites are the most frequent targets of street-clearing campaigns, such occupation does not encroach on others' space but is a well-established way of claiming ground in the city, especially among migrants. In their understanding—that which is "public" is anything not privately owned—public is what they cannot be excluded from. The extent to which the urban poor and working classes have succeeded in holding space by encroaching has been because of the state's willingness, until recently, to allow occupancy as a right. Such rights, which are represented in land reform measures of the 1950s and 1960s, have increasingly conflicted with property rights (as owners seek demolition of encroachments on their property) and with middle- and upper-class norms pertaining to the use of public space. For urban elites, the meaning of "publicity" with respect to space derives from civic and educational discourses that reiterate nationalist pasts and the value of their representation as "history."[61] That which is "public" is somehow tied to, or sacralized by, the nation-state and political modernity, and it is these associations with which conduct, habitation, and bodily comportment should conform.

INTACH's specific designation of Marundeswarar's temple grounds as a "public" space and its broader promotion of heritage are both contextualized by the latter usage of publicity, though it has been a source of conflict. Some members argued pointedly against demolition of encroachments: because they represented work sites, it was reasoned, encroachments were vital to the livelihood of the poor. Most, like bureaucrats and property owners, were not inclined to tolerate the encroachments but recognized that vested interests, including local politicians and party organizations, were represented among some of those "encroaching" on the temple grounds and were circumspect in their recommendations. The plan, in the end, represented a compromise position in favor of relocation rather then outright demolition. Despite INTACH's ostensible commitment to the principle of open-access, these (mainly) lower- and working-class users of the temple embodied a plebeian style of occupation at odds with INTACH's vision of the type of public that might take shape in and around the temple. The encroaching structures, besides violating property rights, constituted visual and temporal transgressions: they concealed the temple's distinctive profile and surfaces from the gaze of passersby, making it difficult to recognize the architectural differences between the old temple and its newer surroundings. In other words, encroachments diminished the temple's value as a marker and reminder of another time and space, a site of productive nostalgia, because without clear boundaries, the temple's value as an edifying anachronism—an island of "then" in a sea of "now"—was nil.

Also significant was that, in considering how commitments might be sought locally, INTACH focused on those whose presence was legally recognized, whose "rights" included those devolving from property ownership, and who were engaged, in some way, with temple-based praxis, whether as devotee or appreciative onlooker. They also speculated that old photographs of the area would pique local interest in and support for their proposal. Said Jaya, during the above-mentioned February 2000 meeting: "We really need pictures of the street houses. People will relate to them, especially if they or their relatives lived in one." Those who lacked such grounds for remembrance—vendors, for example, who claimed space along temple perimeters to sell vegetables, bangles, plastic cups, or postcards—were not among the stakeholders whose interests INTACH hoped to invite. The plan, with its attention to tanks and processional routes as definitive features of temple geography, accommodated both the kind of miraculous excess that for orthoprax Hindus the temple embodied and the heritage appreciation that consumer-citizens have come to voice.

The View from the Street

Older residents of Tiruvanmiyur with whom I spoke had vivid memories of the area prior to its commercial growth in the 1970s. Their comments, even more than INTACH's stated goals and activities, reveal the class-bound sense of publicity that attached to the temple and the porosity between religious and secular spatial practices that this publicity involved. They consistently recalled the temple's rural environs and its geographic and psychological distance from the city. Some emphasized its loneliness and isolation; they welcomed the area's modernization, which, rather than a threat to the temple's condition, would bring more devotees.

"Yes, I remember it well," began Sarala, a middle-class Brahman woman in her late fifties. Though she had been brought up in Mylapore, she was familiar with Tiruvanmiyur and had considered purchasing a housing plot there in the 1970s. Since the early 1990s, she had lived in one of Tiruvanmiyur's multistory flat complexes with her husband, son, and daughter-in-law. Speaking of the seventies, she remarked, "It was so isolated! How could you imagine living in such a place? It was all forest, all brush-covered. There were no conveniences—how could we have gone about day to day life? No electricity, no buses . . . so different from the way it is now." A seventy-nine-year-old man, Kannan, lived in a small hut near the temple's east *kōpuram* from which he sold provisions for household rituals and various Ayurvedic preparations. He concurred with Sarala's recollection of the area's isolation: "I came to this place thirty-eight years ago. It was empty then, really scary. There were not many people. Now it's different. Lots of buildings have come up. Then there were no buildings, just a few houses, a bus stop and this place [his house/shop]." The Muslim proprietor of a temple provisions shop abutting the tank's east compound wall had arrived to the area more recently from Dindugal, a large town in the western part of Tamil Nadu. The shop that he operated had been in his family for twenty years, however. "Now, there's more development, more 'officers' [Eng]," and he added, appreciatively, "it's definitely come up."

Others found deep satisfaction in remembering the village that Tiruvanmiyur had once been. For them, the village was a space of naturalized difference, a space in which caste and ethnic differences were constituted and preserved. Although they acknowledged that these differences existed as part of more enduring patterns of conflict or exploitation, they considered the political narrative incidental to the bigger story, in which caste was articulated with temple praxis forming a sensory cartography of difference. Indeed, caste difference of the past, they suggested, was a matter of order and stability; it was the mitigation of difference in the present that yielded disorder and conflict.

A seventy-year-old Brahman man, "Muthuswamy," who had been born in Tiruvanmiyur recalled: "We were eight miles from the city center, eight miles from Fort St. George. There was a sand-covered road and only bullock carts were plying. I had no fear, no feeling of isolation, only peace. From the Pallava times, it was like that, a village." We were speaking in his third-floor flat, located a few blocks from the temple, and as he spoke he pointed out the window, contrasting the landscape of his past with the present layout: "It was all paddy to the south, from Valmiki Street to where the Jayanthi Theater now stands. It was *tattam tōṭṭam,* [a revenue garden] owned by the temple and rented to cultivators. North of the theater, toward Indira Nagar, there was a lake, now dry." To the east, "it was dry, only gooseberries and cashews could be grown. So many snakes, too, in that cashew grove. My own father's sister was bitten by a cobra in that place." A rain-fed irrigation system watered the paddy, which he described with a Tamil proverb—"*vāṉam pārttu pūmi*" ("earth that looks to the sky for rain"). Pointing to nearby flats and businesses, he recalled the coconut and casuarina groves that once stood in those places. His family lived near the west tank, and he remembered the tanks as being full of water most of the year and surrounded on all sides by coconut trees.

Woven through Muthuswamy's account of the area was a narrative of its social geography, articulated with sensual memories. He recalled that the streets were named after the castes that resided on them, and his descriptions of those places were imbued with the habits and materiality of their residents. "Valmiki Street had Etathurs, the *mada* streets were for the upper castes, the Brahmans and Vanniyars. Anna street was for the toddy-tappers." He remembered only a few big landowners in the village, men named Babu Gurukal and Ramnathan Gurukal, both temple priests. He went on with his caste census: Another street, recalled for its cow sheds, had been home to a low-caste group of herders (Yadavs) who provided dairy products for the village and beyond. Inextricable from his account of that group's socioeconomic and ritual status was his memory of the cows' exquisitely flavored milk, and the yogurt and butter made from that milk. He recalled the proximity of another low-caste family, oil pressers, by remembering the sound of the bullock-operated mechanism and the earthy smell of the oil being released and pressed into cakes, commenting, "It was pure, not like now."

Reiterating comments much like those I have heard from other Brahmans, this man voiced nostalgia for the "affection" that he felt had once existed between caste communities: "It was peaceful then—no fights, no tensions. Now," he asserted, "there is no more affection, only mistrust." He elaborated:

> Then, "SCs" [Scheduled Castes] were not ill-treated. They voluntarily were respectful, they removed their footwear in our presence. SCs would walk only on the last step of the tank, *kaṭaci paṭi* [farthest from the temple]. On West Tank Street where I lived, the SCs were not allowed to beat their drums. Even on buses, SCs would not sit when higher castes were present, now it is the opposite.

The story he told was one of harmonious difference, of a place inscribed by each person's knowledge of and attachment to her or his place. The past that he recalled was at odds with the norms of the liberal democratic statecraft that India's constitution mandates and that it seeks to establish with policies of positive discrimination. At the same time, essentialist differences and aestheticized hierarchies such as those that Muthuswamy described sustain and pervade the class-based distinctions of the modern capitalist order to which India is committed.

Other narratives marked the temple as a space remembered through Hindu praxis. When I asked one man, a retired businessman named "Vijay," about what he considered memorable or important about this temple, he began, like Muthuswamy, in a historicist vein, contrasting the landscapes of "then" and "now" to describe a past suffused by Brahmanic praxis and sensibilities. He recalled that Marundeswarar Garden Lane, now a residential street, covered the traces of what had once been a garden where flowers were cultivated for ritual use. An apartment block occupied a site that formerly housed a school, where Brahman boys had once assembled to chant the Vedas, sacred Hindu verses. He then shifted to a narrative about his devotion to the temple's deity, Marundeswarar, entwining the ontology of the deity's agentive power as a healer with the past of his own body. "I go daily to the temple. I had a slipped disc in my back and could not move or even sit. One doctor told me that I had to have an operation but I hesitated. Instead, I went to the temple, I put myself in the lord's care. Now it has been cured."

Vijay went on to praise the temple's festivals for their singularity; these he also recalled as embodied memories. It was, he said, the presence of another manifestation of the temple deity, Tyagarajar, that set this temple apart from others. During festivals, Tyagarajar is carried in a procession that circumambulates the temple complex. Unlike other processional deities, however, Tyagarajar is not tied to a platform but is secured only within an open bamboo frame. This is done because the deity manifests himself by dancing. As in other processions, devotees bear the deity figure, but this procession is especially demanding and unpredictable because of this deity's kinesthetic powers. Vijay recalled his own excitement when he himself had held that deity during the festival: "I was carrying him when, suddenly, he was there. I felt it, like a jolt, when he arrived." For Vijay, it was nothing less than the miraculous, that which exceeded nature, that made the place important.

For INTACH, the heritage that the temple embodied was of a piece with the heritage of the city's colonial core. Both spaces represented the cultural contours and genealogy of national community. Their preservation offered a kind of primer for enacting citizenship, from the implicit elements embodied in ways of inhabiting public space to explicit features, such as how to represent one's interests to government bureaucrats and how to conceptualize an interest in heritage as a matter of rights. These aims were not extricable from gentrification. What conservation and historicism did was invite a nostalgia, at least for some, for the lifeways of the village in which everyone knew his or her place. This was a nostalgia that concealed the structural violence of gentrification by overlaying the space it produces with the veneer of tradition, making it part of the public of the nation and its past.

The public quality that was both the warrant for INTACH's involvement and the result of conservation was understood also in terms of the accommodation (and blurring) of both religious and secular meanings and uses. Thus miraculous excess was accommodated by the conservation plan, which defined the boundaries of the temple grounds and thus the heritage zone on the basis of the procession route. The narrative space of the temple's past was figured in individual stories such as Vijay's and by collective stories that made up its *sthalapurana*. In an atmosphere in which strident Hindu nationalism was becoming normalized, INTACH members were groping for a way in which Hindu social space might be the touchstone for a pluralist public rather than the familial public of Hindutva or Dravidianism.

Religion in the Secular State

INTACH aimed to partner with the state in the management of those sites, including temples, that embodied heritage, but it was a complex and uneven partnership. The possibility of the Marundeswarar Temple being conceived as public in the way that INTACH proposed arose within a historical context shaped by more than a century of state management of Hindu institutions and practices. INTACH's interests also conformed to the Indian state's valorization of southern Indian temples as national icons. Against this backdrop, the proposal for Marundeswarar was envisioned as a secular endeavor, different from both the mythico-historicism of Hindutva, with its strident, violent tactics of reclaiming Hindu religious sites from Muslim and Christian "colonization," and the mythico-historicism of Dravidianism, with its core of commemorative piety (see chapter 3). However, the kind of public space that INTACH members hoped to create by preserving Marundeswarar as a heritage site was delimited by Hindu visual and spatial praxis and by the exclusionary spatiality of gentrification with its inscription of both class and caste privilege. Also, the very possibility of carrying out the project was entangled with the Tamil state's patronage of the temple. The same mythico-history and "corruption" that INTACH's members disparaged were vital sources of visibility and support for the project. The following discussion historicizes INTACH's project within postcolonial state formation, with special attention paid to those processes involving the development of a legal-bureaucratic apparatus for the regulation of Hindu religious institutions.

The ambiguities of the secular norms to which INTACH appealed characterize secularism's career in postcolonial India, consistent with what Arvind Rajagopal has described as its variegated interpretation. In the electoral system, secularism amounted to the prohibition of religious language; in public institutions, it was invoked to justify fair and inclusive treatment of different religious groups; in the courts, it was interpreted as the grounds for protecting religious sensibilities from various kinds of offenses.[62] This ambiguity, he maintained, was strategic and served to mask the contradictions that arose from the state's intervention in religious organizations. He noted,

> The Indian state saw its mission as a modernizing one, and was thus unavoidably committed to intervening in the affairs of religious communities even if only to eventually transcend the need for intervention. At the same time the presence of a Hindu majority and the legacy of violence against Muslims during the partition rendered the adjudication of minority religions a delicate matter . . . the precise meaning of secularism was thus too contentious at this point to be legislated upon, and remained as a political problem, if for a while a dormant one.[63]

The doctrine of secularism embraced by the postcolonial Indian state was defined, as in other liberal democratic models, in accordance with principles of liberty, equality, and neutrality. Partha Chatterjee explained that, according to these principles, the practice of any religion is permitted within limits set by the basic rights that the state protects; nor does the state give preference to any particular religion or involve itself in religious affairs.[64] In practice, however, these conditions have been rarely, if ever, met in any self-declared secular polity. Chatterjee elaborated on these observations in his comments about India's Constitution, which, he noted, acknowledged the liberty principle in asserting the "right to freely profess, practice, and propagate religion" and granted "collective rights of religion" to denominations, allowing them to establish and administer their own educational institutions.[65] Those rights, however, were limited in practice by the state's own capacity to regulate financial, economic, and political activity associated with religious practice, to provide for social welfare, and to make Hindu religious institutions accessible to all caste communities. The codification of religiously based personal law and the state's administration of Hindu temples then followed upon the above qualifications of the liberty principle. The equality principle underlay the constitutional prohibition of discrimination on the basis of religion or caste (except in provisions for positive discrimination). The limits on this principle have emerged in state projects of Hindu reform, in legislation, and in religiously based personal laws. The third principle, separation, inhered in the prohibitions of an official state religion, of religious instruction in state schools, and of taxes to support particular religions. Nonetheless, the state has become increasingly involved in the support of Hinduism through its management and patronage of Hindu institutions and schools.[66]

India's enactment of secularism, therefore, has been inseparable from the legal-bureaucratic apparatus that has been built to monitor, regulate, and administer Hindu religious institutions. While the meaning of secularism may have been left vague, the legal-bureaucratic regulation of religious institutions that had been established in the colonial era was quite specific. The retention of this apparatus was not simply to control the dangers of religious "excess" but also recognized the possibilities of vernacular modernity that religious identity and practice contained. It was following independence that the national state sought to draw back to itself the nationalist energies and affect that, earlier, had been mobilized against the colonial state. In the 1950s and 1960s Hindu temples were identified as sites for the pedagogies and performances of postcolonial nationalism and the processes of state formation in which it was embedded.[67] Tamil Nadu, known then as Madras, earned special mention. The 1961 Census included an enumeration of Hindu temples, one of a number of special projects undertaken "to highlight the social and cultural heritage of India."[68] The authors suggested that Hindu temples, particularly those of southern India, represented the cultural space of the nation and its past and, further, that they engendered attachments that informed citizenship and national belonging. "South India," they wrote, "has been least affected by the series of invasions, which India witnessed because of its geographic isolation, and the Hindu culture has been preserved in its most pristine form in Madras State."[69]

The 1961 Census report, exemplifying the discourse of publicity that had long underwritten the state's legal and political claims on Hindu temples, was one among several modalities by which the postcolonial state sought to reinvent the nation through, rather than against, the state. Temples, homes, and schools were deemed critical sites for nationalist pedagogies and performances. A series of committees were convened by the central government to survey these institutions and to recommend ways that they might better fulfill their role in nation building. Temples, even more than schools and homes, however, seemed redolent with tradition. In the new map of the nation, they were remade into artifacts of an Indian past but were shorn of unprogressive features. Pluralism and tolerance were foregrounded as the defining qualities of Hinduism, and it was treated as a fountainhead of indigenous nationalism. In state-sanctioned discourses, some differing little from those of militant Hindu nationalists of prior decades, Hinduism was treated less as sectarian identity and more as an ensemble of territorially bounded cultural traits. Hindu temples, represented as expressions of the inherent religiosity and assimilative character of Indian civilization, were described by the Hindu Religious Endowments Commission (HREC) as the foundation of the nation.[70] By promoting their charitable as well as didactic and ritualistic functions, the authors of that report argued that it would be possible to "effect that integration of Indian endeavour and that sublimation of ideals which are of special significance to resurgent India."[71]

That same commission also reviewed existing forms of temple administration in all of India's states and recommended appropriate modes of state oversight. Authors concurred with the census report in treating southern Indian temples as exemplars and proposed that the agencies developed in Madras State, as it was then known, be adopted elsewhere in independent India.[72] The report's authors justified their recommendations for more extensive state surveillance with the observation that temples were "public trusts in the sense that the public or a section thereof are [materially, psychologically, and spiritually] interested in and have the right to enforce their proper administration and management."[73]

Temples, as this brief discussion indicates, have figured prominently in postcolonial modernization efforts undertaken by both central and individual states' governments. Although the officially secular state of the 1950s and 1960s could not go as far as promoting conversion to Hinduism, under the broader rubric of consumption it encouraged other practices by which India's Hindu and non-Hindu populations could be exposed to a Hindu national culture. Thus, in its report, the HREC urged that the government facilitate religious pilgrimage among Hindus, and that it promote Hindu temples as tourist destinations for the wider population.[74] It advocated that India's Archaeological Survey, another artifact of colonialism, be given a greater role in maintaining and publicizing the national heritage that temples were deemed to bear. Temples and associated ritual practices were not simply resources to be managed but have offered grounds for the cultivation and expression of citizenship and ethnicity in ways that employ while deferring sectarian identity.[75]

Subtending the HREC's recommendations were notions of the instrumentality of temple functions and, relatedly, of an instrumental rationality on the part of worshipers. These potentialities made temples and Hinduism itself susceptible to modernity. A passage from the HREC report described temples as "occult laboratories where certain physical acts of adoration, coupled with certain systematized prayers, psalms, mantras and musical invocations, can yield certain physical and psychological results as a matter of course."[76] The authors placed a culturally specific, ratiocinating individual at the heart of Hindu practice, as spectator, beneficiary, and performer of ritual. Temples, like schools and worksites, were meant to be venues that relied upon and engendered a modern subject, a secular subject. Religion was thus re-imagined as a site of incipient modernity, as a glue that would bind nation and state through virtue and through the shared past that it made visible.

By the fiftieth anniversary of India's independence, Hindu spaces, practices, imagery, and discourses suffused a range of political projects, from Hindu nationalism to Dravidianist populism. The state's reliance on Hinduism as nationalist glue created openings for the mobilization and normalization of Hindutva throughout India during the 1980s and 1990s. In southern India, this was hastened by the increasingly close relations between Tamil Nadu's ruling parties and nationalist organizations, and by a resurgence of popular Hinduism, indexed by the popularity of epic tele-serials, increased temple building and renovation activities, and the growth of temple-based voluntary associations.[77] Under Jayalalitha's AIA-DMK government (1991–1996, 2001–2006), which enjoyed the broad support of Hindu nationalist organizations, legislation to ban conversions was introduced, public and private programs for temple building and renovation expanded, and a social welfare scheme launched that used temples as distribution points.[78] The DMK party, which led the government between 1996 and 2001 and was reelected in 2006, has been less accommodating to nationalist interests but struck a formal alliance with the nationalist Bharatiya Janata Party, which, between 1998 and 2004, led the ruling coalition at the center.

Temples throughout India had figured in Hindu nationalist efforts to mobilize popular support. Festival processions and pilgrimages, especially, were used to inscribe space as Hindu territory and thereby create a social horizon flooded by Hindu iconography and spatial practice. This has extended to Chennai, where, since the early 1980s, the annual Vinayaka Chathurthi festival and procession has become an important staging ground.[79] It was popularized in Maharashtra during the anticolonial struggle but has spread across India following its resurrection by Hindu nationalists and their sympathizers.[80] Following its inception in the early 1980s, Chennai's festival has been coordinated with similar events in other cities and towns in Tamil Nadu. As organized by the Hindu Munnani, a local affiliate of the RSS, the festival in Chennai continued for six to nine days, with a procession on the last day. During the days prior to the procession, images of Vinayaka (another name for Ganapati) were displayed and worshiped in public places, and on the final day of the festival the images installed around the city were carried in a procession to Marina Beach and immersed.

Not all appropriations of Hindu social space have been tailored to meet the aims of Hindu nationalism, however. Hindu-inflected political performance extends to the employment by central and state government authorities of the spatial logic and practices of temples in other contexts of political ceremony.[81] Reflecting the hegemony of regionalist parties in Tamil Nadu since the late 1960s, temple architectural elements and design principles have been appropriated to assert Tamil ethnicity at some ceremonial and commemorative sites (see chapter 3).[82] The practical vocabularies of worship are also part of the commemorative activity. Consider the DMK leader M. Karunanidhi's memorialization of the early Tamil moralist and poet, Tiruvalluvar.

Tiruvalluvar authored the Tamil ethical tract, *Tirukkural*, and is said to have been born in what is now Chennai during the third century CE. In Chennai alone, Karunanidhi has commissioned several sites dedicated to Tiruvalluvar. The largest is a temple and a monumental assembly complex, the Valluvar Kottam, which uses architectural features and design principles ordinarily found in temples, including the incorporation of a massive temple car as a structural element.[83] He also commissioned a huge statue of Tiruvalluvar in the waters off Kanyakumari, a town located at India's southern tip, likening the figure to the U.S. Statue of Liberty in its scale and representational significance. During the unveiling ceremony in January 2000, Karunanidhi, a self-identified atheist, larded his speech with idioms alluding to the strategies of naming, seeing, and surrendering that permeate Hindu devotionalism:

> I have prayed for this for twenty-five years. My dream is now fulfilled. . . . When I pressed the inaugurating button, I forgot myself. I am told over 300 nadeswarams were played at that moment. I never heard them. I was in another world. I spoke for forty-five minutes. I knew only from the paper the next day what I spoke of . . . I have meditated on Tiruvalluvar from childhood. I have ever remembered and stressed the genius in the philosophy, I built Valluvar Kottam for him, and I dedicated the day after *Poṅkal* [a Tamil holiday marking the first rice harvest] to Tiruvalluvar. I displayed his poems on buses and in bus stations. I translated the 133 verses of his Tirukkural. For twenty-five years, I have waited, yearningly, for this installation.[84]

Dravidianist ritual repertoire has also included the patronage of Hindu institutions and festivals. As already noted, J. Jayalalithaa, during her first term as chief

Figure 4.5. Valluvar Kottam Temple car, Chennai. *Photograph by author.*

minister (1991–96), initiated a temple maintenance project, launching it with a personal donation amounting to one month's salary; the fund was reinstituted during her subsequent term. Contemporaneously, under the banner of its new "Citizens' Charter," the HR & CE department embraced an ambitious roster of temple maintenance, welfare, and renovation activities and has also made special efforts to incorporate temples within the spaces of statecraft by using them as welfare distribution sites.[85] Under Jayalalithaa's AIA-DMK government, temples' precincts have been used as crèches for destitute children (Karunai Illam), old-age homes, dispensaries, and free meal delivery sites.[86] The latter services are tied closely to Hindu praxis. Not only were children to be brought to temples to receive and consume weekly meals, but the meals were accompanied by religious education sessions. The program was initiated in 2003 at 63 temples, including Tiruvanmiyur's Marundeswarar Temple, and expanded shortly thereafter to 108—numbers that are both deemed auspicious within Hinduism—and the aim was to extend it to all the state's temples.

Temples have been subjects of long-standing public debates about the domain of state authority and the nature of citizenship; indeed, over the past century, a public realm of Hindu imagery, activity, and sentiment has been produced under the sign of secular modernity, even while reworking the meanings of those terms. Hindu temples were stages on which colonial statecraft sought to redirect the communal attachments of its subjects. Temples have continued to be inscribed by the ambiguities of the postcolonial state's secular commitments. Not only does the state use temples as platforms for representing national culture, but, no less than government offices, temples are sites on which the state is encountered and imagined through the intimate, everyday encounters by which individuals engage the collective pasts that undergird ethnicity, citizenship, and sectarian identity and the nation-state itself.

The political claims on the social space of Hindu temples, as well as the discourses and practices of state ceremony, besides defying categorical distinctions between political and religious realms, point to the plural pasts that are imagined and enacted in the making of Tamil and Indian modernities, modernities that encompass but are not contained by Hindu nationalism. In other words, even as they are put forward as modern, they solicit subjectivities, desire, and memories that rest uneasily, if at all, within the boundaries of modern. It is this uneven terrain on which new heritage discourses and activities arise. I argue that the state's relation to Hindu temples should be understood as both seeking to contain sectarian threats ("communalism") to the modern secular order and to appropriate popular attachments to Hinduism within the discursive practices of national belonging and citizenship, practices negotiated increasingly through consumption. Put another way, the development of an institutional apparatus for temple management indexes the genealogy, and the ambiguity, of secularism in India.

Such encounters, institutionalized through administrative structures, through the formation of combined pilgrimage and tourism circuits, and through the nationalization of Hindu iconography, shape the condition of possibility for INTACH's conservationist attention to Hindu sites but also for Hindutva's normalization.

Conclusion: Heritage and the Space of the Secular

Over the past three decades, heritage consciousness and memory discourses have become global concerns, fueling tourism and heritage industries as well as exclusivist ethnic and religious movements. In India, the organized heritage movement described in this chapter developed in tandem with a resurgence of Hindu nationalism. Despite their different sociopolitical agendas, both register alarm at the loss of spaces and practices that represent India's past. The growth of religious nationalism, in particular, has meant that the ritual practices and social spaces of Hinduism have become matters of intense public scrutiny and contestation; these debates, in turn, have influenced the goals and methods of heritage conservation efforts. Centrally figuring in Hindu nationalist discourses are the histories of particular temples, which are narrated and visually represented to argue that, although "Hinduness" emanates from and suffuses the territory of the Indian nation-state, Muslim and Christian "others" have systematically sought to erase Hindus' claims on these spaces.

In response to the bloody consequences of Hindu chauvinism and to the need for principled and unambiguous responses to it, liberal and left-wing intellectuals and activists have debated the value of religiously grounded political action and religiously informed designs for collective life. Although rightly alarmed by the implications and effects of nationalist mobilization, some critics of Hindutva have often appealed to an Orientalist dichotomy that pits superstitious and retrograde "traditions" against secular and rational "modernity." In these secularist and implicitly historicist narratives, temples represent anachronistic holdovers of a premodern era.

I contend, however, that such analyses are limited insofar as they ignore the range of ways that modernity has been framed and encountered through religious practice and vocabularies, especially as religious sites and practices have been impacted, since at least the eighteenth century, by the transformations of colonialism and capitalism.[87] More serious, dominant theories of modernization can be criticized for ignoring the plurality of ways of being in the world that exist contemporaneously, both now and in the past. In this light, it is crucial that critiques of Hindutva attend to the long history of mutual implication of state and religious institutions in southern Asia and to the heterogeneous, vernacular modernities that have been enacted in these spaces.

Though ostensibly concerned with architectural history and conservation, projects such as INTACH's conservation plan for Marundeswarar are informed by more than a century of debate about the publicity of religious space and action. Under the sign of heritage, temples have become stages, I argue, on which the relation between religious and secular norms and institutions in modern India are being revisited. Other debates on secularism, for example, liberal and leftist critiques of fundamentalism or neo-traditionalists' rejection of secular modernity, take as their point of departure the problem posed by the entry of religious subjects into a putatively secular arena. Even their different resolutions—embrace or rejection of the secular—are predicated on a notion of the secular as a space wholly disjunct from the space of religiosity.

By contrast, the new, consumer-friendly heritage discourses documented here imagine, interrogate, and debate the secular within the socio-spatial and pragmatic terrain of Hinduism, albeit a Hinduism that has been long entwined with statecraft. Current projects have roots in the colonial curatorial state's intervention in temple life, which involved conflict adjudication, administration, and financial oversight, and now exist alongside (and are enabled by) the bureaucratic control exerted by the postcolonial state. Even with the privatization of many state functions in the wake of structural adjustment, the state has not relinquished its role in temple administration. Indeed, Tamil Nadu's government patronage and surveillance of temples have grown as Dravidianist ruling parties struggle to maintain a populist profile. State programs dedicated to the "protection" of temples (physical maintenance and ritual activities) expanded, and temples were selected as sites for the delivery of welfare services. Heritage conservation groups work within this domain, and, in many cases, have sought to expand it, by institutionalizing public-private partnerships of the sort understood to index neoliberal reforms.

The representation of temples as embodiments of heritage therefore continues efforts initiated at mid-century to enroll temples in pedagogies of political modernity, which Dipesh Chakrabarty glossed as "the rule by modern institutions of the state, bureaucracy, and capitalist enterprise."[88] Bringing political modernity into being were norms and institutions associated with citizenship, civil society, the public sphere, human rights, equality before the law, individuality, publicity and privacy, democracy and popular sovereignty, scientific rationality, and social justice—all entailing the "unavoidable and indispensable universal and secular vision of the human" that Chakrabarty attributed to the intellectual and theological traditions of Europe.[89] The possibility of enacting secularism through heritage activities and ideas arises because of the historicism that subtends the secular and grounds its ontology and social spaces.[90] Chakrabarty identified this convergence as a product of the "ontological assumptions entailed in secular conceptions of the political and the social."[91] The first of these assumptions was that "the human exists in a frame of a single and secular historical time that envelops other kinds of time"; the second was that "the human is ontologically singular, that gods and spirits are in the end 'social facts,' that the social somehow exists prior to them."[92] Political modernity thus nurtures and depends on historicist discourses and their indexes of progress.

The case I have analyzed was a pedagogical project performed by, but designed to fashion, modern citizens, like the author of the article quoted in this chapter's epigraph, by introducing a historicist orientation toward religion and thereby containing it within the projects of secularization. In both language choice and the specific lexicon employed, INTACH projects are allied with historicism. At the same time as it serves the ends of political modernity, however, heritage makes an appeal to memory, which in turn invites subjects to imagine and locate themselves in the past in ways that are incompatible or incommensurable with historicism.[93] The technologies of memory associated with the conservation of temples arise from Hindu praxis and entertain the possibility of a "now" inhabited by gods, thereby re-sculpting the secularist presumptions of modernity. This is the conundrum—the everyday career of historicism within political modernity and its entanglements with memory—that this chapter has explored. The conservation plan for the Marundeswarar Temple amalgamated the spatial practice of Hindu ritual with that of modern citizenship and envisioned a hybrid representational space in which historicist values of heritage could be braided with the memory-work of Hindu praxis. This project and others like it are, along with Hindutva, the progeny of political modernity, albeit subscribing to different goals and aligned with different political positions.

Such developments belie the predictions of the secularization hypothesis, especially the expectation of the emergence of a neutral public sphere of which of the modern state acts as executor, even as they invite consideration of the ways that temples are implicated within a secular imaginary. For besides demonstrating the conditions of possibility for majoritarian Hindu nationalism, this rudimentary genealogy of the secular shows that history of state intervention in temples has been less about the consignment of religiosity to a domain understood as "private" than about the creation of a "public" realm in which the diverse and competing claims of religious subjects (individual and collective) are accommodated and adjudicated. Rather than relegating India to the ranks of the incompletely modern or treating the conjunction of religion and publicity as a symptom of the malignant return of the premodern, it is more useful to consider the discourse on publicity around temples and their heritage as a particular unfolding of the secular imaginary, with its ragged edges and irresolvable contradictions.

Part 2
Restructured Memories

5
Consuming the Past: Tourism's Cultural Economies

For the attention of foreign tourists
Finally, Kancheepuram has got what it needs most—Kanchi
Kudil—near Kailasanadar Temple
A place to relax when you visit Kancheepuram
Witness the lifestyle of a bygone period
Visit an authentic old Kanchi house, with its simplicity
and functional elegance
See the ancient furniture, craft and artifacts—
You can even buy them
Learn of Kancheepuram history and its temples in the
backdrop of a traditional ambience and music
All this with international standard toilet with wash and
change facility for overseas group tourists
Entrance Fee: Rs.20[1]

Toilet Talk

Thus read the flyer I picked up at Kanchi Kudil. News of the toilet traveled by word of mouth, too. Before the "heritage house" had opened to the public, I had heard of it from friends who emphasized its facilities and praised the forethought of the house's owner. Toilets, not just Kanchi Kudil's, figure in many conversations and articles about tourism in India.[2] I refer here not to guidebooks like Fodor's or Lonely Planet that cater to international visitors, although it is those guidebooks, their authors, and their readers that these conversations implicitly or explicitly engage.[3] Instead, I have in mind the conversations that take place among the professional hosts of the tourist industry and between them and tourist guests, conversations that re-deploy and are framed by state and corporate representations of tourism and its products.[4] For instance, in a public presentation on March 28, 2000, I listened as R. Kannan, the director of the Government Museum, included in his discussion of the museum's conservation facilities and new exhibitions a lengthy excursus about the museum's plans to refurbish its public toilets:

> This is neglected and it is distinctive of the Indian psyche to neglect it. Good families do not have good toilet training. But, if a toilet is clean then it is a sign that a house is clean. We should get luxury toilets, we should follow Kerala's example with a pay-and-use principle.

Further, in an interview, Ashok, a longtime government tour guide and president of a guides' professional association, broke off from telling me about new tour circuits to point out, with evident disgust, that "there is not one clean toilet between Trichy and Madurai."[5] He asserted that toilets, as much as roads and decent hotels, were crucial before tourism could take off as its proponents hoped it would.

Tourism, like anthropology, is always a comparative enterprise, whether explicitly or implicitly. For tourists, the pleasure of travel is found in the gulf between the here of home and the there of the destination. Tourist hosts—the guides, tour agency managers, drivers, craftspersons, vendors, and hoteliers who mediate and deliver the tourist product—are also involved in projects of comparison. Tourism is made up of quotidian encounters and many moments filled with toilet talk and its sister discourses. Among these interactions are the provision of food, personal services, and transportation, hotel check-ins, sales of souvenirs and crafts, and guide services. Within the space of these encounters, tourism providers imagine luxurious, sanitized "elsewheres" from which tourists arrive, even while revisiting the "local" through the imported gaze of the tourist. With these devices, they come to name, and traverse the distance between, "development" and "underdevelopment," and "modernity" and "tradition."

Toilet talk, along with the other discourses associated with tourism, is an instance of what Michael Herzfeld termed "cultural intimacy": the sharing of known and recognizable traits that define insiderhood but are also felt to be disapproved by powerful outsiders.[6] Cultural intimacy affords spaces of both identification and dis-identification with collective institutions, principally, for Herzfeld, the nation-state. He offered it as a heuristic with which to engage, ethnographically, with state formation, nationalisms, and other forms of powerful, institutionalized collective representations. While nationalism, following Benedict Anderson, may be so compelling that its subjects are willing to die for what they imagine the nation to be, the pragmatics that engender that identification are not fleshed out in Anderson's work nor are the possibilities of dis-identification.[7] In response, Herzfeld proposed that in the social poetics that structure expressions of cultural intimacy, an engine of both reification and creative dissent exists.

Tourism's encounters are spaces of cultural intimacy in which the qualities that putatively distinguish the Indian nation-state and the Tamil ethnos are made tangible. Toilet talk, like the talk of food, disease, clothing, and family, arises in the context of touristic encounters. These discourses are signals of cultural intimacy and the translations, linguistic and ethical, that it performs. They are the media with which speakers imagine the nation-state and the modernist project that it enacts. The allusions, in toilet talk, to bodily functions share qualities of other nationalist and communitarian discourses that imagine society and polity through the lens of the body and embodied relations of kinship. More important, however, toilet talk works as cultural intimacy through its particular commingling of self-recognition and disavowal, or, as Herzfeld has put it, its "rueful self-recognition."[8]

The chapters in part 1 of this book concerned living memory in the formal city—the ways that everyday notions of the past were interrupted, recomposed, and formalized as heritage with the formalization of the city. This chapter and the two that follow track the connections between memoryscapes of the urban core and the city's expanding peri-urban fringe, a zone in which patterns of land use and consumption are being rapidly transformed with the adoption of neoliberal economic policies. I begin with tourism, understood as an industrial sector and body of labor and leisure practice closely associated with political and economic development. The work of tourist hosts represents a type of service-oriented labor that has become increasingly common in the neoliberal economies; it comprises spaces of cultural intimacy, particularly in its enactment of regional and national "branding." I attend most closely to the voices of those who produce and provide tourist services and goods—guides, travel agents, and curators—in an effort to consider both the institutional functions of the tourist industry and the cultural discourses with which tourist hosts reify national and regional identities through ambivalent constructions of heritage. Threaded into the discussion of the work they do, the chronotopes they represent, and the composition of tourism's labor force are accounts that speak to the cultural intimacy engendered by such labor.

Tourism and the Postcolonial Project: The Work of Cultural Intimacy

Tourism and the Developmentalist State

The simultaneously economic, cultural, and political orientations of tourism, both domestic and international, were inscribed soon after independence.[9] Domestic tourism was particularly valued as a pedagogy of the modern: a means to display the cultural and linguistic diversity encompassed by the nation-state and to educate India's populace about that diversity by giving them tools to see themselves and others within the spectrum of state-managed difference. The government institutionalized its role as a tourism provider in 1966, with the formation of the Indian Tourism Development Corporation (ITDC) and corresponding state-level agencies (TDCs), which oversaw a growing network of tourism offices, hotels, restaurants, and handicraft shops. One of the first priorities of the ITDC had been to draw tourists away from the "Golden Triangle" of Delhi–Agra–Jaipur and into under-visited areas of the country in order to diffuse the economic and infrastructural benefits of tourism.[10] Tamil Nadu was an early beneficiary of these efforts. Chennai (then named Madras) and Tiruchirapalli were designated regional gateways, having been declared ports of entry for immigration purposes. The Tamil Nadu Tourism Development Corporation (TTDC) was created in 1970, and in 1972 began to offer conducted tours of the city of Chennai (then Madras) and nearby Kanchipuram and Mamallapuram (then Mahaballipuram), as well as a multi-day state circuit that included the large temple towns in the state's rural south. Hotels and youth hostels in the more heavily promoted destinations were built over the following decade.[11]

Tourism was meant to create employment opportunities with both formal and informal sectors for skilled and unskilled workers, from drivers and bag handlers to hoteliers, caterers, and guides.[12] Guides were sought among the educated, English-speaking strata of the population. That labor, though skilled, was seasonal and part-time, with salaries inadequate to support a family. As a result, elite women, whose own negotiation of modernity was mediated by families who valued education but disapproved of women working outside the home, tended to outnumber men among the recruits for these types of jobs.

India's central government regulated both the supply of guides and the demand for their services. Tour guides, a new category of public-sector worker, were recruited and credentialed by the central government, through the ITDC. Recruitment was regionally based and carried out at irregular intervals, on an as-needed basis. Applicants were solicited through newspaper advertisements, and their English-language skills were screened during interviews.[13] Those who did well in their interview and whose families were deemed "respectable" were invited to participate in a two-week training course after which they were tested. Those who completed all steps successfully were certified as "Regional Guides," a status allowing them to conduct tours in any of the states within the region; for the south, this included Tamil Nadu, Andhra Pradesh, Karnataka, and Kerala. A continuing need for guide services was assured by the regulation that Regional Guides lead all conducted tours, whether government-sponsored or private. Further, tour groups were not allowed to enter national monuments unless accompanied by a Regional Guide. Each regional office maintained a roster, with available guides listed, which managers consulted in assigning work. Assignments were rotated among guides, often with short notice.

In the actual conduct of tourism, guides' mediation was crucial and remains so, despite the increased presence of guidebooks and Web sites that provide travel information. Virtually all tourist sites lack their own professional interpretive staffs. Guides, whether working with individual travelers or tour groups, are often the only interpreters of museum collections, historic sites, or monuments. Besides providing linguistic translations, guides are also translators of monetary and aesthetic value and knowledge. Guides typically broker commercial transactions between tourists and vendors; they communicate information about etiquette and are expected to run interference between tourists and various locals, panhandlers, and touts, who also seek to benefit from the presence of tourists.[14] Some guides acquired reputations for their scholarship and specialized in working with foreign scholars and school groups, sometimes in collaborative research ventures. Beyond the job's formal criteria, guides brought personal knowledge and interests to their work. Among those I interviewed, some had combined their work as guides with careers as artisans or performers. For others, tourism provided a space for religious or intellectual endeavor. The comments of one Regional Guide, "Urvashi," serve as illustration.

Urvashi was recruited as a Regional Guide in 1972 and was part of the first cohort in southern India. When I spoke with her in 2000, she was seventy-one years old, married with two adult sons, and lived in a comfortable flat in one of Chennai's newer residential divisions. Like other Regional Guides, she was proud of her fluency in English, which she spoke flawlessly. She had earned a bachelor's degree in natural science in the early 1950s and, shortly after her marriage, in 1955, had taught briefly at Ethiraj College, a private women's college in Chennai. Her family's disapproval of work outside the home and the birth of her two sons took her out of the labor force until 1972, when, to help with the family's expenses, she applied for certification as a Government of India Guide.

> I went into tourism because it did not have a minimum age restriction for entry positions. I was forty-two and could not have gotten an office job, I was too old for that. . . . But I was a graduate and had skills in English, so I was well suited for [work as a guide]. You had to be from a good family, a respectable family—they inquired into that—and there, too, I was qualified.

Urvashi recalled that, in 1972, there were many openings for guides:

> I was scared when I went for the interview, but I got through it and I was approved to take the course. It was nothing much, very simple. It lasted for fifteen days. On each day, we listened to a lecture on one subject but not much was covered. When I started off as a guide, I did not know very much but, in the course of it, I slowly, slowly began to pick up more knowledge. People would ask questions that I didn't expect and so I would go to the library and look up the answer. Like this, it kept on, with my own study, little by little.

The work was irregular, "about ten days per month [because] at that time there were not that many tourists coming to India." In her class, women exceeded men: "Women from good families, who had attended college and did not work because of family restrictions, these were the ones who applied." Those same family restrictions intervened to keep many of the women who earned certification out of the labor force: "About thirty guides were trained in my class but only four continued to work as tour guides. The others dropped it because their families objected."

She herself came from a low-caste but affluent family, and she had spoken with pride about their self-conscious embrace of "modernity," particularly her parents' willingness to educate her. She recognized that it was an ambivalent embrace, however. Modernity was associated with foreign values and lifeways, and with colonial domination. Work as a guide exposed her to frequent encounters with modernity in the form of foreign tourists. Such encounters exposed an India—in the trope of family—that was "not yet" modern:

> To work with foreigners was a problem. People in India had images of foreigners because of movies and magazines, so there was some disapproval of women working in close contact with them. Some in my family objected: "Why should Urvashi work with foreigners?" My own husband hesitated, but he realizes now that the work has value and respectability.

This narrative of respectability, especially as it arose from and reflected back on the family, was also realized in representations of guides as scholarly collaborators. This transforms foreignness into a source of respectability and reflects the positive valence of "guide" which, in Indian English, is used like "guru" or "mentor." Urvashi spoke at length about her work with a German scholar, which was both collaborative and personally absorbing because of the kinds of religious and aesthetic experiences it offered, both for her and the scholar:

> One thing happened, I would call it a miracle. We had worked for ten days and were on our way back to Madras. But the German lady had obtained some brochure, I don't know how she got it. It was about a temple, one dedicated to the Saivite saint . . . Manikavacakkar. She wanted to return to see that temple. I agreed to it. On that day was a celebration of a special *pūja*—full day from sunrise to sunset, it was a full day *pūja* for Saint Manikavacakkar. That was a call to her. When we got to the temple, the priest came forward. I had my doubts about what he would do, usually they will just come and pay attention to a white face hoping for some extra money. But he did not ask or do anything. He just came forward and brought her back into the sanctum. Now Manikavacakkar is known to have had a palm leaf on which he inscribed his songs and poetry. In this temple, they have kept that leaf and coated it with silver—his very own leaf. The priest invited her to come forward and touch the leaf. She declined, she felt unworthy to touch it. Through guiding her to that temple, I found that there was a special power there. I have felt it in other temples, also.

For Urvashi and other guides, the wage labor of tourism allowed for the pursuit of one's own interests while generating spaces of cultural intimacy in which various kinds of "others" and national "selves" could be imagined. In the discourse on tourism, as in many other nationalist discourses, "family" was a key trope for representing Indian-ness. Moreover, in guides' accounts of their work and aspirations, family concerns were not only weighed but reworked, as guides negotiated the contrasts between the foreign world of tourism and the intimate spaces of domesticity. Respectability, a quality in which personal achievement was entwined with familial well-being, might be threatened by work in tourism, but that same work could also add value to a family's social and cultural capital and so enhance its claims to respectability. As is elaborated further in the next section, "family" served as a critical medium of translation and comparison, as guides negotiated the spaces between tradition and modernity, between national self and foreign other.

Tourism and National Integration

The modernist character of tourism was tied to its capacity to foster historicist knowledge and appreciation of India's past and of its regional diversity of culture and language. Tourism, domestic tourism especially, was a vehicle for producing a new, *national* culture. These principles were asserted, more strenuously, following the Emergency (1975–77), as Congress and later Janata governments attempted to use the discourse of culture to manage regional, ethnic, class, and caste difference and inequality. Through its Department of Culture, opened in 1977 under the aegis of the Ministry of Education, Social Welfare and Culture, the Indian government initiated programs that showcased and marketed regional cultural forms.[15] Later, in conjunction with its support for the international Festival of India (1984–86), the department inaugurated a tourist attraction in the form of an annual six-day festival, Lok Utsav, in 1984 that brought performers and artisans from throughout India to New Delhi.[16] Smaller-scale state undertakings were planned, and craft and cultural appreciation curricula were developed for schools. The National Handicrafts and Handlooms Museum, originally opened in New Delhi in 1956, was refurbished as a site for cultural tourism, offering craft demonstrations and sales, and was reopened in 1984. Also in 1984 the Indian National Trust for Art and Cultural Heritage (INTACH) was founded with a mandate to conserve natural, cultural, and historic resources (see chapter 4).

In the early 1980s, as had occurred a decade earlier, the government tried to increase its pool of certified guides. In 1982 another round of recruitment was launched, and another cohort, largely composed of under- or unemployed elite women, was recruited. Among the guides trained during that session were "Asha" and "Lalitha."

Lalitha, a Brahman college graduate, described a path from unpaid labor for a family business to the flexible labor of tourism:

> I needed more money for the [three] children. That was one thing. But, more than that, I was sitting idle and I could never take that. I like working with the public. We [the family] had a textile business and I was helping out with it, with the accounts, but it did not keep me busy. . . . I started going out, house to house, to get people interested in buying. I even learned to cycle so that I could ride. All of this propaganda and publicity, I enjoyed. I knew one lady, she was a guide and she encouraged me to apply and she also coached me. From her, I learned the details about history, culture, all that, and I continued, on my own, to keep building my knowledge.

Comparable entry narratives emerged in conversations with other guides from the 1980s cohort. Asha, an unmarried woman in her mid-forties, had earned a bachelor's degree in economics. Like Lalitha, she was a Brahman and had been discouraged from working outside the home until she proposed part-time work as a guide. She resided in what she called, with a laugh, a "typical, traditional joint family." Being unmarried, she was vulnerable to the taint of disrespectability; her emphasis on "traditional" living arrangements seemed aimed at dispelling any doubts about her moral character that her work as a guide might have invited. Similarly, even while the characterization of her household's typicality suggested ironic distance from tradition, she located her own tastes and talents within streams of classicized, high-caste styles of cultural performance. Her special knowledge, as a Regional Guide, underwrote the authority of claims about what was, and was not, authentic. She cast her work in tourism as a kind of cultural translation, by explaining her interest in guide certification as an outgrowth of her pursuit of another passion, art. In 1982, when she completed the training class, she was also enrolled at the Kalakshetra School, a non-degree institution founded to promote visual and musical culture historically associated with Brahmanic devotional practice.[17]

> In [19]82 I joined [the] Kalakshetra school and studied fine arts. That same year, I took the government course and qualified as a Regional Guide. Painting was my main subject, but, as a minor subject I studied flute. I was enrolled at Kalakshetra from [19]82 to [19]86 [and] I learned Tanjore painting, flat tempera on cloth, Kalamkari, miniature, wash painting, miniature on wood, Chinese lacquer work; I also learned Western styles—seascape, landscape, and portrait. I was doing all this at the same time that I was leading tours for the ITDC. I continue to paint and play flute. I sell Tanjore paintings to individuals and to shops, but I also like to experiment with other styles. I have done some frescoes, on the walls of my brother's flat. One was in the style of Chola painting and another was in the Kerala style. . . . I do my art in [the] early morning and late at night, but I need inspiration. I play devotional music to get into the right frame of mind, to bring the images into my mind. I'm not married but, even though, it's hard in a joint family—we are Brahman—to dedicate myself as much to painting as I would like.

Asha's talents and tastes, which predisposed her for work in tourism, were themselves shaped by her Brahman identity, despite the occasional hindrances that Brahman family life posed for her. Caste was reconstituted in tourism's cultural intimacies by other guides as well. Urvashi was anxious to make her low-caste family's respectability visible and to challenge claims of Brahman hegemony, such as those implied by Asha, by accruing cultural capital through her work as a guide. Lalitha, the saleswoman-turned-guide quoted earlier, told me of the resentment she felt toward non-Brahman guides and supervisors who, she suggested, tried to exploit Brahmans' superior understanding of the region's history and culture:

> LALITHA: (*Speaking of a non-Brahman manager*) This one, Narasimhan, he corners us; he tries to corner Brahmans.
>
> MARY: What do you mean, he "corners" you?
>
> LALITHA: It's like this. We have the knowledge about all the temples and the history and culture, it is natural for us. He goes after our knowledge to improve his own. And then, he sidelines us—he gives us assignments that pay less.

Her position echoed complaints I had often heard from Brahmans: that their merit was not properly rewarded because of positive discrimination policies that guaranteed jobs and seats in educational institutions to non-Brahmans.[18] Culture, at least for Asha and Lalitha, was a "Brahman thing." And although Urvashi may have challenged such presumptions, she was no less attentive to differences of status between educated elites and those who lacked respectability.

Together, these entry narratives illustrate important features of labor in tourism's formal sectors during the 1970s and 1980s—its character as marginal work, temporary and part-time, and its reliance on female labor. Women like Urvashi, Lalitha, and Asha were sought as guides because they provided a low-cost, easily exploitable but still high-status labor force. The restrictions and norms associated with the "respectability" that elite families claimed mediated their entry to the labor force and the work they performed as guides, even as household organization and its moral economy were occasionally reorganized, or even undermined, by that work. For educated, under-employed women, the work of tourism provided a financial supplement but also a measure of autonomy, achieved both by acquiring more latitude for acting on one's interests and talents and, in some cases, by gaining a lexicon for historicizing one's relation to powerful cultural institutions.

The ways that family life and "respectability" entered their accounts point also to the cultural intimacy of tourism. These women negotiated work in tourism through and in the family even as they revisited familial ideals, often with the rueful self-recognition that cultural intimacy begets. "Family" furnished a trope for reifying India and imagining a national culture that distinguished Indians from its foreign visitors. For Urvashi, family represented a space of Indian modernity, its respectability the means to cast doubt on Brahman claims to hold a monopoly on national culture. By contrast, Asha's family—in her words: "typical," "traditional," "joint," and "Brahman"—was a space of immersion in classicized art forms and devotional expression, whose elite, high-caste associations frequently underwrote Brahmanic accounts of national identity. And it is Lalitha's resentful account of Narasimhan's "cornering" her that brings these two perspectives together, revealing the ongoing frictions of caste difference and the claims on regional culture and its pasts that caste identity mediates.

Privatization and Tourism

Working conditions for guides changed with the privatization of the tourist industry. Tourism had been one of the first government-sponsored industries to be privatized, a move heralded by the government's declaration that the 1990s were to be the "Decade of Tourism."[19] Officials were optimistic about its potential to generate foreign exchange and domestic revenues, and in 1998 a new national ministry, charged with planning and management of tourism, was formed. It was anticipated that tourism services, especially in its unorganized sectors, would absorb large numbers of under- and unemployed people and generate new jobs. In Tamil Nadu, planners shared these same hopes, maintaining in their Tenth Five-Year Plan that tourism was a major engine of economic growth through both employment generation and poverty alleviation. Both central and state plans anticipated major increases in domestic and international tourist arrivals by 2007, and, according to preliminary reports, these goals have been met.[20]

Although India's central government has continued to train Regional Guides and to regulate demand for their services by stipulating that certified guides accompany groups touring national monuments, the burden for provision of tourist services and infrastructure has been shifted to the tourism development corporations of individual states and to the private sector.[21] The ITDC, under the central Ministry of Tourism, is charged with functions such as advertising and coordinating tourism services. The recruitment and training of Regional Guides by the ITDC continues but, since the mid-1990s, guide training has been assumed also by state-level agencies. Pay scales for guides are now set by state TDCs, and, in Tamil Nadu, the salaries of Regional Guides were reduced in the mid-1990s. At the same time the number of guides—and the competition among them for assignments—has increased. Newly hired guides with Tamil Nadu's Tourism Development Corporation learn the ropes by accompanying more experienced guides on a few tours; however, there are no assigned texts or standardized assessments. Further sharpening the competition among guides has been the recognition by India's central government of another category of guide, the "monument" or "hereditary" guide. The latter are persons, such as watchmen or priests, who claim hereditary rights to control public access to certain monuments and whose claims, in some cases, may supersede those of Regional and TDC Guides and thereby supplant the need for the latter services at some national monuments.

As government subsidization of tourism has declined, guides' job security has been further eroded. Virtually all guides now work as freelance contractors and those with whom I spoke described working conditions as humiliating. "It's like going out with a begging bowl!" complained one veteran guide. As had been the case previously, travel agencies and government tourism offices maintain rosters and solicit guides and drivers, often with only a few hours' notice, for individual jobs that range from a half-day to several weeks' duration. Guides increasingly try to maintain advantage by personal contacts with agents, making visitation rounds simply to cultivate hospitable relations among managers. Some have abandoned work as guides and instead have invested in car services or become full-time drivers, both of which offer more steady income streams than does guide service alone.

One of the long-standing attractions of work in tourism's front lines was access to foreign-made consumer goods and to the "black money" (undeclared income) of the informal economy. This continues, and, with liberalization, the exposure to other potential business opportunities has also increased. Guides expected and received tips of cash and luxury goods; it was not unusual for guides working with international tourists to augment their earnings by collecting commissions from shopkeepers. Some brokered business arrangements between locals and foreign visitors. For "Sanjeev," the proprietor of an agency specializing in alternative tourism (discussed below), assisting foreign entrepreneurs in locating craft producers enabled him to lend support to artisanal modes of production. By contrast, several other guides described their own subtle efforts to use their contacts with foreign travelers to expand business networks for family members and friends. "Sujata," a Regional Guide with twenty years' experience, told me how she engineered a complex series of "coincidences" to put her son-in-law, a jewelry broker, in contact with a Swedish wholesaler, a "VVIP" tourist whom she had escorted on a city tour. She concluded: "I set it up, I can do no more than that—it's in God's hands, now, isn't it?"

The deregulation of India's tourist industry brought with it the multiplication of private travel agencies, hotels, and other attractions, intensifying the competition among providers.[22] Most of Tamil Nadu's travel agencies are headquartered in Chennai and recruit staff, guides, and drivers from the metropolitan area. Those targeting upper-end consumers (elite Indian citizens, international visitors, business travelers, and temporary residents, including the wealthier, often higher-caste Non-Resident Indians from North America) contract with foreign or multinational travel agencies, like Cox and Kings, Cook's, or Abercrombie and Kent. Like their state counterparts, private agencies are obliged to use the services of government-authorized guides, though Regional Guides are usually preferred because of their language skills and training.

Below the uppermost tier of providers was the large and growing number of private agencies that serve middle- and working-class domestic tourists, many of whom travel in family groups and combine pilgrimage with leisure travel. These companies furnish transportation by bus or van (often equipped with video screening facilities) to a mix of religious and leisure sites. The TTDC aims to reach the same market and one segment of the international market—ethnic Tamils residing outside India—with a roster of conducted bus tours and a network of moderately priced hotels and hostels in popular destinations. State-certified guides accompany these groups but they function more as activity coordinators rather than as interpreters of cultural or historical sites. Guides with whom I spoke attributed this to domestic tourists' disinterest in such details.

"Daniel," a TTDC guide hired during the mid-nineties, elaborated on his experiences. We had met in 2000 during a visit to Chennai's Government Museum, when Daniel, then in his mid-thirties, approached me and my friend, Mythili, near the entrance and offered his services as a guide. We agreed, and he accompanied us through the museum's major galleries, offering lengthy and detailed explanations of the exhibitions. As is customary, I tipped him at the going rate (for foreigners) of Rs.100 per gallery, about twice the rate expected from Indian tourists.

We shared a soft drink in the park outside the museum entry after our tour, and he told me a bit about his background,

> I was trained as a TTDC guide, but that training is very poor. I only watched other guides and read things on my own. Ninety percent of what I know I have taught myself—I have an interest in South Indian history. I quit TTDC in [19]99. There was not much work and I no longer wanted to go on long tours. And it was humiliating to always be begging for assignments from the managers. Now, I work on my own, here at the museum and for special clients. I still lead some tours for TTDC, but only for Indian groups from Malaysia and Singapore. Americans tip better, but the Malaysians make less demands. They don't want

> to hear so much about history. The main things for them are temples—a tour is good as long as they can get *darśan* for at least a few minutes.

Like other guides who spoke with me, Daniel characterized tourists in terms of national character. A similar ethno-sociology also emerged in managers' comments. "Chitra," a manager at "Elite Travel," a private agency, had gained clear ideas about the styles of consumption typical of different ethnic and national segments of the tourist market through her supervisory duties. She had this to say about her international clientele:

> Germans insist on knowing all aspects of the culture . . . Dutch come for a cheap holiday . . . Americans come for fun, but don't want to be educated about the country. . . . We deal mostly with Japanese tourists, who come to visit astrologers and for [Sathya] Sai Baba.[23] We've earned over four lakhs from the Japanese tourists coming for Sai Baba.

"Raj," an assistant manager at the Chennai headquarters of the TTDC, made these observations about the domestic market that his agency targeted:

> Most of the Indians who take the tours are not so much interested in history or architecture but in the temples, in receiving the gods' blessings. Our most popular offerings are the city sight-seeing tour, the Mahaballipuram-Kanchipuram day trip, the fourteen-day Sunny South tour and the Tirupathi tour, which advertises "special *darśan*" for TTDC clients.

Raj contrasted the tendency of foreign visitors to travel alone, in couples, or in small groups of friends with what he regarded as the more typical Indian preference for family travel. This, he pointed out, was recognized by the government. In an effort to encourage domestic tourism, India's central government launched a program of vacation subsidies for public-sector employees during the mid-1990s. Through this program, Leave Transfer Concession (LTC), employees were reimbursed for the costs of TTDC vacation packages, which typically encompassed travel, conducted tours, and accommodations.[24] After he explained the procedures, Raj praised its family focus:

> The LTC is a good approach, more wholesome, because it encourages family vacations. They can't just get the money and spend it on drinking or waste it. And, with LTC, people who work together can mix with each others' families, not like the traditional socializing with relatives.

Work in India's tourism sector in the 1990s, while considerably more competitive and consumption-oriented, continues to be an engine for a national imaginary tied to state formation. Within the larger story of postcolonial state formation, tourism has been claimed for purposes of "development" and "national integration" because of the labor it absorbs, the revenues it generates, and its traffic in well-worn tropes of cultural intimacy. "Family"—its obligations and constraints, the depth of its emotional currents—surfaces repeatedly across tourism discourses, as it does in other arenas of public culture, as a key signifier of and surrogate for the nation-state. "Family" was engaged and recomposed in the comments of some guides (Urvashi, Asha, and Lalitha) about their entry into the world of paid labor. Raj resituated the family as the consumer of that quintessentially modern experience, the vacation. Indeed, he suggested that by being made a part of family life the vacation was Indianized, and family life was modernized by being exposed to wider social networks.

Cultural intimacy, recycled in guides' ethno-sociology of national character, furnished both marketing tools and spaces for reifying comparison. While "others" were brought into focus, the national "self" remained implicated and pressed into service for branding India's tourist product, whether in the enumeration of the special appeal that astrology and god-men held for foreign tourists or in the devotional orientation and familial commitments of Indian travelers.

Tamil® Culture

> The southern state of Tamil Nadu is the most "Indian" part of India. The Aryans never brought their meat-eating influence to the extreme south, so this is the true home of Indian Vegetarianism. Hindu architecture here is at its most vigorous. . . . The home of Dravidian art and culture [is] characterized best by the amazingly ornate temples with their soaring towers known as gopurams.[25]

India's Ninth Five-Year Plan had identified tourism as a commercial and moral endeavor that advanced the goals of liberalization while still containing it within the integrationist message of cultural nationalism.[26] The tourist product—destinations, accommodations, performances—and the infrastructure that would make those products accessible to consumers, domestic and international, was increasingly left to private enterprise, while state agencies defined tourism's goals and parameters. To these ends, each state was charged with developing "brand equity" by crafting a rubric within which their tourist attractions could be marketed. With the drop in international tourist arrivals following the 9/11 attacks in the U.S., the Tourism Ministry intensified its efforts, marketing the attractions of individual states within its "Incredible India" campaign.[27] Complementing the campaign was a new program, "Atithi Devo Bhavah," dubbed as a social awareness campaign and designed to change the attitudes of tourism providers, skilled and unskilled, through training in hygiene, integrity, and courtesy.[28] The boot camp in emotional labor that the ministry outlined was a seven-point program whose Sanskrit keywords were glossed using the vocabulary of motivational and self-help discourses. The training program itself was framed as a memory exercise, an organized recollection of India's "tradition" of hospitality. Workers, termed "stakeholders," were asked to (re)learn integrity, etiquette, and hygiene. This new attitude and its anticipated spillover effects were described as keys to creating brand equity for and greater revenues from Indian tourism.

Tamil Nadu's Tenth Five-Year Plan echoed national plans with its confident assertion that tourism was "one of the three leading socioeconomic and service businesses of the new century."[29] With language that differed little from the prose of earlier plans' celebration of culture, planners stated their expectations that tourism, especially domestic, would contribute "to national integration and to the creation of [a] harmonious social and cultural environment, [and would encourage] respect for and preservation of monuments, heritage properties and art, craft, and culture."[30] In recognition of the "deep-rooted and innate relationship between Tourism and Culture," Tamil Nadu was branded as a destination for heritage or cultural tourism.[31] The slogan "Enchanting Tamil Nadu—Experience It Yourself" was proposed as the brand name for products that included ecotourism, pilgrimage, and resort-based health and leisure pursuits.[32]

The designation of Tamil Nadu as the "most Indian part of India" extends the characterizations made shortly after independence, when, seeking an integrationist rubric for nationalism, the Indian government enumerated religious institutions within its states and territories as part of the 1961 census. As noted in chapter 4, the report for Madras had lauded the authenticity of its Hindu practice and institutions, and attributed it to the region's insulation from Mughal influence.[33] Similarly Tamil Nadu's current brand identity marks the region's inhabitants, like the territory itself, as bearers of a Dravidian culture that, contrary to the stance of some Dravidian nationalists, is fully and originally Hindu.

Tourism planning and policy, at both state and central levels, continue to take account of the industry's bifurcated market, with its international and far larger domestic streams.[34] While international tourist arrivals have increased since the post–9/11 drop, India's share of the global international tourist market remains less than 1 percent, with 4.5 million arrivals estimated for 2006. Greater growth has occurred in domestic tourism, which reached an all-India level of 382 million tourist visits in 2005.[35] Tourism officials in Tamil Nadu hoped that heritage tourism would attract more international visitors and encourage higher levels of consumption among domestic tourists. For the international market, the region's UNESCO World Heritage sites and national monuments were highlighted.[36] High-end options for lodging, dining, and transport have multiplied in those locales, with the focus remaining on improved, modern infrastructure; toilet talk frequently appears in plans in their appeals to the "pay-and-use" principle, "hygiene," and "convenience."

As pitched to the domestic market, nearly half of which is drawn from middle-income groups, "heritage tourism" refers primarily to pilgrimage, with Hindu sites the main focus, an association that became firmer in the late 1990s with the electoral successes of the Hindu nationalist BJP. Just as India's Congress government had sought to promote national integration by modernizing pilgrimage in the 1950s and 1960s, the BJP-led government initiated efforts, in the late 1990s, to market Hindu pilgrimage sites as tourist attractions by upgrading transport, accommodations, and infrastructure, and by incorporating leisure travel destinations within pilgrimage circuits. Although the BJP lost to the Congress Party in 2004, the central government's promotion of religious tourism has not diminished, though it has expanded to include non-Hindu sites.[37] These moves built on long-standing practices that entwined pilgrimage and commerce but outfitted them with explicit consumerist messages. In this new context, pilgrims became "tourists" and priests, vendors, and touts became "hereditary guides." Domestic heritage tourism, by incorporating and expanding pilgrimage, at once inflates tourist markets, employment levels, and revenues while asserting that religious practice is modern by virtue of its contribution to economic productivity and nationalism.

Chennai: "Gateway to Southern India"

Much of the work of representing and sustaining the Tamil brand takes place in Chennai. Most tourist activity is initiated and concluded there, in keeping with its moniker as the "Gateway to Southern India." Making the city more accessible and more legible as a tourist product has been among the goals of formalization. In a refurbished and assertively modern city, one with both heritage attractions and tourist services, in addition to industrial and financial advantages, higher revenues from tourism are anticipated. Such a city, with what planners lauded as its "imageability" and navigability, would, in turn, be more appealing as a destination for investor capital, including investment in tourism, an industry in which 100 percent foreign direct investment is now permissible. Chennai's transport, commercial, and administrative services make it a gateway in a practical sense. Beyond that, its sites of public memory function as narrative gateways, framing the pasts that lend value and authenticity to Tamil Nadu's heritage-branded products, services, and knowledge.

Whether they rely on government tourism services, private agencies, or guidebooks, tourists (as I myself experienced) are channeled through a standard set of sites around the city and its environs. These include Fort St. George, the Government Museum complex, state-commissioned memorials and monuments, Mylapore's Kapaleswarar Temple, Guindy National Park, and the Birla Planetarium. Some stops, such as the Gandhi Mantapam Memorial, remind visitors of the nationalist struggles of the first half of the twentieth century and echo the national government's frequent invocations of the country's Gandhian legacy. The memorials to Tamil Nadu's political leaders along Marina Beach tell a different story, which focuses on the regional autonomy movements that developed contemporaneously and in contention with Gandhian nationalism. Commodity consumption, especially of handicrafts, is a critical element of tourism, and Chennai offers plenty of opportunities to shop for textiles, furnishings, jewelry, and decorative objects at state and national craft emporia and private handicrafts boutiques.[38] This basic tour circuit has changed little since its launch in 1972. Differences in accommodation, transport, consumption, and guide services, however, create heterogeneous tourist experiences and forms of cultural intimacy. The formal city, an emblem of the state's brand equity, is also a prismatic space in which different cities appear.

Domestic Circuits

Domestic tourists and ethnic Tamil tourists from Southeast Asia treat Chennai as a gateway but employ other framing discourses, mostly familial in origin and

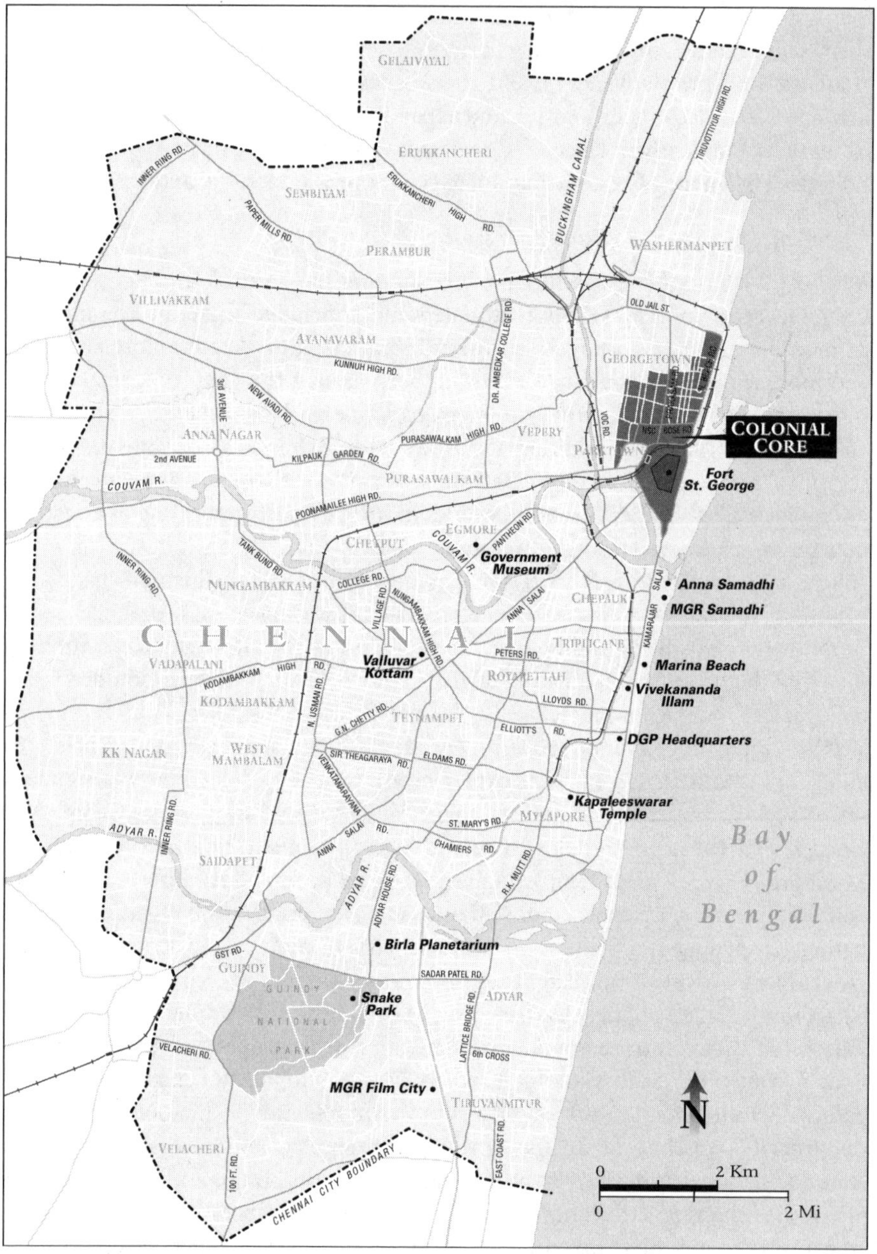

Map 3. Tourist sites in Chennai. *Map prepared by James Craine.*

often centered on pilgrimage. Following state efforts to redefine pilgrimage as tourism, Hindu temples are the main attraction for the middle-class and mostly Tamil consumers of state tourism offerings. Between 1996 and 1999, for example, the numbers of conducted tours offered by the TTDC increased from thirteen offerings to twenty-six; in 2005, twenty-seven tour packages were advertised, in addition to sixteen budget-priced "student" packages.[39] Of the packages on offer in 2005, twelve were dedicated to Hindu temple circuits and expressly marketed to Hindus (Indian citizens and Non-Resident Indians) for the purposes of worship, and ten others combined pilgrimage and sightseeing. Private agencies serving the domestic market also include pilgrimage but mixed those offerings more liberally with visits to theme and amusement parks, memorials, zoos, beaches, and shops.

The central attractions of pilgrimage tours are the stops at temples where *darśan* is guaranteed, though they also include meals and shopping opportunities. For example, the TTDC's "One-day Sakthi Tour" is scheduled on specific days (Tuesdays, Fridays, Sundays, and Full Moon days) when special rituals are performed to propitiate goddesses, and the tour advertises stops at nine goddess temples located in Chennai and its outskirts. In 2000 only one tour was dedicated to non-Hindu pilgrimage, this to the Roman Catholic shrine dedicated to Annai Vailankanni (the Virgin Mary in the form of Our Lady of Good Health) in southern Tamil Nadu. By 2005, that tour had been dropped and additional Hindu pilgrimage circuits were in the works.[40] Other available tour packages, although not marketed as pilgrimage, included temples in the mixes of leisure and historical sites on offer.

Many newer attractions are found in the outskirts, along the new IT-corridor southwest of the city. The themed amusement parks outside Chennai draw an almost exclusively domestic audience. Kishkinta, named after the idyllic forest kingdom, described in Ramayana, is located in Tambaram, just west of Chennai. Another, one of the region's earliest theme parks, VGP Golden Beach Resort, named after founder V. G. Paneerdas, was opened in 1975. It lies about fifteen kilometers south of Chennai on the East Coast Road and consisted initially of dispersed pavilions, gardens, and groves, populated by statues and carvings depicting deities and historical figures and events. Over the years the resort's spaces have served as film sets for Tamil movies, and, during the past decade, thrill rides and overnight accommodations have since been added. Its management estimates that the site is visited annually by more than a million people: domestic tourists from Tamil Nadu and other states, as well as local residents who can reach the site by city bus. A few kilometers south of VGP Golden Beach is another popular theme park, MGM Dizzee World, and day trippers can easily visit both.

Another kind of pilgrimage that state and private agencies catering to domestic markets accommodate is that which focuses on popular politicians and cultural heroes. Such circuits include memorials honoring deceased Dravidianist party leaders and monuments, such as Valluvar Kottam, dedicated to the Tamil sage, Tiruvalluvar. Because Tamil cinema has been an important vehicle through which film stars, screenwriters, musicians, and others have forged political careers, the sites visited by domestic tourists may enable them to recall the cinematic

Figure 5.1. Government Museum grounds, Chennai. *Photograph by author.*

mediation of the past as well as the lives and deeds of politician-heroes. The reconstructed classical pavilions at VGP Golden Beach, for example, are well known to movie fans as sets for song-and-dance routines. Visitors often recalled the filmic episodes and, through them, the classical scenes they portrayed. Another themed site, MGR Film City, located in a southwest suburb of Chennai, traded on the popularity of M. G. Ramachandran, the state's former chief minister and, before that, a major film star in Tamil cinema. MGR's political persona was entwined with the Robin Hood–type characters he portrayed in film. Although MGR Film City is now closed, it had been built as a full-service film production campus.[41] It appealed to domestic tourists with old film sets from MGR's movies, which visitors could view, pose with, and photograph.

The heritage encountered in these touristic experiences is not a chronologically ordered account of regional history but rather a revisitation of familial pasts, of the mythico-historical pasts of Sanskritic and Tamil epics, Puranic stories, and folktales, and of the pleasures and fantasy worlds of the cinematically mediated past, with its retinue of cultural heroes, celebrities, and film star–politicians; that is, visitors arrive at sites already knowing their significance, their context, and their histories. The appeal of Chennai's Government Museum typifies this. Although a standard offering on all circuits, the museum also serves the local population as a place for family outings and picnics. Although the chronological narrative represented by its collections is presented through labels composed in English and literary Tamil, I was told by the museum's staff and guides that the labels were read mostly by foreign tourists. Of more interest to Indian visitors were the collections themselves because of the opportunities they furnished to touch, literally, the remains of the region's ancient civilizations.

The tour guides who mediate these places and activities provided little in the way of interpretation; their duties involved managing the group's transportation, dining, and so forth. For their part, the domestic tourists who utilized TTDC and other private services generally did not expect interpretation; most came with their own understandings of the sites and the pasts they represented, which they gained orally and through television, cinema, popular and scholarly journals, and comic books. For its consumers, therefore, domestic tourism was a pleasurable way to fulfill various aims. People wished to teach their children about India's independence struggle and about Tamil Nadu's own form of cultural nationalism. They sought a particular deity's *darśan* or aimed to fulfill vows; they desired merit or blessings of a general sort or wished to satisfy specific wants or needs. Sometimes they wanted to consult special religious practitioners such as mediums or spiritual guides. Alongside these goals, they often intended to purchase special saris or carvings or to visit relatives; some simply wanted the experience of a thrill ride at an amusement park.

International Circuits

Affluent tourist-consumers (international as well as Indian elites), often escorted by Regional Guides like Asha and Lalitha, are routed to sites that celebrate southern India's imperial past and its present-day artisanship. Elite tourists generally find high-end accommodations near the city's financial and communications core areas.[42] In Nungambakkam, where Anglo-Indian bungalows once stood, there are now five-star hotels such as the Chola Sheraton Hotel and the Taj group's Coromandel Hotel. Their designs, like their names, evoke stereotypes of precolonial imperial opulence with their sumptuous guest rooms and lobbies, themed restaurants, bars, and clubs. Jewelry shops and boutiques are on the properties or within easy walking distance. There consumable heritage appears in the eighteen- and twenty-two-carat gold chains and gem-studded rings, necklaces, and bracelets, and also in the cotton and silk handloom textiles—bolts of running fabric, tablecloths, curtains, and napkins in addition to saris and salwar sets—displayed among brass utensils and figurines, and carved rosewood furniture. Picking up on a recently popularized heritage template in Europe and the U.S., an INTACH-published guide, *Madras: The Architectural Heritage*, outlines walking tours in different neighborhoods throughout the city.[43] The guide invites visitors to decode the complex history of this global city through its mix of vernacular, colonial, and modern architecture. Copies of this and other guidebooks are available in the hotels' gift shops.

Many international tourists have purchased tour packages that include locally furnished guide services. Regional Guides, like Urvashi, Asha, Ashok, and Lalitha, are engaged for these contracts. During the high season for international arrivals, November through February, many of Asha's workdays begin in

Figure 5.2. Bronze Gallery, Government Museum, Chennai. *Photograph by author.*

the lobby of one of Chennai's five-star hotels, where, dressed in a chic sari, she waits near the concierge desk to meet the group to whom she has been assigned escort. If the group is small, say, three or four people, they will travel in an air-conditioned Ambassador sedan or in one of the foreign makes, such as a Hyundai or Ford, now manufactured just outside the city. For larger groups, a Maruti van or small coach would be hired. When her group arrives, Asha introduces herself and inquires about preferences. Often European visitors wish to see colonial sites, the Fort Museum, the city's Christian churches. Asha told me about one woman keen to visit the cemetery near St Mary's Church at the Fort, where some of her own ancestors were buried. If the tourists have any interest in the region's history, she recommends that they stop at the Government Museum: "I can give them the whole picture that way, from the Indus Valley, through each dynasty, and on to the present. The bronzes, especially the Chola bronzes, are very good for this." It was not unusual for Asha to travel several times a week to Kanchipuram to show tourists the town's Pallava-era temples and assist them in purchasing handloom silk or cotton. Just as frequent were trips to Mamallapuram, a UNESCO World Heritage site, where, focusing on the most detailed of the site's bas-relief carvings, Arjuna's Penance, she would weave together the story of the Mahabharata epic and a narrative of India's pre-British history.

The same civilizational achievements that are mediated architecturally and artifactually at these sites are also represented in music and dance forms coded as classical and marketed to international visitors as emblems of the city's branded heritage. Since the 1920s the city has hosted an annual Music Festival during the Tamil month of *Māṟkaḻi* (mid-December to mid-January) dedicated to the performance of music and dance styles historically associated with upper-caste performers and patrons. As an artist herself, Asha, enjoys the opportunities to introduce tourists to these aspects of local culture:

> I have very strong interests in art, a strong feeling and attachment. Sometimes, I find that my involvement is at a different level than the tourists—they want a more superficial account. I have to monitor myself, to be sure that I don't go overboard.

Heritage sites, cultural and natural, are increasingly packaged for elite consumers as part of a resort experience. The five-star hotels in the city's center bill their services as all-inclusive, with boutiques, restaurants, spas, pools, and clubs contained within their (usually heavily guarded) grounds. Eager to follow the lucrative leads of Goa and, more recently, Kerala, Tamil Nadu's international tourism providers also emphasize beachfront resorts, catering to well-heeled international tourists and proffering consumable tradition in the form of handicrafts, folk performances, and themed environments within their precincts or in close proximity. These sites offer friction-free encounters with Tamil Nadu's "brand" with minimum contact with the Tamil citizens who live and work in the city.

Several themed cultural environments, located outside the city, are also part of elite tour circuits. DakshinaChitra, the outdoor museum and cultural center that opened in 1997, is the most renowned of these sites. Because this site is analyzed in detail in the next chapter, here I include just a few comments to place it within the geography of tourism. Located south of the city, it comprises reconstructed buildings, complete with furnishings and mannequins, arranged to represent southern Indian rural life in the nineteenth century. While representing "tradition," its exhibitionary praxis—similar to outdoor museums in North America, Europe, and Japan—is markedly modern (and, for some Tamilians, foreign) in function, spatial syntax, and design.

Lalitha, like Asha, escorted foreign tourists and occasionally Indian businessmen and government officials to DakshinaChitra once or twice a week during the high season. The entry fee (Rs.175 for foreigners) is high relative to that charged at other museums and some guides were critical of the value-for-price. Said Lalitha: "175 rupees? That's too much, especially for what it is. You can spend about an hour or an hour and a half there, max." She went on, "They've done it well, I won't deny that. But, if they are going to charge that much, they should have guides to give the explanation." Irked, perhaps, by the fact that employees were salaried and enjoyed health and retirement benefits, unlike Regional Guides, she then confided: "I decided that I would not escort the visitors into the houses anymore. I just take them to the reception and ask for one of the museum's own guides and let them take them through. Then, I go have some tea or have a look in the gift shop until they are finished."

More like the five-star hotels that its visitors patronize than domestic tourist attractions, DakshinaChitra is not included in tours conducted by the state's tourism department nor, with the exception of school groups to whom it offers free admission, is it patronized by the lower classes who make up the majority of Chennai's population. It is, however, prominently advertised in the brochures and guides available in the guest rooms of five-star hotels and in the guidebooks and Web sites consulted by foreign travelers, and increasingly by Chennai's own middle- and upper-class residents, where it receives stellar reviews as a "must-see."[44] In the context of Chennai-based tourism circuits, it sustains, extends, and makes materially real the rural idyll that the city's museums, hotels, restaurants, and guidebooks present as the region's past.

Although perceived, even by some Regional Guides, as "foreign," DakshinaChitra sits comfortably—by virtue of exhibitions as much as its location on the IT corridor south of the city—within a circuit of hotels and resorts that fold heritage into the tourist experience they offer. In the 1990s the Taj Group, a large hotel and resort chain, enlarged its Fisherman's Cove Resort, just south of DakshinaChitra, with craft shops, music and dance performances, and themed public spaces.[45] On a much smaller scale, some owners of ancestral properties in other towns have declared those buildings "heritage homes" and opened them to international tourists; Kanchi Kudil, the site mentioned in the epigraph to this chapter, is one such site. In some of these house museums, household items and furnishings are offered for sale in improvised gift shops; occasionally meals and overnight accommodations are provided.[46]

Affluent tourists, international and domestic, thus experience Chennai as a network of English-mediated, air-conditioned spaces that allude, materially, to an imperial past in architecture, furnishings, interior design, and cuisine. Tradition, in the form of ethnic authenticity, is delivered in handloom textiles and other artisanal products and performances; likewise, spirituality is on offer through the services of god-men, gurus, mediums, and astrologers. The mosaic of spaces at which they encounter these pieces of the past are organized into a linear, historicized chronology by guides, by tourism-oriented print and electronic media, and with the help of the glass-cased and labeled displays at the Government Museum. Images and narratives presented in the city anticipate and help frame the sights, sounds, and tastes encountered in the touristic spaces one comes across in travel circuits that extend beyond the city. Finally, in their accounts of regional history, elite guides may also embed genealogies of their own caste-based authority as indigenous literati and spokespersons for the region's classical forms of music, dance, drama, and material culture, thus performing acts of status production even while engaged in the waged labor and informal economies of service provision.

Alternative Circuits

Among the state's private providers, a minority has emerged with offerings styled as "alternatives" to the standard tourist fare. Like the elite agencies, they also target the international tourist market, but, working through networks of alternative tourism practice, they seek clients through NGOs, university-based organizations, and churches. The tour packages are tailored to the clients' goals and interests but typically include visits to craft cooperatives, self-help projects, and eco-resorts, combined with big-ticket attractions like large temple complexes or UNESCO World Heritage sites.

Urvashi had been engaged as a tour leader by one such agency, and she described the tour that she designed for a student group. She took them on the standard city tour—the Government Museum, the Fort, the Kapaleeswarar Temple—but included another stop not usually part of this circuit, the fishing community hamlet near San Thome:

> I want them to see how the fisherfolk live, what their way of life is and how they stick to it, even now. They don't value education, their only skill is building boats, fishing and they work hard, it's a hard life. It's not a pretty picture for the tourists, it's dirty and the fisherfolk, they are arrogant. Even still, they are vital in the city, so the tourists should see this. I make sure that they do!

The group she escorted had booked their tour with a local provider, Vanakkam Tours,[47] operated by Sanjeev Das since the early 1990s. Vanakkam specializes in bookings within the "alternative" stream of the international market. Sanjeev organizes and conducts the tours, and his wife, "Sarala," assists with bookings and accounts. Sarala, from Ahmedabad, studied history through the postgraduate level and is from a well-to-do non-Brahman family. Sanjeev has a degree in chemistry and hails from an affluent, low-caste Christian family. His previous career, with a U.S. multinational corporation, along with family resources has enabled him to maintain his business at a low-volume. "Culture" he told me, "is my hobby. I'm not trying to make a living doing this; it's a way to make tourists aware of what is really here, who Indians really are."[48]

An interest in philosophy and religion combined with his love of travel and the critique of capitalism developed while working for the multinational corporation drew him to alternative tourism. It began, he said, through a connection with an NGO, Equations, headquartered in Bangalore. Through them, he was introduced to the Oakland, California-based Center for Responsible Tourism, which, in turn, helped him broker contracts to provide tour services for a few small groups. He did not advertise, but by the late 1990s he had developed a small client list. He arranged tours for and escorted three or four groups annually, school and church groups as well as groups from nonprofit and fair trade organizations, whom he assists in their businesses by locating suppliers among local artisans. Typical of the latter, he told me, was

> a woman who runs an NGO [Global Village] in Japan that markets handloom textiles. She gets organic cotton from small growers in Nagpur and the cotton is then spun to thread, woven and dyed by a women's cooperative in southern India. I'll arrange her travel, take her around, help her get contacts for the work—things like that.

He considers that an important part of his work is educating foreigners about the real India, its history and the critiques of modernity and development that have been a part of that history. Thus he distributes books such as the Tamil classic, the *Tirukkural,* or the more recent, *Why I Am Not a Hindu,* by the Dalit activist Kancha Ilaiah.[49] Trips to conventional heritage sites, such as the Brihadeswara Temple in Tanjavur, are intermingled with visits to small-scale local industries (e.g., artisan cooperatives), to Dalit organizations, to musical performances. He described a tour he had organized for the employees of the above-mentioned NGO, a tour in which they encountered methods and materials that allowed for neither the standardization of product quality nor labor value:

> The tour is to reward the employees who perform well, but the NGO's customers can also join, for a fee.[50] I take them around to the craftspeople here, to the villages. They can see the actual materials and the techniques that the craftspeople use and the ways that they work, no regular workdays or production quotas. It makes them closer, it puts the employees in direct contact with the suppliers. Employees, customers, craftspeople—all of them are now more connected. Otherwise, the selling of these things, it's anonymous, isn't it?

These experiences are designed to privilege a real that is visceral and embodied. Sanjeev wants visitors to stay in villages and eat and live as villagers do, even if only for twenty-four hours. The phenomena that mainstream providers often encode as marks of the not-yet modern (i.e., dirt) here become matter-in-place, culturally grounded, identifying phenomena as opposed to the sanitized environs of resorts and heritage hotels. In Sanjeev's words, the latter may correspond to elite (often Brahmanical) representations of the region, but they do not encompass the full reality of southern India. The organizing trope, for Sanjeev's cultural intimacy, is work—the work of locals was the tourist product and signifier of an Indian real. He elaborated:

> Supporting organic cotton farmers and handloom and artisanal crafts is to bring to the attention of all industrialized moderns that it is these persons who historically generated the wealth of India and cotton was indeed the fabric of industrialization. . . . [T]he money looted and accumulated by exploiting this is what heralded the birth of the so-called industrial revolution in UK. Today these very wealth-creators whose craft and toil changed the face of the earth are at the bottom of the economic ladder driven to suicide. . . . My work with the fair trade movement to promote their products in the West and also in India springs from this concern.

The encounter with India that he sponsored was thus an encounter with laboring bodies, and with it he wanted to invite critical reflection about the political and moral economies that such work sustained.

While disparaging elite versions of Indian culture, however, Sanjeev remained skeptical about the claims of ethnic authenticity that pervade Hindu and Tamil nationalisms. As he observed: "I suppose that none of us is really Indian, are we? We're all in some identity crisis now, with globalization!" He attributes this, in part, to his own upbringing, characterizing himself as a "language orphan": "I think only in English and . . . so tend to be alienated from the majority of Tamils in my state and so tourism allows me to try to reconnect with what I have lost through the tourist as my vehicle!" Indeed, he told me that part of the pleasure in his work comes with sustaining the give and take of hybrid identity through his contacts with international tourists. For him, this ranged from acquiring new books, journals, or CDs to an occasional bottle of Jameson's whiskey. Within this mix, his aim is to create opportunities for visitors to engage directly with ordinary people and social activists, and to nurture local development paradigms, alternatives to those endorsed by the neoliberal state.

Though interested in a historicized chronological frame for the region, tourists in the alternative stream also seek direct contact with artisans and laborers, with co-religionists, and with educational and welfare associations and their clients. Cultural intimacy, forged through proximity and face-to-face engagement, generates a real that resists reification and invites tourists themselves to join in rueful self-recognition.

This chapter has outlined the major ways that memory, objectified as heritage and mediated in tourism, is produced as an effect of liberalization in Chennai—as a marketable legacy of objects, knowledges, relations, and spaces. It is not uncommon for popular discourses on "heritage" to relate changes in the urban-built environment to the influence of liberalization, as I have shown, in chapter 4, in the discussion of the Marundeeswarar Temple's conservation. Stalls, markets, sidewalk vendors, and shrines disappear as streets are widened and overpasses built to accommodate automobile traffic. Colonial-era public buildings fall into disrepair and are abandoned. Temple tanks are emptied as new water storage and distribution systems drain some sections of the city to enrich new industrial and residential areas elsewhere. Bungalows and street houses are demolished to make way for flat complexes, hotels, and malls. The poor are removed forcibly from settlements that they have called home for generations and are relocated at the city's outskirts. These absences are marked in discourses, such as narratives that describe the way a neighborhood once looked, and in images that contrast the presence of "then" with the absence of "now." These ghostly reminders of the past invite mourning and, at times, desires to conserve, refurbish, or violently remake some spaces or objects.

"Heritage," however, is not only that which is *lost;* it is *produced* and *marketed* in the context of economic development, as tourist product and as gentrifying status symbol. Tourism has become an especially important site for the work of memory in the neoliberal setting of the formal city and its peri-urban extensions. Tourism produces heritage by strategically crafting discourses of both modernity and tradition, framing the city as a destination for investment. "Modernity" is represented in its labor markets, amenities, and infrastructure, and in the touristic pleasure afforded by its accessibility, navigability, affordability, and safety. "Tradition," in the form of vernacular architecture, temples, handicrafts, and luxury goods describes a valuable tourist product that can be packaged for different class, ethnic, and national niches of the tourist market. Heritage-marked goods and services circulate among various class segments, signaling status achievements and aspirations through distinctions of taste among citizen-consumers and their international counterparts. Citizens, moreover, are invited to enact their identities through touristic action and sentiment, as both hosts and guests, as they adjust to everyday life in the formal city. The heritage-themed environment of DakshinaChitra, introduced here as part of the elite tourism circuit that connects Chennai to its hinterland, is examined in the next chapter as an illustration of the ways in which nostalgia is evoked within and against the formal city and its industrializing suburbs.

Toilet talk, a semantic point of entry for many tourists, was also this chapter's point of entry. Like other major industries, tourism was inaugurated as a state-sponsored enterprise, geared to the goal of national integration and designed to harness nationalist sentiment for the work of state formation. Domestic tourism was long the principal focus of India's Tourism Development Corporation, and it remains a major concern, even with the more concerted efforts to increase international tourist flows. In the contexts of tourism, as in other institutional areas of state formation, the designated hosts speak with the voice of the state, reiterating its (modernist) ambivalence about tradition. The cultural intimacy of toilet talk, however, also positions the speaker as a national subject, as a self-consciously modern Indian, who can recognize the residues of tradition in embodied practices and landscapes, and name them as "problems," linked to structural conditions of daunting poverty and inadequate housing. At the same time she herself, outside the spaces in which tourism's emotional labor is performed, may share that same tradition and its bodily habitus.

This attention to tradition, whether cast as irony or tragedy, takes account of the multiple others addressed. For the target audience of those tourists whose modernist sensibilities are imagined to be fully and seamlessly embodied, the tourist host mimes the stereotypes that express their distaste, with references such as Kannan's to the "Indian psyche," with its disregard for proper bodily comportment. But there is also another audience, not directly addressed, perhaps, but imagined by her as collateral listeners. They who are spoken about are also invited to participate in the emotional labor of hospitality, to see themselves as "stakeholders" and as tourist "hosts." This is made explicit in the newer efforts that look to tourism as an employment generator for unskilled and semi-skilled labor. In the cultural intimacy of toilet talk, *these* stakeholder-hosts might, in a moment of recognition, be persuaded or scolded into disavowing tradition, at least in the matter of toilets, and fall in line with the promises of neoliberalism.

6
Recollecting the Rural in Suburban Chennai

An Arrival

Nothing but a small sign, tinted in earth tones, announces that you have reached the entry of DakshinaChitra, a cultural center dedicated to the re-creation of southern India's premodern rural lifeways. The center, situated thirty kilometers south of Chennai, would be easy to miss, especially if you were distracted by the bold signage and amplified pop music spewing from the amusement park, MGM Dizzee World, that adjoins the site.[1] DakshinaChitra's different, though still global, exhibitionary order contrasts with the carnivalesque space of Dizzee World as well as with the actual villages surrounding it.

These contrasts are sharpened by DakshinaChitra's proximity to both kinds of space. Not only is it abutted by Dizzee World, an acoustic and visual presence that can be perceived from within DakshinaChitra's exhibition space, but real villages lie close at hand. The re-created vernacular structures that form the site's chief attractions are clustered several hundred meters east of the highway, concealed behind a low rise. Visible to passing travelers, however, is a squatter settlement that occupies the expanse of open land between the highway's edge and the parking lot built for DakshinaChitra's visitors.

You turn east into the center's access road and drive toward the ocean, arriving at a parking lot where a few other cars, a scooter, and the museum's van are parked. Your visit begins in the reception center that faces the parking area, with the purchase of an admission ticket. The young woman who greets you suggests that you begin your visit by viewing the orientation video, *A Vision of the South*, screened hourly in a small theater adjoining the entry lobby.[2] As you make your way to the theater, you notice the large, well-stocked gift shop, its shelves laden with bolts of handloom textiles and ready-made clothing, its display tables covered with handcrafted toys and musical instruments.

The video concludes and you leave the reception area, stepping outside into a large, semi-enclosed courtyard. Ahead you see an amphitheatre and snack bar, and, in the distance, a glimpse of the re-created village spaces that make up the site's outdoor exhibitions. Some are newly crafted replicas of traditional buildings; others are period structures that were disassembled on their original sites and rebuilt on DakshinaChitra's grounds. The exhibitions may remind you of open-air museums elsewhere in the world, and, as is the case at many of those institutions, DakshinaChitra's staff is ambivalent about characterizing the site as a museum. Its Web site banner proclaims it to be an event, a "celebration of culture," rather than simply a site.[3] Its own version of staged authenticity rests on its uneven capture of the rural real. Though lacking the costumed interpreters that serve both as guides and living exhibitions at other outdoor museums, DakshinaChitra's front regions are nonetheless filled with persons at work. Some, like the potter who demonstrates his craft, are part of the preïndustrial world of artisanal production, ecological sustainability, and tolerance that the center aims to re-create. Most, however, are laborers recruited from nearby villages to construct or maintain the exhibitions. In one house, the woman cleaning the floor with a twig broom greets you in Tamil with an invitation to "come inside," "*Uḷḷe vaṅka!*" Another woman rests on a verandah; two men trim shrubbery. In one of the site's unfinished exhibitions, a group of masons whitewash a wall, laughing loudly.

Conjunctures of urban and rural, local and global, suffuse DakshinaChitra. Nestled among villages now being transformed by the uneven penetration of urban infrastructure and services, the site comprises a montage of residues of other, more distant villages and towns. Indeed, despite having salvaged some of its exhibited structures from towns, the center uses displays of vernacular architecture, landscapes, and furnishings, as well as the living exhibition of laboring rural persons to create a simulacrum of *village* India. That generative trope of Indian nationalism, the almost-forgotten village, is made tangible. Insistently local, the site is nonetheless a fixed space of transnational culture. Created by and for the nostalgic gaze of cosmopolitan elites, national and transnational, it is laid out in the style of new, interactive museums across the globe. It exists as a space in which the rueful self-regard of cultural intimacy is leavened with and transmuted by nostalgia.

Heritage-themed environments like DakshinaChitra can now be found throughout the global South.[4] Many are found in urban hinterlands, the mosaics of villages and globalizing suburbs in which urban and rural lifeworlds are being rearticulated under neoliberal globalization. India now boasts Disney-style theme parks, craft villages, and historic homes and palaces. Such sites exist within a global exhibitionary complex that evokes the nation-state within a global order of nations.[5] The complex, however, has expanded from the museums, department stores, and expositions that mediated cultural projects of nation-state formation in the nineteenth century to encompass interactive and virtual museums, video arcades, theme parks, malls, and IMAX theaters. Using global technologies of memory, these newer sites consciously assert the possibility of a "local"—a local tied to particular representations of the past and affective orientations to the past—in a world of global consumer practice.

This chapter considers this problematic as it has unfolded in the social space of DakshinaChitra.[6] I am interested in the wider, affectively charged fields associated with neoliberal nostalgia, a formation that infuses not only the ersatz historicity attached to the names and facades of the new industrial landscape, but also the economy of heritage entrepreneurship and the practices of consumer-citizenship that it underwrites. I begin by situating DakshinaChitra within the globalizing suburban spaces of Chennai's hinterland. I then turn to the specific pasts that DakshinaChitra mediates, visually and materially, and to the forms of consumer-citizenship that underwrite those pasts. DakshinaChitra, I argue, illustrates the relations between the nostalgia that restructuring engenders and the roles that new exhibitionary complexes play in the expanding service sectors that have been hallmarks of neoliberal transformation.

Restructured Production and Recombinant Heritage

Global Appetites for Local Pasts

DakshinaChitra's international notoriety has often eclipsed its local profile. Coverage in Chennai's English-language press has expanded since its opening (1997), although its visitation levels lag behind those at the city's other large museums.[7] It has garnered international attention and accolades, however, with a sophisticated Web site, joint exhibitions at international venues, and international seminars.[8] Typical of the latter was an event I attended, "Old Cities, New Cultures," hosted jointly by the Friends of DakshinaChitra and the British Council, and held in Chennai in March 2000. It illustrated the sort of reaction formation that the heritage industry represents within the dynamics of neoliberal globalization. Deborah Thiagarajan, DakshinaChitra's founder and the president of the Madras Craft Foundation, the private nonprofit organization that administers the museum, was among the featured speakers.[9] Along with the other presenters, who included museum and arts administrators, journalists, performers, educators, and preservationists from India, Scotland, and England, she reiterated the by then widely circulated notion that entire cities can be packaged as tourist destinations with themed environments consisting of refurbished public and commercial spaces and planned events like festivals and walking tours.[10]

During the Chennai seminar, both the Edinburgh Festival and Glasgow's designation as U.K. City of Architecture and Design were discussed alongside DakshinaChitra as templates for salvaging the material past from the creative destruction wrought by global capitalism. Participants just as easily might have pointed to Boston's Fanueil Hall or Singapore's Chinatown to name only two among many well-publicized examples of this sort of refurbishment. Such themed spaces, which often serve as anchors for what Dennis Judd has called the "tourist bubble," present selective accounts of local, regional, and national histories through carefully wrought montages of visual images, narratives, and built environments.[11] These accounts, usually framed as "heritage," celebrate and advertise the culturally distinctive, but always safe, comprehensible, and consumable, experiences that urban encounters can offer. Those assembled were optimistic about transferring global models of heritage entrepreneurship to India, and some identified comparable, albeit nascent, ventures already initiated in Chennai and other Indian cities.[12]

Like the urban arts and heritage districts, interactive museums, and festivals discussed at the 2000 seminar, DakshinaChitra was designed as an environment in which heritage preservation and commodity consumption could be tightly interwoven. Like them, it responded to the exigencies and challenges of a national economy characterized by increasing levels of consumption, expanding service and manufacturing sectors, and the deregulation of industry and trade. DakshinaChitra, unlike most museums in India, is privately operated and receives limited state support. Relative to open-air museums in Europe and North America, its entry fees are modest (although higher than other Indian museums).[13] That, coupled with low visitation, means that the center has had to secure funds for its operations, capital expenses, and endowment through focused solicitation and grant writing.[14] Using sophisticated advertising techniques, it targets national and foreign elites as both investors and visitors. The museum's interactive Web site is an important gateway for the museum's translocal audience and potential donors, providing virtual tours, handicraft sales, events scheduling, and donation opportunities.

Although DakshinaChitra encourages and facilitates school group visitation, including public school children, most of the museum's visitors and supporters are part of a foreign or domestic elite, and it is to their tastes that DakshinaChitra's exhibitions, sale items, and performances correspond. DakshinaChitra quickly became a popular destination within the circuits of leisure travel and consumption that, in and around Chennai, connect the five-star hotels, upscale boutiques, and art galleries of the urban tourist bubble with selected heritage sites.[15]

The center's administration and managerial staff, like its donors and visitors, represent the stratum of urban elites who have been most advantaged by India's liberalization. The center's founder is an American citizen.[16] She has lived in Tamil Nadu since the early 1970s, following her marriage to a Tamil man, a banker and member of a prominent Nattukottai Chettiar family.[17] Most other members of the museum's upper-level, managerial, and educational staff hail from one of the south Indian states and are members of the region's globally connected elite. Like educated, nationalist elites of the past century, and in some cases their actual descendents, most have lived, worked, or been schooled abroad or elsewhere in India. They are literate in both English and Tamil, and some speak other languages. Many are tied by kinship, occupation, and educational experiences to the museum's affluent base of visitors and donors.

DakshinaChitra's reliance on elite sponsorship and audiences is evident in its exhibitionary modes, which rely on templates drawn from metropolitan museums in India and abroad. These forms of representation make its projects legible within global discourses on heritage. It is, for the most part, an English-mediated space, notwithstanding bilingual signage and labels, and the large number of front-line personnel—craftspersons, housekeepers, gardeners, and drivers—who speak only

Tamil. The site's spatial syntax, which corresponds to that found in other interactive museums throughout the world, will also be familiar to its cosmopolitan visitors. To reach its open-air exhibition and performance spaces, visitors are routed by a gift shop and theater, both placed near the main entry, and then past the snack bar that lies in the threshold space between the entry regions and the outdoor exhibitions. The site's exhibition areas are themselves bifurcated, with artifact display cases and a rotating exhibition of contemporary art in the reception region, adjacent to offices and seminar rooms. The outdoor exhibitions are organized in accordance with newer norms, as immersive spaces of interactive pedagogy and performance. As is also found in newer types of museal spaces, continuities exist between DakshinaChitra's curatorial and commercial components: it has a well-stocked gift shop from which visitors can select hand-crafted goods of the sorts displayed in the houses; cassettes of its orientation video program are available for purchase; and the museum grounds can be hired by outside parties for benefits and other events, such as weddings and banquets.

DakshinaChitra's global template has earned both praise and derision, with some conservation architects and cultural tourism proponents calling it a "Disneyfied" version of south India's past. Thiagarajan herself acknowledges the influences of sites in the United States, Europe, Japan, and Rumania on DakshinaChitra's formation but traces her commitment to the project to deeply felt concerns about the loss of vernacular architectural, performance, and craft traditions with the rapid industrialization of the south.[18] She is quoted on the center's Web site: "From 1970–1998, I traveled extensively to villages in Tamilnadu. . . . I understood that artists were turning away from these arts because of lifestyle changes and lack of appreciation of their skills. Something needed to be done . . . and I knew I had a role to play."[19] She intends DakshinaChitra as a critique of the effects of liberalization, a force that she, like many, associates with the homogenization of place and the collapse of history. Nonetheless, under her direction, the center approaches conservation as an entrepreneurial activity, governed by competitive norms of private enterprise. Thiagarajan expects that the mix of leisure, consumption, pedagogy, and performance that DakshinaChitra represents will ensure its financial stability and success, and so contribute to sustaining the ongoing evolution of southern India's distinctive artisanal traditions. The museum, in short, is premised unabashedly on consumerist hopes, sharing with pro-liberalization businesspersons and analysts the expectation that by enhancing economic growth, a free-market economy will revitalize local cultural production and conservation.

A National Locality

DakshinaChitra's very existence is indicative of the gentrification that has transformed Chennai's hinterland. It is located along a new industrial corridor that connects Chennai with points south: the UNESCO World Heritage site of Mamallapuram, and the ports, industrial estates, fish farms, and power facilities beyond. Most of these developments date from the early 1970s, when India's central government established the Indira Gandhi Center for Atomic Research in Kalpakkam, a village about eighty kilometers south of Chennai.[20] The corridor's development accelerated in the mid-1980s, with the addition of the Madras Atomic Power Station to Kalpakkam's research center and a wave of residential and commercial construction.[21] Within a decade, information and bio-technology campuses and gated communities appeared.[22] Capitalizing on the success of new information technology ventures and on the pool of professional talent associated with the Chennai branch of the elite Indian Institute of Technology, the region is now aggressively promoted as India's Biotech Valley. Its name, a deliberate play on San Jose's Silicon Valley, where thousands of ambitious Indian professionals settled in the 1980s and 1990s, holds out the possibility of globalization in a nationalist key. By pressing forward with such ventures, Tamil Nadu's ruling parties and its corporate sector hope to retain those skilled workers who once traveled abroad for high-paying employment and to repatriate the resources, affective and financial, of India's diaspora, especially affluent Non-Resident Indians.

DakshinaChitra's own origins can be traced to the same forces—deregulation, privatization, decentralization—that have been responsible for the transformation of the corridor between Chennai and Mamallapuram (see chapter 2). Planning for DakshinaChitra commenced in the mid-1980s, contemporaneous with a cautious turn toward liberalization by the Indian state. Central and state governments lent token support to DakshinaChitra's development at this point, but the bulk of funding for the site's development was solicited from private donors and from educational and philanthropic foundations. In 1997, when the site opened, neoliberal policies were firmly in place. Like other private businesses and deregulated government agencies, DakshinaChitra has continued to seek investors from the private multinational corporate sector, from international foundations, and, increasingly, from among India's own mobile, cosmopolitan elites, especially NRIs who are tapped as underwriters and nostalgic consumers of India's territorial past.[23]

Together, the social space of DakshinaChitra and the peri-urban development to which it has contributed call attention to the ways that globalization has reorganized the relations between city and countryside in the postcolonial world. Just as global cities serve as command and control centers in a global economy, so, too, have various spaces in the urban periphery, variously known as suburban, ex-urban, and peri-urban, been formed in the convergence of national and transnational cultural and economic flows. Anthony King has been particularly attentive to the globalization of suburbia in the postcolonial world. Following Hopkins, he has referred to these spaces, which include gated communities, resorts, and corporate campuses, as "postcolonial globurbs," defining them as:

> Forms and settlements on the outskirts, origins of which (social, economic, cultural, architectural) are generated less by developments in city or even in country and more by external forces . . . in form of imperialism, colonialism, nationalism and diasporic migratory cultures and capital flows.[24]

Like suburbs that preceded them, globurbs continue to be represented by their developers and residents as spaces apart from both the failed modernism of nearby cities and the stagnant "localism" that pervades surrounding villages and towns.[25]

DakshinaChitra corresponds in form and function to the settlements, such as gated communities and industrial campuses, that typify the postcolonial globurb. It is enclaved and exclusive while still globally connected; its spatial syntax and amenities are tailored to meet international standards of comfort and efficiency. DakshinaChitra, along with other globurban outcrops, makes up a "landscape of consumer modernity" (after Taylor) in which combinations of then and now, here and there, enable developers to engage with diasporic cultures and capital flows, to attract investors and clients with promises of both status and nostalgia.[26] On these sites, the global aspirations of both the state and corporate sector are inscribed within a national narrative articulated with neoliberal globalization. DakshinaChitra, no less than the glass-and-steel campus of Cognizant IT Solutions, a multinational business outsourcing firm also located along the corridor stretching southward from Chennai, is meant to be a space in which the nation—refurbished, lean, competitive—could be exhibited and celebrated within a wider world of nations.[27] What distinguishes DakshinaChitra from its avowedly modernist neighbors is its evocation of the nation through material signs of (rural) absence, through the performance and discourse of salvage, and its solicitation of affective commitment to the nation through the mournful reenactment of loss and recovery.

Continuities exist between the national imaginary embodied in DakshinaChitra's material and performative landscapes and that found in other craft-oriented museums in India. Its template and closest precursor is New Delhi's National Handicrafts and Handlooms Museum, popularly known as the Indian Crafts Museum. The Crafts Museum, managed by the central government, was founded originally in 1956 but was expanded and reorganized in the mid-1980s. It curates representative craft products, conserves craft techniques, and facilitates the marketing of crafts to urban consumers.[28] The Crafts Museum's "living" exhibitions include a rotating roster of craft producers recruited from all over India to conduct on-site demonstrations for visitors. The Crafts Museum's mission is framed, explicitly, by the official nationalism of the postcolonial Indian state; accordingly, it represents India as a mosaic of distinct regional cultures and languages, and it treats crafts and performing arts as the emblems of India's "unity-in-diversity." It participates in state formation in more pragmatic ways as well; its on-site craft demonstrations, marketing, and fairs are among the institutional mechanisms by which the state enacts its commitment to rural development.

DakshinaChitra, though distinct from the Crafts Museum in its regional orientation, is similarly committed to the tropes of the nation-as-mosaic and the village as wellspring of national community. What state funding it receives has come from the Development Commissioner for Handicrafts, which has awarded regular grants to DakshinaChitra for its craft education and marketing operations. By encapsulating the diversity and common threads of southern India, it claims a place for the south *within* the territorial bounds and official cultural narrative of the nation-state. More than that, it redeploys a regional stereotype—the conservatism of southern India—to create an exemplar of a possible India.

DakshinaChitra has mined the past of southern India for narratives of national possibility. Its national imaginary avoids the Tamil exceptionalism that lies at the heart of Dravidianist public culture, and, not surprisingly, Tamil Nadu's state government has shown little interest in its programs.[29] DakshinaChitra re-creates southern India as a space of artisanal lifeworlds, ethnic pluralism, Hindu religiosity, and self-sustaining consumption. Its account updates the well-worn trope of Gandhian nationalism, the village republic, with a dose of cosmopolitanism. Though the anticolonial nationalism of Mohandas Gandhi is not explicitly invoked at DakshinaChitra, the center's re-created rural world resonates with the popular imagery of Gandhism. Gandhi envisioned independent India as a polity based not on the European nation-state but rooted in the self-sufficient "village republics" that he considered indigenous to the South Asian subcontinent.[30] Central to this vision were the small-scale settlements and craft-based economic institutions of the sorts that DakshinaChitra presents as emblems of southern Indian history. Though Gandhian nationalism has had a negligible impact on the economic and social policies on the postcolonial Indian state, the imagery and keywords of Gandhism have been invoked repeatedly by elected officials and by government institutions to characterize their own nationalist commitments and values, particularly in discourses on the management and representation of India's rural communities. DakshinaChitra's vision of southern India draws liberally on these same values and images.

A genealogy for a globally connected nation is fashioned by appealing to craft as both sign of and modality for the imagined national community. With this, DakshinaChitra constitutes southern India as the subject of a new national narrative. India's turn to neoliberalism is rewritten within DakshinaChitra's immersive specular order not as the latest chapter of colonially engineered loss of self but as the retrieval of an indigenous trajectory that encompassed but did not originate with European imperialism.

Technologies of Memory

Though ceremonially unveiled in December 1996, DakshinaChitra was only opened to visitors in early 1997.[31] My first visit, in November 1996, was to a museal space that was entirely a back region: it was a busy workplace where masons, carpenters, and electricians maneuvered around one another, amid partially laid footpaths, piles of bricks, and stacks of wooden beams. The center's Tamil Nadu and Kerala sections were close to completion; the Tamil region even included a small Ayyanar temple, built in 1992. Later visits, in 1999 and 2000, brought me to a more populous, built-up but still incomplete site, where educational programming was already entwined with fund-raising. By 2007 the museum's outdoor exhibitions comprised nineteen buildings—houses, outbuildings, and shrines—distributed among its four "states," although the Karnataka and Andhra Pradesh

Figure 6.1. Courtyard houses, Tamil Nadu section, DakshinaChitra. *Photograph by author.*

sections remained incomplete. Each section's spatial organization, construction materials, and design were chosen to be representative of regional ecology and social organization, and all exhibitions, with the exception of Karnataka's and a projected section of Andhra Pradesh, depicted rural settlement forms. Footpaths meandered within and between the regional exhibitions, with no explicit boundaries marked between "states."

The museum's layout was the product of a conceptual plan prepared by the architect Laurie Baker and implemented by DakshinaChitra's site architect, Benny Kuriakose, one of Baker's associates. Baker was India's foremost proponent of cost-effective architecture, an approach based on local materials, environmental adaptability, and affordability, and inspired by a commitment to Gandhian nationalism, with its norms of self-sufficiency and limited consumption.[32] DakshinaChitra's endorsement of cost-effectiveness is evident in the decision to retain and reconstruct existing building stock, in the textual and visual references to the ecological sustainability of premodern lifeways that are spread throughout the museum, and in the museum's attention to artisanal modes of production. As I discuss later, however, it has been more selective in its implementation of the methods of work that Baker advocates.

With its eight buildings, Tamil Nadu's is the densest exhibition; in addition to the above-mentioned temple, residences of wealthy merchant and agriculturalist families, Brahmans, skilled craftspersons, and laborers are represented. The most integrated presentation of the principles of sustainability and adaptation are found in a gallery attached to one of the rebuilt houses. The exhibit has five sections

Figure 6.2. Thatch house, Tamil Nadu section, DakshinaChitra. *Photograph by author.*

Figure 6.3. House in Kerala section, DakshinaChitra. *Photograph by author.*

based on the metaphoric landscapes according to which classical Tamil poetry is typologized: forests, mountains, cultivated fields, seashore, and desert waste.[33] In poetics, each region is associated with certain plants, deities, seasons, and kinds of love. In the gallery, each landscape depiction combines references to classical poetry, ecology, and human modes of subsistence, using poetic excerpts, samples of agrarian tools, and handicrafts, and enlarged photos of landscapes, buildings, and their inhabitants.

"Kerala" is sparsely settled in comparison with "Tamil Nadu." It features three residences—a Syrian Christian house and two Hindu dwellings from northern and southern Kerala—and a separate granary and cowshed. Unlike the densely settled village of the Tamil section, Kerala's depicts the rural settlement pattern of that region's landowning class, with dispersed residential compounds graced by sloping roofs and wide verandahs. Each house is surrounded by open lands and cross-cut by water channels. The Karnataka section, unfinished as of 2007, consists of two residences (part of a single domestic compound) and a shrine, and depicts the home of an extended family of weavers. To complete that exhibit, four additional structures were sought, including a colonial bungalow. Finally, Andhra Pradesh is represented by a weaver's house and a cluster of two, circular, mud-walled huts typical of the modest homes of coastal fishing communities. In 2007 it, too, remained unfinished, with three more structures, including a Muslim house, sought to complete that exhibition.

Although its administration chafes at DakshinaChitra's designation as a "museum," faulting the term as both derivative and deadening, the site shares with other museal spaces a focus on the collection. Its reconstructed buildings form a taxonomically ordered whole that refers, metonymically and mimetically, to southern India. The most inclusive category, the ethnic and linguistic state, comprises households, each defined by cross-cutting socio-demographic characteristics (occupation, community, sect, wealth). The taxonomic logic of the collection is also asserted in the breach, with frequent references on the museum's grounds and on its Web site to *gaps* in its offerings. The incompleteness of both the Andhra and Karnataka sections, for example, is acknowledged by detailed descriptions of the structures that should be added but that still remain outside the boundaries of DaksinaChitra. These not-yet-salvaged casualties of industrialization await the proper care and conservation that the museum will afford. The Web site includes appeals for assistance in locating appropriate structures and for financial support for the work of disassembly and reconstruction:

> Help us complete the Heritage Houses collection. . . . What can you do? You could give us information about the . . . houses if they are available for relocation to DakshinaChitra. In cases where we have already identified the house you could help in donating towards the relocation/building of the house at DakshinaChitra.[34]

In alerting visitors, virtual and actual, to still empty spaces, the museum communicates the rationality of its own organization and planning apparatus; it also enrolls its cosmopolitan patrons in commodified memory work by asking them to donate by adopting houses, crafts, and educational programs. As it builds its collection, then, DakshinaChitra completes the cycle of creative destruction: gathering the residues of industrial expansion and enrolling its active agents and beneficiaries in the work of imagining and conserving heritage.

Authentically Postcolonial

With its mix of vernacular structures, exhibition galleries, and demonstration and performance spaces, DakshinaChitra is reminiscent of open-air museums elsewhere in India, as well as in Europe, the United States, Japan, and Southeast Asia. As is the case on these other sites, DakshinaChitra's immersive exhibitionary space represents a regional and historical whole by reordering and displaying fragments of that whole. The center produces the effect of rural reality through its "creative geography," its carefully wrought spatio-temporal montage.[35] Unlike some of its foreign counterparts, however, it does not claim to represent a discrete temporal span (e.g., the continuous present of 1627 at Plimoth Plantation). Instead, its exhibitions span the late-eighteenth to the mid-twentieth century, framing that vaguely bounded period of intensive British colonization as a "before" for which the creative destruction of the present is the terminus ante quem. That "before" is embedded, literally, in DakshinaChitra's recombinant rural real, with salvaged originals and painstakingly reproduced copies.

The real south India to which it lays claim was, in the mid-nineteenth century, an agrarian, artisanal society, albeit one embedded within larger imperial networks of commerce, industry, and administration. The museum tracks the effects of colonial modernity on regional life-worlds with a historical narrative built through in-context strategies, such as labels, audio-visual guides, and catalogs, that frame the built environment as a collection and furnish visitors with interpretive principles.[36] The merchant house in the Tamil section is one of the spaces used to develop this theme. It was the ancestral home of the Nattukottai Chettiar family and, like other such residences, had been built with earnings acquired by participation in colonial trading networks.[37] Such houses, along with patronage extended to temples, choultries, and schools, were means by which the wealth acquired by the community was transmuted into status. Texts posted on the website and on the museum grounds elaborate on these relations, using the hybrid material culture of the dwellings—their Burmese teak columns and European tiles, their architectural plans that fused colonial bungalow and palace—to comment on the range of transactions, between colonizer and colonized, brokered by the merchant community.[38] The Syrian Christian house, in the Kerala section, acknowledges similar hybrid origins. In these ways DakshinaChitra, like other new museums in India, claims a specifically postcolonial genealogy that recognizes the spatio-temporal ruptures of colonial modernity even while asserting the possibility of a nationalist future built on material continuities with both colonial and precolonial pasts.

The linchpin of its enactment of postcoloniality, however, is DakshinaChitra's employment of in-situ representational conventions with its reconstructed dwellings and on-site workers.[39] Thiagarajan has emphasized, in conversation with me and in published texts, that the museum's immersive environment is both a window on the region's preindustrial, artisanal economy and an incubator for maintaining those bodies of knowledge and practice. Craft, she argues, is not rote reproduction but a body of knowledge and practice based on continuous adaptation and innovation. Like the eco-museum as conceived by Pierre Rivière, DakshinaChitra treats cultural knowledge and artifacts as the means to cultivate and assert community identity.[40] It is, nonetheless, craft as object—its production professionalized and its circulation commodified—that fills the center. And distinguishing its personnel from costumed interpreters elsewhere who merely perform authenticity, DakshinaChitra asserts that craftspersons, as living signifiers of preindustrial India, prove that while the world of "before" may have been forgotten by inattentive urban elites, it is not yet past.

The Aura of the Copy

DakshinaChitra's reality effect rests on rhetorical strategies that are mediated both materially and discursively. Its incorporation of originals, treated as relics, is carefully marked in texts, labels, and on its Web site. The auratic quality with which residues of originals are outfitted invites engagement with Benjamin's well-known formulation of the properties of "the work of art in the age of mechanical reproduction," especially the "tactile seeing" that the center's immersive environment and technologically enhanced vision (e.g., its video and Web site) ensure.[41]

DakshinaChitra, like other living museums that aim for mimetic realism through a combination of salvage and reproduction, exemplifies what Benjamin argued was a resurgence of the mimetic faculty within the commodity form.[42] In another, incomplete work, the notes assembled as *The Arcades Project*, Benjamin pursued this phenomenon in the commodity landscape of the Parisian arcades, seeing those spaces as dialectical images in which old and new interpenetrate, and in which the wish images of capitalism and its residues are conjoined.[43] Brought into being within the technological and economic orders of modernity, heritage-themed environments reengage the mimetic faculty, through "dialectical images" that evoke and satiate nostalgia. Among these dialectical images are exhibited materials (the reconstructed originals) and the mass-mediated visual representations (photographs, videography, digital images) that provide interpretive frameworks for both actual and virtual visitors. These dialectical images, like their precursors in the Parisian arcades, register the simultaneous absence and presence of the past by copying and offering contact with its residues within the immersive, multimedia environment that forms the global template for new, interactive museums.

Within DakshinaChitra's immersive order, several rhetorical strategies are deployed to produce the effect of the real. These strategies include the *mimesis* of the mirror image, the *metonymy* of the reassemblage, and the *typicality* of the statistically normative. Eight buildings referred metonymically to rural originals.[44] These structures had been reassembled on DakshinaChitra's grounds from materials culled from period structures dispersed across southern India. Five of these buildings had been disassembled at their original sites and reassembled on-site; the others were recombinant structures in which new structural elements were augmented by features such as doors or windows salvaged from one or more period buildings scheduled for demolition or in disrepair.[45] The remaining eleven structures were wholly new re-creations that mimicked vernacular structures. Some, like the Ayyanar shrine (Tamil Nadu) and the weavers' houses (Andhra Pradesh), were detailed copies of specific buildings, with identical features, plans, and dimensions. Others sought authenticity by virtue of statistical typicality, by re-creating vernacular styles deemed representative of particular regional or occupational communities.[46]

DakshinaChitra's authenticity, however, was not solely a matter of architectural style or materials but depended on the presence, in back and front regions of the site, of laboring bodies, mainly rural artisans and locally recruited maintenance staff persons. Among these laboring bodies, moreover, are visitors themselves, whose participation in hands-on craft and performance workshops is also framed as a means by which craft traditions are sustained. What I am calling the aura of the copy depended critically on the center's exposition of back-region activities, especially the employment of rural artisans in on-site construction activity. Just as the structures are metonymically and statistically *of* particular regions, so also were many of the craftsmen recruited to rebuild them.

Consider the somatically encoded authenticity attributed to the Ayyanar shrine in the site's Tamil Nadu section. That shrine is modeled on another Ayyanar shrine, located in a village south of DakshinaChitra, though the logic of its replication arises from Hindu praxis rather than museological conventions. New Hindu temples are often constructed as offshoots of existing ones. Their actual construction involves ritualized transfers of substances, such as soil and icons, between the donor temple and the site under construction. For DakshinaChitra's temple exhibit, the priest of an existing Ayyanar village temple had been engaged as a builder. The museum's Web site makes careful note of the builder's priestly status and the ritual procedures he followed in erecting the new temple:

> To prepare for the shrine, the neem tree, itchli tree, peepul tree, banyan tree and *vembu maram,* were planted at the site, in accordance with the priest's instructions. Back in Melkapoondi, the priest did a *pūja* (with beads and bones) to ascertain whether the god was willing for another shrine to be built. He was. Then the priest came to Madras to see if the DakshinaChitra site suited Ayyanar. It did.[47]

With these sanctifying procedures, DakshinaChitra's shrine was no less real than any other Ayyanar temple.

A similar reality effect is sought by employing regional artisans in exposed back regions. This technique conforms to the architect Laurie Baker's emphasis on local materials and knowledge but recontextualizes it within museal space. As a case in point, one might consider the on-site construction activities. Encoded in the rubric of cost-effectiveness is the notion that construction is done by and for those who reside in and use the space. Baker advised that the architect generate a conceptual plan which he or she then brings to fruition as built form by working with builders and modifying as needed, making the end result a materialization of a series of interactions rather than an objectification of the architect's idea.[48] At DakshinaChitra, Baker's design principles are retained but, as noted earlier, the modes of work he advocates are not. Uneven skill levels are partially responsible. For example, Thiagarajan told me that workers from Kerala had been able to reconstruct that state's exhibition area in its entirety but that Tamil workers had shown less skill in the execution of vernacular design. She ascribed the difference to the more extensive use of industrialized methods of construction in Tamil Nadu. Besides uneven skill levels, the center's administrators also cite reasons of efficiency and cost control, for the dialogic relation between architect and builders advocated by Baker usually results in longer construction times than are typical in conventional work.

Although the built environment of DakshinaChitra creates an architectural shell in which the past can be evoked, the presence of the past, its immediacy, veracity, and authenticity, rests on the distribution of bodies at work throughout the exhibitionary complex and on strategic merging of front and back regions that labor reveals. In frankly acknowledging its mix of period originals with recently fabricated copies, DakshinaChitra asserts authenticity not in spite of these recombinant forms but because of them, especially the labor, both of research and construction, that they represent and the participation in the neoliberal order that they make possible. The persons hired as front-region performers make obvious contributions to this project, but those brought on-site as construction and maintenance workers are also enrolled, as are visitors themselves. Together, these different categories of people and the work they do dominate the site's specular order and, as they traverse front and back regions, their presence endows the copy with auratic value that subsumes and eclipses that of the original.

The Mediated Past

A Vision of the South

DakshinaChitra's recall of southern India's rural past is meant to be an instructive and nostalgia-infused contrast with the urban present of Chennai. Visual technologies, its orientation video in particular, are critical to its mission, especially in the absence of on-site interpreters. The video contains the visual and narrative cues that allow viewers to frame their on-site experience in terms of a re-embedding in regional, national, and familial pasts. The orientation video, *A Vision of the South,* uses English subtitles and voice-over to introduce the region to an English-speaking audience.[49] Its segments include "A Day in a South Indian Home," "Harmony with Nature," which depicts the annual Hindu festival cycle, and "Cycle of Life," which presents the individual life cycle as bracketed by Sanskritic Hindu ritual. It introduces India's southern states with images of cultural performances set against rural backdrops and with emblematic landscapes—Tamil Nadu's mountainous interior, Kerala's lush coastal backwaters—anticipating the environmentalist message of the outdoor exhibitions.[50] The opening images of ocean and mountain are accompanied by a voiceover recitation of passages from the Rg Veda confirming humans' inseparability from nature; the reliance on natural foodstuffs and agricultural techniques is asserted in "A Day in a South Indian Home"; "Harmony with Nature" outlines the natural cyclical pattern of temple and domestic ritual. Contemporary environmentalism is thus outfitted with indigenous (and, implicitly, Hindu) roots.

Throughout the video, visual elements—landscapes, buildings, and bodies—are juxtaposed to contrast the "now" of modernity and city life with the "then" of tradition and village life, and to interweave DakshinaChitra's rural simulacrum with the rural real beyond its grounds. Scenes of present-day Chennai are visual foils that establish distance between "then" and "now," and sharpen nostalgic desire for "then." Modernity is represented as a time and place of anonymous crowds as distinct from the smaller-scale, implicitly familial world of the past. Spaces coded as modern are filled with images that connote the atomization and rapid pace of urban existence and its degraded quality of life: exhaust-spewing cars and scooters, department stores, and garbage-filled streets.

Whereas the world of "now" is set in contemporary Chennai, DakshinaChitra's reconstructed buildings serve as sets for many of the scenes from "then." In scenes shot on the museum grounds, actors are shown pursuing tasks deemed typical of premodern village life—meals are prepared and eaten, and life cycle rituals performed. Life is shown bounded by familial and ritual concerns, even as villagers' incipient nationalism and awareness of their place in Britain's colonial empire are signaled with visual devices such as newspaper headlines.

The video represents southern India as an imperial borderland and as a space of caste, sectarian, and occupational difference. It nonetheless emphasizes solidarity over conflict or exploitation and locates that solidarity in upper-caste cultural hegemony. In a region known for the success and longevity of non-Brahman political movements and parties, and for periodic eruptions of populist anti-Brahmanism, the video reiterates Brahmans' own claims to be exponents of southern Indian culture. Affinities, in tastes, modes of piety, cultural endowments, between Brahmans and other high-caste communities, such as Chettiars, are established as well.

We learn from the video that the past continues to be lived in some twentieth-century lives. Upper-caste communities are depicted as leading lives that are infused by cultural sensibilities of the past, as sharing (perhaps inspiring) the museum's mission. The Brahman dwelling in the Tamil section, salvaged from Tirunelveli district near the temple city of Madurai, is shown in the video as a space in which Hindu ritual binds southern India's past and present. In footage that depicts the rituals of house building and domestic life, we learn, through voiceover, that DakshinaChitra has retrieved and restaged these practices in the course of constructing its own exhibitions. We also learn that the twice-born body—performing Vedic ritual, preparing vegetarian meals, adorned with the sacred thread, attired in nine-yard saris—is a repository of southern Indian culture.

Other lower-caste non-Brahmans are introduced as craft producers, and caste relations are portrayed as governed by functional, integrative, and unconflicted interdependence. The video invites viewers to recognize that craft, no less than Brahmanic ritual practice, is an index of the socio-moral values and material concerns that bound preindustrial communities in the past and offer the promise of solidarity in the future.

As the video rolls, however, it becomes apparent that its real work is not in the establishment of contrast between then and now but rather in establishing DakshinaChitra as a site of *continuity* between then and now. The visual vocabulary of difference is recomposed to create identity between DakshinaChitra's built environment and the pastness of the rural. Scenes shot at the museum and in Chennai's streets, temples, and homes, for example, use the same actors.[51] Gradual fades between scenes also diminish the differences between staged events on the museum grounds and naturalistic footage shot on location in Chennai. Further, throughout the video, rural footage alternates with that shot at DakshinaChitra. The museum's mimetic relation to rural life is asserted not only with landscape but even more insistently with bodily labor, for example, in a series of scenes that shift between potters at work on location, in Pudukottai district, and DakshinaChitra's master potter, Ramu Velar, at work on the museum grounds.

By oscillating between the presentation and dissolution of spatio-temporal difference, the video suggests that DakshinaChitra is not a passive mirror of rural lifeways but the key to their persistence—that rural lifeways are more real at the center than they are in the countryside. Images of empty, seemingly deserted village homes, for example, are followed with images of such activities as construction or basket-weaving at DakshinaChitra. Such sequences imply that although traditions may be lost in the real world, they persist within the center's precincts. Indeed, while such images are metaphors for the museum's work, they are not only that. They remind viewers of the actual work of retrieving and reconstructing rural buildings undertaken by the museum, and solicit their affective and financial commitments to such projects.

The Gender of Memory

Among the most plaintive and affecting images of the video are those of women. Femininity, especially as embodied by mothers and grandmothers, is often deployed as a touchstone for personal and community pasts. In the video, women recur in the "then" scenes of village life. In "A Day in a South Indian Home," women's ritualized labor, namely, cooking and worship, creates a leisured, unhurried temporality and spatiality. Women's bodies, adorned with aesthetic emblems (nine-yard sari, *kuṅkumam,* jewelry) that encode their esteemed status as upper-caste *cumaṅkali,* women with living husbands, are signs of this past and its persistence. Women's work brings the past to presence.

Images of such women provide visual continuity and narrative anchors, as figures of loss and recovery. In the video's opening sequence, after its evocation of the Vedic account of creation, the scene shifts to the interior courtyard of a large traditional home, in actuality the reconstructed Nattukottai Chettiar house in the Tamil Nadu section of DakshinaChitra. The foreground holds an elaborately carved and polished wooden swing, suspended from the ceiling with heavy chains. Swings like this can be found in older, more affluent homes and carry a strong mnemonic charge because of their association with Hindu mythology and with weddings, during which newly wedded couples swing together in a ritualized reenactment of the amorous play of Krishna and Radha. The camera remains trained on the woman on the swing as she rocks pensively; her downcast face and crumpled posture suggest resignation or sorrow. The voice-over explains that such scenes once were prevalent and remain so in the "interior" (here, conflating the "interiors" of geography and domestic architecture) but that they are fading, that the past is disappearing. The scene fades. The next scene opens in the same domestic space but now without any human presence. The woman is gone; the swing, still gently swaying, seems to have been abandoned. The woman's absence is made palpable by the movement of the swing but is left unexplained.

The narrative thread introduced in the video's early scenes is picked up later, in the overview of DakshinaChitra's Tamil section, when we learn in voice-over about the depopulation of Chettinadu, the region of southern Tamil Nadu claimed by the Nattukottai Chettiar community as their homeland. The image of the woman, alone in the house, recurs and, as in the earlier sequence, that scene is followed with a shot of the same interior space, now empty. The narrative's resolution comes only in the video's closing sequence. Night has fallen, and we are told that it is time to prepare for a "new beginning." We return to the courtyard with its swing, now occupied by the woman we witnessed at the beginning. She is no longer idle, however, but seems contentedly absorbed in prayer, fully alive. And DakshinaChitra's re-created rural real has become a space to realize what viewers themselves are losing—to remember not only what they have forgotten but the fact of its forgetting—and to reclaim it.

The video solicits the cosmopolitan, high-caste viewer's nostalgia with its mournful images of loss. These scenes use the iconic imagery of the upper-caste female body to evoke a past erased and a past recovered. Its erasure is condensed in images that suggest death or abandonment, and invite mourning. And because it is not any death but that of a woman who could be one's own elderly mother, grandmother, or aunt, mourning can be easily solicited. With its visual concordance of womanhood/village/childhood, the video aims at transference, at displacing the mourning for one's parents and one's own childhood to the mourning for a countryside transformed by industrial growth and urbanization. It frames DakshinaChitra as redemptive by intimating that it is the threshold between past and present, village and city. For the center's target audience, this claim is even more persuasive because of the personal memories and desires it may draw forth. Urban Hindus, especially from orthodox and upper-caste families, make a point of returning to their ancestral villages for the performance of certain life-cycle rituals, and the museum visit offers a convenient (and secularized) reenactment of such a return to the space and time of childhood and familial intimacy. The video appeals to urban and transnational elites not only with its English voice-over but also with its use of the cinematic conventions and narrative frames of documentary, rather than those of melodrama or epic, to name two of the more popular genres among India's monoglot lower and middle classes. The video, with its documentary "truth," its intimate forms of address, its gendered visual rhetorics, and its affective economy, coaches viewers to identify with the story of the past told at the museum, to make it their own story.

Like the heritage houses displayed on its grounds, DakshinaChitra's orientation video aims to offer a copy of the space-time of the past that the center strives to re-create. It works with the architectural re-creations by soliciting viewers' affective participation and by holding out the possibility of tactile seeing. The on-site footage draws viewers into an enchanted space. It depicts the grounds of DakshinaChitra not in the rather desolate, uninhabited form that they are likely to encounter when they leave the screening room but as an animated space, filled with figures who are at once ancestral and fully contemporary. With the mnemonic overlay of the video, viewers themselves can be reembedded, if only for a moment, in what went before.

Embodied Pasts, Embedded Labor

DakshinaChitra's design and its mediation have arisen within a world of global consumer practice. It is an ethnoscape in which interactions between workers, visitors, guides, and staff sustain a hybrid institutional identity as educational foundation, service-sector business, performance space, and museum. The conditions in which the mimetic faculty is engaged and given affective force are not only by-products of visual technologies but rest on the labor that sustains the center's material and performative infrastructures. A fixed space of transnational culture, DakshinaChitra in both its back and front regions comprises a space of encounter structured by wage labor, touristic consumption, philanthropy, and research.

In the front regions of the museum, visitors can see handicrafts, tools, and raw materials exhibited in their contexts of production and use; they can also witness folk performances and craftspersons at work, and purchase handcrafted goods directly from their makers. With calculated expositions of back-region activities, the museum also communicates that crafts are conserved in the work of exhibition construction and maintenance that artisans and other less-skilled laborers perform. Back-region operations are also exposed in the museum's efforts to expand the market for craft goods and to shape consumer desire for craft products and knowledge. As part of its professional recruitment and training, DakshinaChitra launched an arts management internship program in 2004; in collaboration with the Madras Craft Foundation's Institute for Arts Management, the center offers professional certification for future curators, educators, and managers. Back-region activities also focus on training for artisans, who are coached in rationalized forms of production. Thus, even as it anticipates the cosmopolitan gaze of the consumer-citizen, it also is space where rural subalterns, mainly craftspersons and various unskilled laborers, encounter and comment upon the consumer-citizen, now recognized by the neoliberal Indian state as an ideal national subject.

Craft in the Consumer Gaze

Since opening in 1997, DakshinaChitra has catered to urban tastes for handicrafts and for what the global consumer market glosses as "indigenous" styles of architecture and design with information about craft production and with retail sales of handicrafts. It does this in an organizational context that, under the monitoring and evaluation of international foundations and corporate funders, has become more professionalized. By-laws have been drafted, and all employees receive written contracts; salary and benefits scales have been standardized according to function; a general manager has been hired to run the daily operations. With this, DakshinaChitra's own corporate identity has gained a sharper profile, including the introduction of the DaCh brand name for some of the goods produced by contracted artisans. Most artisans who participate in public programs are hired on a temporary basis, in connection with special projects or sales, which, by 2005, occurred monthly. A few artisans are members of the museum's permanent staff and are expected to engage in regular on-site craft production. Home-based production and the work of rural cooperatives are also represented in commodities available in the gift shop and at the craft bazaars that the museum sponsors in its capacity as a broker bringing crafts producers and urban consumers together. The museum, however, is not merely a sales venue but intervenes more actively in the production and marketing phases. Museum staff members occasionally assist craft cooperatives with financial planning and marketing. This assistance includes advice about designs favored by the museum's clientele as well as the museum's marketing of some products under its DaCh brand name.

With all these interventions, DakshinaChitra aims to enlarge rural artisans' participation in a neoliberal economic order, both as producers and consumers. In our conversations, Thiagarajan spoke frequently and with genuine fervor about professionalizing craft production, including the introduction of market-rate pricing, which she felt would ensure the desirability of craft products: "unless it's costly, they [consumers] won't recognize that it's worth buying—and they definitely won't think it worth conserving as heritage."[52] The museum's promotional material asserts its goals of improving the living and working conditions of southern India's craft producers by enlarging the markets, in India and abroad, for the goods they produce. Though reaping a share of revenues from the sale of its DaCh-branded products, the museum takes no commission from those craftspersons who sell their work at DakshinaChitra's crafts bazaar and at occasional fairs. Donations from supporters can be targeted to developing and sustaining "a base of resource people and programs associated with crafts and provide for marketing, production, product development, design and packaging."[53] In fact, at DakshinaChitra, as at the Indian Crafts Museum, it has proven more difficult to support craft production than to cultivate urban markets for craft products.

Craft products and techniques are central in the relations the museum seeks to establish with its urban clientele. Lecture-demonstrations dealing with craft techniques have proven to be key sites for cultivating visitors' affective and somatic investments in craft, and they are common weekend events at DakshinaChitra. A lecture-demonstration on indigo dying that I attended in December 1999 can illustrate. The proprietor of a Chennai handloom boutique (a member of one of Chennai's leading industrialist families) had been invited to explain the process by which indigo pigments were produced and the cloth dyed. The lecture coincided with special exhibition-cum-sales of indigo fabric and ready-made clothing at DakshinaChitra's gift shop, at the speaker's boutique, and at several other city boutiques. Attending were about forty women, ranging in age from the late teens to the sixties. Most were Indian, but also present were a few European women, associated with foreign consulates and the British Council, which had donated generously to the center. All were exquisitely dressed in saris or salwar-kameez sets of fashionable vegetable-dyed, handloom material.[54] Near the seminar site, a small gallery displayed a donated collection of indigo clothing, representing various regional designs and styles. A closer look at the labels revealed not only the object's provenance but also its current owner and market value. Not surprisingly, the owners of the clothes were among the seminar's attendees and organizers. Before the seminar concluded, visitors were reminded that DakshinaChitra would feature another special event a few weeks hence. An indigo vat, for processing the pigment, was to be built, and, once the pigment was prepared, people would be able to come to the museum for a special interactive exhibition-demonstration at which they could watch cloth being dipped and, for an extra fee, dye fabrics themselves.

Events like the indigo lecture-demonstration continue to be pitched as major attractions at DakshinaChitra, along with handicraft sales and dance and music performances. Most lectures and craft sales were free with museum admission; special educational programming for students from village schools and from Chennai's Corporation schools was also offered at no cost. Other workshop-type events were priced anywhere between Rs.500 and Rs.2,500, depending on the event's duration, the materials used, and the presenters' skill levels.

The number of special events at DakshinaChitra has increased substantially since its 1997 opening, with care taken to develop topical themes around which educational programming, performances, and special sales activities could be coordinated. Between September 1998 and August 1999 the museum's public programming included eleven special events. These were scheduled at approximately monthly intervals to coincide with Hindu and Christian festival periods. In conjunction with some events, the museum offered overnight "heritage experience" stays that included sessions on yoga and Ayurveda fundamentals. In 2007 the special events programming had expanded to include seventeen festivals (Hindu, Christian, and Muslim), and a roster of related workshops and lecture-demonstrations. Folk dance and theater, as well as Indo-European fusion styles, were part of the regular performance schedule. Upon advance request, the museum would also arrange private workshops, performances, and lectures. These on-site activities were complemented by art exhibitions and museum-led field trips to villages and eco-resorts.

DakshinaChitra's growth has been hastened by competition with the nearby Fisherman's Cove resort, which predated DakshinaChitra.[55] Indicative of the direction that this competition has taken, according to Thiagarajan, was the resort's signage, which dwarfs DakshinaChitra's own. She described other aspects of their relation, which had grown more fractious in the late 1990s. DakshinaChitra had contracted with the Taj Group for its on-site food service for the first two and a half years of the center's operation. The Taj Group then terminated the contract because of its low profitability.[56] Subsequently, the Group attempted to recruit some of the center's staff for its Fisherman's Cove resort, which was being upgraded with the addition of a craft bazaar and new programming that mimicked DakshinaChitra's own. Though it was unsuccessful in its effort to hire away the center's resident artisans for its own craft exhibition, the Group managed to hire the center's educational director by offering her a better-paying position in the craft shop, Khazana, at its central Chennai property, the Taj Coromandel Hotel. Competition has continued to simmer with the appearance of additional resorts and restaurants along the East Coast Highway, many of which now include craft demonstrations and products among their offerings.

DakshinaChitra, like themed environments and resorts across the globe, also rents its facilities to corporate groups and private individuals for fund-raising and other events. This aspect of its business operation has grown as the corridor on which it is located has developed. The center's Web site boasts of hosting more than five hundred such events between 2000 and 2005. Mindful of the success of nearby resorts, DakshinaChitra enthusiastically markets its guest quarters for overnight stays.[57] The same nostalgic longings that the orientation video plays on are solicited in advertising pitches on the Web site. Families are invited to rent the site's facilities to celebrate life-cycle rituals, such as a married man's sixtieth birthday observance, which is celebrated by Brahmans and other upper-caste communities. A similar affective chord is struck in the targeted giving opportunities detailed on the Web site, such as the invitation to "adopt" houses, crafts, and educational programs. In offering visitors and donors a shared space of nostalgia-laced consumption, DakshinaChitra cultivates elite patronage while shaping consumer tastes and linking handicraft consumption to class status. Though the museum's representation of rural life acknowledges the existence of deprivation and poverty, it binds it within a "past" of village self-sufficiency, a past evocative of Gandhian nationalism. In turn, with its handicraft sales, demonstrations, and displays, the museum makes these values and emblems of Gandhism available to urban consumers, as *swadeshi* chic.[58]

Craft as Performance

DakshinaChitra was initially envisioned as a living craft community, in which knowledge and skills could be developed and taught; there were plans to house families of craftspersons on-site, and to exhibit and sell their work. The museum's administration, however, was able to recruit only one family to live on-site, a difficulty that reveals the contradictions of the museum's craft conservation mission. Some criticisms came from regional craftspersons (and their advocates), who resisted the museum's efforts at conservation because it would have isolated them, geographically, from their extended families and communities. Some were wary of the objectifying experience of being on display. Other, more pragmatic objections were raised. A historian, engaged as a consultant in the mid-1990s, told me that he had refused to assist them in gathering information about craft communities because he did not think that the museum's intervention in their community life would have offered any significant or lasting benefits.[59] As a result of these difficulties, the museum's administration abandoned the idea of re-creating an entire community as part of its exhibition. It prominently advertises the fact that some craftspersons and families reside on grounds in well-made, spacious quarters that include both individual units and dormitory-style accommodations. Master artisans on staff are permanent residents, but most, such as visiting craftspersons and performers, reside temporarily in these quarters.

Despite its inability to recruit a permanent craft community, the center has remained optimistic about the beneficial effects of marketing crafts. Thiagarajan argues that craft skills can be sustained and revitalized, and artisans empowered, through professionalization, especially by adopting rationalized financial planning and more sophisticated marketing techniques. Moreover, in a departure from the visual rhetorics of the video and exhibition spaces, she recognizes that the craftspersons involved in DakshinaChitra's programs had been producing for a market economy prior to their encounter with the museum. She thus dismisses arguments against professionalizaton that appeal to the image of the timeless village, maintaining instead that craft is dynamic and innovative but mainly in need of a deeper and broader market.

Prior to liberalization, craftspersons' participation in the market economy was organized by various rural development and handicrafts promotion agencies associated with central and state governments. The rural development programs that characterize the welfare state of the 1950s, 1960s, and 1970s continue to operate but now under the banner of "empowerment" and with the mediation of a growing number of NGOs and private distribution and marketing concerns. These programs, which are cloaked with a fusion of Gandhian village republic and Nehruvian developmentalism, include central government projects dedicated to training and employing craftspersons, who constitute a significant segment of India's rural population.[60]

DakshinaChitra's operations have benefited from the support for crafts marketing afforded by such programs. The central government subvenes the costs that craftspersons incur traveling to the museum's Craft Melas (exhibition-sales) and has assisted in some costs of reconstruction and curation. DakshinaChitra's marketing of craft, therefore, has not radically departed from the relations of exchange in which craftspersons were already embedded. It is apparent, though, that the museum, like the Indian state, has sought to gain access to and sustain craft *products*—which can complement and "Indianize" modernity—but is more ambivalent about sustaining the socially embedded ways of producing those objects.

The craftspersons themselves were also eager to participate in some of the economic opportunities that museum work offers. Employment by the museum increases craftspersons' class mobility: artisans on permanent staff in 1999–2000 were paid monthly salaries of Rs.4,000–5,000 and received retirement and health benefits as well as paid leave. The job also allowed a range of aesthetic and technical experimentation that village employment did not. At the same time, work at DakshinaChitra complicated their status in other ways, especially as they negotiated the distance, physical and social, between the world of the museum and that of their home communities. These contradictions pervaded the specular order of the exhibition, in which they were not only seen by tourists but were also witnesses to and marginalized participants in the consumer citizenship emblematized by the museum's cosmopolitan visitors. Their comments are indicative of their conjunctural positions.

The only resident artisan, a potter named Ramu Velar, had worked at DakshinaChitra since 1996. Like many villagers, his formal education had ended early, at the fifth standard. He was proud, and rightfully so, of his ability to read and write Tamil, as those are skills that fewer and fewer of the state's citizens, rural or urban, can claim. He lived on site with his son, daughter-in-law, and grandchild but periodically visited his home village where his wife, other children, and extended family dwelled.

Velar's work as a potter, at DakshinaChitra and in previous contexts, mediated both his territorialized identity, his status as village priest, and the de-territorialized identity of a nomadic artisan. Though his status was inherited, having learned from his father how to throw pots, he had accepted temporary employment by the state in the mid-1980s, when he participated in children's pottery-making workshops. His notoriety increased in the early 1990s, when he was again engaged by the state government to create massive terracotta figures to decorate the venue for the World Tamil Conference. It was this work that brought him to Thiagarajan's attention.

His comments in one of our conversations were symptomatic of the cultural intimacy that his work engendered, by revealing his awareness of being an object of the consumer-citizen gaze, but also of being a participant, even if marginal, in more globalized practices of consumption. He asserted that he was pleased by the chance to work for DakshinaChitra because of the opportunities for innovation and experimentation it offered.[61] Some of these possibilities arose from the mechanized technology available to him at the center. There he used an electric wheel, something he noted he could not afford when he was in the village. The reference to mechanization was one allusion to the "modernity" that the museum represented for him. More specifically, he spoke also of the "modern" [Tamil, *navīṉam*] goods that he produced, indexed as such by the greater range of styles and designs than would have been possible in his village. Also marking DakshinaChitra as a space of the modern was his reference to the center as the "company" [English]—a term

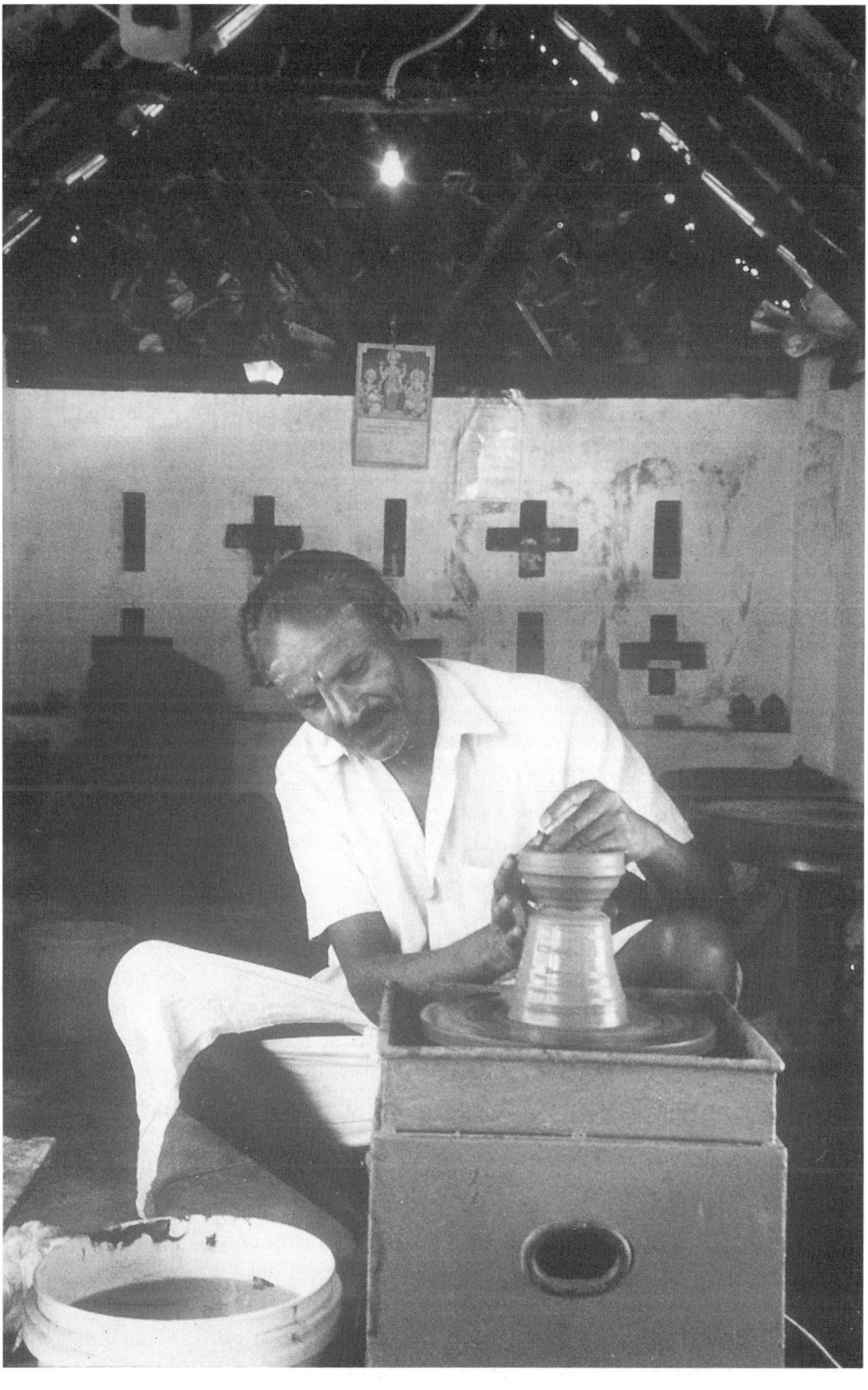

Figure 6.4. Ramu Velar, Master Potter, DakshinaChitra. *Photograph by author.*

suggestive of his back-region experience of it as a bureaucratic organization. At the center, his work garners recognition and admiration from a wide spectrum of cosmopolitan consumers, who appreciate innovation and artistry. "*Iṅke taṉ veḷḷikaraṉ ellāme varaṅkaḷ!*" ("All the foreigners are coming *here!*"), he exclaimed. He continued in this vein, explaining that it was not only foreigners who visited but India's own celebrity elite, including the Tamil actress Revathi.

Though all the possibilities associated with modernity were appreciated, as was the regularity of income and benefits (which included his and his family's accommodation on-site), he acknowledged that museum work did pose certain risks for the life he continued to lead in his village. Here he returned to the tension between the territoriality of his vocation and the de-territorializing direction that his work had taken him. As a hereditary potter, he was also a priest and was bound to return for festivals in order to reconfirm and maintain that status, for his own sake and for the welfare of his family. He was a rural person who had grown increasingly conversant with the de-territorialized practices of consumer citizenship, but who also retained territorialized subjectivity of villager.

Another craftsperson, a weaver (Ramaswamy), commuted daily from a village in Chennai's outskirts to his job at DakshinaChitra, which he had held since 1997. His regular travel between the globurban terrain of the museum and his own village was part of already developed mobility typical of villagers whose settlements have been absorbed into Chennai's peri-urban belt. Like Velar, he was a hereditary craftsman, having learned from his father, who continues to work in the village. Also like Velar, he was literate in Tamil, though his own formal education through the SSLC (Secondary School Leaving Certificate) level exceeded Velar's.[62] Until the mid-1990s he had worked, along with his father and brothers, on home-based cloth production, supplying bolts of handloom fabric, saris, and smaller pieces to some of the region's large handloom distribution and retail corporations, mainly Kumaran Silks. He had also taken advantage of state-sponsored training offered in Chennai to expand his technical and stylistic repertoire, and had obtained certification entitling him to referrals and placement services through the central government handicraft agency. He said that his skill exceeded the limited demands made by the museum, and, unlike the potter, he was frustrated by the limited opportunities for innovation or artistry that museum work afforded. Though trained to weave saris and running fabric for clothing, his output for the museum during most of the time he had worked there had consisted of table linens, handkerchiefs, and so forth, which were used at museum functions and in displays. Though paid for the latter, he told me that he felt slighted by the assignments, given his ability to take on the more complex and demanding tasks of weaving saris in various regional styles: "At home, I have made so many styles, combining cotton and silk, cotton and polyester. Why not here?"

The comments of both artisans reveal the forms of cultural intimacy that employees negotiated on-site through idioms of work and livelihood. Adopting a foreigner's gaze, Velar imagined the village as a space of pastness, social insularity, and stasis, comparing it to the desirably "modern" space of DakshinaChitra.

Ramaswamy, by contrast, refused to cast the village as a space of traditional labor and consumption. Working-class consciousness shaped his recognition of the museum as a space of constraint, in which he was compelled to reinvent a "tradition" that had no mooring in the actualities of his own life as a rural subaltern citizen. Thus, while the DakshinaChitra's specular order was designed to assist urban visitors in seeing traces of the past, it afforded rural laborers glimpses of modernity and the dilemmas of consumer citizenship.

Back-Region Labor and Front-Region Narrative

Construction of buildings and maintenance absorb skilled and unskilled rural labor, on both temporary and long-term bases. These less-skilled laborers are not employed in the high-profile operations that craftspersons are, but they are prominent parts of the visual field, comprising about half of DakshinaChitra's paid staff. It is from villages in the peri-urban fringe that the museum's temporary construction laborers and permanent maintenance staff are recruited. The village where DakshinaChitra is located, Muttukadu, is home to about three hundred families and, in the course of planning, the Madras Craft Foundation (MCF) commissioned a study of its socio-demography.[63] The unpublished report outlined the caste and occupational composition of the three hamlets that made up the village. Dalit and low-caste populations predominated; most men worked as casual construction laborers or fishermen, though a minority was employed as clerks, drivers, and bus conductors. The latter job opportunities followed the extension of the East Coast Road, with its hatcheries, dairies, and aquaculture farms. Women worked in construction and in home-based, piece-work manufacturing. The report proposed that DakshinaChitra hire villagers as unskilled laborers and as handicraft producers.

The museum's incorporation of local women and men as laborers (like its effort to market work of local, small-scale handicrafts producers) is framed, explicitly, with discourses of empowerment consistent with that of voluntary associations and state welfare organizations, especially with the turn to neoliberal governmentality. Being hired by the center represented the formalization of domestic and handicrafts labor. Tied, therefore, to the museum's ongoing efforts to document, conserve, and represent the rural real are activities designed to build skills and revenue-earning capacity among rural people, and thus enable them to turn local knowledge into a knowledge of locality that could be circulated and consumed in the global marketplace.

In fact, the presence of rural subalterns on-site confirms DakshinaChitra as part of the familiar horizon of creative destruction now seen throughout Chennai and its outskirts in the bodies of construction laborers and the spaces of squatter settlements. Even more familiar to elite visitors were the village women who prepared snacks at outdoor snack bars and who cleaned the dwellings that make up the outdoor exhibitions. These women are trained not only to clean the houses but to greet visitors and to lend credence to DakshinaChitra's claim to be a living museum by drawing *kōlam* at their thresholds.[64] With no interpretive staff stationed in the outdoor exhibition area, housekeepers' charge sometimes extended to supplying basic information to those visitors capable of understanding Tamil. Administrators, anticipating such situations, provided rudimentary training to its housekeeping staff about house construction and everyday rural life. Salaries (Rs.500–800 in 2000) were comparable to that earned by domestic servants, and, for some, the job of housekeeper at DakshinaChitra was preferable because of its regularity, proximity to their homes, and less arduous labor.

The familiarity that is encoded by the housekeepers' presence invites reflection on the continuities between present-day rural settlements and those depicted at the museum. In several conversations, Thiagarajan underscored the "authenticity" of these workers, the housekeepers in particular. She explained that, as villagers whose own way of life and material culture were not far removed from the preindustrial world that DakshinaChitra simulates, they may be the "most authentic" features of the center. She remarked, specifically, on the women's familiarity with the types of houses exhibited on-site. They were well suited to the work of housekeeping, because it involved performing chores that they would ordinarily do in their own homes. She did admit, though, that the very things that made them "authentic"—their ties to rural locales—could interrupt their performance of DakshinaChitra's real on occasion. For example, she pointed out that Tamil housekeepers stationed in the Kerala section refused to wear the white saris that were appropriate for that section, because white, the color prescribed for Tamil widows (and for widows in some other regions of Hindu South Asia), connoted deep inauspiciousness.

Another source of familiarity was never explicitly acknowledged by anyone with whom I spoke at DakshinaChitra, visitor or staff. Rural women's employment as housekeepers mirrored not only their own domestic routines but also the paid labor, as domestic servants, that many poor women rely upon. Women's housekeeping at DakshinaChitra reproduced the familiar domestic world of middle- and upper-class urban dwellers, which relied on maidservants' labor for its daily functioning. This leads to even denser intersections between the simulated space of the museum and the real spaces of domestic life. Along with the orientation video, in which women (marked as high caste) were figures of nostalgia, such images exposed the gendered project of the center's memory work. For a visitor, the emptiness of DakshinaChitra may seem to betray the video's promise that the center is a "new beginning." The presence of women on-site, in domestic roles, however, picks up where the video narrative leaves off, their bodily labor subsumed in DakshinaChitra's meticulous work of recovery and rebuilding.

Conclusion

The nineteenth century exhibitionary complex, encompassing metropolitan museums, galleries, expositions, department stores, and arcades, was tied to the spatial, political, and economic formation of the modern, territorial state. In similar ways it can be argued that the new global exhibitionary complex, which includes interactive, living museums like DakshinaChitra, along with video arcades, cineplexes, malls, and the virtual worlds of cyber-space, is tied to the neoliberal nation-state—to its constitutive spaces, its political economy, its founding narratives and pedagogies. The contradictions of heritage within such contexts are well known. Its creation and consumption is fueled by, and solicits, nostalgia—home-sickness—for the "before" that modernity has displaced. Nonetheless, the formation of heritage as a specific type of state project, for instance, national trusts with their registers of historic places, and arena of popular consumption are obvious indicators that heritage arises within, not against, the capitalist modes of consumption and mediation that have been tied so intimately to the rise of the nation-state. This dynamic, consolidated in the nineteenth century, shows no sign of abatement though it unfolds, now, in the globalizing neoliberal order, trafficking in memories that are bound to both local and cosmopolitan imaginaries. In adopting self-consciously modern, global templates to define, represent, and conserve tradition, new heritage sites of the global South through the cultural intimacies of touristic experience produce territorialized pasts that bind nationalist affect. At the same time, through the creative destruction wreaked by the political economy and the rueful self-regard of cultural intimacy, these same sites disavow the past and anticipate the global connections of the unfolding neoliberal order.

Rather than being a project to counteract the declining urban fortunes associated with de-industrialization, DakshinaChitra is an integral part of the new economy that the Indian nation-state, decentralized and deregulated, has embraced. The center's mission is framed in terms explicitly critical of the effects of industrialization, though its critique does not take the form of outright resuscitation of artisanal mode of production. Instead, by salvaging the material remains and embodied knowledge of preindustrial lifeworlds, it poses a counter-narrative that recalls (selectively) what modernity has displaced. DakshinaChitra's location within the new industrial landscape that characterizes Chennai's peri-urban fringe is a crucial index of the terms by which it organizes its project of recovery and remembrance. A memento of another space-time in the midst of the modern, it completes the cycle of creative destruction by gathering the residues left in the wake of industrial expansion and recombines them to yield a rural real that can be mined for signifiers of local resilience, persistence, and adaptability in a new global order.

The exhibitionary spaces and practices on the grounds of DakshinaChitra point, similarly, to the close but conflictual relation between the center's formation and the region's neoliberal restructuring. No less globalized than the new industrial spaces surrounding it, DakshinaChitra's distance from the city center, its global exhibitionary template, and the creative geography of its grounds all herald its global legibility. It is a space of leisure, where international standards of cleanliness, comfort, and connectivity are the norm. More specifically, it is a recognizable example of the new wave of interactive cultural centers that, since the 1970s, have sought to break away from the previously hegemonic Victorian museal model. With its fusion of education, entertainment, and spectacle, the center is part of a recognizable genre of leisure destinations now marketed to cosmopolitan audiences. Moreover, it is a decidedly nationalist space: offering rural southern

India as synecdoche of the nation-state. Its technologies of memory, which borrow Gandhian idioms, frame the nation-state as a homely space, a remote and only partially translatable rural life-world that invites both detached contemplation and nostalgic attachment.

Its participation in neoliberal globalization, its embrace of a specifically neoliberal nostalgia, and its espousal of an Indian national imaginary make DakshinaChitra readily distinguishable from the heritage templates that have organized the work of preservation and remembrance in the city's colonial core. The differences are telling. State-sponsored public memory projects near Chennai's commercial core take the form of monuments, museums, and commemorative sites (see chapters 2, 3, and 4). The city's major museum, the colonial-era Government Museum, situated near central Chennai's government and financial districts, is a repository of salvaged architectural features, bronze and stone figures, coins, paintings, and photographs. Its collections are organized to serve as signifiers of the region's past civilizational achievements. That museum's specular order, fashioned in the early twentieth century, embodied the racialized logic of imperial statecraft. Only slightly refurbished over the past hundred years, it has continued to attract tens of thousands of visitors, most of them local residents. More important, because of its location in one of the city's few well-maintained parks, it is valued by the urban poor and working classes as a space of recreation and is a popular destination for holiday outings and picnics.

Other spaces of public memory—memorials, statues, and monuments—have been constructed since the 1970s by Dravidianist political leaders. These sites function as spaces of political ceremony and popular pilgrimage, and, stylistically, they fuse modernist abstraction with neo-traditionalist references to the architecture of palaces and Hindu temples. They are part of a spatial and inter-ocular field dominated by the popular imagery of cutouts, cinema hoardings, and devotional chromolithographs and, like them, afford what Pinney has called "corpothetic" engagement, a tactile visuality that, though not reducible to *darśan,* participates in its substantive, transactional logic.[65] These are social spaces in which a Dravidian community of imagination, understood as continuous with the classical Tamil civilization that predated both Aryan and European incursions in the region, is visually mediated and ceremonially recalled.

DakshinaChitra, a sanitized simulacrum of southern India's past, aims to convey that past with clarity and force *because* of its separation from the spaces of ongoing urban life. Its designers have emphasized the visual and pragmatic disjunctions between the center's social space and the sites of popular memory in Chennai. The glitzy, celebratory, hybrid nature of nearby amusement parks is disparaged. Instead, DakshinaChitra comments on the social landscape of the city it adjoins by presenting images of what it once was, and by reminding viewers of the city's rural other. At DakshinaChitra, encounters with the past are unencumbered by the exhaust fumes, litter, beggars, construction debris, and honking buses of Chennai's streets. Equally absent are the signs of industrialization, the factories and power plants, that lie just beyond its grounds.

Despite these assertions of spatio-temporal and moral distance from urban India, DakshinaChitra embodies a modernist logic for representing, assessing, and consuming the past. It engenders cultural intimacy by inviting a contemplative, at times mournful and even ironic, remembrance of the pasts that modernity conceals, whether through occlusion or erasure. At the same time, it rests on the effectivity of what Benjamin called the mimetic faculty, the disposition to seek contact through the production of likeness.[66] Here I extend these insights to the immersive themed world of DakshinaChitra. How is the mimetic faculty engaged at DakshinaChitra? Like the operations of disciplinary history, which can be read as signs of the modern, the past that is narrated and visualized in the immersive environment of DakshinaChitra confirms the possibility of modernity by fashioning its "before." Armed with interpretive cues gleaned from textual guides, the Web site, and the orientation video, visitors enter a space in which encounters with that "before" are guaranteed in the form of reassembled material traces of the rural real and in the form of rural laborers.

DakshinaChitra, aimed avowedly toward ends that are both secularist and historicist, does not invite the participatory, tactile seeing that is constitutive of Hindu ritual. It nonetheless invites visitors to contemplate such transactions as signs of an authenticating "before" from the distanciated vantage infused by both irony and nostalgia. As visitors overwrite the center's recombinant rural with the space-time of the gendered pasts of family and community, they endow these images and spaces with auratic value. The notion of tactile seeing, predicated on the possibilities of both copy and contact that mimesis involves, offers a fruitful direction for thinking about the properties and capabilities of the interactive technologies of memory associated with living museums and immersive cultural environments as both outcomes of and reactions to the commodification of memory. Benjamin's vocabulary, which struggles to convey both the affective and material claims of commodity capitalism, helps unpack the workings of what Huyssen has described as the uneven ethical and cognitive demands posed by the globalization of memory.[67]

DakshinaChitra's geography, its design, the labor that sustains it, and the goods and services offered on its grounds are means by which cultural intimacy with a world of global consumer practice is gained. It participates fully in the neoliberal project with its emphasis on service-sector industries and in its commitment to deregulation and public-private partnerships in economy and governance. This introduction of heritage into the industrializing hinterland inscribes the rural with signs of modernity, and the center's effect is not unlike that of nearby factories and information technology campuses. Visitors, seduced by neoliberal nostalgia, encounter the nation as handicrafts; workers may encounter it as a space at which modernity and the possibilities of consumer citizenship are presented. Consumer-citizenship, as a socio-moral discourse and subject-position, is encoded in the "modernity" that work for the "company" offers, and in the visitors whom the center's rural workers encounter. In tandem with the residential and industrial developments of globurbia, whose names and designs are meant to evoke imperial pasts, DakshinaChitra both encapsulates and authenticates the home that India's urban elites and off-shore citizens desire, while ensuring that its authenticity, its pastness, remains legible within global cultures of consumption. It celebrates a past that anticipates, not without hesitation, the ethos of consumer-citizenship even as it laments the loss of the rural life-world. The next chapter moves to that life-world, asking how cultural memory is made and remade by rural subalterns as they make claims on space and citizenship in Chennai's socio-spatial margins.

7
The Village as Vernacular Cosmopolis

A Global Village

Kuthambakkam

Google the term "Kuthambakkam," and in a tenth of a second links to 599 postings from news sources, organization Web sites, and Web blogs appear.[1] Visits to these sites reveal Kuthambakkam, a village of about five thousand that lies about thirty kilometers west of Chennai, to be one of Tamil Nadu's "model villages," selected for participation in a multi-sectoral rural development program, Anna Marumalarchi Thittam. The village boasts small-scale industries, good-quality infrastructure, and a one-of-a-kind Panchayat Academy, where panchayat (village council) officials from around the state are brought together to share their knowledge and learn from one another's experiences. Kuthambakkam's leaders are optimistic about reducing high levels of malnutrition and illiteracy through innovative self-help programs. Among the most visible fruits of recent development efforts are the village's *pukka* (permanent) houses, including those making up the samathuvapuram (equality village) constructed in one of the village's seven hamlets in 2000.[2] This experimental mixed-caste housing project is 1 of 132 that were built in Tamil Nadu between 1997 and 2001 and it has been one of the most successful.

Many of the Web sites I located in late April 2007 using Google's search engine included details of the personal story of the village's energetic young panchayat president, Rangaswamy Elango, a Dalit man, who retired from a successful career in chemical engineering to seek office.[3] Indeed, Kuthambakkam owes its virtual visibility largely to Elango's efforts to secure development funds transnationally. Much information about Kuthambakkam is found on Web sites of NGOs based in the United States and operated by and for expatriate Indians, from whom he has obtained grants, fellowships, and donations.[4] Included among the postings are descriptions of presentations that Elango made during a 2002 visit to the United States on a trip that combined fund-raising and consultation with experts on local governance.[5] The trip engendered cultural intimacy, virtual and face-to-face, as he outlined his vision for Kuthambakkam's development. That vision, *gram swaraj* (village self-rule), was borrowed from the lexicon of Gandhian nationalism; it combined high-tech futurity with a conscious and selective reinvention of rural tradition.

Kuthambakkam's recent growth, like that of other villages now engulfed by Chennai's peri-urban fringe, has followed upon the economic restructuring of the 1990s and the political decentralization that accompanied it. Deemed a "model village" with respect to the state's developmentalist aims, a now globally networked Kuthambakkam also models the cosmopolitan possibilities touted by proponents of liberalization.[6] Panchayati raj, Dalit political activism, and transnational discourses of human rights have converged to make the village a space of Dalit self-assertion, a fragile negotiation of militancy and assimilation that has emerged in different forms throughout India over the 1990s. In Kuthambakkam, new expressions of cultural memory have arisen alongside strategic erasures of the past. Once the fourth-largest site for distillation of illegal arrack, it is now a site for distillation and recirculation of Gandhian neo-traditionalism.

The Urban, the Rural, and the Rurban

"Urbanization," considered quantitatively as a process in which the habitation of urban space steadily increases at the expense of rural areas, invites images of desolation, of the inevitable and progressive eradication of rural life. The city, with its connotations of worldliness and connectivity, is envisioned as emerging geographically and semiotically against the remoteness of the countryside beyond its edges, a rendering that helps sustain the stubborn fiction that the "global" and the "local" are discrete spatial categories. The experience of urbanization in India from the colonial era forward suggests, however, that urbanization may be better viewed as a process in which the spaces of urban and rural life are continuously rearticulated in ways that evoke what Ramanujan has described as the "rurban" quality of many cityscapes.[7] Cities are larger and more numerous but the geographic boundaries between city and countryside have become blurred and discontinuous as have the spatio-temporal framing devices—the "modernity" of the urban/global and the "traditionalism" of the village/local—that are commonly used to describe the relations between urban and rural worlds.

Maps of Chennai reveal clear lines of geopolitical separation between the municipality and the administrative units that lay farther afield. In the built environment, however, the boundary between urban and rural does not lie at the geographic edge of the municipality but exists in the form of multiple, dispersed zones of contact where urban meets rural, within and outside the municipality. Chennai's moniker as "the city of villages" acknowledges its growth by accretion between the seventeenth and nineteenth centuries, as the East India Company annexed villages and temple towns of the surrounding countryside. Over much of the twentieth century, even as it acquired a more typically urban landscape, it continued to be dotted with new outcrops of village life, as rural migrants formed squatter colonies near the city's port facilities and factories. And, since the 1970s, features characteristic of urban space have spread beyond the city's municipal boundaries. Manufacturing and residential clusters have appeared in the municipality's western and southern margins. Slumdwellers, evicted from urban core areas, have been resettled in tenements outside the city limits.

While rural spaces continue to be made in the heart of the city, settlement forms and features typically associated with the city have spread into the surrounding countryside, extending the state's apparatus of governance, control, and surveillance. Villages like Kuthambakkam, that once lay outside the city geographically and experientially, have been incorporated into the city's peri-urban fringe, with infrastructural development and with the new communications and transportation networks that create closer connections between the metropolitan core and its hinterland. Kuthumbakkam itself is adjacent to a site recently designated for one of the new "satellite towns" intended to decentralize Chennai and decongest its urban core.[8] The making of a new, "rurban" settlement form has been hastened as well by the closer ties that have been forged between rural communities and the machinery of the nation-state, with the combined effects of development programs and political decentralization leaving villages more visible to and penetrable by the state. Chennai and the countryside surrounding it have long been articulated by state-level party machinery, especially the fan clubs that mobilize supporters around its film-star politicians. And since the 1950s, villages have been sites for state-sponsored development projects that brought new infrastructure, housing, and schools—all of them contact zones between the state and its rural citizenry.

In the 1990s further transformations in the relations between the state and the rural populace came with the political decentralization mandated by economic restructuring. Under the new "Panchayati Raj" provisions of the Indian Constitution's Seventy-third Amendment, ratified in 1994, many villages were empowered as self-governing units with budgetary and policing authority. Some were reserved as Dalit constituencies, and Kuthambakkam, where Dalits make up 55 percent of the population, was one of these. Electoral reservations, designed to promote Dalit autonomy, often have had the opposite effect, however. There has been backlash against Dalit officials by the dominant caste factions who had formerly exerted de facto and de jure power. Rigged elections, and non-cooperation with and violence against Dalit panchayats, including the murder of one panchayat president and his associates, have been reported.[9] Thus, as villages have been "modernized" through the provisions of panchayati raj, rurban political worlds have become more volatile: sharpened caste boundaries, continued discrimination, and heightened violence create a context in which the rural and largely Dalit poor navigate among strategies of assimilation, self-assertion, and militancy.

Rurban Pasts

This chapter explores the making and unmaking of cultural memory in the built environment of rurban Chennai, focusing on Kuthambakkam. How are pasts deployed to make claims on space and citizenship at Chennai's spatial and social margins? And how do these renderings of the past compare to other templates for heritage, such as the living museums, memorials, and urban heritage zones that have arisen with the restructuring of the urban landscape?

For their inhabitants, rurban villages such as Kuthambakkam represent deprivation, but not only that. They are also made, comprehended, and perceived through the work of memory, encoded in expressive culture, such as oral narratives, performances, and artisanal products (some of which earn the approving label "folklore"), and in spaces of everyday life: the homes, religious sites, workplaces, and schools that make up the built environment. These are the spaces that, as zones of contact between state and rural populace and between dominant and subaltern communities, have been made modern by state surveillance and discipline. They are sites of developmentalist statecraft, destinations for projects designed to address the persistence of poverty, discrimination, and violence, especially as these issues affect Dalits, described in administrative parlance as "Scheduled Castes," who now make up 23 percent of the state's rural population.[10]

Despite their diverse functional objectives, a common aim underlies such projects—the eradication of the pastness that poverty and caste discrimination represent. At the same time, the political fields in which the projects are conceived and implemented have been shaped by the rise of political parties representing the interests of the rural poor, including autonomous Dalit parties, by denser NGO networks connecting villagers to national and transnational bodies of human rights activists and discourses, and by the formation of Dalit media space. These projects and organizations are shot through with new forms of (often) counter-nostalgic cultural memory and worldly aspiration.

Technologies of memory used in Dalit activism include conventional commemorative praxis. In some locations, memorials have been raised to honor Dalits who have been murdered, injured, and jailed in the course of struggles for land, dignity, and political voice.[11] The 1990s saw an upsurge in the commemoration of B. R. Ambedkar (1892–1956), the anticolonial nationalist and Dalit leader, in the built environment, in print and digital media networks, and performatively, with public events on the anniversaries of his birth and death, and his conversion to Buddhism.[12] Ambedkar, a conjunctural figure, embodies what Racine and Racine have called the dialectic of oppression and emancipation that Dalits negotiate, with its competing strategies of assimilation and autonomy.[13] Born into the Mahar community, which was treated as "untouchable," Ambedkar, a Columbia University–educated lawyer, is best known as one of the authors of India's constitution and for his activism against untouchability, which relied on an incisive and uncompromising critique of Hindu ideology and the caste system.[14] He sought, through modern statecraft and, later, through Buddhism, to abolish the caste system and fashion remedies for its inequities. Those aspirations are recalled across India in what has become Ambedkar's iconic image; the statues and portraits depicting him in an orator's pose, clad in a Western-style business suit and eyeglasses, and holding a law book in his outstretched hand.[15] His frank embrace of modernity put him at odds with Mohandas Gandhi, the neo-traditionalist, ascetic leader of the Indian National Congress who, though opposed to untouchability, remained staunchly devoted to Hinduism (albeit in an eclectic and recombined form) and to its caste order.

Less conventional technologies of memory are present in various development programs, and it is these that are addressed in this chapter. I argue that memory, its politics and practices, is also incorporated in state-administered, rural housing programs for poor beneficiaries. The programs' aims—to erase a past of discrimination, deprivation, and inequality, and the memories (embodied and semantic) that sustain it—have often involved the introduction of "modernity," in the form of tenement housing for the rural poor, nearly half of whom are Dalits. The "equality village," or samathuvapuram, represents memory work of this sort and illustrates its mediation of the dialectic of oppression and emancipation. The program, framed as a remembrance of the anti-caste reformer E. V. Ramasamy, known as EVR or Periyar (Great One), introduced mixed-caste group housing as a way of combating the persistence of untouchability in rural Tamil Nadu. While nominally commemorative, its experimentalism—shock therapy to erase the body memory and spatial practices of caste—was informed by the tenets of architectural modernism. Its modernism also extended to the design of living spaces, which were standardized units (tenement complexes and single family houses) of reinforced concrete. The program, in other words, was designed to *remember* EVR and the Dravidian movement he is credited with founding by *forgetting* caste boundaries and the Hindu principles with which they were associated. Other kinds of memory trouble have also been engendered in the course of site construction and habitation, in residents' reintroduction of caste segregation and untouchability, and in the vernacular design elements that some project architects have incorporated in new structures.

Kuthambakkam's samathuvapuram was one of two in the state that adopted vernacular design, and it can be read as an expression of the Gandhian praxis that the panchayat president appropriated and reworked. Usually associated with the cost-effective architecture movement and its originator, the Kerala-based architect Laurie Baker, this revisitation of vernacular form has a commemorative dimension, albeit less conventional than that of memorials, statues, or portraits. In its use of local materials and design traditions, and its commitment to low-tech construction techniques, it expressed the norms of self-sufficiency, artisanship, and limited consumption that formed the core of the national community as Mohandas Gandhi imagined it. Gandhi's nationalist philosophy made eclectic and unorthodox use of Hindu principles, which he combined with elements of Jainism, Buddhism, Christianity, and Islam to forge an ethos that he regarded as pan-Indian.[16] He advocated non-cooperation with the colonial administration and proposed programs of economic self-sufficiency, political autonomy, and social reform including women's education, religious tolerance, and the abolition of untouchability. The latter was ambiguous for, while seeking abolition of untouchability, he also praised Brahmanic orthopraxy and the guild-like principles of caste, which he saw as the bedrock of the village republics that he imagined as political alternatives to the bureaucratic power of modern state institutions. Gandhi envisioned India as an agglomeration of self-ruling "village republics," sustained by a self-sufficient, artisanal economy, a perspective in sharp contrast to Ambedkar's famous castigation of the village as a cesspool.[17] Unlike Ambedkar, Gandhi was deeply skeptical of modernity, which he understood as bureaucratic institutions of statecraft, an industrial economy, and ever spiraling consumption, all regarded as foreign impositions. The critique of modernity embodied in cost-effective architecture, I maintain, represents a novel form of public memory, envisioned as both commemoration and enactment of Gandhian practice. It reclaims the spatio-temporal remoteness of the vernacular as a space of worldly aspiration.

The Equality Village

Development's Pasts

In new rurban nodes beyond the city's borders, tenements for resettled slumdwellers lie aside chemical and automotive plants, fortified IT campuses, and elite gated communities. Each, in its own way, is an outpost of the urban modern. Other signs of the modern reach even deeper into the rural world. Under a social welfare program, Periyar Ninaivu Samathuvapuram, launched in 1997 by Tamil Nadu's DMK government, Dalit-majority villages in twenty-seven of the state's thirty districts were upgraded with new housing projects.[18] The projects were experiments in social engineering intended to introduce a new, caste-integrated settlement pattern to rural Tamil Nadu where segregation and violence, both symbolic and physical, have long supported persistent inequalities between caste communities, between landholders and landless laborers, and between sectarian groups.[19] Within the equality villages, families of different communities were to reside in adjacent units and share a single set of common institutions, such as schools, child care centers, playgrounds, burial grounds, and stores.[20] The installation of statues of religious and political figures was forbidden, as was the construction of exclusive places of worship.[21] Moreover, the program offered its beneficiaries tangible resources: once occupants had paid back a portion of the construction costs (about Rs.10,000), they could obtain the title to the house and plot.

By 2001, when the state's DMK government was voted out, 132 such villages had been completed in twenty-seven districts, though the results of this experiment were mixed.[22] In several widely publicized cases, owners of the new homes had violated the program's terms by renting the houses to others while they themselves resided off-site.[23] More common were cases in which caste boundaries and caste-based discrimination were reinscribed in residential geographies, employment, and consumption, sometimes as part of the backlash against Dalit panchayats.[24] In a report evaluating rural development programs across the country, E. Karuppaiyan took aim at its beneficiaries, concluding that the "real picture" in samathuvapurams deviated sharply from the program's goals because beneficiaries had been unable to "break their social traditions [and] to live among different caste groups."[25] Samathuvapurams, moreover, remained an enclave economically, perpetuating the structural inequalities from which the rural poor suffer.[26]

The program's name, with its allusion to E. V. Ramasamy, known popularly as Periyar, enacts the filial piety that is often expressed in the politics of nomenclature. The scheme was conceived as a remembrance (*niṉaivu*) of the figure claimed by Dravidianist parties as a founding father. An early Gandhian nationalist, Ramasamy broke with that movement because of its high-caste leadership and its gradualist approach to social reform. He then founded southern India's atheist, anti-caste Self Respect Movement, which yielded the Dravida Kazhagam (DK) or Dravidian Federation, the association from which Dravidianist parties evolved. Among the measures Ramasamy advocated for the abolition of caste, which he saw as a foreign (Aryan) imposition on the original Dravidian population of peninsular India, were closer inter-caste relations, such as "self-respect marriages"—inter-caste, without dowry, and without religious officiants—and inter-caste dining and residence.[27] Ramasamy's attack on caste, like Ambedkar's, was fueled by a broader critique of Hindu religiosity, which he regarded as the foundation for caste inequality; he advocated atheism and was known for his biting criticisms of Hindu epics, mythology, and ritual practices.[28] The DK, organized in the 1940s to pursue these goals, operated as a social movement centered on atheist militancy; it was fractured in 1949, when C. N. Annadurai, who, unlike Ramasamy, accepted the electoral process, broke away, and formed the DMK as a political party.

The Dravidianist parties, DMK and AIA-DMK, that have controlled the state government since the late 1960s have taken pains to memorialize Ramasamy as founding father by affixing his name to places and social welfare schemes, and by other displays of filial piety such as observing the anniversaries of his birth. They have been less successful, however, in accommodating the interests or participation of the state's poorest and most abject communities in the ways he advocated. The parties have sought instead to serve as umbrella organizations that include Dalits, and they have been able to secure Dalit votes through a combination of intimidation and patronage. Signifying the politics of incorporation is the label Adi Dravida, ("First Dravidians"), by which Dalits are identified within Tamil Nadu's administrative apparatus.[29] Dalit support for Dravidian parties began to wane in the 1990s, with the recruitment of poor and low-caste Hindus to the ranks of the Hindu nationalists and with the consolidation of autonomous Dalit parties. The Dravidianist party machines responded with efforts to retain Dalit support, including populist measures for the benefit of the rural poor, pursued even as both parties have aggressively pushed ahead with neoliberal restructuring.

The DMK's sponsorship, in the late 1990s, of the equality village program as well as other programs (Anna Marumalarchi Thittam and Namakku Naame Thittam) was intended to address the problems of livelihood and subsistence that had followed structural adjustment measures as well as the heightened caste violence that ensued after the implementation of panchayati raj.[30] Such programs represented the DMK's hopes of securing the loyalty of the rural poor, Dalits in particular. With their support, party leaders intended to cut into the electoral base of the rival AIA-DMK and to undercut the appeal of nascent Dalit parties.[31]

The samathuvapuram plan acknowledged the power of memorial praxis both in its name and in the breach, with its prohibition on the installation of political and religious statues in the new villages. The DMK government hoped to dampen commemorative attention to Ambedkar, whose statues and memorials had become popular rallying points for Dalit organizations, and reclaim Dalit loyalty. In an unexpected turn, however, the plan's commemorative masthead was supplemented by references to Gandhi in two of the new samathuvapurams, both of which were constructed in accordance with the principles of cost-effective architecture.[32] In Kuthambakkam, discussed below, architects working with the village's Dalit panchayat president, Rangaswamy Elango, sought to create a material metonym of Gandhian praxis and the national imaginary that it sustained, a nation with roots in "*gram swaraj,*" self-governing village republics, self-sufficiency in production, and limited consumption.

Worldly Villages

The vast majority of equality villages housed residents in single-family units or tenements; primary schools, child care centers, and ration shops were also included on many sites. The new structures, made of poured concrete, resembled the slum board housing that is found throughout India and had been erected using conventional modes of construction, financing, and labor. State agencies were responsible for their construction, often contracting with commercial builders who bid competitively for the jobs. As was also standard practice, architects or engineers or both were engaged to prepare plans and low-skilled, temporary laborers hired for the actual construction.

The hundredth samathuvapuram, destined for Kuthambakkam, was to be a departure from the norm in both its design and mode of construction.[33] In other respects, however, it showcased the program's aims and methods. Kuthambakkam's equality village enacted state-sponsored development within the broader context of liberalization. Tiruvallur, the district adjacent to Chennai in whose eastern reaches Kuthambakkam was located, was a case study in rurban modernity. The district's professionally mounted Web site boasted of an electronically networked administration and proclaimed Tiruvallur to be "one of the fastest developing districts in Tamil Nadu in terms of Industrial Development."[34] The district's status as a destination region for a number of recent industrial ventures combined with high levels of agricultural sector employment made it typical of the rurban belts that have formed near cities with India's greater participation in global capitalism.[35] Also typical, however, were the high rates of illiteracy, low sex ratio (970/1000), and prevalence of hunger among its poorer citizens, among whom Dalits were overrepresented. In Kuthambakkam, Dalits, though making up 55 percent of the village's population, owned only 2 percent of the productive land, a proportion consistent with statewide figures. Like the majority of rural Tamilians, most of Kuthambakkam's residents worked as agricultural and construction laborers, though some were employed in a nearby chemical processing plant.

Kuthambakkam's samathuvapuram was part of a wave of reforms that followed the strengthening of panchayat governance. By 1999 the village's panchayat president, Rangaswamy Elango, had already launched a crackdown on the manufacture of illicit arrack and initiated infrastructural renovation and micro-development projects, all of which generated employment by relying on local labor for their implementation. Later during that same year, after Kuthambakkam had been awarded a samathuvapuram, the People's Architectural Commonweal (PAC), a Chennai firm, was invited by India's Housing and Urban Development Corporation (HUDCO) to design Kuthambakkam's samathuvapuram.[36] The proposal PAC presented had been drafted after visits to other samathuvapurams and interviews with residents, and it differed radically from the plans of other samathuvapurams. In accordance with the principles of cost-effective architecture, its design vocabulary favored the rural vernacular, with most structures composed of locally produced brick and mortar rather than poured concrete. Also distinctive was the architects' interest in training and working with local laborers in the site's construction, a condition that panchayat president Elango had insisted upon.

Construction on the new equality village began in early 2000, and, on October 7 of that year, the samathuvapuram was officially unveiled by the state's chief minister, M. Karunanadhi. The village, built to resettle a group of squatters who had previously resided on the site as well as residents recruited from Kuthambakkam's other six hamlets, totaled one hundred houses. Residences, all duplex units, were laid out in a grid and grouped into several blocks. The site plan included a large community building near the center of the development, as well as plots for community gardens and social forestry; a post office, ration shop, child care complex, and workshops were also part of the new village.

The buildings, both residential and institutional, were constructed with mud-brick walls, supported by wooden joists, and covered by tile roofs typical of the rural south. Each home, with a plinth area of 286 square feet, was larger than those built in other samathuvapurams and consisted of a single room, with a rear courtyard and wide front verandah, screened by a perforated brick wall called a *jali*. To ensure thermal comfort in the region's subtropical climate, openings, including a full-sized window, were positioned for cross-ventilation. The window placement also minimized the need for artificial lighting inside the house. Building exteriors featured exposed brick, but interior walls were plastered and whitewashed. Functionality governed the design of house interiors; each had built-in shelves, hooks, and benches. A space for cooking was created in one corner of the verandah and bathing/toilet areas were located in separate structures, behind the homes.

PAC's architects had made decisions about house layouts consultatively. They knew, from previous projects, that many villagers were accustomed to cooking outside the house and strongly preferred the verandah location for this chore. Their interviews with Kuthambakkam's residents and with residents of other samathuvapurams revealed similar sentiments. The latter villagers had been particularly dissatisfied with the "modern" (Western-style) indoor toilets because of their flushing mechanism and their proximity to cooking areas, both of which they found unclean.[37]

Figure 7.1. Kuthambakkam house, under construction. *Photograph by author.*

The attention to local materials and design, and the allied goal of self-sufficiency, involved the reuse of building materials, including the use of random rubble masonry for foundations and plinths. Further, architects sought to establish a close relation between buildings and the site's natural terrain. Variable topography was accommodated by placing buildings at different elevations; the plan also included spaces for gardens and groves. Lacking precise topographic surveys, architects expected to do some design work on-site and visited weekly to train and consult with workers and participate in construction.

The Shock of the Old

Re-socialization was sought in Kuthambakkam by introducing a modernist spatial syntax with duplex residential units and a grid-like layout. These patterns contrasted with the circular settlements ordinarily found in rural hamlets. Spatial defamiliarization was tempered, however, by the inclusion of familiar elements in the form of features derived from the rural vernacular and emblematic of Laurie Baker's style of cost-effective architecture.[38] The tile roofs and the brick exteriors and *jalis* were familiar sights in rural India. Like the brise-soleil favored by Le Corbusier, the *jali* protects sections of buildings that are most exposed to sunlight and is a distinctive feature in Baker's work. Baker himself described it as a vernacular solution to the problem of the window, because it caught light and air and diffused glare while still furnishing privacy and security. He considered the *jali* and other, comparable, perforated walls to be distinguishing features of India's own architectural traditions.

A vernacular design vocabulary was also evident in the community center, a building meant for meetings, weddings, and other gatherings. It was a large, single-storey structure, with a clerestory that allowed natural light to flood its interior. With its central courtyard design, the building mimicked the layout and appearance of a rural dwelling, though on a grander scale. The east-facing main entry led into the large central hall; cooking and food storage spaces were situated in the northeast corner of the compound, and spaces for dining were placed along the north wall of the main hall. Courtyards adjoined the hall on its north and south sides, and guest quarters were situated in the compound's northwest corner. Additional spaces for workshops and sheds were located in its southwest corner. The architects told me that they had deliberately adhered to domestic design norms because of the traditional use of homes for wedding ceremonies; they also wanted to avoid making a "modern" or "grandiose" statement with the structure. Though larger than other structures, it closely resembled them in style, with visual continuity maintained by the center's mud-block construction and tile roof.

The architects' work on the site, their reliance on local materials and labor, and their attention to local skills-enhancement accorded with Baker's Gandhian approach and adhered to the conditions set out by the panchayat's president. The production of most building materials—mortar, brick, and cement joists—was completed on site by workers trained by the architects. Nearly all the construction workers were recruited from the village of which the new settlement was to be a part, and those selected as future occupants included a group of squatters (about twenty-four families) who had been residing on the building site for a number of years. The principal exception to the use of local labor was the recruitment of skilled artisans from Tirunelveli district in southern Tamil Nadu to lay roof tiles.

Ethical Convergences

The prominence of vernacular elements in the samathuvapuram's design, materials, and construction methods was a hallmark of the People's Architectural Commonweal. At the time of the Kuthambakkam project, the firm's four partners included three architects (Sudhir and Vishnupriya, a married couple, and Nyas, a long-time associate) and the head of a local construction workers' union (Dominic, a former mason). Their small office was located in a section of the couple's home in Shenoy Nagar, a neighborhood in one of Chennai city's newer, western divisions.

In one of my conversations with the architects, they explained that they had welcomed the opportunity to participate in the community housing experiment, for it was aligned with the architectural training they had received in the early 1980s and with several projects they had subsequently undertaken in connection with the declaration of 1987 as the International Year of Shelter for the Homeless. All, with the exception of Dominic, had received professional training at Anna University's School of Architecture and Planning. There they had worked with architects and

Figure 7.2. Brick making, Kuthambakkam. *Photograph by author.*

Figure 7.3. House building, Kuthambakkam. *Photograph by author.*

geographers associated with the Center for Human Settlements, many of whom had been strongly influenced by John Turner's criticism of slum clearance policies and his advocacy of community-based upgrading.[39] They, like their teachers, were committed to ideals that had both Gandhian and socialist roots. Sudhir put it this way:

> Very early on in our undergraduation, we were extremely uncomfortable with the way that things were in the architectural profession: the quality of work that we were seeing around us and the attitudes that were involved. . . . That kind of dislocation and sense of alienation led to all of us hanging on to each other and trying to find a way more relevant to take part in the profession.

The firm's sympathy for the methods and goals of community housing, and their interest, both political and aesthetic, in vernacular architecture and the artisanal production methods it employed were influenced by Laurie Baker, who had gained national attention in the mid-1970s, with his influential designs for St. John's Cathedral and the Centre for Development Studies, both in Kerala.[40] In the late 1980s, Vishnupriya, Sudhir, and Nyas, joined by other colleagues who had worked with Baker-trained architects in Kerala, formed a cooperative with the idea that they would specialize in rural community architecture based on consultative design praxis and local labor.[41] In these projects, they established the consultative model, including detailed observations of existing settlements, augmented by interview and meetings with beneficiaries, that they applied in the samathuvapuram project.

In the course of these jobs they developed antipathy toward conventional contracting and what they regarded as its design counterpart, architectural modernism. In this they echo the sentiments of a generation of Indian architects, including Baker, who became disenchanted with modernism and with the postcolonial cityscape with which it was most closely associated. Modernism's departure from the norms of the colonial-built environment, its internationalist vocabulary, its functionalism, and its association with a narrow set of standard building types had recommended it as a postcolonial architectonic, especially given the enormity of the need for adequate housing. Le Corbusier's internationalism had famously inspired the design of Punjab's capital, Chandigarh, and from the 1950s to the early 1970s the Public Works Departments (PWD) across India reiterated the design vocabulary of modernism in thousands of structures, institutional and residential. Modernist materials and features were soon criticized, however, as inappropriate for India's climate, infrastructure, and notions of privacy.[42] PAC's architects shared this view; they maintained that the industrialized building technology and modernist design favored in PWD construction projects were inappropriate for most rural settings. Commenting on their experience in rural housing design in the late eighties, Sudhir explained:

> The group houses and the type of designs that they used were not preferred by the villagers. Basically they had brick work with masonry walls, brick with cement mortar and plaster on both sides; they had cement floors and often an RCC [reinforced concrete] sloped roof. Those consisted of the inputs from an

> expert's point of view. Those styles had failed to make any dent in the kinds of preferences that people had.

The contracting system in which the projects were implemented was also rife with corruption, as project funds were regularly siphoned off by subcontractors and officials, leaving minimum allotments for actual construction and resulting in shoddily built and often incomplete structures. Because many of these projects focused solely on Dalits' housing needs, they inadvertently reinforced existing inequalities by erecting Dalit-only tenements on the sites of existing, segregated colonies. The PAC partners' experiences in rural housing convinced them, in short, that modernist solutions to India's housing problems were inadequate. The alternative, they felt, was to be found in vernacular design and building technology.

We spoke at length about a rural community housing project that they completed between 1988 and 1990.[43] When I asked whether those villagers ever sought "modernist" innovations, Vishnupriya acknowledged that, although two or three families had expressed a desire for "town" houses, that is, poured concrete structures seen in urban areas, most preferred more familiar designs. Sudhir added:

> The innovations [by villagers], if at all, were in the form of reviving references to the past that were extremely relevant. This ended up giving us very similar houses on the outside. . . . They had to have a front door right in the center of the front wall and a window facing the front door. The kitchen would be on the verandah. This was in the front—they always had the verandah in the front . . . all told people were using a . . . pattern of design that was extremely deeply rooted in their consciousness. Somehow they felt that that was what they were comfortable with, that it suited them. . . . It was a rejection of the government's modern group housing style.

Nyas pointed out that the assertion of preferences and the claim on the house as property were themselves signs of a greater political voice and could be interpreted as positive outcomes of the pilot study:

> Opting for the kind of houses that they had been used to, having a say in determining the kinds of houses that were built and in the process of planning it out—all this had a huge political impact during the time of the project. They could say, "this is the house we bought, this is the house we built. This we did by ourselves. And we've got the money, we have used it. And we have done this." Usually money does not reach these people. Funds, even if [from] a government program, hardly any get into their hands. Here, it was six thousand rupees. It was a meager sum, but they got it and it made an impact.

Their work on rural housing solidified their conception of architecture as a broader, more transformative set of practices than those taught in most professional schools. According to Sudhir:

> Our feeling was that we should find some way in which we could remake the practice of building. We did not feel like calling it architecture only or engineering only or building only. . . . So we thought that one way in which we could broaden the base of an organization dealing with construction and architecture

> was to make it a cooperative that would involve workers as equal shareholders in the business.

They acknowledged the difficulties of translating their goals into action. Regardless of their own commitments, participation by construction workers was limited by several factors, including the pervasiveness of structural inequality and exploitation. As Sudhir observed:

> The prevailing ethic . . . is not just an attitude promoted by the interest groups, it is also an attitude that has deeply permeated the workers themselves. They also are looking for the shortest possible end, the best gain in the shortest time, least effort. . . . Another large part of the problem is because it has been so stratified, every person does a specific job and the division of labor is so stratified that each person does not really know what his contributions mean in the entire scheme. . . . So you can't really expect that you can build identification—that you can build it in relation to the work that you are doing.

By the mid-1990s they realized that the practice's financial viability could not be sustained with community housing projects, particularly given their unwillingness to work within the norms and specifications of conventional contracting. Since then, they have worked, almost exclusively, on private commissions, designing and building single family homes.[44] They still hoped that cost-effective architecture could lead to what Sudhir called a "rejuvenation of the craftsman sort of ethic," though they realized that what they were seeking was a profound change, not only of ethos and subjectivity, but also in structural conditions of the architectural profession and of the construction industry on which it depended.

The partners were attracted to the samathuvapuram project because it hearkened back to the projects of the previous decade. According to Vishnupriya, it offered a chance to put their Gandhian principles into action, even if on a limited scale:

> We're taking as much time off from the work on the job to explain to them . . . as much of the process as we can . . . basically to rejuvenate interest in detail so that we can show that their own skills have meaning, have relevance and offer scope for dignified work, for a dignified role in the process of building.

Their participation in the project, however, owed less to their own intentions than to the goals of Kuthambakkam's reform-oriented panchayat president, Rangaswamy Elango, a chemical engineer who had worked during the 1980s for Oil India and later for the Council of Industrial and Scientific Research (CISR), based in Chennai. Elango, a Dalit, had taken up grass-roots reform projects in the village since his youth and, even after moving away, had returned regularly to the village. In 1994 he quit his job to contest the panchayat presidency in the village's first such election, mandated by the Constitution's Seventy-third Amendment.[45] He won on a reformist platform that advocated greater educational opportunities, economic growth, and transparency in governance. Recognizing that prosperity depended on infrastructure development, he proposed micro-development projects and sought to cut costs by utilizing local labor without the intervention of contractors. This approach he felt was consistent with the sort of self-help programs that were, at that point, being inaugurated by the state's DMK government.

His commitments acquired a Gandhian dimension as a result of a controversy that had erupted around an infrastructure project completed during 1998. By sidestepping government-approved contractors and using local labor and recycled construction rubble, the project, a drainage canal, was completed under budget but in violation of regulations pertaining to the expenditure of grant monies. Contractors complained, and Elango was suspended from office. Hoping that it would encourage him, his wife urged Elango to read Gandhi's autobiography. Gandhi's struggle, about which he had known little previously, inspired him to challenge his ouster in Gandhian fashion by sitting *dharna* (a sit-in) at the Secretariat building in Chennai. He did this to pressure the government to hold a plenary session of the village before deciding on his guilt or innocence. The session was held, after which he was cleared of corruption charges and reappointed to the panchayat's presidency.

In an August 2002 interview with Asha Mahesh of India Together, an association of Non-Resident Indians in the U.S., Elango reflected on that crisis:

> I do not say that I am a 100% Gandhian. Maybe 40%, 50%, some such number. What I mean is that I find many of Gandhi's ideas . . . to be a source of strength and . . . I believe that many of the problems I face can be solved by applying that thinking. . . . It is not merely in making the panchayat self-sufficient that I draw strength from Gandhi, it is also to assert that *dharma* [moral order] is essentially more important than law. . . . Because I know the laws and understand them, I can see the purposes for which they [stand]. That purpose is more important than the law. . . . Yes, I did not follow the law [in constructing the drain without obtaining bids] but I believe that a just thing was done.[46]

Shortly after Elango's exoneration the village was selected as a site for a samathuvapuram, an honor he accepted on the condition that he have a say in the design and construction, and that local labor and materials be used.

The construction of the samathuvapuram offered work and training for locals and exemplified the "best practice" model for self-rule and economic self-sufficiency that Elango aimed to develop in his village and export to other panchayats. Kuthambakkam's samathuvapuram was successful as an inter-caste residential space and in terms of skill acquisition. Villagers, in fact, applied the same techniques to other projects after the samathuvapuram was completed. The samathuvapuram also offered media visibility to the village and enhanced Elango's credibility as an effective and honest leader. Following its completion, Elango pressed forward with an ambitious effort to foster more autonomy, accountability, and effectiveness among panchayats. He built a panchayat federation in the state and launched a support and training program, Panchayat Academy, for panchayat presidents. In 2002 he was recognized as a "social entrepreneur" by the Ashoka Foundation, and, with his fellowship money, he set up the Trust for Village Self Governance to support his goals, which he regards as ongoing enactments of Gandhian imagined community.[47] Gandhian economic principles inform his embrace of self-sufficiency, and toward this end he has continued to use infrastructure development to generate employment and has set up various small-scale industries, including a small dairy and production units for foodstuffs, jute products, and footwear.

In his pursuit of economic and political autonomy for his village, Elango has cultivated wide, transnational networks for funding and publicity, making the village globally visible.[48] After being named an Ashoka Fellow, he traveled to the U.S. where he was hosted in NRI forums across the country, making presentations and giving interviews about his achievements in Kuthambakkam and his plans for its development.[49] In conversations such as the one with Asha Mahesh, quoted above, Elango encountered NRIs' and other Westerners' nostalgic attachments to Gandhian nationalism and, especially, to the images of village India to which those attachments are often bound. In those conversations, his own class privilege relative to other Dalits and his English-language abilities and Gandhian values (though embraced with equivocation) were supplemented by a broader fluency in the language of technocratic modernity—gained through his experiences as scientist, planner, and elected official. The interaction between Elango and his Western supporters engendered cultural intimacies in which Elango both re-created and deconstructed the "village," nurturing Gandhism without relinquishing the pragmatism of rural subaltern citizenship. These strategies enabled him to navigate within broad political and class spectrums and to connect with Western and upper-caste audiences, especially those that sought a channel to express their Indian roots and extend the benefits of modernity to a homeland that many knew only through brief encounters.

The samathuvapuram, one among several reform projects launched under Elango's leadership, contributed to the village's welfare and enhanced his reputation for transparent, accountable governance, making Kuthambakkam's equality village one of the few that the government considered a success in terms of the program's goals. All samathuvapurams were conjunctural formations that mediated the state apparatus and the lived world of the village. At each equality village, the worldliness of the urban modern met its rural "other," constituted as both vernacular and remote. Kuthambakkam's, however, also represented a convergence among ethical horizons—the Gandhian aspirations of the architects and panchayat president, the homesickness of NRI donors, and Dalit villagers' own ambiguous attachments to place.

Architecture as a Gandhian Project

Though Elango has often commented on the Gandhian tenor on his economic and political principles, he has not remarked on its relation to the built form of the samathuvapuram or the later structures that were modeled on its style and techniques. The Gandhian dimensions of cost-effective architecture are widely claimed by practitioners, however. Like Gandhian nationalism, which freely recombined regional and sectarian traditions but still claimed spatio-temporal continuity with village India, cost-effective architecture arises from cosmopolitan appreciation of rural lifeways. Laurie Baker explicitly attributed the guiding principles of cost-effective architecture to Gandhi, who sought models for Indian nationhood in its rural spaces and lifeways in his quest for a future outside the telos of Euro-Western modernity. Gandhi resignified vernacular architecture as a national emblem when he observed that the ideal house in the ideal village should be built of materials found within a five-mile radius. Baker reclaimed that principle as the core of appropriate building technology and developed a genre of design and construction that relied on locally produced materials, such as mud-brick, lime mortar, palm thatching, stone, granite, laterite, and local timbers, and their parsimonious use.

Although cost-effective methods could be applied to any type of structure, Baker and his followers have regarded community housing as closer in spirit to the tenets of cost-effectiveness.[50] This is because of its perceived affinity with the space of collective life, the intentional community of the ashram, most closely associated with Gandhi. Gandhi himself resided in a series of ashrams after returning to India in 1914 up until his death in 1948, and treated them as the cell-form of the village republics which he regarded as bedrocks of a national community.[51] Gandhian economics, as developed by J. C. Kumarappa, takes an ashram-type community as its basic unit.[52] It outlines an economy predicated on the self-sufficiency of local units, with consumption limited by resources and norms of local modes of production, rather than profitability.

Baker's long-standing interest in the design and construction of community housing and his involvement in India's community architecture movement of the 1970s and 1980s carried forward, but resituated, the ashram model within the public housing programs of the postcolonial state.[53] This brought its own conditions and compromises, including working within the terms of the conventional contracting system, which Baker found antithetical to the aims of cost-effective work.[54] Baker stated that cost-effective principles should extend across the entire industry, although he and other practitioners acknowledged the impossibility of that goal given the incompatibilities of scale and the realpolitik of India's electoral system. They strove instead to create alternate ways of working that favored a less hierarchical and more consultative process. As it stands now, cost-effective work exists within the industrialized construction system in the form of islands of alternative practice, reliant on locally available labor and resources.

Within the domains of cost-effective practice, architecture is understood, like the social space of the ashram, as experimentation. Architecture does not denote the final product of building but encompasses the interactions between builders and occupants, and between the conceived space of the architectural plan and the lived space of the built form. These dense relational webs and the improvisational quality of the work accords with Gandhian praxis, particularly its core modality of experimentation. This was not meant as experimentation in the terms defined by Western science but as moral experimentation. It was in such activities that the possibility of progress outside the telos of Western modernity lay. Gandhian projects, both individual and collective, were designed as experiments to test participants' resolve and grasp of truth, and to further the moral growth of the individual and the moral solidarity of the group. The term by which these various experiments were categorized was *satyagraha*. This neologism, coined by Gandhi, is often translated as nonviolence. Gandhi's own English gloss was more subtle, however. He defined satyagraha as "firmness in adherence to truth." The forms that this moral firmness could take were grounded in Hindu praxis, in austerities (*tapas*), devotion (*bhakti*), and vision (*darśan*), but they were always evolving. *Satyagraha* was, in this sense, always experimental. The actions to which *satyagraha* came to refer over time included marches, fasts, work strikes, sit-ins, and craft production. *Satyagraha* also included negative actions, such as nonpayment of taxes and refusal to purchase goods of European manufacture. Much of the work of nationalist mobilization, of resistance to colonial authority and cultivation of Indian subjectivity, was conducted through various combinations of these activities.

In the case of cost-effective architecture, experimentalism has extended beyond the realms of design and materials. Projects influenced by Baker, including Kuthambakkam's samathuvapuram, demonstrate Gandhi's influence in their attention to integrating the work of design and building, and to creating close relations between architects and the construction laborers, masons, carpenters, and tile setters who executed the plans and hailed, mostly, from low-caste and Dalit communities. The active presence of PAC's architects during construction, incorporating, and adjusting according to the context was in keeping with conditions stipulated by Baker, who maintained that, through negotiation, the design should evolve over the course of construction. This put their work fundamentally at odds with the standard contractual model in which bids were made for jobs on the basis of plans and detailed projections of finance and labor. This approach, which integrated architecture and construction, was also meant to counteract the de-skilling of construction labor that had occurred with its industrialization.

As this indicates, Baker's objections to the conventional contracting system lay in its organization of labor, as well as in its typically modern products. Cost-effectiveness, besides its hallmark traditionalism in style, was a form of praxis that sought to create relations with workers that enhanced their skill levels and the dignity of manual labor. Cost-effective practice also aimed to demystify the work of the architect by encouraging greater dependence between design and construction. These were approaches that Baker regarded as consistent with the traditional role of the architect in Indian society and with Gandhi's valorization of manual labor in general and craft in particular. The same principles were evident in PAC's approach, both in their inclusion of a construction worker as a partner in the firm and in their on-site work at Kuthambakkam. In the same spirit, panchayat president Elango cited Gandhi and the Gandhian economist J. Kumarappa in outlining an approach to increase employment and revenue in the village by employing locals in the various infrastructure development projects that he launched.

Troubled Nostalgias

The normative style and praxis of cost-effective architecture, with its dialectical relation to conventional design and construction, carries with it a critique of modernity and a strategic retention of tradition, both promulgated by Gandhi in his 1909 tract, *Hind Swaraj*. Its title refers to Indian self-rule—moral self-rule of the person and the political self-rule of the nation. There he asserted that Indian traditionalism was morally superior to Western modernity. However, the traditional institutions and principles that he supported were in some cases expedient inventions, that is, he recombined elements of different moral and economic systems in order to hold out aspirations which he regarded as both appealing and plausible to ordinary Indians.[55]

The critique of modernity made implicitly and explicitly by proponents of cost-effective architecture is similarly selective and, in Gandhian terms, experimental. On the one hand, its concerns for functionalism and efficiency unabashedly embrace modernism. On the other hand, the modernist reliance on steel and glass has been dismissed as inauthentic and inappropriate for Indian conditions. Baker and his followers have been critical of "facadism"—the use of nonfunctional decorative elements—as being arrogant and dishonest. Baker maintained that the reuse of existing structures, along with vernacular design and materials, enables people to recall and reinterpret the past within contemporary settings, and to strategically *enact* the past as material memory. He did not advocate whole-scale re-creation or preservation but a selective gathering of pieces of the past as part of a living present. Baker's position was wholly in keeping with Gandhi's insistence on India's exceptionalism and, he maintained, his embrace of its traditionalism and "immoveability," qualities that revealed the limits of worldviews that valued progress and its historicity. History, Gandhi asserted, was merely "a record of an interruption of the course of nature. Soul-force, being natural, is not noted in history."[56]

Gandhian keywords and iconography continue to serve as a currency for nationalism in India and its diaspora. Not surprisingly, Baker's cost-effective style, with its Gandhian overtones, has won praise (and contracts) from India's Housing and Urban Development Corporation. Such patronage is wholly consistent with the ways in which emblems of Gandhian nationalism have been recycled in official nationalism, even as the Indian state has pursued large-scale planned development and, more recently, free-market policies, both of which are at odds with Gandhian economics and governance.

Baker, his associates, and his sympathizers aimed to shape the built environment in ways that would enable the Gandhian national imaginary to be recalled implicitly and enactively, in building and inhabiting their material surroundings. As had Gandhi, the architecture selectively quoted the past, with features that evoked, even as they recombined, the familiar world of rural hamlets. This strategy folds together the nostalgic appropriation of rural as the wellspring of tradition, but it is bound to a counter-nostalgic understanding of past (and continuing) oppression and to aspirations that the panchayat's president, evoking Gandhi, tagged "*gram swaraj*," village self-rule.

Because of the moral principles of his projects, Gandhi is often considered utopian, though that may not do justice to his thinking and to the materiality of his projects, for example, as demonstrated in the bodily mediation of Gandhian nationalism. The idea of utopia suggests a pipe dream, a soporific lacking a critical edge and oppositional energy. But there are other ways of engaging the idea of utopia that can shed light on Gandhian projects and their present status. David Harvey, a geographer and social theorist, argued that utopia, conceived dialectically, could be understood not as a retreat but as a site of struggle; Richard Fox, similarly, stressed the improvisational and experimental character of Gandhian formulations of utopia.[57] Harvey employed the figure of architect to describe the agent of dialectical utopia. Here he meant the architect in the literal sense of one who designed the built environment. But he also meant it in the figurative sense of a person capable of translating critical discourses and oppositional ideals into an actual way and space of living—who, in other words, ceased to be an abstract planner and adopted the limited, provisional, and compromise-ridden stance of action.

This lends insight into Gandhi beyond the simple binary of alienating consumerism versus authenticating self-sufficiency. Gandhi's utopia was ambiguous not so much because it was an immaterial, esoteric, or disembodied spiritualism but because it sought material mediation and, to an important degree, could only be expressed through the material world and in bodily activity. Apart from the body itself, the ashram was the template and exemplar of such praxis. Gandhi intended the ashrams as workshops in which *satyagraha* could be tested and a national community shaped. It was to be an experiment that translated ethical aspirations into the material spaces of everyday life. In his illuminating interpretation of Gandhi's own writings on ashram life, Ajay Skaria makes a case for the ashram as a locus for "neighborly nationalism":

> In the Gandhian vows of the ashram—which constituted it as a set of political practices, not simply a place—we can read an opposition to this logic of transcendence, a constituting of the nation through a politics of *ahimsa* (literally nonviolence: better understood as "neighborliness."[58]

Skaria's reading of the Gandhian ashram acknowledges its conceptual debt to both Hindu orthopraxy (ashram, as in *varṇāśramadharma,* refers to the phases of the normative [male] Hindu life cycle) and to the models for intentional communities that, in the context of anticolonial reformist and nationalist movements, consciously and selectively recuperated past forms of Hindu praxis. He maintained, however, that the Gandhian ashram was reworked to enact both a national imaginary that existed as a critique of the secular commitments of liberal nationalism and the chauvinist exclusion of Hindutva.[59] As a space of moral experimentation, the ashram was organized around the bodily repertoire of Hindu praxis (service, self-abnegation, devotion, vision) but, rather than seeking to reconstitute a specifically Hindu community or to neutralize differences of caste, sect, ethnicity, or gender, aimed to generate "neighborliness" among those whose differences—of religion, ethnicity, culture—were absolute. Neighborliness, then, was the product of radical engagement with difference, in this instance through the shared suffering of *tapasya* (self-abnegation).

The politics that emerged from neighborliness, Skaria writes, "was nothing if not about everyday life.... Much of Gandhi's work lay precisely in seizing upon the fugitive (and supplementary) forms of everyday life, and in infusing them with a rigorous antidisciplinary discipline that allowed them to no longer be fugitive."[60] It is in this context that the significance of architectural mediations of Gandhism, such as Baker's, can be appreciated as mnemonic enactments of Gandhian praxis. The ashram and the architectural experiments that have followed are intended as spaces (conceptual and material) and practices that relate the "local," understood as the space-time of daily life, to the abstract space-time of the nation. What Skaria calls "neighborly nationalism" is irreducibly local insofar as it exists in and is constitutive of the social space of the ashram, a built environment in which consumption, rest, labor, recreation, devotion, and discipline are carried out. Community housing projects conceived by Baker partake of these aspirations. That such architectural mediations of Gandhism are meant as spaces of reorganized habitus, moreover, points to their status as technologies of memory; that is, these architectural experiments can be understood as a way of remembering Gandhi, for they privilege the enactive, embodied memory that Gandhi himself advocated in his selective retention of tradition and skepticism about history. Gandhi's own transnationalism and mobility, his willingness to experiment with ways of living, and his compromised utopias may have value as models for Indians who recall, through him, earlier moments of experimentation, of radical newness, of friction-filled hybridity.

In Kuthambakkam, then, Gandhi was remembered not by conventional commemorative media, such as iconography or anthems, but materially and pragmatically, in the production of a vernacular future. This nostalgia sought to recapture a once-imagined future. It made Kuthambakkam's samathuvapuram a template for cultural memory that was less about representing heritage than it was a revisionist effort to make the past selectively present as a force in the community's revitalization, as a space of cultural intimacy borne of dialogic engagement between the village's residents and urban elites, and as an emblem for its global audiences of donors.[61]

Conclusion: Memory, Place, and Voice

Within the wider context of the city's neoliberal restructuring, both its rurban expansion and the redevelopment of its core, the past has become scarce and superabundant. It resides in what neoliberal nostalgia recaptures but also in what it forgets: Heritage is invented and celebrated even as other signifiers of modernity's "before" are swept away. The poor, especially, are caught within the juxtaposed temporalities of neoliberal nostalgia. Villagers, as well as urban slumdwellers, are cast (and cast aside) as residues of the pasts of city and nation, making them touchstones for personal and national pasts as well as being what its modern consumer-citizens hope to leave behind, sooner rather than later. The erasure of the past—in the accelerated pace of forced evictions, the demolition of old building stock, and the re-sculpting of the streetscape—invests these terms of recognition with material effects.

While the recognition of the poor, urban and rural, in popular and official discourses is shaped by the pasts that they are understood to embody within dominant discourses, claims to citizenship and to the space of city and nation by the poor rely also on strategic representations of the past. Articulated with the neoliberal nostalgia that animates NGOs dedicated to heritage preservation are other nostalgias, more reflective than restorative, to use Boym's parlance, many authored by slumdwellers, Dalits, and workers. These efforts, which sometimes are carried out collaboratively with urban elites, engage critically with the spatiality of oppression and underwrite political projects of various sorts—claims of entitlement to resources, demands for greater enfranchisement—by pressing for changes in terms of recognition and by developing more capacious forms of political voice.

The Periyar Ninaivu program, under whose auspices Kuthambakkam's samathuvapuram was built, melded social welfare with commemorative piety and electoral calculus. Equality villages were designed to alleviate caste-based discrimination, conceived as a vestige of tradition, with the modernist prescription of defamiliarization. In most, mud-thatch or brick houses were replaced with multi-unit tenements of reinforced concrete. Along with these architectural signs of modernity, villagers were promised schools, shops, and clinics, services they associated with "town." The samathuvapuram's modernity lay also in its scientistic experimentalism. The break with the architectural past was, like the demolition of a slum, a razing of the quotidian world in which caste segregation and inequality had persisted. In common with nearly all populist measures launched by Tamil Nadu's major parties, the samathuvapuram program was nominally commemorative, the choice of Periyar as namesake announcing the DMK's opposition to caste and its essential Tamil-ness. What differed in Kuthambakkam was the samathuvapuram's harnessing of commemorative impulse to both a name and to the village's very materiality. Designed as a collaborative venture between architects, residents, and the village's panchayat, it recalled not only Periyar, but Gandhi, implicitly, through the material mediation and experimentalism of cost-effective architecture.

For the rural and largely Dalit poor, who were the beneficiaries of the samathuvapuram and other self-help programs, the political and economic transformations associated with the making of rurban space have not undone long-standing forms of inequality and stigma. They are sites of nostalgias that exist conjuncturally, at the spatio-temporal interface of the rurban itself and in the relations, across the boundaries of caste, class, and nation and between state and populace. In association with shifts in political participation, formal and informal, however, they have introduced opportunities for political and cultural self-assertion, sustained and mediated by new cultural memories.

The experimental vernacular design of Kuthambakkam's samathuvapuram existed within a wider field of memory work that has mediated political and cultural associations among poor and Dalit groups. For example, in response to evictions and resettlements, which accelerated over the 1990s, slumdwellers across the city mobilized to challenge evictions, often with the support of national and international human rights organizations. In these legal challenges, the past of slum settlements, as part of the historically emergent cityscape, has been advanced as a basis to challenge evictions and to claim rights to place and citizenship. The court cases, though usually decided against slumdweller petitioners, offer insight into the ways in which some representations of the slum's pastness can operate as tactics of visibility that counter neoliberal erasure of the poor—that make the social space of slums visible without lapsing into nostalgic, romanticized, or celebratory accounts. The very existence of such challenges hints at the ways that slums, like any other habitation, may be made "place-ful," their dense ties of kinship, sociality, and struggle treated as loci of cultural belonging even as their abject, demeaning conditions are denounced. Place attachment, expressed and sustained in the quotidian practices by which place is made, is a source of the commitments and aspirations that lead slumdwellers to challenge evictions and resettlement and to forge new cultural memories.[62]

Political mobilization among "backward" and "Scheduled" communities during the 1990s has drawn on these nostalgias in the formation of political parties as well as in the thickening of culturally based associational life and media.[63] Dalit history has been made visible, critical perspectives on caste and Hinduism introduced, and Dalit cultural memory nurtured. Through written text and images, these cultural media have promulgated a popular understanding of a Dalit past by recirculating works of Ambedkar and Phule, and by recovering hidden pasts (e.g., Dalit cricketers, ancient Dalit heroes). Wider alliances have been sought; in some instances, efforts have been made to enroll others, such as Muslims, Christians, women, and other non-Brahmans, in a shared oppositional consciousness, as non-Hindus.[64] These alliances have transnational reach, through the networks, coordinated by human rights NGOs, that were galvanized in response to backlash against panchayati raj and in preparation for the UN-sponsored World Conference Against Racism in Durban, in September 2001.[65]

Besides opening a space in which the poor and their histories are made visible, these developments, along with the housing experiments discussed in this chapter, also suggest ways to think about how pastness may be harnessed to the cultivation of voice. Political voice—participation in governance by communicating one's interests, expectations, demands, and dissent to fellow citizens and to officials—rests on the existence of institutional channels for representation as well as on individual agency and the capacity of persons to aspire.[66] In development discourses, the formation of political voice is often envisioned as the fruit of neoliberal economic development and as a break with the past.

Such approaches to development have been influenced by Amartya Sen's notion of "capabilities," which referred to the institutional means by which the health, well-being, and political participation of citizens could be assured.[67] Building on Sen, Appadurai underscored the necessity of a capacity to aspire, part of the broader, ethical horizon that gives meaning, substance, and sustainability to concrete capabilities.[68] The psychological sense of agency and the relational and institutional contexts for its expression are at the heart of the capacity to aspire, which rests on the ability to plan, to explore the connections between means and ends, and to act with effects. With this intervention in development theory, Appadurai sought to introduce a richer, more nuanced understanding of culture to the work on culture and development, one that heeded the underdetermined and improvisational qualities that make culture a zone of contestation and possibilities, rather than simply a matter of rules. While rightly stressing the centrality of innovation and creativity within culture, however, he ignored the fluidity of the past itself and the possibilities for cultural critique and invention that the work of memory may yield. It is to these possibilities that I have sought to speak with the materials of this chapter.

I argue that discourse and activities associated with the recognition of pastness are part of the cultural and ethical horizons in which the capacity to aspire arises and political voice is cultivated. They may form sites around which aspirations, interests, and collective identities are negotiated, sites for mobilization and coalition building, avenues for engaging with state and public authorities and learning how to navigate their systems. As such, they may offer models for political dissent. Whereas Kuthambakkam's samathuvapuram mined vernacular pasts for a future outside the bounds of modernity, slumdwellers, in challenges to eviction and in strategic attention to commemoration, sought to realize the promises of modernity by making historical pasts visible. Commemoration has played a role as catalyst in associational life and place attachment, with the multiplication of statues, memorials, and portraits of prominent figures such as Ambedkar, Periyar, and Phule, as well as of those killed or injured in past struggles. In addition to cultivating affect that may energize struggles for recognition and voice, commemoration of these figures recalls their oppositional praxis—itself formed through historical bricolage—for present projects.

The senses of the past that Chennai's rurban poor have developed in articulation with state and market development arise through the interaction of social and psychological domains and work both implicitly, by means of *enactments* of the past through labor, acts of protest, imagery, and the built environment, and explicitly, through the shared knowledge about the past, semantic memory, to which people appeal in making decisions, executing actions, and planning. As rights to the city are circumscribed by market principles, pastness has emerged as a resource for making alliances and for imagining alternatives to current conditions, for thinking that things can be different because they once were.

8

Conclusion: "How Many Museums Can One Have?"

"Anita" posed that question during a conversation with me about Tamil Nadu's recently mooted Heritage Act. An architect and a member of INTACH's Chennai chapter, Anita was exasperated by the ways that some in that organization viewed preservation. "Whom does it benefit?" she asked, referring to activities such as the listing and conservation of monuments and colonial-era structures. She continued:

> Suppose this preservation of heritage precincts becomes a law, and suppose that many more NGOs start to get involved in preservation efforts. The whole thing will be "clean up the pavement," "clean up the street." There's a whole load of people—vendors, tailors, cobblers—they will all be thrown out and they add something to the character and even to the beauty of the street. This is what I'm saying, this whole . . . process has to be rethought. You can't just model [it] . . . on something that has been borrowed from another country, even if it has worked there.

The problem lay not only the foreignness of the models, but in the ways that their implementation exacerbated already existing structural inequalities. As she explained: "These conservation projects they always come from the upper end, they always come in an authoritative mode."

Conservation, she thought, could be carried out in a way that enhanced the dignity and well-being of the poor and working classes, but only if they were able to participate in its conception and implementation. She drew selectively on Euro-Western models, having earned a degree in conservation architecture at a British university, but she sought to formulate methods tailored to India's needs and challenges. Her efforts to imagine how conservation of this sort might work were marked by the hesitations and ironies of cultural intimacy, particularly because she remained resolutely skeptical of both exclusivist nationalisms and what she viewed as the tendency, among conservation architects, to romanticize craft.

Those uncertainties surfaced again in a conversation a few weeks later, as we discussed a recent public presentation. The speaker, K. T. Narasimhan, was employed by the Archaeological Survey of India and specialized in the conservation of Hindu temples. Narasimhan had described several projects of restoration—repair, repainting, and so forth—in which the aim had been not the exposition of their antiquity but the renewal of their facades through re-plastering, painting, and structural repair. Such activities, while serving as routine repairs, were also associated with the periodic, ritual renewal of temples' sacrality. His talk had been studded with Sanskrit phrases, *slokas* (verses) from the ritual manuals that governed temple construction. His quotation of Sanskrit sources was to emphasize that they alone furnished guidelines for conserving temples and other ancient monuments; his mastery of those sources was also an assertion of his authority, as a Brahman, in such matters. Anita, also a Brahman, regarded him with ironic detachment:

> Do you remember Narasimhan's talk . . .? He showed a slide of some *kōpuram* that he and his team had restored and he said that when he visited the site with some archaeologists from abroad, no one was able to figure out whether the thing was newly built or ancient. He was proud of the fact that he was able to renovate like that, wasn't he? But it's not like that, you should show the time factor. In a living culture where a *kōpuram* undergoes renovation periodically, it cannot be a neutralizing sort of conservation.

Where Narasimhan's approach to conservation drew on Hindu praxis to stress the continuity of past and present, Anita understood conservation as a response to and preservation of temporal disjuncture. Anita's criticism of Narasimhan, moreover, stemmed not only from her ideas about proper conservation techniques, ideas shaped by formal training in conservation architecture but also from a pluralistic ethos. She assumed that competing claims to authenticity existed and that such pluralism was both necessary and desirable.

My own experience of hearing Narasimhan's talk illustrated what was at stake in a slightly different way. I had invited an acquaintance, Lalitha (a Brahman tour guide introduced in chapter 5), to come to the talk with me, thinking that she would be interested in what Narasimhan had to say. I was not wrong—she had listened carefully to the entire presentation, at points gesturing in enthusiastic agreement. As Narasimhan concluded, she had turned to me: "That was superb! He knows the authentic reasons for the temples, for the ways that they were built. Why aren't we [tour guides] given such information? We should know all this to be able to answer tourists' questions." Like Lalitha, I also found Narasimhan to be a knowledgeable and engaging speaker. Lalitha's appreciation of his "authenticity" went beyond a generalized respect for his knowledge, however. She had often shared with me her own views on Brahmans' cultural superiority, especially in matters of heritage, and Narasimhan's presentation merely confirmed the truth of what she already knew. Between Lalitha's pleasurable affirmation and Anita's rueful self-regard is the conflicted ground on which pasts take shape.

Narasimhan's projects and goals fulfilled, but revalorized, a set of expectations, long held by foreigners and Indian citizens, about Indian traditionalism. Stigmatized as "ahistorical" during the colonial era, measures of the sort that Narasimhan prescribed attracted the opprobrium of ASI officers such as Alexander Rea (discussed in chapter 2). Now, however, some of those same techniques have been retrieved by British colonial officers' Indian successors. Moreover, Narasimhan's approach to conservation privileges the selective account of Brahman-authored tradition with which some Indians, Brahman and non-Brahman, buttress a sense of national identity.

As the differences between Lalitha's, Anita's, and Narasimhan's perspectives suggest, the nostalgias of the present harbor multiple modes of engaging with the past. Drawing on a cosmopolitanism that straddles former colonial divides and contemporary nation-state boundaries, some conservation advocates, like Anita, find Narasimhan's agenda parochial and tied to a system of unequal privilege with which they maintain a conflicted cultural intimacy. While disavowing the traditional lifeworld in which Hindu religiosity and caste inequality were locked together, they remain divided about the translatability of templates (e.g., museums, heritage registers) borrowed from Europe. Moreover, these positions hardly exhaust the kinds of past-consciousness expressed among Chennai's citizens, from the automotive plant workers inhabiting its rurban villages to the "foreign-returned" who patronize Nungambakkam's discotheques and coffee bars. As I have shown in this book, cultural intimacies of the present rely on pasts—known, seen, heard, and embodied—of ritualized commemoration, vernacular architecture, bodily labor, archives and museal spaces, commodities and brand logos, oral narratives, and place names.

Anita's dilemma, while resting on the experiences of a narrow stratum of Chennai's elite, can be read as a prism on issues taken up in the book, revealing the dialectical relations between heritage projects and capitalism's creative destruction, and the cultural intimacies with the past that those dialectical relations sustain and trouble. While her dilemma indexes the ways that heritage projects engage, reinforce, and undermine the intersecting inequalities of caste, gender, and class, it serves as an object lesson about the nostalgias that neoliberal globalization has released. Anita and like-minded colleagues participate in projects that draw on knowledge and resources that are available because of India's turn to neoliberalism. However, as Kim and Mike Fortun have pointed out, such work also grapples with the problems that this turn has created and offers a critical analysis of these conditions.[1] To quote Fortun and Fortun, symbolic analysts like Anita recognize that "national borders mean something different than they once did, [but] they remain committed to 'Indian alternatives'—alternatives to [modes of] national development that [. . .] merely mimic the West and exclude most Indians from both economic prosperity and political authority."[2] The sort of home-sickness that their activities communicate is expressed in different registers: it can be read in the persistent insecurities of slumdwellers' claims to a home in the city and in a Non-Resident Indian's aesthetic regard for the signs of antiquity that an eighth-century Hindu temple discloses. And the dilemmas that have accompanied the nostalgic formation that neoliberal globalization engenders have only become more pressing over the years that I researched and wrote this book.

The Planning State, 2007

> Modern India's political and economic experiences have coincided most dramatically in its cities—symbols of the uneven, hectic and contradictory character of the nation's modern life. . . . They have emerged out of an intricate, discontinuous history: remade by the will of the Raj, with its shifting, precise and—for most Indians—bewildering sense of what a city was; rearranged again by a nationalist conception of what the modern Indian city should be; and now, once again subject to rearrangement by new post-nationalist ambitions.[3]

With this passage, Sunil Khilnani captured both the historically changing forms of India's cities as well as the ways that cityscapes encode narratives on their own pasts and futures. In a similar spirit, I have argued that Chennai has been a stage for world historical change from its colonial appearance as "Madras" to its current claim to be one of India's "mega-cities."

Chennai's planning authority, in its most recent draft master plan, echoed Khilnani's characterization: "Cities are engines of development. They are also loci of the most important impacts of globalization and hence the places of change and expectations for the future." That plan, subtitled Vision 2026 and discussed in chapter 2, prescribed how Chennai could be made "more livable, economically vibrant and environmentally sustainable and with better assets for future generations." The engine for growth, planners wrote, was Chennai's embrace of the "new economy," of IT-led development and its strength in the "old economy" of industry and manufacturing; both were hailed as departures from the state-sponsored developmentalism of previous decades and as the keys for realizing, through free-market capitalism, the promises of future prosperity. This optimism is grounded, planners argued, in the history of Chennai's development which they reinterpreted as having a free-market orientation, even under the centrally planned economy of India's postcolonial state: "Unlike other major cities . . . public sector led growth and development process was not envisaged . . . but [planners relied on] private involved growth process to achieve the objectives of town planning."[4]

More than its predecessors, however, this plan was attentive to Chennai's history and included specific provisions for the listing, grading, and conservation of heritage sites, and for creating incentives for such activity. The plan's provisions for defining and regulating the use of heritage sites have been welcomed by some within INTACH and allied organizations. Events like the INTACH-CMDA seminar, discussed in chapter 4, seem to have borne fruit. City planners now concur with INTACH that heritage preservation can contribute to economic growth—not only through revenues yielded by tourism and leisure consumption but also by indirect contributions to infrastructure development through such mechanisms as transfers of development rights. Dilemmas such as those voiced by Anita, however, will only be intensified. Whose heritage will be showcased? Who will be called upon to define the past? What futures will new spaces of heritage anticipate? Will the authorship of community pasts enlarge democratic participation and enrich civic culture?

This book's genealogy of the present has tracked the state's institutional investment in spaces of public memory, arguing that those investments themselves mark transformations in statecraft from the planned welfare state of the fifties, sixties, and seventies to the neoliberal designs of the nineties. While aiming to get a handle on contingencies that have made heritage conservation part of India's planning state, I have also sought to explore broader questions about how and why past-consciousness and the social spaces that it creates matter for citizenship.

India's cities, like those of any nation-state, form a connective tissue that lend form and force to the state, both as idea and institution. They are administrative switchpoints, where the state's surveillance and its regulation of populace and territory are translated from its center to various localities and regions. Attention to the pasts that are made present in cities, however, reveal that the city is not just an artifact of state function and ideology: its lifeworlds are built on collective pasts and futures.

Critical to the ways that cities serve as mediators of the state effect are their representations of its genealogy, in official and unofficial sites of public memory. These sites may present statements, by governing bodies, about the origins, core values, and telos of their power of rule. As material signifiers of the state, they condense and localize what is usually encountered as a depersonalized and disaggregated bureaucracy; they may embody the state's own myths of origin, representing both its temporal durability and its sometimes sacralized transcendence. Such spaces are designed to work rhetorically: to argue and persuade, to enroll people within particular political projects and models of sovereignty, and to make certain forms of citizenship vital and desirable. They are also theaters on which competing images of sovereignty and citizenship struggle for ascendancy, especially in moments of political crisis and transformation, emplotting both logics of rule and modes of dissent within morally compelling stories and imagery. If, under conditions of neoliberal globalization, states cede some parts of sovereignty, they must continue, perhaps in more intensified ways, to retain the loyalties and affective attachments of citizens through the same forms of commemorative praxis, as exemplified in MGR's memorialization, discussed in chapter 3.

Cities, however, are not only nodes of statecraft but places to which attachments are formed through work and leisure, through walking, seeing, and hearing, and deepened through remembrance. Smriti Srinivas's work on festivity and the making of civic space in Bangalore is a reminder of the embodied persistence of place attachments, defined as the psychodynamic forces by which people define, emotionally and cognitively orient themselves to, and derive satisfaction from the environments, built and natural, that they occupy.[5] Such attachments are formed over time and expressed through memory, through individual and social acts of remembering, and the objects, words, images, sounds, smells, and tastes that encode and represent personal and collective pasts.[6] The power of place attachment can underwrite the chauvinism of religious nationalism—think here of the blood-drenched territoriality of Hindutva—as well as the praxis of self-sufficiency that proponents of cost-effective architecture sought to enact.

That Chennai is a city comprising a multiplicity of places and attachments was implied in an e-mail message I received from one INTACH member regarding the 2006 celebration of "Madras Week," staged to celebrate the city's 1639 founding:

> The Madras Week raises questions as to what heritage will it celebrate? From its own definition and limitation of history, heritage of Chennai starts with the 17th century. What will happen to the ancient vrshni heroes deified in the Triplicane temple? How do we deal with the legend of Thiruvalluvar and Pei Alvar's birth at Mylapore? What happens to the ancient ports of Tiruvottriyiur and Mylapore? Do we have to forget the earlier Portuguese contribution in the making of Santhome and thus Chennai?[7]

Consider, for a moment, Mylapore, one of the original temple towns annexed by the East India Company. Mylapore is often thought of as a Brahman locality, owing to the prominent Brahman writers, lawyers, and politicians who have resided there over the past two centuries, and to the iconic signifiers of Brahmanic Hinduism seen on its streetscapes: temple priests on scooters, the open storefronts of ritual provisions shops, older women in traditionally tied saris. But Mylapore's actual population is far more diverse than its reputation suggests. Scheduled Castes make up 19 percent of the division's population, and there are numerous hut colonies and tenements; residents of one such colony, which occupied land on which a new commuter rail station was planned, had taken their challenge to Chennai's High Court, as well as to the streets and parks, to assert their historic rights of occupancy.[8]

In interviews and informal conversations, I learned that Mylapore's many non-Brahman residents regard it with as much affection and attachment as do its Brahmans. "Raji," for example, was a member of the non-Brahman Mudaliar community who responded to my query about her memories of her neighborhood, by asserting: "*Ellam ceḷakkiyam!* [Everything is good!]." She added, "You won't find anyone who will say that things are bad here." As was the case throughout Mylapore, new flat complexes stood among smaller, independent houses; what Raji appreciated was its intimate scale, its sacred spaces, and the vibrancy of its commercial and cultural life. Besides its proximity to the massive Kapaleswarar temple complex and many smaller shrines, the street and adjoining lanes held ubiquitous provision stores and vegetable carts; there were also coffee vendors, a small appliance depot, an eversilver shop, a goldsmith, and an instrument repair shop. Such features had persisted over the thirty-plus years of her residence there.

Differences of caste and class within the division's population were complicated by their sectarian diversity. Again, despite its Hindu reputation, Mylapore's residents include significant concentrations of Muslims, Jains, and Christians. In 1994 a gleaming Jain temple was constructed to meet that population's needs; San Thome, the former Portuguese enclave, is home to mixed-race descendents, and its cathedral, built atop the burial chamber of St. Thomas, is a Christian pilgrimage site.[9] Further, Mylapore's proximity to the land formerly granted to the Nawab of Arcot had brought Muslim families to the area, many occupying the commercial and residential streets that adjoin Bazaar Road. A Muslim saint's tomb and shrine adjoins a Muslim burial ground near the San Thome section of Mylapore. Modest homes are clustered near the tomb, and the elderly man who spoke with me asserted that the shrine was "more than four hundred years old."[10] Like many poor, minority communities this one had been forced to resettle numerous times—settling finally near the burial ground in the hope of forestalling eviction. Another older man whom I interviewed identified himself as a Marwari, having migrated from Rajasthan in the 1920s, but also as a devotee of Tamil language and literature. He captured the cultural diversity that, for many Mylapore residents, was its distinctive feature, when he praised its having seven sites for each of the major religious sects: "Here, only, you'll find seven churches, seven Pillaiyar temples, seven Siva temples, seven Vishnu temples, seven masjids [mosques], and seven tanks. Mylapore and Triplicane are oldest and best . . . the originals!"[11]

Mylapore's pasts were encoded in the mnemonics of place, mnemonics encountered in everyday experience. These encounters did not yield single, orderly narratives but story threads. Typical of the acts of remembering that sustain place attachments, these rely on both implicit and explicit forms of recognition that produce (rather than simply recall) images, words, and sensations associated with other times, with times not-present and with the futures that were once anticipated. The notion that multiple temporalities inhabit any given place inspires new, embodied templates for heritage conservation, for example, walking tours and hands-on participation in conservation work. To this end, Anita has helped create a series of walking-tour maps for neighborhoods in older divisions of Chennai that are rarely, if ever, visited by tourists. The intent was not just to provide a novel experience for international and domestic tourists but also to bring everyday lifeworlds into focus and to capture the everydayness of difference—the situated cosmopolitanisms of working-class as well as more privileged citizens. A similar hope animates the reengagements with Gandhian praxis described in chapter 7. In that context, a template for cultural memory was created that was based not on representing "heritage" but—following the revisionist remembering of Gandhian nationalism—sought to make the past selectively present as a force in the community's revitalization.

The still present pasts of "historic districts" and vernacular settlements may invite their designation as *milieux de memoire*. That category, however, exoticizes and romanticizes tradition in ways that both misrepresent pasts and make temporal Others of present-day lifeworlds. Instead, there are possibilities of seeking in expressions of place attachment the taken-for-granted, everydayness of some pasts and of the futures that were once anticipated. Given the scale and pace of gentrification, however, will spaces in the formal city be able to accommodate these pasts? And in what ways will the ambiguous powers of commemorative praxis be expressed? In the compulsions of mourning and re-mourning the absent "father"? Or in enactive, material memories that recall once-living hopes?

Memory on the Global Stage

The argument of this book, while grounded empirically in Chennai's history and social spaces, has engaged with broader issues surrounding cultural politics and economic change. Heritage formations of the 1980s were shaped by a worldwide boom in the construction and refurbishment of themed cultural environments, including museums, theme parks, malls, downtown arts districts, historic precincts, and decommissioned industrial sites. Heritage was produced and exchanged as a profitable commodity within the expanding service sectors of de-industrializing regional and national economies in North America, Europe, and Japan. In the former Soviet bloc and South Africa, revolutionary political transitions upended received histories and invited new nostalgias—processes mediated by the production and circulation of heritage in the form of new place names, monuments and counter-monuments. In the global South, heritage was marketed in the service of cultural identity politics and revenues, especially in regions like India, where structural adjustments had been mandated by the World Bank and International Monetary Fund.

Andreas Huyssen characterized the shared spatial, visual, and narrative templates for producing representations of the past together with the global flows of mnemonic objects, images, and narratives as the "globalization of memory."[12] With it, he captured the simultaneously localizing and universalizing ambitions of heritage conservation; he also wedded economic dynamics to a political problematic. He recognized that the globalization of memory can be regarded as a reaction formation to economic globalization, as resistance to the rapidity of change and the ruptures in the spaces of daily life, as well as a means of meeting consumerist demands for signs of the authentically local. It is not *only* reactive, however, and Huyssen's observations are worth quoting at length. He wrote:

> Politically, many memory practices today counteract the triumphalism of modernization theory in its latest guides of the discourse of globalization. . . . They express the need for spatial and temporal anchoring in a world of increasing flux in ever denser networks of compressed time and space. . . . Slowing down rather than speeding up, expanding the nature of public debate, trying to heal the wounds inflicted in the past, nurturing and expanding livable space rather than destroying it for the sake of some future promise, securing "quality time"—these seem to be unmet cultural needs in a globalizing world, and local memories are intimately linked to their articulation.[13]

New spaces of public memory in Chennai, which include museums, memorials, shrines, and historic structures, reveal the entanglements of these contradictory desires, goals, and images. These new sites are intended to assert the futurity of "India Shining" by presenting a past that anticipates India's present global ambitions.[14] The past, however, is never singular; rather, multiple, competing pasts are called forth to sustain different futures by underwriting different logics of rule and different possibilities for political engagement. Though often meant to be educational, entertaining, and consumable, some sites work also as critical reminders of traumatic events. While some mask the authoritarian power of the state with infantile or mythic imagery, others seek to enlarge democratic participation or to open spaces of dissent. These sites contain, as well, remnants of the entwined local and national histories that unfold in the city, chapters that have been elided in the narratives on the past that dominant political interests have authored. All sites are (potential) nodes within the increasingly profitable and culturally and politically diverse industries of heritage and tourism; they are also spaces for the formation and representation of "traveling culture," an expression that signals both the cultural significance of traveling and the mobility of cultural images, goods, and styles.[15]

New spaces of public memory are diagnostic indicators of the reorganization of governance under neoliberal globalization and of the contradictions that these changes engender. On their terrains, different and competing conceptions of sovereignty are remembered, imagined, and contested. Such developments belie, or at least complicate, fears that the postmodern turn has replaced historical consciousness with pastiche. In this book I have argued that history, defined broadly as represented past(s), is diffusing and proliferating, not only as scholarly discourse but, in the global-local conjunctures of urban memory, as entertainment, consumer good, political project, and homecoming.

Notes

1. Making the Past in a Global Present

1. See, for example, Lyla Bavadam, "To Save the Coast," *Frontline* (online edition), vol. 22 (February 11, 2005), http://www.flonnet.com/fl2203/stories/20050211006513300.htm; S. Gopakumar, "'A Good Occasion for Change': Interview with Prof. John Kurien, fisheries economy expert," *Frontline* (online edition), vol. 22 (February 11, 2005), http://www.flonnet.com/fl2203/stories/20050211005601800.htm (accessed June 14, 2005).

2. In this book I define memory as acts and products of representation and understand memory as having both individual (psychological) and collective (social/cultural) dimensions. I focus most attentively on what scholars have referred to, variously, as "collective," "social," "cultural," and "public" memory: narratives, images, and sites that represent and serve as grounds for debate about shared pasts and about the diverse identities and sociopolitical, economic, and cultural agendas that are formulated with reference to those pasts. The literature on these topics is voluminous and growing. Key works include Svetlana Boym, *The Future of Nostalgia* (New York: Basic Books, 2001); Thomas Butler, ed., *Memory: History, Culture, and the Mind* (Oxford: Blackwell, 1989); Paul Connerton, *How Societies Remember* (Cambridge: Cambridge University Press, 1989); Maurice Halbwachs, *The Collective Memory*, ed. and trans. L. Coser (Chicago: University of Chicago Press, 1992); Andreas Huyssen, *Twilight Memories: Marking Time in a Culture of Amnesia* (New York: Routledge, 1995); Jacques LeGoff, *History and Memory*, trans. S. Rendall and E. Claman (New York: Columbia University Press, 1993); Pierre Nora, "Between Memory and History: Les *Lieux de Mémoire*," *Representations*, Special issue: *Memory and Counter-Memory* 26 (winter 1989): 7–24; Marita Sturken, *Tangled Memories: The Vietnam War, the AIDS Epidemic, and the Politics of Remembering* (Berkeley: University of California Press, 1997). An exhaustive review of the literature (in the social sciences and humanities) on memory can be found in Barbie Zelizer, "Reading the Past against the Grain: The Shape of Memory Studies," *Critical Studies in Mass Communication*, 12, no. 2 (1995): 214–239.

It bears noting that the representations that constitute shared pasts inevitably entangle both recollection and erasure, an observation that suggests both the parallels and intersections between psychological understandings of memory and approaches taken by anthropologists, sociologists, and historians. I have adopted in this book some of the analytic vocabulary of cognitive psychology to distinguish between different memory processes and functions: "Implicit memory" glosses the embodied, sometimes unconscious knowledge exhibited in habitual activities, dispositions, or feelings; "semantic memory" refers to shared bodies of knowledge, such as facts about the world around us; "episodic memory" denotes the capacity to recall specific events. These categories are useful in highlighting both the different ways that individual and collective memory intersect and the necessary interdisciplinarity of any inquiry about memory. A useful review of recent research in the psychology of memory can be found in Daniel Schacter, *Searching for Memory* (New York: Basic Books, 1996).

3. On "creative destruction," see David Harvey, *Spaces of Global Capitalism* (New York: Verso, 2006); Joseph Schumpter, *Capitalism, Socialism, and Democracy* (New York: Harper and Row, 1962 [1942]); Sharon Zukin, *Landscapes of Power* (Berkeley: University of California Press, 1991).

4. Boym, *The Future of Nostalgia*, xv, xvi.

5. Lefebvre argued that social space, as an analytic category, corresponded to everyday spatial knowledge and experience. He wrote: "From the point of view of these subjects, the behaviour of their space is at once vital and mortal: within it they develop, give expression to themselves, and encounter prohibitions; then they perish, and that same space contains their graves. From the point of view of knowing . . . social space works . . . as a tool for the analysis of society." Social space, whether dedicated to public memory or other functions, encompasses *representations of* space (space conceived as maps, emblems, plans), *representational* space (the reifying spatial metaphors used as everyday descriptors), and *spatial practice*. See Henri Lefebvre, *The Production of Space*, trans. D. Nicholson-Smith (Cambridge: Blackwell, 1991), 33–34, 36–37.

6. Halbwachs, *On Collective Memory*, 182.

7. See, for example, David Glassberg, *Sense of History: The Place of the Past in American Life* (Amherst: University of Massachusetts Press, 2001); Edward Linenthal, *Preserving Memory: The Struggle to Create America's Holocaust Museum* (New York: Viking, 2001); Roy Rosenzweig and David Thelen, *The Presence of the Past: Popular Uses of History in American Life* (New York: Columbia University Press, 1998); Daniel Walkowitz and Lisa Knauer, eds., *Memory and the Impact of Political Transformation in Public Space* (Durham, N.C.: Duke University Press, 2004).

8. See Kerwin Klein's thoughtful review, "On the Emergence of Memory in Historical Discourse," *Representations* 69 (winter 2000): 127–150; see also ground-breaking works by David Lowenthal—*Possessed by the Past* (Cambridge: Cambridge University Press, 1998), and The *Past is a Foreign Country* (Cambridge: Cambridge University Press, 1985)—and by Raphael Samuel, *Theatres of Memory* (London: Verso, 1994).

9. The past-consciousness to which I allude has been characterized by Svetlana Boym as "nostalgia," which she glosses not as "history without guilt" (following Kammen) but as a "yearning for a different time" and the "ache of temporal distance and displacement" (*The Future of Nostalgia*, xv). Although symptomatic of modernity, it is expressed as a "rebellion against the modern idea of time" (44). To capture the different ways in which that yearning is expressed, Boym created a typology according to which nostalgia could be characterized as either "restorative" or "reflective." The former "stresses nostos" [home] and "attempts a transhistorical reconstruction of the lost home" while asserting its own truth-value; this sort of nostalgia is at the core of many nationalisms. The latter "thrives in algia, the longing itself" and "delays the homecoming—wistfully, ironically, desperately" while calling any singular or universalized truth into doubt. This sort of nostalgia is expressed in personal narratives and in aesthetic engagements with ruins and other fragments of past experience (xv, xviii, 41–49). While not adopting Boym's typology, I share her view of the productivity and mutability of past-consciousness; I am also informed by her historicization of "nostalgia," which she describes as appearing in European contexts in outbreaks, following revolutionary upheavals. Initially understood as medical pathology, it came to gloss aesthetic and political orientations, for example, the linguistic nationalisms of the nineteenth century and Ruskin's celebration of ruins, in which contexts it engendered an "off-modern" critique—"a critical reflection on the modern condition that . . . allows us to take a detour from the deterministic narrative of twentieth century history." Although the scope of Boym's discussion is limited to modern Europe, the conditions she describes are relevant to Europe's colonial periphery, because this "off-modern" critique, codified in knowledges and institutions dedicated to the recovery and conservation of heritage, was transferred to colonized domains, including British India. There it served to further the "civilizing mission" of imperial domination, even while engendering critiques in the form of anticolonial nationalisms and hybrid cultural formations, which, in turn, form the historical grounds and templates for the current expression of past-consciousness. In her study of the transnational career of the idea of Lemuria, including its presence in some Dravidianist representations, Sumathi Ramaswamy relies heavily on Boym's formulation of nostalgia. See Sumathi Ramaswamy, *The Lost Land of Lemuria* (Berkeley: University of California Press, 2004).

10. Michael Hardt and Antonio Negri, *Empire* (Cambridge, Mass.: Harvard University Press, 2001); Fredric Jameson and Masao Miyoshi, eds., *The Cultures of Globalization* (Durham, N.C.: Duke University Press, 1998).

11. Monuments need not be built as such. A landscape or an office building may be re-signified as "monumental" by changing the ways that it is used, entered, or controlled, or by refashioning its

framing narratives. The trauma of war, natural disaster, or terror may make a "monument" of an empty field or a leveled city. Monumentality may be realized episodically, as well, in an assembly or in a march, with its fluid streams of bodies and its larger-than-life processional figures and vehicles.

12. Ernst Cassirer, *The Myth of the State* (New Haven, Conn.: Yale University Press, 1961 [1946]); Philip Corrigan and Derek Sayer, *The Great Arch: English State Formation as Cultural Revolution* (Oxford: Blackwell, 1985); Philip Abrams, "Notes on the Difficulty of Studying the State, (1977)" *Journal of Historical Sociology*, 1, no. 1 (1988): 58–89. See also recent work including Begoña Aretxaga, "Maddening States," *Annual Review of Anthropology* 32 (2003): 393–410; Wendy Brown, *States of Injury: Power and Freedom in Late Modernity* (Princeton, N.J.: Princeton University Press, 1995); Timothy Mitchell, "The Limits of the State: Beyond Statist Approaches and Their Critics," *American Political Science Review* 85 (1991): 77–96; Michael Taussig, *The Magic of the State* (New York: Routledge, 1997); Michel-Rolphe Trouillot, "The Anthropology of the State in the Age of Globalization," *Current Anthropology* 42 (2001): 125–138.

13. Abrams, "Notes," 77.

14. Timothy Mitchell, "Society, Economy, and the State Effect," in *State/Culture: State Formation after the Cultural Turn*, ed. George Steinmetz (Ithaca, N.Y.: Cornell University Press, 1999), 95.

15. Aretxaga, "Maddening States," 398; Bruce Grant, "New Moscow Monuments, or States of Innocence," *American Ethnologist* 28, no. 2 (2001): 332–362.

16. David Morgan, *The Sacred Gaze* (Berkeley: University of California Press, 2005); Marita Sturken and Lisa Cartwright, *Practices of Looking* (Berkeley: University of California Press, 2003).

17. As Bruce Grant has observed, monuments, by representing the state as a transcendent agency standing outside the nitty-gritty world of realpolitik, are both effects of and rhetorical media for the power wielded through state institutions ("New Moscow Monuments," 336–340).

18. Diana Eck, *Darśan: Seeing the Divine Image in India* (New York: Columbia University Press, 1998); Sandria Freitag, "The Realm of the Visual: Agency and Modern Civil Society," In *Beyond Appearances? Visual Practices and Ideologies in Modern India*, ed. Sumathi Ramaswamy, 365–397 (New Delhi: Sage, 2003); Christopher Pinney, *Camera Indica* (Berkeley: University of California Press, 1997).

19. James Ferguson and Akhil Gupta identified mundane bureaucratic practices as contexts in which this spatialized imaginary was made commonsensical ("Spatializing States," *American Ethnologist* 29, 4 [2002]: 981–1002).

20. Fernando Coronil, *The Magical State: Nature, Money, and Modernity in Venezuela* (Chicago: University of Chicago Press, 1997), 114.

21. Advertising flyer for Kanchi Kudil, published by Deccan Tourism. Collected February 2000.

22. Geoff Crowther, Prakash Raj, Tony Wheeler, Hugh Finlay, and Bryn Thomas, *India: A Travel Survival Kit*, 5th ed. (Singapore: Lonely Planet Publications, 1993), 991.

23. While several studies confirm the historical and cultural specificity of Indian civil society and outline the policy implications of its analysis—for example, Narendra Subramanian, *Ethnicity and Populist Mobilization* (New Delhi: Oxford University Press, 1999); Ashutosh Varshney, *Ethnic Conflict and Civic Life* (New Haven, Conn.: Yale University Press, 2002); and John Harriss, *Power Matters: Essays on Institutions, Politics, and Society in India* (New Delhi: Oxford University Press, 2006)—they invite questions about the kinds of pasts and futures that both everyday and associational forms of civil society engender as they mediate and mobilize collective interests and identities. Both historians and anthropologists have taken up these questions. These works include Daud Ali, ed., *Invoking the Past* (New Delhi: Oxford University Press, 1999); Kelly Alley, *On the Banks of the Ganga* (Ann Arbor: University of Michigan Press, 2002); Dipesh Chakrabarty, *Provincializing Europe* (Princeton, N.J.: Princeton University Press, 2000); Sandria Freitag, ed., *Collective Action and Community* (Berkeley: University of California Press, 1989); David Ludden, ed., *Making India Hindu* (New Delhi: Oxford University Press, 1996); Janaki Nair, *The Promise of the Metropolis: Bangalore's Twentieth Century* (New Delhi: Oxford University Press, 2005); Sumathi Ramaswamy, *Passions of the Tongue* (Berkeley: University of California Press, 1997); and Smriti Srinivas, *Landscapes of Urban Memory* (Minneapolis: University of Minnesota Press, 2001).

24. Andreas Huyssen, *Present Pasts: Urban Palimpsests and the Politics of Memory* (Stanford, Calif.: Stanford University Press, 2003), 27.

25. Michael Herzfeld, *Cultural Intimacy: Social Poetics in the Nation-State* (New York: Routledge, 1997), 94.

26. Herzfeld, *Cultural Intimacy*, 3.

27. The label "NRI" has usually been reserved for those affluent Indian professionals (and their descendents) who have emigrated to the United States, the United Kingdom, Canada, and Australia since the late 1960s in search of employment and education. The Indian state's invention, in mid-1980s, of the NRI as a category of off-shore citizen dovetailed with national efforts to attract foreign investment and repatriate the human and financial capital that had been lost over several decades of emigration. Since the 1990s, NRI investment has been sought to enable India to move forward aggressively with its New Industrial Policy. *India Today International* (March 13, 2002) estimated that the total number of POIs (People of Indian Origin, including Non-Resident Indians) was 20 million; 3 million of that number were North American or British Non-Resident Indians (cited in Anthony King, *Spaces of Global Cultures: Architecture Urbanism Identity* [London: Routledge, 2004], 139 n. 4). At that time annual remittances from the Indian diaspora were estimated to be about U.S.$10 billion, and NRI deposits in Indian banks about U.S.$23 billion.

28. Annapurna Shaw, "Emerging Patterns of Urban Growth in India," *Economic and Political Weekly* 34 (1999): 969–978.

29. Renato Rosaldo, "Imperialist Nostalgia," in idem, *Culture and Truth* (Boston: Beacon Press, 1991), 68–87.

30. "Dalit," a Marathi word, means "oppressed" or "downtrodden," and it is used by groups formerly called "untouchable" as a title in order to signal both social position and oppositional consciousness.

31. See Amos Rapoport, "A Framework for Studying Vernacular Design," *Journal of Architectural and Planning Research* 16, no. 1 (1999): 52–64.

32. A. K. Ramanujan, "Towards an Anthropology of City Images," in *Urban India: Society, Space, and Image*, ed. Richard G. Fox, 224–244 (Durham, N.C.: Monograph and Occasional Papers Series, Monograph 10, Duke University Program in Comparative Studies on Southern Asia, 1970), 242.

33. In part, this is a matter of opportunity. The open spaces beyond the city's municipal boundaries offer open space for the construction of such sites; the improved transportation infrastructure that came with industrialization allows easy access from urban core areas; and the proximity of new business and residential sites ensure pools of potential consumers and donors.

34. Pierre Nora, "Between Memory and History."

35. M. D. Muthukumaraswamy, "From the Director," *National Folklore Support Centre Folk Festival 2002 Souvenir* (March 2002): 3.

36. Writing about a folk festival sponsored by Chennai's National Folklore Support Centre (NFSC), the NFSC director M. D. Muthukumaraswamy stated: "oral narratives, folk paintings, musical instruments and puppetry become . . . metaphors for our national life. It will not be an exaggeration if I were to say that this festival is a metaphor of the nation we are today" ("From the Director," 3). Founded in 2000 with the generous support of the Ford Foundation, the NFSC sponsors conferences and seminars, publishes a monthly bulletin, collects and records examples of folklore, and coordinates the work of many smaller organizations, including college and university departments.

37. India's rate of urbanization, 27.8 percent in 2001, has increased almost threefold since 1901, when the urban population constituted 10.8 percent of the total population of British India. See "Rural-urban Distribution of Population," *eCensusIndia* 14 (2003), http://www.censusindia.net/results/eci14_mail.html (accessed May 20, 2007).

38. See, for example, the recent Dalit life history, Viramma, Josiane Racine and Jean-Luc Racine, *Viramma: Life of an Untouchable*, trans. W. Hobson (New York: Verso, 1997).

39. See Rachel Dwyer and Christopher Pinney, eds., *Pleasure and the Nation: The History, Politics, and Consumption of Popular Culture in India* (New Delhi: Oxford University Press, 2002).

40. For example: Bernard Cohn, *An Anthropologist among the Historians and Other Essays* (Oxford: Oxford University Press, 1987); idem, *Colonialism and Its Forms of Knowledge* (Princeton,

N.J.: Princeton University Press, 1996); Ranajit Guha and Gayatri Spivak, eds., *Selected Subaltern Studies* (New York: Oxford University Press, 1988).

2. Governing the Past

1. The astute reader will recognize my reference here to the opening sentence of Clifford Geertz's groundbreaking essay, "Deep Play: Notes on the Balinese Cockfight," in idem, *The Interpretation of Cultures* (New York: Basic Books, 1973), 412–453.

2. Consistent with its identity as longtime pilgrimage and market site, it has been an international tourist destination since the nineteenth century when the colonial government, through its archaeological survey service, encouraged visitation. Kanchipuram has been a destination on government-sponsored tour circuits since their inception, exemplifying what was regarded as a salutary combination of pilgrimage and leisure. Perhaps incongruously, in light of its association with Hindu orthodoxy, Kanchipuram also served as launching place of the Self-Respect movement, an anti-caste, rationalist movement headed by E. V. Ramasamy (known as "Periyar" or "EVR"), a figure commemorated with statues and plaques all through the town.

3. The *Imperial Gazetteer of India* in 1908 described Madras as a "fortuitous collection of villages, separated from the surrounding country by an arbitrary boundary line" rather than "a town in the usual sense of the word" (*Imperial Gazetteer of India,* [new edition], 16 [Oxford: Clarendon, 1908], 364). In 1977 P. V. Venkatakrishnan, the director of Town and Country Planning, Government of Tamil Nadu wrote: "Madras, then, is a story of how sheer accident changed the future of a fishing village. . . . The fact that Madras is an artificially stimulated growth and not a naturally evolved organism explains why the growth of Madras has been at the expense of the region in which it is set" ("Madras City in its Regional Setting," *Civic Affairs,* Special Issue: *Madras on the Move* (December 1977), 25.

4. See, for example, Susan Lewandowski, "The Built Environment and Cultural Symbolism in Post-Colonial Madras," in *The City in Cultural Context,* ed. John Agnew, John Mercer, and David Sopher, 237–254. Boston: Allen and Unwin, 1984.

5. Chief among the English-language periodicals was *Madras Musings,* launched in 1991; a Tamil-language example can be found in a short book by K. Pakavati, *Ceṉṉai* (Ceṉṉai: Ulakattamiḻ araycci Niruvanam, 1995).

6. Madras Metropolitan Development Authority, *Master Plan for Madras Metropolitan Area—2011,* Draft (Madras: Madras Metropolitan Development Authority, 1995), 47–49.

7. The Tamil Nadu Legislative Assembly approved the bill authorizing the name change on August 31, 1996. "Assembly Nod for Name Change," *Hindu,* September 1, 1996, 4.

8. For example: "Chennai versus Madras," *Hindu,* Metro Section, July 29, 1996, 1; "Why 'Chennai'?" *Hindu,* Metro Section, July 9, 1996, 1. The Indian National Trust for Art and Cultural Heritage (INTACH) was founded in 1984 with the support of Rajiv Gandhi to document, preserve, and promote India's regional craft, performance, and artistic traditions. Originally funded by the central government, it is now a private voluntary association.

9. As Susan Neild observed: "What emerged [over the eighteenth century] . . . was not merely a collection of separate quarters, but two or even three distinct societies with their own characteristic ways of organizing space. . . . The outstanding feature of Madras was that these cultural units—colonial European, indigenous urban and rural societies—in many cases shared the same territory without actually merging together or losing their distinctive characteristics" ("Madras: The Growth of a Colonial City in India, 1780–1840," Ph.D. diss., University of Chicago, 1977, 377).

10. "Black Town" was the place name used by the British after 1676; before then, references were made to "Gentu (Telugu) Town" (S. Muthiah, *Madras Rediscovered,* 4th rev. ed. [Chennai: East West Books, 1999], 11).

11. "The firman granted Mr. Day for priviledges in Medraspatam by the Nague Damola Vintutedra," from Original Correspondence Series, India Office Library, cited in Henry Davidson Love, *Vestiges of Old Madras, 1640–1800,* 4 vols. (London: John Murray, 1913), 1:16–18.

12. Darmala Venkatapati was a vassal of the Raja of Chandragiri, a representative of the Vijayanagara king.

13. San Thome was named after St. Thomas the Apostle, whose burial site was reputed to be there.

14. The historiography of Vijayanagara and its successor kingdoms is extensive. See Burton Stein, *Peasant, State, and Society in Medieval South India* (Delhi: Oxford University Press, 1980); Nicholas Dirks, *The Hollow Crown: Ethnohistory of an Indian Kingdom* (Ann Arbor: University of Michigan Press, 1993); Pamela Price, *Kingship and Political Practice in Colonial India* (New York: Cambridge University Press, 1996); and Joanne Waghorne, *The Raja's Magic Clothes: Re-visioning Kingship and Divinity in England's India* (University Park: Pennsylvania State University Press, 1994). For historiography that takes a transregional perspective, see Sanjay Subrahmanyam, *The Political Economy of Commerce: Southern India, 1500–1650* (Cambridge: Cambridge University Press, 2002); Sanjay Subrahmanyam, *Penumbral Visions: Making Polities in Early Modern South India* (Ann Arbor: University of Michigan Press, 2001); and Sanjay Subrahmanyam, Velcheru Rao, and David Schulman, eds., *Textures of Time* (Oxford: Oxford University Press, 2001).

15. Love, *Vestiges*, 1:83–85; V. Raghavan, "Notices of Madras in Two Sanskrit Works," in *Madras Tercentenary Commemoration Volume*, 107–112 (Madras: Humphrey Milford/Oxford University Press, 1939), 112.

16. "Limits of Madras as fixed on the 2nd of November, 1798 . . . Scale of 1800 feet to an inch" (Madras: Survey Office, 1904). Reproduced with permission of the British Library.

17. Susan Neild's excellent dissertation (cited above) deals with Madras during the critical period between 1780 and 1840 and I have relied on it as a definitive work on land use changes during this period.

18. Love, *Vestiges*, 2:614, 3:512.

19. Besides the Fort and Black Town, the city encompassed ten villages acquired by the East India Company from local rulers, several other villages created by Company officials and numerous small hamlets (Neild, "Madras," 18). The population in the early nineteenth century was estimated by Neild at 236,500. Half that number resided within Black Town, another thirty thousand in Triplicane, and the remainder in dispersed settlements whose populations ranged from a few hundred to several thousand (Neild, "Madras," 30–31). Neild indicates that the 1822 Census listed thirty-five villages within Madras, excluding Black Town and hamlets of low caste and "Untouchable" groups, and that the 1871 Census identified fifty-eight villages within the municipal boundary.

20. "Bungalows" were styled after the domestic architecture of rural Bengal but were appropriated and modified by British settlers as a way of adapting to the tropical climate while also aspiring to an aristocratic style of domestic life. The bungalow offered its British occupants a cultural refuge, bounded by racial and class difference. See Anthony King, *The Bungalow: The Production of a Global Culture*, rev. ed. (New York: Oxford University Press, 1995 [1976]).

21. "Mrs Kindersley's Letter XIX," in Love, *Vestiges*, 3:617–618.

22. See Indira Peterson, "Eighteenth-century Madras through Indian Eyes: Urban Space, Patronage, and Power in the Sanskrit Text *Sarva-deva-vilasa*," paper presented at the Annual Meeting of the Association for Asian Studies, Chicago, March 25, 2001.

23. Peterson elaborates on the complexity of these social spaces based on her close reading of *Sarva-deva-vilasa*, a Sanskrit literary text (known as a *campu*, in which prose and verse alternate) on subjects of travel, social life, and topographical description supported by Nayak and Maratha patrons. This one, dating from the late eighteenth to the early nineteenth century, unfolds as dialogue between two pandits who are discussing the patrons that might be approached in the city. It is largely panegyric, in which the pandits laud potential patrons. Travels of the pandits are described, as are the travels and processions of their patrons, which are likened to the circumambulations with which kings declared the limits of their domains. Peterson interprets this text as a documentation of connections that wealthy, city-based merchants and dubashes maintained with outlying villages through temple patronage and the territoriality produced through these connections (Peterson, "Eighteenth-century Madras through Indian Eyes").

24. Neoclassical architecture was common in Europe by the late eighteenth century and influenced the design of public buildings. This was adopted by Company architects initially in imitation of European fashion but later acquired more intense symbolism meant to distinguish the different origins of rulers and ruled (Neild, "Madras," 298).

25. Ibid., 7, 295.

26. William Hodges, *Travels in India during the years 1781, 82, 83* (London: n.p., 1873), 1–2, cited in Neild, "Madras," 295.

27. *The Oriental Annual or Scenes in India,* comprising Twenty-two engravings from original drawings by Wm Daniell, R.A. and a descriptive account by the Rev. J. Hobart Caunter, B.D. (London: Edw. Bull, 1834), 5.

28. Thomas Daniell, *Oriental Scenery: Twenty-four Views in Hindoostan,* drawn and engraved by T. Daniell (London: William Daniell, 1795–1801); Thomas Daniell and William Daniell, *A Picturesque Voyage to India, by way of China.* (London: Longman, Hurst, Rees, and Orme [etc.], 1810).

29. Thomas Daniell and William Daniell, "Government House, Fort St. George," aquatint published by Thomas Daniell, March 1798; from the British Library, P Series, P 944 (India Office Library X432/2/9). Reproduced here with permission of the British Library. The aquatint has been reprinted in Mildred Archer, *Early Views of India: The Picturesque Journeys of Thomas and William Daniell, 1786–1794* (London: Thames and Hudson, 1980), 99.

30. Thomas Daniell and William Daniell, "Western Entrance to Fort St. George," aquatint published by Thomas Daniell, September 1798; from the British Library, P. Series, P 947 (India Office Library X432/2/12). Reproduced here with permission of the British Library. Reprinted in Mildred Archer, *Early Views of India: The Picturesque Journeys of Thomas and William Daniell, 1786–1794* (London: Thames and Hudson, 1980), 130.

31. Population estimates for the seventeenth and eighteenth centuries were not based on systematic census counts. On the basis of revenue accounts, the population in 1639 was estimated at about seven thousand. By 1691, according to East India Company records, it had risen to four hundred thousand, and a 1791 letter estimated a population of three hundred thousand (Love, *Vestiges,* 3:557). Regardless of actual numbers, Europeans constituted a miniscule portion of the total throughout the colonial period. In 1750 Madras was estimated to have a European population of about four hundred, three hundred of whom were soldiers; by 1800 the total was thought to be between four hundred and five hundred (Neild, "Madras," 271).

32. The original Black Town was razed in 1758 to allow for an extension of the Fort. This forced residents and businesses to relocate in the adjacent villages of Peddanaikenpet and Muthialpet, though the name "Black Town" remained in use.

33. "Chennai" or variants also appear in descriptive essays and literary works as names for the city that the English know as Madras. The *Visvagunadrasa Campu,* (composed between 1650 and 1700) and *Anandarangavijaya Campu,* (composed in 1752) refer to the settlement as "Chenna Kesava Pura" and to "Chenna Patna," and the *Sarva-deva-vilasa* uses the term "Cennapuri" or "Cennapuram" as the place name (Peterson, "Eighteenth-century Madras through Indian Eyes"). In the 1840s an organization titled Chennappatnam Hindu Videya Pareyalochan Sabha (Hindu Council of Education) established Tamil and Telugu schools in various parts of the city (Neild, "Madras," 242).

34. Black Town's central temples, Chenna Kesava and Chenna Malleswarar, typify late medieval styles of temple construction in the many sub-shrines, *maṇṭapam* (pillared halls) and carved pillars but depart from those styles in lacking *kōpuram* (entry arches). See Joanne Waghorne, "The Diaspora of the Gods: Hindu Temples in the New World System, 1640–1800," *Journal of Asian Studies* 58, no. 3 (1999): 648–686.

35. Europeans, for example, purchased agricultural lands in Mylapore and adjacent villages and converted them to garden houses; the southeast section of Muthialpet (the eastern portion of Black Town) was also a European enclave. See further discussion in Neild, "Madras," 310–327.

36. The British provincial rulers divested the Nawab of his title and his jurisdictional authority following the Company's defeat of Tippu and its annexation of his Carnatic holdings. The Nawab and his descendents were granted a title (the Prince of Arcot) and pension, and a portion of the estate was allocated for their use. The estate's main palace, Chepauk Palace, was purchased by the British administration in 1855 and converted to government offices, and it continues to be used in this way. See Love, *Vestiges,* 3:529; and Neild, "Madras," 257–260.

37. S. E. Runganadhan, introduction to *The Madras Tercentenary Commemoration Volume,* xiii.

38. The term "historical mindedness" is from Stephen Bann, *Romanticism and the Rise of History* (New York: Maxwell Macmillan International, 1995).

39. The population of the city, as reported in the 1871 Census, was 367,552; in 1881, 405,848; in 1891, 452,518; in 1901, 509,346; in 1911, 518,660; in 1921, 526,911; and in 1931, 647,230.

40. *Imperial Gazetteer of India,* 16, 371.

41. The *Imperial Gazetteer of India* reported the intensification of the urban character of Madras in the early years of the twentieth century, noting that 30 percent of the city's population was between the ages of twenty and forty and that the sex ratio was 98/100.

42. Early leadership of the Indian National Congress, and its forerunner, the Hindu Mahajana Sabha, was based in Madras and the city had hosted early meetings of those organizations. The high-caste residents of Madras were also prominently represented in the Home Rule League, a Gandhian organization with strong ties to the Theosophical Society, headquartered on an estate in Adyar, about nine kilometers south of the city's urban core. See D. Sadasivan, *The Growth of Public Opinion in Madras Presidency* (Madras: University of Madras Press, 1974).

43. In the 1910s references to conservation undertaken by merchant communities appear in Archaeological Survey of India reports. The "Conjeevaram Ekambaranadhar Temple" and the "Tirupallathurar Siva Temple" in Trichinopoly taluk, were both being extensively repaired or rebuilt by Nattukkottai Chettiars (*Annual Progress Report of the Archaeological Survey Department, Southern Circle, for the year 1905–1906,* Alexander Rea, Director [Madras: Government Press, 1906], 12, 14). The Archaeological Survey of India (ASI) Report for 1915–16 mentioned Nattukkottai Chettiar renovation of "Siva temples of Puranic fame on a very large scale" (*Annual Report of the Archaeological Department, Southern Circle, Madras, for the year 1915–1916* [Madras: Government Press, 1916], 34). The ASI Report for 1917–18 alluded to "three applications for demolition and renovation of certain ancient monuments by Nattukkottai Chettiars and trustees" (*Annual Report of the Archaeological Department, Southern Circle, Madras, for the year 1917–1918* [Madras: Government Press, 1918], 2). Those temples included the "Kadambavaneswara Temple," in Kadambarkoil, Kulittalai taluk, Trichinopoly district, an Amman shrine connected to the "Panchanadeswara Temple" at Tiruvadi, in Tanjore district and a Siva shrine in the center of Kamalyam tank at Tiruvalur, Negapatam taluk in Tanjore district.

44. See Eugene Irschick, *Tamil Revivalism in the 1930s* (Madras: Cre-A, 1986), 20–237; and David Washbrook, *The Emergence of Provincial Politics* (Cambridge: Cambridge University Press, 1976), 282–287.

45. C. W. Ranson, *A City in Transition: Studies in the Social Life of Madras.* (Madras: Christian Literature Society for India, 1938), 78.

46. The Tamil film industry's history is summarized in Sara Dickey, *Cinema of the Urban Poor in South India* (Cambridge: Cambridge University Press, 1993). The first production studios were set up in the 1920s and 1930s; with the advent of sound, regional cinemas (i.e., those in languages other than Hindi or English) quickly gained in popularity. The first theaters were built in the 1910s on Mount Road, in Georgetown and in Purasawakkam. By 1927 the city had nine theaters; in 1941 that number had risen to twenty. See S. Theodore Baskaran, "Cinema Houses of Chennai," in *The Unhurried City: Writings on Chennai,* ed. C. S. Lakshmi, 75–86 (Harmondsworth, U.K.: Penguin, 2004), 77.

47. By the first decade of the twentieth century, 125 newspapers and periodicals existed in the Presidency; of that total, 65 were vernacular (Tamil, Telugu, or Hindi) or bilingual publications (*Imperial Gazetteer of India,* 345–346). The city itself had 5 daily newspapers at that point, all English-language; 3 (*The Hindu*, *The Madras Standard*, and *The Indian Patriot*) were published and edited by Indians.

48. Neoclassical details abounded in the statues of colonial officers and British royals that appeared during the course of the nineteenth century, in public buildings, in the city's new parks, and along its major roadways. These began to appear at junctions in the city in 1839 and later in parks and on the grounds of government buildings. In the *List of Statues, Monuments, and Busts Erected in Madras* (Madras: Government Press, 1898), the city is listed as having ten statues, all having been erected by the colonial government. The 1908 *Imperial Gazetteer* noted that a statue dedicated to an Indian High Court Justice, Muttuswami Ayyar, was added to the list (*Imperial Gazetteer of India,* 367). It was not until after independence, however, that additional statues commemorating Indian cultural heroes and political leaders appeared in public spaces.

49. Thomas Metcalf, *An Imperial Vision* (Berkeley: University of California Press, 1989), 8, 11–12, 15. Neoclassicism was also adopted for projects sponsored by indigenous patrons: Pachiayappa's Hall, a school built in 1840 in Black Town, was modeled on the Athenian Temple of Theseus and was funded by the bequest of an Indian merchant whose name it bears (ibid., 15).

50. Metcalf explained that Madras's governor Napier developed the conceptual parameters of Indo-Saracenic style in 1870. Dissatisfied with certain features of southern Dravidian style, particularly its "over-abundance" of solid ornamentation and horizontality, but finding it otherwise "picturesque," he called for designs in which "Saracenic" features, such as arches and domes, were introduced to create a more pleasing and balanced style. Designs submitted by one of the Presidency's consulting architects, Robert Chisholm, corresponded to the hybrid form that Napier imagined, and Chisholm was commissioned with the renovation and design of a number of buildings, public and private, in Madras. Despite Chisholm's own professed admiration for indigenous architectural principles and styles, and his encouragement of traditional architectural craftsmanship while director of the Madras School of Industrial Art, his innovation resulted in a landscape of power based on eclectic imperialism, which placed European rule within a descent line that was global in scope (Metcalf, *An Imperial Vision*, 51–59). Tillotson pointed out that the same hybrid style was also adopted by India's princely rulers; the combination of elements asserted both Indic cultural roots and British imperial reach, and suggested loyalty to British rule as well as modernist aspirations. See Geoffrey Tillotson, *The Tradition of Indian Architecture* (New Haven, Conn.: Yale University Press, 1989), 2–6.

51. Historicity was asserted as well with commemorative nomenclature (Love, *Vestiges*, 3:564–574).

52. Its inception in Europe was precipitated by the identification of the cityscape with an ailing "body," with tuberculosis, drunkenness, and violence regarded as symptoms of the malaise of industrialization. The interests of public health, of individual bodies and the body politic, demanded the intervention of town planning.

53. Henry Lanchester, *Town Planning in Madras* (London: Constable, 1918).

54. Ibid., 105–115.

55. Ibid., 5.

56. Ibid., 35, 94. The decline of traditional spatial norms was also attributed, with unreflective Orientalism, to the religiously sanctioned "passivity" of Indians, "who regard the lapse of a great city with more equanimity than would be felt in Europe" (ibid., 94).

57. Lanchester, like his colonial contemporaries, conflated racialized and sectarian categories, dividing the indigenous population into "Brahmin," "Other Hindu," "Musalman," "Eurasian," and "European," and further subdivided according to occupation, noting that "occupational groups claim distinct positions in city area and many have recognized activity centers (*Town Planning*, 27–28, 33). As justification, he cites the "Hindu Sastras" as mandating that the four varnas be in different areas of the city but also noted the practicality of residing near one's workplace. Lanchester regarded the caste system, which he understood as a distribution of occupational duties rather than a matter of differential privilege, as impervious to reform and as a source of order and stability, opining that "no encouragement should be offered to measures trying to break up the Indian social system" (ibid., 73–74). Caste, he maintained, was integral to India's distinctive artisanal economy (72).

58. Lanchester, *Town Planning*, 108.

59. Ibid., 93.

60. Ibid., 110.

61. Ibid., 41.

62. Ibid., 36.

63. Museums appeared in a number of colonial cities in the latter part of the nineteenth century. By 1911 there were thirty-six in British India; twenty-five years later there were 105. Government of India, *The Conference of Orientalists, including Museums and Archaeology Conference* (Simla: Government Press, 1911); Sydney Markham and Harold Hargreaves, *The Museums of India* (London: Museum Association, 1936).

64. A. H. Longhurst, *Annual Report of the Superintendent, Archaeological Survey, for 1916–17* (Madras: Government of Madras, Home Department (Education), 1917), 4.

65. Thurston was appointed as the first full-time superintendent in 1885 and served until 1910. The connections between colonial knowledge and colonial rule were particularly evident in Thurston's career. Not only was he responsible for collection and curation of material remains—displayed to reveal the chronology of civilization and its decline in southern India—he was an energetic ethnographer of the "salvage" variety. He relied on the investigative efforts of a local assistant, K. Rangachari, to prepare a seven-volume work, *The Tribes and Castes of South India* (Madras: Government Press, 1909), an encyclopedia of the region's ethnic and caste communities. He turned this information to administrative ends by working with the Census commissioner Herbert Risley to design the 1901 census survey instrument that employed the ethnographic categories and produced additional data that were analyzed, according to then canonical tenets of scientific racism, to identify "racial" difference through the analysis of co-variation of physiognomy and caste status.

66. *Imperial Gazetteer of India,* 373.

67. It was subsequently dissolved and reinstituted in 1866.

68. In subsequent years, administrative orders from the Government of India refined the scope, made budgetary provisions, and defined the organization and relations with other agencies.

69. The agency's jurisdiction was delimited by statute and Government Orders were the devices with which "national monuments" were designated.

70. Address of 20 December 1900, delivered by Lord Curzon at the Asiatic Society, Calcutta from file No. 54 of 1900, National Archives of India, New Delhi; cited in B. P. Singh, *India's Culture* (New Delhi: Oxford University Press, 1998), 164.

71. Most of the churches are sites within Thomist hagiography. The church at Little Mount is said to be the site of a miraculous spring, marking the spot where St. Thomas took refuge from pursuers; the Portuguese church at St. Thomas Mount, dated to 1547, is described as important because of the stone cross the Portuguese claimed to have discovered on the site. San Thome's significance owes to the presence of St. Thomas's grave.

72. Archaeological Survey of Southern India, *List of Ancient Monuments Selected for Conservation in the Madras Presidency in 1891,* comp. Alexander Rea (Madras: Government Press, 1891), 2.

73. Ibid., 3–4.

74. Ibid., 7.

75. Archaeological Survey of India, *Annual Progress Report of the Archaeological Survey of Madras and Coorg for the Year 1904–05,* Alexander Rea, Director (Madras: Government Press, 1905), 25.

76. Henry Cole, *Preservation of National Monuments, Madras Presidency* (Simla: Government Central Branch Press, 1881), 13, 19. A related intervention, sanctioned by temple managers and priests, was the paint (usually whitewash) that was periodically applied to sculpted features as a restorative and auspicious type of cleansing (Cole, *Preservation,* 12, 13, 14, 16, 19, 20, 21, 22, 23).

77. Other collections deemed to be of value were the arms and armor from the Arsenal in the Fort and from Tanjore palace, and the museum's large coin collection (*Imperial Gazetteer of India,* 373–374).

78. Archaeological Survey of Southern India, *Lists of Antiquarian Remains in the Presidency of Madras,* Vol. 1, comp. Robert Sewell (Madras: Government Press, 1882), 175.

79. J. Talboys Wheeler, *Madras in the Olden Times* (Madras: Graves, 1861–62).

80. The 1905–1906 report enlarged the list of significant, albeit modern, features existing in Madras. Listed features include crosses and tombstones at Christian cemeteries in Purusawakkam, Teynampet, St. Thome, and near St. Andrew's Church; iconographic details and structural features of various public and private buildings; and images in some of the Hindu temples. Archaeological Survey of India, *Annual Progress Report of the Archaeological Survey Department, Southern Circle, for the year 1905–06,* Alexander Rea, Director (Madras: Government Press, 1906), Appendix D.

The 1912–13 report lists boundary pillars (Tondiarpet, Washermanpet), obelisk near old town wall, cannon near Mylapore, and "old building" at St. Thome. Archaeological Survey of India, *Annual Report of the Archaeological Department, Southern Circle, Madras, for the year 1912–1913.* (Madras, Government Press, 1913). The Cornwallis memorial near custom house is included in a subsequent report (1914–15), and a few other inscription stones and obelisks marking original city boundaries. Archaeological Survey of India, *Annual Report of the Archaeological Department, Southern Circle, Madras for the years 1912–1915*, Appendix C, (Madras, Government Press, 1915). The 1915–16 report adds tombs of Elihu Yale and Joseph Hymnners, both in the compound of the Law College, being that both "were historical personages, having both acted as governors of old Fort St George." Archaeological Survey of India, *Annual Report of the Archaeological Department, Southern Circle, Madras, for the year 1915–1916* (Madras: Government Press, 1916), 45.

81. Love, *Vestiges*. Other examples include William Foster, *Founding of Fort St. George* (London: Eyre and Spottiswoode, 1902); Frank Penny, *The Church in Madras* (London: Elder, 1904).

82. John Murray, *A Handbook for Travelers in India, Pakistan, Burma, and Ceylon* (London: Murray, 1892).

83. Glyn Barlow, *The Story of Madras* (London: Humphrey Milford, 1921).

84. Ibid., 77.

85. Caste histories appeared in the late nineteenth century and became more common in following decades to substantiate claims on status, property, and caste-based entitlements, as well as to advance populist critiques of Brahman hegemony.

86. *Tondaimandalam uyartuluva veḷḷāḷar carittira curukkam* (The short history of the Superior Tuluva Veḷḷāḷars of Tondaimandalam) (Madras: MLV Press, 1911); quoted in Neild, "Madras," 5–7.

87. By the late 1930s all the nationalist movements had generated historiographical writing. Poetry, essays, plays, and fiction, as well as aural and visual representations (maps, cartoons, lithographs, sculpture, songs, film); all were generative of politically infused historical consciousness. See S. P. Sen, ed. *Historians and Historiography in Modern India* (Calcutta: Institute of Historical Studies, 1973). See also Gyan Prakash, "Writing Post-Orientalist Histories of the Third World: Perspectives from Indian Historiography," *Comparative Studies in Society and History* 32, no. 2 (1990): 383–408, for a compelling analysis of these developments.

88. Irschick, *Tamil Revivalism;* Ramaswamy, *Passions of the Tongue.*

89. Ramaswamy, *The Lost Land of Lemuria*, 97–181.

90. S. Krishnaswami Aiyangar, "The Character and Significance of the Foundation of Madras," in *Madras Tercentenary Commemoration Volume*, 39–50, 41.

91. C. Achyuta Menon, "Dravidic Studies in Madras," 393–406.

92. In the 1937 provincial elections, nationalists associated with the Indian National Congress had gained a legislative foothold and C. Rajagopalachari, a lawyer and Congress nationalist, was the Presidency's premier between 1937 and 1939. In an effort to advance the pan-Indian nationalist cause, he had introduced legislation making study of Hindi compulsory in the Presidency's secondary schools. In the course of the protests, twelve hundred persons were incarcerated, and, in 1939, two men died in prison. They were hailed as martyrs and mourned with elaborate funeral processions in Madras. Ramaswamy, *Passions of the Tongue*, 198–204.

93. Their sentiment was encapsulated in poems such as this: "[Our] mind is Tamil; [our] entire body is Tamil; [our] life is Tamil; [our] pulse is Tamil; [our] veins are Tamil; [our] flesh, muscle, everything is Tamil; everything in [our] body is Tamil, Tamil, Tamil" (S. Subramanian, *Tamiḻ Veṟi* [Passion for Tamil] [Madras: Saddhu Accukuttam, 1939], 15–16; quoted in Ramaswamy, *Passions of the Tongue*, 6).

94. "Assembly nod for name change," *Hindu*, September 1, 1996, 4.

95. Tamil Nadu, India's southernmost state, is also its sixth most populous (http://www.censusindia.gov). In the decade between 1991 and 2001, the state's population increased by 11.19 percent. As of the 2001 Census, the state's urbanization level was 43.86 percent, an increase of almost 10 percent from 1991, when it was 34.2 percent. These rates differed sharply from the levels of the preceding two decades, which R. Rukmani characterized as a phase of declining urbanization following the earlier "agglomerisation" period and its associated industrial development. The rate of urbanization in Tamil Nadu was 30.16 percent in 1971, and in 1981 had risen by less than 3 percent, to 32.96 percent ("Urbanisation and Socio-Economic Change in Tamil Nadu, 1901–91, *Economic and Political Weekly* 29 [1994]): 3263–3272, 3264. These features are consistent with Tamil Nadu's industrial development since Indian independence. The state's Human Development Index of .657 is indicative of its relatively high levels of literacy (73.47 percent overall, with male literacy at 82.33 percent and female literacy at 64.55 percent) and its sex ratio (986/100, with lower rates in those districts having lower female literacy levels and high incidence of female infanticide).

Government of Tamil Nadu, *Tamil Nadu Human Development Report* (Delhi: Social Science Press, 2003). The statewide poverty level (21.12 percent) represents a reduction of 25 percentage points since 1973, when it was higher than the All-India average.

96. After Mumbai, Chennai is India's second most popular destination for investment. During the 1990s, domestic, foreign, and multinational corporations, including Phillips Ltd., Sony, Hyundai, Hindustan Motors, and Mahindra Ford, as well as a number of software development firms (Pentafour, Alcatel, EDS, IBM, Infosys, and Wipro) opened production sites and offices in or just outside Chennai (See N. Bajpai and N. Radjou, *Raising the Global Competitiveness of Tamil Nadu's Information Technology Industry,* Development Discussion paper no. 728, Harvard Institute for International Development [Cambridge, Mass.: Harvard University Press, 1999]; N. Bajpai and N. Radjou, "IT Industry: Great Prospects Ahead, II," *Hindu,* March 30, 2000, 12). Chennai also has a large and growing services sector, accounting for over 40 percent of the total organized sector employment (Madras Metropolitan Development Authority, *Master Plan for Madras Metropolitan Area—2011,* 36–49; G. Chidambaram, *Madras 2011: Policy Imperatives—An Agenda for Action,* 11 vols. [Madras: Madras Metropolitan Development Authority, 1991], 5:12).

97. "Urban Agglomeration" and "Metropolitan Area" are census categories that describe an area of continuous urban spread, comprising a city and its adjoining outgrowths.

98. http://www.environment.tn.nic.in/chn.htm (accessed June 10, 2005).

99. The Gini coefficient is a measure of wealth or income inequality within a population. A Gini index of "0" denotes perfect income equality; "1" denotes perfect inequality. Chennai's GINI index, at .33, is the highest in the state (Government of Tamil Nadu, *Tamil Nadu Human Development Report,* 7–8, 13–15, 31–38).

100. Shaw, "Emerging Patterns of Urban Growth in India."

101. Chennai was a site for national and international pilot projects in sustainable urban development, including the Jawaharlal Nehru National Urban Renewal program, and the UN's "Sustainable Cities" program. It has been a recipient of World Bank aid for both specific projects and financial institution building. The latter goal represents a direction embarked upon by the World Bank in the late 1990s. The Bank now seeks to "develop and deepen state-level reform agendas" by establishing or strengthening agencies that set development policies, administer funds, and evaluate specific programs and their sponsors (municipalities, statutory boards, and private investors) in light of the goals of liberalization. By intervening in and restructuring the financial, administrative, and managerial performance of municipalities, the Bank expects to make cities more credit-worthy. The first such project in India, in 1998, was an economic restructuring project in Andhra Pradesh ("India: Country Framework Report for Private Participation in Infrastructure," *Country Brief: India* [Washington, D.C.: World Bank, 1998]; see also S. Maitra, "Financing Urban Development," *Economic and Political Weekly* 35 (2000): 4647–4655. In 1999 the World Bank approved Tamil Nadu's Urban Development Project, which included investments valued at about U.S.$270 million; it has been renewed subsequently and is currently active (through March 2011) as the "Third Tamil Nadu Urban Development Project" (Project ID: PO83780). Available at http://www.worldbank.org/L67WLT8H3 (accessed June 28, 2007). See also "India—Tamil Nadu Urban Development Project II," Project Information Document (Report No. PID 6850), Washington, D.C.: The World Bank, 1998; "India—Tamil Nadu Urban Development Project II," Project Appraisal Document (Report No. 18400-IN), Washington, D.C.: The World Bank, 1999; "Tamil Nadu Urban Development Project III," Project Information Document (Report No. AB734), Washington, D.C.: The World Bank, 2004.

102. Madras Metropolitan Development Agency, *Master Plan for Madras Metropolitan Area—2011,* 133–143.

103. Although the state's working population increased between 1991 and 2001 (from 24.2 million to 27.8 million), the overall work participation rate has declined over the past forty years, from 45.7 percent to 44.8 percent. Responsible for the increase in working population is the rise in marginal workers (from 1.4 million in 1991 to 4.1 million in 2001). And among main workers, over 90 percent are employed in the unorganized sector (Government of Tamil Nadu, *Tamil Nadu Human Development Report,* 26–29).

104. Ibid., 58–66.

105. Lawsuits have been brought against these developments, and the state's High Court issued rulings limiting some development in the estuarine area ("Court Offers Hope for Adyar Creek,"

Madras Musings, August 16–31, 2001, 1, 7). Given the resistance of state and private corporate interests to growth curbs, however, there is little hope that coastal zone development will abate or be reversed (Hari Babu, ed., *Dossier on Tourism: Issues in Tamil Nadu* [Bangalore: Equations, 1997], 34–47); Bharat Jairaj and K. Mehta, "One Five Star or One Fifty Villages: Tourism on the East Coast Road," *CAG Reports,* October–December 1999, 8–9.)

106. In his 1996 election campaign the city's mayor, M. K. Stalin (son of the then chief minister M. Karunanidhi) promised to make Chennai a clean, Singapore-like city. Once in office, the city's newspapers bore regular visual reminders of Chennai's progress toward this goal, with photographs of earth-moving machinery demolishing huts and collecting garbage ("Pavement Hawkers Removed from NSC Bose Road," *Hindu,* November 28, 1996, 3; "Hawkers on Poonamallee High Road Evicted," *Hindu,* December 4, 1996, 3; "Traffic Moves Faster after Clearance," *Hindu,* December 5, 1996, 3; and "Squatters to be Rehabilitated Outside the City," *Hindu,* December 5, 1996, 3). Shortly thereafter, the city entered into negotiations with a Singapore-based company for privatized waste collection and disposal—putatively a cheaper and more efficient option than the existing public conservancy system ("Garbage, Garbage Everywhere," *Hindu,* Metro Section, January 6, 1997, I).

107. Special Housing Committee, *Report of the Special Housing Committee* (Madras: Corporation of Madras, 1933).

108. Ranson, *A City in Transition,* 116–122.

109. Ibid., 125, 126.

110. Ibid., 126. The Town Planning Schemes under Section 4(K) and (L) of Madras Town Planning Act provided for house sites and construction but no funds were allocated.

111. These included Hindu Religious Endowments Commission, *Report of the Hindu Religious Endowments Commission* (New Delhi: Government of India, Ministry of Law, 1962); Committee on Emotional Integration, *Report of the Committee on Emotional Integration* (New Delhi: Ministry of Education, 1962); and Committee on Religious and Moral Hygiene, *Report of the Committee on Religious and Moral Hygiene* (New Delhi: Ministry of Education, 1959).

112. Tamil Nadu Slum Clearance Board, *Socio-economic Survey of Madras Slums* (Madras: Tamil Nadu Slum Clearance Board, 1975), 175. By 1977 twenty-three thousand tenement flat units had been constructed. The agency's focus then shifted to the provision of serviced plots on which residents were assisted in building their own homes. However, the number of slums targeted for resettlement or improvement dropped sharply in the late 1970s because of financing shortfalls. Paul Weibe, *Tenants and Trustees: A Study of the Poor in Madras* (Delhi: Macmillan, 1977), 70.

113. Mary Douglas, "Secular Defilement," in idem, *Purity and Danger,* 29–40 (London: Routledge and Kegan Paul), 35.

114. In 1967 an *Interim Development Plan for Madras* was authored by the Directorate of Town Planning; the following year saw the publication of the *Metropolitan Plan for Madras.* These were quickly followed by the *Urban Development of Greater Madras* (1970) and *Madras Metropolitan Plan, 1971–1991* (1973). All but the last of these plans focused on the physical aspects of development; the 1971 plan explicitly dealt with both the economic and physical framework of development and called for a comprehensive and multifunctional planning agency. In 1972, contemporaneous with the formation of the Madras Urban Agglomeration, the Madras Metropolitan Development Authority was set up as an ad hoc, inter-agency planning body.

115. *Madras Metropolitan Plan, 1971–1991,* 29–30, 34–35. The city's southward growth and the extensions of its radial road network are among the present-day features that bear the imprint of that plan's recommendations.

116. Ibid., 22.

117. Ibid., 84.

118. Ibid., 86. Echoing this sentiment, the architect, F. B. Pithavadian wrote: "The Marina should be made attractive both aesthetically and physically for our people and not preserved like a dead monument for tourists. . . . We can afford to have many more restaurants . . . small theatres . . . amusement parks." He encouraged more high-rise structures and, impatient with development control regulations, declared that "the main aim and target should be to start the process of redevelopment and once the process is on its way more stringent regulations could be introduced to control it." See F. B. Pithavadian, "An Architect's View," *Civic Affairs,* Special Issue: *Madras on the Move* (December 1977): 32–33.

119. Many of the recommendations of the 1973 plan were not implemented because of infrastructural inadequacies and the planning agency's own limited jurisdiction. In the late 1970s a consulting firm was hired to assess existing plans and the planning apparatus; it recommended strategic changes in policy making to ensure coordination of various implementing agencies (Madras Metropolitan Development Authority, *Structure Plan for Madras Metropolitan Area,* 2 vols. [Madras: Madras Metropolitan Development Authority, 1980]). The 1980 document identified the central problem for planning as population growth and the decline in formal sector employment coupled with low earnings in the informal sector; these were accompanied by a widening gap between housing supply and demand and the growth of slums. Economic growth was argued to be the key factor in solving these interconnected problems.

120. *Master Plan for Madras Metropolitan Area—2011,* 138–140.

121. Ibid., 47–48.

122. Chennai Metropolitan Development Authority, *Draft Master Plan II for Chennai Metropolitan Area* (Chennai: Chennai Metropolitan Development Authority, 2007), http://www.cmdachennai.org/SMP.html (accessed June 19, 2007); A. Srivathsan, "Government tells CMDA to Prepare Fresh Draft Second Master Plan," *Hindu* (online edition), January 12, 2007, http://www.thehindu.com/2007/01/12/stories/2007011207940100.htm (accessed March 13, 2007); idem, "Chennai's Long Wait for a Master Plan" *Hindu* (online edition), January 13, 2007, http://www.thehindu.com/2007/01/13/stories/2007011300200100.htm (accessed March 13, 2007); idem, "Chennai Master Plan Is Ready" *Hindu* (online edition), March 6, 2007, http://www.thehindu.com/2007/03/06/stories/2007030617180300.htm (accessed March 13, 2007). At the time of this writing (December 2007), the 2007 Plan remained under review.

123. Proposals similar to CMDA's draft plan were found in another planning instrument, the 2006 City Development Plan, which had been prepared in response to a central government initiative, the Jawarhalal Nehru National Urban Renewal Mission; like the Master Plans, it was prepared without public consultation and released for public review only in April 2007 (Jawarhalal Nehru National Urban Renewal Mission, City Development Plan [New Delhi: Government of India, 2006]), http://jnnurm.nic.in/cd_apprep_pdf/CDP_Appraisals_ASCI/CHENNAI/May_2006.pdf (downloaded May 19, 2007).

124. See, for example, Hema Vijay, "Housing Board Flats Make Way for Gentrification," *Hindu* (online edition), July 29, 2006, http://www.thehindu.com/thehindu/pp/2006/07/29/stories/2006072900050100.htm (accessed May 20, 2007); "Real Estate Rush," *Frontline* (online edition), August 25, 2006, 23, 16, part of a special feature: "Boom Time in Chennai," http://www.flonnet.com/f12316/stories/20060925003310600.htm (accessed May 20, 2007).

125. Through its cultural media initiatives, the Ford Foundation has lent support to the National Folklore Support Centre and DakshinaChitra. An English-language biweekly, *Madras Musings,* dedicated to increasing public awareness of cultural and environmental conservation in the city, is funded almost entirely with the financial support of fourteen major corporations. The Chennai Heritage Trust, established in 2000 with support from the same corporate bodies, finances a range of conservation activities, including the documentation of historic buildings, precincts, and other architectural features. These and allied cultural conservation activities tend to be English-mediated and are spearheaded by an elite core group affiliated with INTACH.

126. Some of this activity takes place in the areas where supporters live and work, such as Mambalam. In an effort to build a nationalist constituency among poor and low-caste Hindus, however, slums adjacent to Muslim-majority areas also have been sites for the latter projects.

127. From the mid-1980s on, Hindu nationalist groups affiliated with the Rashtriya Swayamsevak Sangh had orchestrated festivals and processions in connection with Vinayaka Chathurthi, extending to Madras the same strategies that they had used in other cities to mobilize popular support for Hindutva. The events, which were organized so as to make claims on Muslim and Christian social spaces—for example, with procession routes that led by mosques—had become more frequent in Madras, and also increasingly violent. Despite their use of generalized narratives on Hindu tradition in colonizing public space, however, Hindutva's promulgators showed little interest in the city's history. See chapter 5 for further discussion.

128. The only exception to this was the attention lavished on Tiruvalluvar, a Tamil sage said to have been born in Mylapore sometime between the first and third century CE.

129. It also coincided with the DMK's political control of the city itself. For the first time in nearly twenty-five years, municipal elections were held. DMK contenders, led by the mayoral candidate M. K. Stalin, son of the chief minister, easily won the election with the support of the party's working-class base. For a recent discussion of the cultural politics of the name change and its implications for historiography, see R. Venkatachalapathy, ed., *Chennai not Madras: Perspectives on the City* (New Delhi: Marg, 2006).

130. The text posted on the Web site explains that Venkatapathy sought access to British trade partners, and so granted to the company's representatives a fishing village, Madraspatnam, and surrounding territory. The fort, built south of Madraspatnam, came to be known to Indians as Chennapatnam, after Venkatapathy's father, "either in deference to the wishes of Damarla Venkatapathy or because the site originally bore that name" ("History of Madras," http://www.chennaicorporation.com/madras_history.htm, p. 3 [accessed March 12, 2005]). The Web site accounts for the use of the name "Madras" over the prior 350 years as the product of "confusion," asserting that the original place names were inexplicably reversed, with Chennai taken to refer to the fishing village and Madras to the fort and environs and that, as a result, historians drew the erroneous conclusion that Madras was the more accurate name.

131. See, for example, "CM Promises to Make Chennai Asia's Premier City," *New Indian Express*, September 26, 2003; "Budget Speech 2007–2008," http://www.tn.gov.in/budget/dubsp07_08.htm (accessed April 20, 2007).

132. Muthiah, *Madras Rediscovered*, 6.

133. Here, I modify Roland Robertson's useful neologism, glocalisation, coined to capture the articulation of global and local forces ("Globalisation or Glocalisation?" *Journal of International Communication* 1, no. 1 [1994]: 33–52).

3. Memory, Mourning, and Politics

1. *Mōrkuḻampu* is a stew made up of vegetables in a spicy coconut-buttermilk sauce, *racam* is a spicy lentil broth, and *poriyal* is a fried vegetable.

2. An expression translated as "Revolutionary Leader" and one of the praise names by which MGR was popularly known. It is sometimes transliterated as "Puratchi."

3. On the hermeneutics of modern temporality, see Reinhard Koselleck, *Futures Past* (New York: Columbia University Press, 2004 [1985]); see also Ramaswamy's *The Lost Land of Lemuria* for a discussion of discursive and cartographic representations of modernity and loss in Tamil nationalism.

4. Aretxaga, "Maddening States," 398.

5. Ibid., 403.

6. Giorgio Agamben, following Schmitt, considers states of exception to be "caesurae and divisions" within the body of law, such as emergencies and periods of martial law, that "by means of their articulation and opposition allow the machine of law to function" (*State of Exception*, trans. K. Attell (Chicago: University of Chicago, 2005), 35; Carl Schmitt, *Political Theology*, trans. G. Schwab (Cambridge, Mass.: MIT Press, 1985 [1922]). Agamben, noting their increased prevalence in the twentieth century, probes the dependence of law on its antithesis, the exception, likening the exception both to what Derrida categorized as the "supplement" and to the ritual condition of "liminality," and traced its political genealogy to the episodes of disorder associated with public mourning upon the death of the sovereign (Agamben, *State of Exception*, 37–40, 65–73).

7. See Thomas Markus and Deborah Cameron, *The Words Between the Spaces* (London: Routledge, 2002).

8. The Tamil term for a gravesite, such as MGR's, is *camāti* (sometimes transliterated as *samadhi*); memorials, including those that are not burial sites, are also referred to as "*niṉaiviṭam*" or "*niṉaivālayam*." Both compounds are based on the verb, "*niṉai*," meaning to think or to remember; the suffix "*iṭam*" refers generically to a space or context; "*ālayam*" refers more specifically to a temple or other sacred place. Politicians associated with both of the state's principal Dravidian parties (DMK and AIA-DMK) regularly commission commemorative sites, including memorials, statues, and galleries; both parties' evocations of Tamil history and culture are similar, despite differences in the specific heroes each celebrates.

9. On emotive institutions, see Geoffrey White, "Emotive Institutions," in *A Companion to Psychological Anthropology: Modernity and Psychocultural Change,* ed. C. Casey and R. Edgerton (London: Blackwell, 2004), 241–254.

10. To date, J. Jayalalithaa has served two terms as the state's Chief Minister. Her first term was 1991–96; her party was succeeded by the DMK in 1996, and M. Karunanidhi held the Chief Ministership from 1996 to 2001. In 2001 the AIA-DMK once again took a majority of assembly seats, and Jayalalithaa returned as Chief Minister until 2006. The assembly elections in May 2006 repeated the earlier sweep, returning the DMK to power.

11. "The Dr. Jayalalithaa Led AIADMK Political Party Official Web Site," http://www.aiadmkindia.org. All pages on the AIA-DMK Web site referenced in this chapter were accessed between October 20 and November 30, 2004, and revisited in February 2007. That Web site was subsequently taken down and replaced with a single-page site, "Official Site of AIADMK Supremo J. Jayalalitha," http://aiadmk.8k.com. At the time of this writing (December 2007), all Web links for the original site were dead.

12. "Assembly Election Manifesto, 2001," 4, http://www.aiadmkindia.org/em2001.html.

13. Lynn Hunt, *The Family Romance of the French Revolution* (Berkeley: University of California Press, 1992), xiii; Sigmund Freud, "Family Romances," In *The Freud Reader,* ed. Peter Gay (New York: Norton, 1989 [1908]), 297–300.

14. The literary form in which this dynamic is expressed is also consistent with Freud's original essay, the title of which used the German term "roman," glossed literally as "novel." See Peter Gay's introduction to "Family Romances," in *The Freud Reader,* 297–298.

15. Though the secession movement of the 1950s and 1960s has never been resurrected, idioms of Tamil exceptionalism remain the basic currency of all Dravidianist parties.

16. M. S. S. Pandian, a sharp critic of MGR's brand of populism and—by extension—the party's (and his successor's) continued cultivation of it, acknowledges its effectiveness: "the political devotion of the subaltern classes to MGR was not because he had pursued radical economic policies . . . effecting major structural changes in the economy and lessening the sufferings of the poor. . . . The AIA DMK government under MGR taxed the poor (and the middle classes) to profit the rich" (*The Image Trap: M. G. Ramachandran in Film and Politics,* [Newbury Park, Calif.: Sage, 1992], 21). Pandian argues that MGR was able to pull this off through skillful exploitation of his screen image to produce an ideology that conformed to the common sense of the rural poor by speaking to their struggles and aspirations, and that this enabled him to secure popular consent for his policies and programs. The invocation of MGR's rule, through commemorative actions and spaces, and its perpetuation programmatically as well as iconographically, has marked the subsequent periods of AIA-DMK rule, under MGR's protégé, Jayalalithaa. The hollowness of this populism has been recognized—in the 2004 elections in which AIA-DMK suffered a complete rout, losing all the constituencies in which its candidates stood. For a detailed analysis of the rise of Dravidianist parties in Tamil Nadu and their styles of political mobilization, see Sara Dickey, "The Politics of Adulation: Cinema and the Production of Politicians in South India," *Journal of Asian Studies*, 52(1993): 340–372 and Subramanian, *Ethnicity and Populist Mobilization.*

17. For a sensitive discussion of DMK political oratory, see John Bernard Bate, "*Mēṭaittamiḻ:* Oratory and Democratic Practice in Tamil Nadu," Ph.D. diss., University of Chicago, 2000.

18. The 2006 state assembly elections were the first since 1967 in which neither the DMK nor the AIA-DMK won a majority of seats. The DMK itself won 96 seats and gained control of the government by leading an alliance that included six other parties, the Democratic Progressive Alliance (DPA). The DPA alliance holds 163 out of the assembly's 234 seats. Analysts Sanjay Kumar and Yogendra Yadav suggest that the hegemony of the two major Dravidianist parties may be eroding because of challenges posed by Dalit voting patterns and by a new Dravidian party headed by the popular actor Vijaykant, though whether changes in political culture will follow remains to be seen (Sanjay Kumar and Yogendra Yadav, "Tamil Nadu's Changing Political Landscape," *Hindu* [online edition], May 10, 2006), http://www.thehindu.com/2006/05/10/stories/2006051008901200.htm (accessed May 20, 2006).

19. "Eṉṉa naṭantālum cilai tiṟappatu uṟuti: Karuṇāniti pēccu," (Whatever happens, the statue will be unveiled: Karunanidhi's speech), *Tiṉatanti,* December 22, 1999; "Kaṉṉiyākumariyil Amaikkappaṭṭa 133 aṭiuyara Tiruvaḷḷuvar cilai: Karuṇāniti, nāḷai tiṟantu vaikkiṟār" (Karunanidhi

to unveil the 133-foot tall statue installed at Kanyakumari tomorrow), *Tiṉatanti*, December 31, 1999; "Em. Ji. Ar. Peyarai Maṟaikkavillai" (MGR's name is not hidden), January 6, 2000; "Putiya Vaḷḷuvar cakāptattai uruvākkavēṇṭum: Karuṇāniti pēccu" (We must usher in a new "Valluvar" epoch: Karunanidhi's speech), *Tiṉatanti*, January 17, 2000; Stapati, Kanapati "Alai ... Kalai ... Tiruvaḷḷuvar cilai" (Waves ... art ... Tiruvalluvar's statue), *Tiṉatanti*, January 15, 2000.

20. T. S. Subramanian, "Promises to Keep," *Frontline* (online edition), June 2, 2006, http://www.flonnet.com/fi2310/stories/20060602002002600.htm (accessed June 15, 2006); "Statue Symbolizes Culture, says Chief Minister," *Hindu*, June 4, 2006. http://www.thehindu.com/2006/06/04/stories/2006060408060600.htm (accessed June 16, 2006); Government of Tamil Nadu, "Policy Note 2006–2007, Demand No. 31, Information Technology Department," http://www.tn.gov.in/policynotes/information_technology.htm (accessed May 12, 2007); "Governor's Address in the Legislative Assembly on 24th May 2006," http://www.tn.gov.in/tnassembly/Governors_address_May2006_2.htm (accessed May 12, 2007).

21. See John Echeverri-Gent, "Politics in India's Decentered Polity," In *India Briefing: Quickening the Pace of Change*, ed. A. Ayres and P. Oldenburg (Armonk, N.Y.: M. E. Sharpe, 2002), 19–53.

22. "Tamil Nadu [has] ... aggressively pursued industrial growth and ... adopted ... pro-investment strategies ... designed to create a business friendly environment.... [but] Tamil Nadu's political leaders have been reluctant to be seen as openly endorsing, let alone embracing liberalization.... In Tamil Nadu, an increasingly fragmented party system has eroded the support bases of the two main Dravidian parties.... The 1990s witnessed intense political mobilization of the OBCs and Dalits, and several new formations emerged.... The instability resulting from this combination of mobilization and fragmentation helps to explain the reluctance of Tamil Nadu's leadership to trumpet its commitment to economic reform. Moreover the left-of-centre and egalitarian political idiom if not ideology of the state's two main parties, and especially their lower caste/class social base, constitutes an additional disincentive to identifying themselves too closely with policies perceived as pro-rich" (Lorraine Kennedy, "The Political Determinants of Reform Packaging," in *Regional Reflections: Comparing Politics across India's States*, ed. Rob Jenkins, 29–65 [New York: Oxford University Press, 2004], 63–64).

23. Ibid., 40–41.

24. Ibid., 52, 64.

25. See George Michell, *Architecture and Art of Southern India* (Cambridge: Cambridge University Press, 1995), 121–154.

26. I described this in my earlier book, *Womanhood in the Making* (Boulder, Colo.: Westview Press, 1999), 77–108; see also Sara Dickey, "Permeable Homes: Domestic Service, Household Space, and the Vulnerability of Class Boundaries in Urban India," *American Ethnologist* 27, no. 2 (2000): 462–489.

27. Programs associated with his government employed his cinematic persona to garner notoriety and cement popular support. This was especially apparent in the Nutritious Noon Meal Scheme, which was publicized as an extension of his personal philanthropy, using a photographic image of MGR feeding a grateful child.

28. Apart from the homepage, there are few visual images. A "Photo Gallery" and a few small illustrations embedded in texts show MGR, Jayalalithaa, and occasionally Annadurai addressing crowds, receiving honors, or dispensing food, clothing, or other goods.

29. The flag comprises two horizontal bands of black and red, with an outline of Annadurai in oratorical pose at the center.

30. An alternate, inclusionary form (*nām*) exists, and its use implies the contemporaneity of readers/hearers and speakers/authors and evokes, by its usage, a shared identity. Use of the exclusive pronoun hails readers/hearers as witnesses of, but not participants in, the immediate, contemporaneous "we" of the speaking subject(s). Web site visitors are such witnesses: of the AIA-DMK party, of the events reported, and of the sentiments and wishes of MGR, and, more often, Jayalalithaa, which are reported in lavish detail. That this reader may not even be a fellow Tamil is implied in the mounting of the English site. Indeed, the transmutation of the real social spaces of political oratory, posters, and pamphlets into the virtual spaces of Tamil and English texts encompasses an audience who, though de-territorialized, can be called into cognitive and emotional co-presence as witnesses.

31. "Assembly Election Manifesto 2001," http://www.aiadmkindia.org/em2001.html. The Tamil version: "*Aṉaittintiya Aṇṇā Tirāviṭa muṉṉēṟṟakkaḻakam uḷappūrvamāka uṟutiyaḷikkiṟatu. Varum kaṭṭamaṉṟa potuttērtalil eṅkaḷ koḷkaikaḷaiyum, kōṭpāṭukaḷaiyum naṭaimuṟaippaṭutti, makkaḷ ukku tūymaiyuṭaṉum toṇṭaṟṟiṭa eṅkaḷukku vāyppaḷikkum vakaiyil, uṅkaḷ nallātaravai nalkuṅkal eṉum vēṇṭukōḷuṭaṉ eṅkaḷ tērtal aṟikkaiyai taṅkaḷ mēlāṉa pārvaikku paṇivōṭu aḷikkiṟōm*" ("Election Manifesto—2001," http://www.aiadmkindia.org/em2001t.html).

32. "Legend MGR,"1, http://www.aiadmkindia.org/legendforMGR.html. The Tamil version reads, "*Tamiḻ nāṭṭiṉ camīpattiya varalāṟu tamiḻ makkaḷiṉ aṉpu, pācam, mariyātai, ākiyavaṟṟuṭaṉ kaṭṭuṇṭu aṉaittintiya aṇṇā tirāviṭa muṉṉēṟṟakkaḻakattiṉ varalāṟṟōṭu piṉṉippiṇaintuḷḷatu.*" ("Legend MGR," 1, http://www.aiadmkindia.org/legendforMGR.html).

33. "History of AIADMK" (hereafter, "History") (http://www.aiadmkindia.org/History/html). The Tamil version: "*Nāṭu muḻuvatum pala itaṅkaḷil em.ji. ār. racikar maṉṟattiṉarum puraṭci talaivar mītu paṟṟum pācamum koṇṭa ti. mu. ka. toṇṭarkaḷum aṅkāṅkē tāṅkaḷākavē karuppu cikappu koṭiyil tāmarai ciṉṉam poṟitta koṭikaḷai ārvattōṭu ēṟṟiṉar*" ("History," 6, http://www.aiadmkindia.org/Historyt/html).

34. Reports on welfare policies, as well as charitable efforts, could be accessed by clicking the links to "MGR Trust," "Welfare Schemes," and "Idhayam Kaappom."

35. "History" 5. The Tamil version: "*Ceṉṉai meriṉa kaṭaṟkaraiyil pērariñar aṇṇā avarkaḷiṉ niṉaiviṭattiṟku pakkattil avarāl 'eṉ itayakkaṉi' eṉṟu aṉpōṭu aḻaikkappaṭṭa ṭākṭar puraṭci talaivar em. ji. ar. avarkaḷiṉ pūta uṭal cantaṉa pēḻaiyil vaittu aṭkkam ceyyappaṭṭatu*" ("History," 6).

36. In 1984, when MGR suffered a stroke, one of the film's hit songs circulated as a prayer for his return to health. Its first lines: "Long may you live / that the country may prosper," like a poem of praise for a king, implicitly treated the leader's body as coterminous with the land and the polity (Pandian, *The Image Trap*, 56).

37. "Living Legend Dr. J. Jayalalithaa," 12 (hereafter, "LL-J"), http://www.aiadmkindia.org/legendformadam.html. The Tamil version: "*Puraṭci talaivi mutalamaiccarāka poṟuppēṟṟatum caṭṭamaṉṟa pēravaiyil puraṭci talaivariṉ tiruvuruva paṭattai tiṟantu vaittumakiḻntār*" ("LL-J," 15, http://www.aiadmkindia.org/legendformadamt.html).

38. These acts included, besides building the memorial, acts of devotion that established Jayalalithaa's political ancestry through MGR to Anna and to E. V. Ramaswamy (or Periyar), the architect of the Dravidian Self-Respect movement. Among them were donations to the Periyar Self-Respect Foundation and to Annadurai's widow (LL-J, 12).

39. During this, her first term of office, Jayalalithaa assumed MGR's populist mantle, continuing the programs he had initiated, though she also embraced a neoliberal agenda that India's central government had crafted with its New Industrial Policy. She remained in office until 1996, when a welter of corruption charges against both her and her party led to losses at the polls.

40. This section summarizes information found in the English dailies, *The Hindu, The Indian Express,* and in the Tamil daily *Tiṉamaṇi.*

41. Bate, "*Mēṭaittamiḻ:* Oratory and Democratic Practice in Tamil Nadu," 183–220.

42. "History," 2.

43. Ibid. The Tamil site version: "*Karuṇāniti atikāra pōtaiyil ūḻal malintavarākavum, carvātikāriyākavum māṟiṉār*" ("History," 2).

44. Ibid.

45. Ibid., 3.

46. Ibid., 2. The Tamil site version: "*Āṉāl em. ji.ār. makkaḷiṉ nāyakarāka manilam muḻuvatum varavēṟkappaṭṭār*" ("History," 2).

47. Ibid. The Tamil site version: "*Avarkaḷiṉ utaviyuṭaṉ appōtu vaḷarntu koṇṭirunta pērācai piṭitta karuṇāniti vantār*" ("History," 2).

48. "LL-J," 2.

49. Ibid. The Tamil site version: "*Makkaḷāl 'ammā' eṉṟu aṉpuṭaṉ aḻaikkappaṭṭa avar kaṭciyiṉ itara talaivarkaḷukku patilāka attokutiyil piraccāram ceyyumpaṭi kēṭṭu koḷḷappaṭṭār*" ("LL-J," 3, http://www.aiadmkindia.org/legendformadamt.html).

50. Ibid., 6. The Tamil site version: "*Ammaṉṟa mānāṭṭu nikaḻccikaḷiṉ muttāyppāka puraṭci talaivarukku āraṭi uyara veḷḷi ceṅkōl oṉṟiṉai talaimai kaḻakattiṉ cārpil tayārittu ataṉai aḷikkum nikaḻ cci amaikkappaṭṭu ac ceṅkōliṉai puraṭci talaivariṭam aḷikkum vāyppai peṟṟiruntār puraṭci talaivi.*

Ac ceṅkōliṉai puraṭci talaivar karaṅkaḷil aḷittār. Puraṭci talaivi aḷitta veḷḷi ceṅkōlai puraṭci talaivar puraṭci talaiviyiṭamē tiruppi aḷitta pōtu māṉāṭṭil tiraṇṭiruntavarkaḷ ac ceykaiyai varavēṟṟu ceyta karavoli iṉṟum aṉaivar uḷḷattilum pacumai māṟāta makiḻcci niṉaivāka uḷḷatu" ("LL-J," 8).

51. Ibid., 6.

52. Ibid., 7. The Tamil site version: "*An nikaḻcciyiṉai tāṉ tamiḻ nāṭṭu makkaḷ taṉakku piṉ tāṉ vakitta poṟuppukaḷai ēṟṟu naṭatta vēṇṭiyatu yār eṉ puraṭci talaivar aṭaiyāḷam kāṭṭiya nikaḻcciyāka iṉṟum karutukiṉṟaṉar*" ("LL-J," 8).

53. Ibid., 7–8. The Tamil site version: "*Illam tēti vanta makkaḷ 'Ammā! Nīṅkaḷ tāṉ talaimaiyēṟka vēṇṭum; eṅkaḷai vaḻi naṭatta vēṇṭum' eṉṟu puraṭci talaiviyiṭam vaitta vēṇṭukōḷkaḷ nāḷukku nāḷ valuvaṭaintu vantaṉa. . . . Avarkaḷ taṉ aṉṉai cattiyā tiruvuruva paṭattiṉ muṉ puraṭci talaiviyai niṟutti avariṭam cattiyam vāṅkiyatai niṉaittu pārttatāl avar uḷḷattil putiya uṟutipaṭu pūttatu. Puraṭci talaivar em. ji. ār. niṟuviya iyakkattaiyum, kaḻaka toṇṭarkaḷaiyum kāppāṟṟa enta tollaiyayum etirttu etir nīccal pōṭuvatu eṉṟu muṭivetuttār*" ("LL-J," 9).

54. Ibid., 9.

55. Ibid., 10. An abbreviated version appears on the Tamil site: "*Urimai piraccaṉaiyai capānāyakar aṉumatikka maṟuttatāl vākkuvātam vaḷarntatu; kūccal, kuḻappam atikarittatu; āḷum karuṇāniti katciyiṉ caṭṭamaṉṟa uṟuppiṉarkaḷum, amaiccarkaḷum oru peṇ eṉṟum pārāmal puraṭci talaiviyiṉ mītu kolai veṟi tākkutal naṭattiṉārkaḷ. Cēlaiyai piṭittu iḻuttu māṉapaṅka paṭuttavum muyaṉṟaṉar*" ("LL-J," 12).

56. Elsewhere Jayalalithaa explicitly likened the DMK chief minister M. Karunanidhi to the Kaurava king Dushasan, who orders the disrobing in the epic (B. Krishnakumar, S. Murthy, and V. D'Souza, "Playing it Dirty," *The Week*, February 10, 1991, 29–31). Her invocation of Draupadi derived salience from the Draupadi's goddess-like stature in many parts of rural south India (Alf Hiltebeitel, "The Folklore of Draupadi: Saris and Hair," in *Gender, Genre and Power in South Asian Expressive Traditions*, ed. A. Appadurai, F. Korom, and M. Mills, 395–427 (Philadelphia: University of Pennsylvania Press, 1994). She was also able to trade on the popularity of the *Mahabharata* teleserial, broadcast in 1989 and 1990. In the latter, as Purnima Mankekar has reported, the episode featuring Draupadi's disrobing invited identification among women viewers by capturing their own sense of vulnerability in male-dominated public spaces (Purnima Mankekar, *Screening Culture, Viewing Politics: An Ethnography of Television, Womanhood, and Nation in Postcolonial India* [Durham, N.C.: Duke University Press, 1999], 239–252).

57. "New Design for MGR *Camāti*," *Hindu*, August 24, 1992, 3.

58. Ibid.

59. The associations with divinity extended to sacralized praise names, which multiplied during the time that she served as chief minister, and to her representation on posters, billboards, and cutouts with iconographic embellishments of divinity. Visual associations with divinity, moreover, find support with some of the programs with which she has sought to garner electoral support. Besides various temple protection measures, Jayalalithaa ostentatiously launched a noon meal program with personal funds that, although meant to continue MGR's signature program, spatially and nominally reframed it as Hindu ritual. Hindu temples were selected as sites of distribution and consumption, and the program was christened with a Sanskritic title, *annadhanam*, a phrase that literally means "gift of rice," and which designates a form of ritual charity often prescribed as the concluding act of a vow. See chapter 4 for further discussion of these devotional themes.

60. Preminda Jacob, "From Co-Star to Deity: Popular Representations of Jayalalitha Jayaram," in *Representing the Body: Gender Issues in Indian Art*, ed. V. Dehejia, 140–165 (Delhi: Kali for Women, 1997).

61. See Christopher Fuller, *The Camphor Flame: Popular Hinduism and Society in India*, 106–107 (Princeton, N.J.: Princeton University Press, 1992); Dirks, *The Hollow Crown*, 55–60, 285–305.

62. See B. Hillier, A. Leaman, P. Stansall, and M. Bedford, "Space Syntax," *Environment and Planning B*, 3 (1976): 147–185; Kim Dovey, *Framing Places: Mediating Power in Built Form* (London: Routledge, 1999).

63. An apt demonstration of this point can be found in Preminda Jacob's description of the billboards and cutouts of Jayalalithaa, mounted for the 1995 World Tamil Conference, held in Tanjavur, an ancient temple town and the seat of the medieval Chola dynasty. One billboard depicts the Chola king, patron of the Brihadesvara Temple, "point[ing] towards a portrait bust

of Jayalalitha [*sic*] whose head is encircled by a halo. In the background, sculptors and builders are shown constructing the temple. . . . At the right, on a slightly depressed plane, is the image of the Chola king directing his queen's (and the viewer's) attention to Jayalalitha [*sic*]. In a sweeping teleological vision Jayalalitha [*sic*] emerges as the direct successor of the politically powerful as well as culturally accomplished ancient Tamil hero" (Jacob, "From Co-Star to Deity," 160).

4. Modernity Remembered

1. Pradeep Chakravarthy, "In Precincts Serene and Green," *Hindu*, June 4, 2004, http://www.thehindu.com/thehindu/fr/2004/06/04/stories/2004060402030600.htm (accessed March 20, 2006).

2. "Thiruvanmiyur," http://en.wikipedia.org/wiki/Thiruvanmiyur/ (accessed February 28, 2006).

3. Current "inventions of tradition" have predecessors in various cultural revitalization discourses. See Ali, *Invoking the Past;* Eugene Irschick, *Dialogue and History: Constructing South India, 1795–1895* (Berkeley: University of California Press, 1994), 81–94; and Joanne Punzo Waghorne, *Diaspora of the Gods: Hindu Temples in an Urban Middle-Class World* (New York: Oxford University Press, 2004), 83–106.

4. The Nehruvian legacy is defined, by Rajagopal, as "the desire to preserve a minimally neutral ground in a society with plural castes and creeds, going around rather than through the complex differences of the different communities, and establishing a political meeting ground removed from these" (Arvind Rajagopal, *Politics after Television: Hindu Nationalism and the Reshaping of the Public in India* [Cambridge: Cambridge University Press, 2000], 81). For a probing and eloquent discussion of the Nehruvian legacy, see Sunil Khilnani, *The Idea of India* (New York: Farrar, Straus, Giroux, 1997).

5. Rajagopal, *Politics*, 81.

6. This chapter is a substantially revised and expanded version of my article, "Modernities Remade: Hindu Temples and Their Publics in Southern India," *City and Society* 14, no. 1 (2002): 5–35.

7. Talal Asad, *Formations of the Secular: Christianity, Islam, Modernity* (Stanford, Calif.: Stanford University Press, 2003), 192–193. Asad explains that the doctrine of secularism arose in early modern Europe as a means to solve problems such as the control of the mobile poor, the governance of mutually hostile Christian sects within sovereign territory, and the regulation of commercial, military, and colonizing expansion of Europe overseas.

8. Oskar Negt and Alexander Kluge, *Public Sphere and Experience*, trans. P. Labanyi, J. Daniel, and A. Oksiloff (Minneapolis: University of Minnesota Press, 1993 [1972]), 2.

9. An extensive literature exists about southern Indian temple architecture, ritual practice, and institutional organization, including Arjun Appadurai, *Worship and Conflict under Colonial Rule* (Cambridge: Cambridge University Press, 1981); Christopher Fuller, *The Camphor Flame* (Princeton, N.J.: Princeton University Press, 1992); George Michell, *Architecture and Art of Southern India*, in *The New Cambridge History of India*, 1:6 (Cambridge: Cambridge University Press, 1995); and Franklin Presler, *Religion under Bureaucracy* (Cambridge: Cambridge University Press, 1987). In this section I intend only a brief overview to set the stage for later discussion and provide context for readers unfamiliar with these structures.

10. In 1996 I tabulated and mapped street shrines in 15 of the city's 150 administrative divisions. I came up with nearly 400, which, if representative, indicates that a total of 4,000 such shrines would not be out of line. In her recent book Waghorne suggested that a minimum of 600 Hindu temples existed in Chennai—presumably referring to larger, propertied sites rather than the more ephemeral street shrines—on the basis of a "general survey of urban temples" (Waghorne, *Diaspora of the Gods*, 9, 21).

11. Nationalist reformers targeted temples with reforms such as the Madras Devadasi (Prevention of Dedication) Act (1947), introduced originally in 1929, and the Madras Temple Entry Authorization Act (1947). With these measures, they sought to curb those forms of religious "excess"—the existence of dancers (devadasis) who often maintained sexual liaisons with temple patrons and caste-based entry restrictions—that threatened to derail modernist projects of state formation.

12. With the passage of the Madras Hindu Religious and Charitable Endowments Act (1951), the agency (the Hindu Religious Endowments Board) was reorganized as the Hindu Religious and Charitable Endowments (HR & CE) Administration Department and placed under the authority of the executive branch of the state government.

13. The Web site of the HR & CE Administration Department reports that 38,396 religious and charitable institutions (including 17 Jain temples) are managed by the HR & CE, http://www.hrce.tn.nic.in (accessed June 27, 2007). Efforts have been launched intermittently, but without much success, to intervene more directly in temple ritual by requiring that Tamil, rather than Sanskrit, be used as the language of worship (Presler, *Religion under Bureaucracy*, 114–118).

14. Statutory measures for the regulation of Hindu temples and other charitable institutions now exist in Andhra Pradesh, Karnataka, Maharashtra, and Himachal Pradesh; they postdate Tamil Nadu's measures.

15. Arun Agarwal and Sunita Narain, eds., *Dying Wisdom* (Bangalore: Center for Science and Environment, 1993), 245–264, 290–312. It was under Vijayanagara rule (1336–1564 CE), in particular, that irrigation works were developed and expanded, and evidence suggests that large temples played pivotal roles, both within the ecological networks of water storage and circulation and in the socioeconomic management of irrigation works.

16. Among the street shrines I surveyed, the vast majority were Hindu, with smaller numbers of Christian sites, dedicated usually to the Virgin Mary in the form of Annai Vailankanni, "Our Lady of Good Health." Mary acquired this title after she miraculously appeared in a village near Nagapattinam in the sixteenth century and was credited with restoring health to many believers. The village now boasts a basilica, which has become a major pilgrimage site, described on its Web site: http://www.annaivailankanni.org (accessed June 12, 2007). A satellite of that church was built in Chennai, in a fishing colony in Besant Nagar. Muslim sites, mainly mosques and saints' tombs, are found throughout the city, though they are spatially enclaved and not readily accessible from the street, either visually or proximally.

17. These shrines are often the work of auto-rickshaw and taxi drivers, marking the spots where they wait for fares. Roadside vendors and repair persons also build small shrines, sometimes seeking patronage as well as financial and in-kind support from local notables, gangsters, and nearby merchants.

18. They may be part of a strategy to extend holdings or to create a barrier to development or occupancy. In one case I recorded, a shrine was built by residents of a slum community near the access road to the slum in order to deter a nearby middle-class housing colony from dumping their garbage on the spot. Shrines may also occupy small niches cut into the compound walls surrounding well-to-do residences and institutions.

19. Mariyamman is ordinarily represented as a lone female, without a male consort. She and other *amman̲* goddesses are represented as being infused by volatile energy—"heat"—built up through unfulfilled sexual desire. She announces her presence in the bodies of her votaries and victims with "heat" of inspired speech, dance, and soaring fevers.

20. "*Agraharam*" is the most common transliteration of this term; the more accurate transliteration would be "*akrakāram.*"

21. See W. Noble, "Houses with Centered Courtyards in Kerala and Elsewhere in India," in *Dimensions of Social Life: Essays in Honor of David Mandelbaum*, ed. Paul Hockings (Berlin: Mouton de Gruyter, 1987), 215–262.

22. Waghorne, *Diaspora of the Gods*, 18–34.

23. Eck, *Darśan*, 59–60.

24. LeFebvre, *The Production of Space*, 68–79.

25. Ibid., 38–39.

26. The Tamil form is *cuyampu.*

27. The "Templenet" Web site lists Marundeswarar Temple as one of a group of seven Tyagarajar shrines in southern India. (http://www.indiantemples.com/Tamilnadu/maruchen.html) (accessed June 20, 2007).

28. A *stapati* is a hereditary designer-builder whose craft is based on classical precepts traced to the Vastu Vidya. For further discussion, see Vibhuti Chakrabarti, *Indian Architectural Theory: Contemporary Uses of Vastu Vidya* (Delhi: Oxford University Press, 1999), 1–34; and Samuel Parker,

"The Matter of Value Inside and Out: Aesthetic Categories in Contemporary Hindu Temple Arts," *Ars Orientalis* 22 (1992): 97–110.

29. Processions in which the deity is carried outside the temple, through surrounding neighborhoods, and then back to the temple exemplify the circumambulation that is a common part of temple ritual. Worshipers walk, crawl, or roll around temple complexes, shrines, or deity images—often repeatedly. These actions recapitulate a pilgrimage that, by approaching and circling the deity, "symbolically attend[s] to the entire visible world of name and form" (Eck, *Darsan,* 63).

30. The place-making capacity that is activated as temples are built and put to use is something that Hindu nationalists have recognized and used to advantage by erecting street shrines honoring the god Ram and his entourage, and using those sites for the Ramshila *pūjas*, during which bricks were blessed in preparation for their use in VHP-sponsored Ayodhya temple construction. In his account of the VHP-affiliated Hindu Munnani's staging of annual processions since the mid-1980s, Christopher Fuller shows how Hindu nationalist organizations have attempted to introduce Vinayaka Chathurti festivals into the spatial lexicon of southern Indian public religiosity and to provoke communal violence ("The Vināyaka Chaturthi Festival and Hindutva in Tamil Nadu," *Economic and Political Weekly* 34 [2001]: 1607–1616).

31. See David Schulman, *Tamil Temple Myths: Sacrifice and Divine Marriage in the South Indian Saiva Tradition,* (Princeton, N.Y.: Princeton University Press, 1980). For a discussion of *sthalapuranas* of Chennai temples, see Waghorne, *Diaspora of the Gods.*

32. I was told that the etymology of the village name Tiruvanmiyur can be traced to Valmiki, that the name is a composite of the terms *Tiru* (holy) + *Vanmi* (Valmiki) + *Ur* (place).

33. A. G. Krishna Menon and B. Thapar, *Historic Towns and Heritage Zones* (New Delhi: INTACH, 1988); B. Thapar, *Our Cultural Heritage* (New Delhi: INTACH, 1989). A British sister organization, INTACH-UK, operates independently of INTACH, and was established in 1987, with a bequest from Charles Wallace, who died in 1916. Wallace's original bequest had been divided between the British government and the Government of British India, and was meant to promote the sharing of knowledge between Britain and its colony about art and cultural heritage. INTACH-UK is administered by ICOMOS-UK and supports British citizens' visits to India related to art and heritage. Funds from the same estate were used to create the Charles Wallace Trust, which supports Indian citizens' travel to the United Kingdom for the purpose of studying heritage conservation.

34. Department of Culture, *Report of the Working Group on Art and Culture for the Sixth Five-Year Plan* (New Delhi: Ministry of Education, Social Welfare, and Culture, 1978); Department of Culture, *Performance Budget* 1985/86 (New Delhi: Ministry of Education, Social Welfare, and Culture, 1986); Richard Kurin, "Cultural Conservation through Representation: Festival of India Folklife Exhibitions at the Smithsonian Institution," in *Exhibiting Cultures: The Poetics and Politics of Museum Display*, ed. Ivan Karp and Steven Lavine, 315–343 (Washington, D.C.: Smithsonian, 1991).

35. One of the group's first major projects was an assessment of pollution in the Ganga River and proposal of mitigation recommendations (http://www.intach.org/history/ [accessed April 4, 2007]; see also Alley, *On the Banks of the Ganga*). Similar projects, focusing on urban waterways, were pursued by regional chapters, including Chennai's.

36. The work of INTACH lies firmly within the ambit of political modernity and its historicist foundations. Published reports describe constitutional precedent for its mission, noting that the "Fundamental Duties of Citizens" (Constitution of India, Part IV, A) stipulate that citizens should value and preserve culture (Thapar, *Our Cultural Heritage,* 8). Authors noted also that India's Eighth Five-Year Plan (1989/90–1994/95) recognized a role for conservation in the context of planned development. Citing these mandates, INTACH has identified lacunae within existing statutory measures for cultural and environmental conservation, noting, for example, that state-level Town and Country Planning Acts (which contain statutory provisions for urban and regional planning bodies and activities) allowed for the definition and protection of special, protected areas, which would include "heritage zones" but offered no specific directions as to how such areas were to be designated and protected (Thapar, *Our Cultural Heritage,* 8–10). INTACH sought to remedy this by offering professional consultancy services for the government; its Charter argues for the efficacy of conservation as a development goal and emphasizes that use of indigenous practices in conservation will ensure that such knowledge is sustained as part of the cultural milieu of heritage sites (Article 2, "INTACH Charter," http://www.intach.org/pdf/charter.pdf [accessed May 20, 2005]).

37. The hybridity of INTACH's charge reflects its relation to the preservation norms and practices institutionalized during the colonial period, notably the formation of the Archaeological Survey of India (ASI) in 1864 (see chapter 2). The ASI was charged with the listing and protection of antiquities and monuments, including forts, palaces, and temples not in active use. Such sites remain under the legal protection of the ASI today. In recent decades, however, concerns have arisen about the fate of more recent structures, including colonial buildings. There are also concerns about the condition of temples that remain in active use, as their conservation is not mandated by ASI rules. INTACH's mission was designed to suture this gap. The organization designates ancient temples and mosques that remain in use as heritage, as well as natural resources and the colonial-built environment, in some cases soliciting support from India's former colonizers to assist in preserving the latter.

38. INTACH Charter, Articles 2.6 and 3.12.

39. Ibid., Articles 1 and 2.

40. Along with other state-sponsored tourism and cultural ventures, INTACH's regional chapters had lost government support by the early 1990s. Its governance was decentralized, with its regional chapters expected to be self-supporting, even though all chapters share a common mandate as defined in the Charter. The Chennai chapter, convened until 1996 by Deborah Thiagarajan and G. Dattatri, proposed several ambitious projects, including an urban waterways assessment, the preparation of heritage zone plans for Mylapore and Mamallapuram, and research and planning for a craft center, later opened as DakshinaChitra (INTACH, *Mylapore: An Approach to Its Conservation,* Final Report [Madras, July 1993]; D. Varacharajan, A *Survey of Mamallapuram: Study Conducted for INTACH* [Madras: Madras School of Social Work, August 1986]). Indicative of the resistance that the group's proposals faced was the fate of the heritage zone plan for Mylapore. INTACH's plan envisioned a pedestrian promenade on the *mada* streets surrounding the temple, and proposed that bus routes be remapped and a large, bustling, open-air vegetable market be relocated. The proposal, prompted by the state's plan to extend the city's commuter rail line to Mylapore, was rejected, and the track extension and new station were completed in 2000.

41. In 1991 a citywide English-language weekly, *Madras Musings,* was launched under the editorship of S. Muthiah, a writer of popular local histories (including commissioned corporate histories) and co-convenor of INTACH's Chennai chapter. An endowment funded by donations from locally based private corporations funds its publication and distribution. In 1994 another group of neighborhood-based papers came on the scene, under the patronage of a single publisher, a retired officer of the elite national civil service corps, the Indian Administrative Service. The printing and circulation of these weeklies is supported by advertisers, most of them purveyors of consumer goods and services, such as clothing, groceries, communications, and Internet access. They contain interviews with local notables, news articles on municipal and ward affairs, and performance, book, and restaurant reviews. Their names (e.g., *Adyar Times, Mylapore Times*) refer to the neighborhoods in which they are distributed, most of them in the more prosperous southern and southwestern divisions of the city.

42. To date (2007), only two states, Punjab and Maharashtra, have heritage acts: the Punjab Regional and Town Planning and Development (Amendment) Act, 2003 and the Maharashtra Regional and Town Planning (Amendment) Act, 1994.

43. At the time of this writing (2008), no such act had been passed in Tamil Nadu, though INTACH representatives were instrumental in the formation, in 1999, of the Chennai Heritage Committee, an advisory group charged with the job of listing heritage buildings and precincts in the city and reviewing the draft Heritage Act.

44. For background on opposition to the East Coast Road project, see Hari Babu, "Dossier on Tourism," 38–40.

45. "Palani Hills Conservation Council, etc. v. The State of Tamil Nadu, etc. and others," 1995-2–*Writ Law Reporter* 737. For background on the case, see T. S. Subramanian, "The Conviction of Jayalalitha," *Frontline* (online edition), 17, no. 4 (February 19–March 3, 2000), http://www.flonnet.com/fl1704/17040380.htm (accessed January 12, 2001).

46. Other initiatives included a conservation plan for Pulicat, a village situated in an estuarine zone north of Chennai (P. Krishnan, M. Ramesh Kumar, A. Azeez, and M. Rajkumar,

Heritage Conservation Plan for Pulicat, [Chennai: INTACH, 2000]). The village had been the site of a Dutch trading post and was slated to be the site for a new power generation facility, and INTACH's plan combined historic preservation and ecological conservation. INTACH had also served as a consulting body for a plan designed to preserve the "girivalam," a circumambulatory procession route at the base of the hill on which the Siva temple at Tiruvannamalai sat (P. T. Krishnan, personal communication). See also "HC order on 'Girivalam Scheme' in Tiruvannamalai Stayed," *Hindu* (online edition), August 7, 2001, http://www.thehindu.com/2001/08/07/stories/0207000c.htm (accessed May 20, 2005); "'Girivalam' Cleanliness Needs Greater Attention," *Hindu* (online edition), March 31, 2002, http://www.thehindu.com/2002/03/31/stories/2002033102340300.htm (accessed May 20, 2005); "ASI Move to Take Over Tiruvannamalai Temple Opposed," *Hindu* (online edition), November 4, 2002, http://www.thehindu.com/2002/11/04/stories/2002110405560700.htm) (accessed May 20, 2005); "Tiruvannamalai Society Takes Up Greening Project," *Hindu* (online edition), August 1, 2003, http://www.thehindu.com/2003/08/01/stories/2003080106050300.htm (accessed May 20, 2005); "Declare Girivalam Path Part of Heritage Town Centre," *Hindu* (online edition), April 7, 2005, http://www.thehindu.com/2005/04/07/stories/2005040709660100.htm (accessed May 20, 2005).

47. A. G. Krishna Menon, "Towards an Indian Charter," *Seminar* 467 (1998): 21–26.

48. See James Q. Wilson and George Kelling, "Broken Windows," *Atlantic Monthly Online,* March 1982, http://www.theatlantic.com/politics/crime/windows.htm (accessed January 20, 2006).

49. In 2004 the city announced plans to give the old bridge a "facelift" in connection with a natural conservation project (K. Lakshmi, "River Conservation Project Nearing Completion," *Hindu* (online edition), April 1, 2004, http://www.thehindu.com/2004/0401/stories/2004040113320300.htm (accessed May 20, 2005).

50. Some accounts of this temple claim that five tanks once inhabited its grounds. One was destroyed or dried up, two existed in the form of wells, and two remain extant, just outside the east *kōpuram.* See, for example, the entry on the Marundeswarar Temple posted on the EPrarthana Web site: http://www.eprarthana.com/temples/Chennai/tn215maru.asp?tid=215 (accessed February 12, 2006).

51. I also attended these meetings.

52. INTACH was not alone in its effort to restore tanks, and the project the group outlined was not the first of its kind. Alarmed by the loss of ground and surface water in and around the city, a number of voluntary associations, community groups, and government agencies—working both independently and in collaboration—had assessed the condition of natural and human-made tanks, rivers, and streams in the 1990s. Most of these water bodies are dry or polluted. The fragmentation of the tank system under British rule had initiated this decline; subsequent urban development and population pressure contributed to additional losses of storage and circulation capacity. During the mid-1990s several organizations, including INTACH, had surveyed the city's 124 tanks (including the 39 temple tanks), and community groups, led by local chapters of the Rotary Club, had sponsored tank restoration efforts at a few temples, including the Marundeswarar Temple. See A. Srivathsan, *Temple Tanks in Chennai: An Inventory* (Chennai: INTACH, 2001); M. Amirthalingam, "Temple Tanks of Chennai: A Survey," *Ecoheritage* (October–March, 2003), http://cpreec.org/pubperiodicals-ecoheritage.htm (accessed February 1, 2006); and M. Amirthalingam, "Status Survey of Temple Tanks of Chennai," *Indian Journal of Environmental Education* 4 (April 2004), http://cpreec.org/pubperiodicals-indjournal.htm (accessed February 1, 2006). The same groups have sought to complement larger-scale government projects (mechanized regional irrigation works, storm drain clearance and expansion, dam and reservoir construction) with local measures such as residential and institutional rainwater harvesting and with community-based efforts to modernize and restore urban tank systems, including temple tanks.

53. The seminar, held in late December 1999, was sponsored jointly by INTACH's Chennai chapter and the Chennai Metropolitan Development Authority, the regional planning agency. The seminar was held in a small amphitheatre-style hall on the campus of Anna University School of Architecture and Planning. Convenors of INTACH's Chennai chapter were on hand, along with several of the more active members. CMDA was represented by several officials. Other presenters included members of INTACH's Hyderabad, Mumbai, and Delhi units. Rounding out the audience were members of local environmental and consumer associations, city-beat reporters from *The*

Hindu, and students enrolled in Anna University's School of Architecture and Planning. The seminar differed little from scholarly conferences I had attended in the U.S. and Europe. Like most public events conducted by INTACH, it was English-mediated—this was not in deference to the presence of foreigners (I was the only non-Indian) but reflected, instead, the transnational legacy of the approach that INTACH takes to heritage conservation and the regional mix of seminar participants, all of whom were part of urban India's English-speaking elite. Over the seminar's two days we in the audience listened to formal presentations by planners and by INTACH consultants; we were invited to participate in question-and-answer sessions and roundtable discussions. The event offered a window on the competing claims on the past occasioned by neoliberal development; it also enacted a form a deliberation that, in endorsing "transparency," "rationality," and "efficiency," illustrated both means and ends of neoliberal governance.

54. For example, in 2001 another Tiruvanmiyur-based voluntary group, TRY (Trees, Rain, and You), developed a system to channel the water that accumulated on streets during monsoon season and harvest it for residential use (Santosh Malliah, "It Rains Ideas," *Business Line* [online edition], September 24, 2001, http://www.thehindubusinessline.com/2001/09/24/stories/102425az.htm (accessed May 20, 2005).

55. During earlier periods of AIA-DMK rule, the temple was also benefited by state patronage. A hereditary temple priest and longtime resident recalled that improvements to the temple paralleled the area's commercial development, with more temple funds allocated during periods of AIA-DMK rule: "After 1965, improvements began in the area. From then, five hereditary priests, forming an association, began to serve in the temple. Between [19]79 and [19]81, the *rajakōpuram* was built. In the mid-1980s, more donors stepped in, more money was collected in the *hundi* [temple donation box] and temple lands began to yield more income for the temple."

56. Despite the longevity of these arrangements, there is abiding resentment among the devotees and priests of many state-managed temples because of what they perceive as state interference with and degradation of temples' sacred spaces and practices, and also because of interference with priests' own perquisites, property, earnings, and status networks. Some claim that "private" temples—those managed by families, sectarian groups, and neighborhood associations without state involvement—are the only sites where Hindu ritual is properly performed today, although the popular revivalism as well as patronage by the state's elected officials have mitigated this sentiment and contributed to a revival of interest and support for large temples. See Christopher Fuller, *The Renewal of the Priesthood: Modernity and Traditionalism in a South Indian Temple,* (Princeton, N.J.: Princeton University Press, 2003); and Hancock, *Womanhood in the Making,* 29.

57. A blogger from Tiruvanmiyur going by the name "blackdatura" offered a poetic description of an evening visit to the Marundeswarar Temple in an entry dated August 28, 2005: "As the sun vanished below the horizon at 6:40 PM, on Wednesday, the 13th of July 2005, [the] temple was transformed into a place of unwinding and rejuvenation for its visitors. A grandfather patiently answering the endless questions of his grandson near the sthala vrksha, groups of clean shaven senior citizens sharing notes at the mandapa steps, youngsters in jeans and chudidars, earnestly going around their pradakshina, a grandmother encouraging her little grandson to climb down from her hip to walk on the sand . . . a lady of gentle stature, pouring her heart out, while rendering the song 'Marakadavalli' in rag Kambodi, as a sandhya kala offering to the feminine deity, were scenes that added color to the darkening dusk" (http://blackdatura.blogspot.com/ [accessed April 12, 2006]).

58. In a conversation with Jaya, for example, I commented on the ambitious scope of INTACH's proposal. She agreed, noting that INTACH needed just one significant success in order to gain public support. She continued: "Democracy is new in India, compared with countries in Europe and North America. People have to learn that they have rights but this takes time. It's so slow . . . it takes generations. It's even more tragic that those who are well aware of their rights often misuse them, there is such corruption."

59. See John Harriss, "Middle-Class Activism and the Politics of the Informal Working Class," *Critical Asian Studies,* 38, no. 4 (2006): 445–465. For a discussion of comparable changes in norms of publicity and class culture in Mumbai, see Leela Fernandes, *India's New Middle Class,* (Minneapolis: University of Minnesota Press, 2006), 137–172.

60. Sudipta Kaviraj, "Filth and the Public Sphere: Concepts and Practices about Space in Calcutta," *Public Culture* 10, no. 1 (1997): 83–113.

61. Ibid., 105.

62. Rajagopal, *Politics after Television*, 21.

63. Ibid., 21–22.

64. Partha Chatterjee, *A Possible India: Essays in Political Criticism* (New Delhi: Oxford University Press, 1997), 241–249.

65. Ibid., 241.

66. Ibid., 241–249.

67. Both anticolonial and post-independence nationalist claims on Hindu temples and associated ritual practices are discussed in greater detail in my book, *Womanhood in the Making*, 177–195, and in an article, "Modernities Remade."

68. P. Nambiar and N. Krishnamurthy, "Report on the Temples of Madras," *Census of India, 1961*, 9, 11–D, xv.

69. Ibid.

70. Hindu Religious Endowments Commission, *Report of the Hindu Religious Endowments Commission* (New Delhi: Government of India, 1962), 6.

71. Ibid., 194.

72. Ibid., 162–168, 170.

73. Ibid., 146.

74. Ibid., 171.

75. In 2004 Tamil Nadu's HR & CE Administration Department posted the following statement on the homepage of its Web site:

> The temples of Tamil Nadu not only serve as places of worship to develop moral rectitude and spiritual awareness but also introduce to the new generations our glorious and hoary cultural heritage and function as institutions for the development of music, art, painting, sculpture, and architecture, and thus endeavour to safeguard the righteousness of society.

In 2007 the Web site was redesigned and that statement was no longer posted.

76. Hindu Religious Endowments Commission, *Report*, 42.

77. The growth of Hindu nationalism in southern India has been documented by many scholars and activists. It is therefore not necessary to review this information here except to underscore the success with which Hindu nationalism has advanced in southern India. This growth has relied largely on the efforts of the Hindu Munnani, a political organization that, like the Vishwa Hindu Parishad ("World Hindu Federation") in the north, serves as a cultural wing for the "family" of groups—the Sangh Parivar—affiliated with the Rashtriya Swayamsevak Sangh or RSS (National Association of Volunteers). Greater receptivity to Hindutva, especially among upper-caste communities, has been documented in Tamil Nadu over the 1980s and 1990s, including among some traditional religious leaders who have allied openly with the RSS and the Munnani. See Fuller, *The Renewal of the Priesthood*, 130–142; Hancock, *Womanhood in the Making*, 221–224; and S. Anandhi, *Contending Identities: Dalits and Secular Politics in Madras Slums* (New Delhi: Indian Social Institute, 1995).

78. The 2002 law, Tamil Nadu Prohibition of Forcible Conversion of Religion Ordinance, was repealed in May 2006, shortly after state assembly elections returned the DMK to power.

79. Fuller, "The Vinayaka Chaturthi Festival."

80. Along with Vinayka Chathurthi, the Ayodhya campaign has mediated this expansion. As public observance of Vinayaka Chathurthi increased in the early 1990s, so also did the incidence of other Munnani-choreographed events staged in support of the VHP's Ayodhya campaign. Prominent among these were the Ramshila *pūjas*—rituals held to consecrate bricks for use in the temple that the RSS wished to build—held in temples and community centers in the city. In October 1992 ceremonial vehicles (*rathas*), decorated with Ram iconography and bearing consecrated bricks destined for Ayodhya, toured the city under police protection ("Rathas Carrying Rama Padukas Start Journey," *Hindu*, October 3, 1992, 3.

81. While the Dravidianist movement acquired a rationalist, atheistic orientation under EVR's leadership, it also incorporated a devotional logic and praxis drawn from the earlier

"*Taṉittamiḻ*" (Pure Tamil) movement, as well as from its privileging of Saivite religiosity as a mark of Dravidian personhood and territoriality.

82. Tamil Nadu authorities commissioned a well-known *stapati* (a traditionally trained architect and builder), Kanapati Stapati, to design and supervise the construction (and renovations) of state-managed temples, memorials, offices, and ceremonial sites.

83. For further discussion, see A. Srivathsan, "Politics of Tamil Monuments: 1968–1975," *South Indian Studies* 5 (1998): 59–82.

84. "Em. Ji. Ar. Peyarai Maraikkāvillai" [MGR's name is not hidden], *Tiṉatanti*, January 6, 2000, 3.

85. The state's neoliberal turn was as evident in HR & CE operations as it was in other agencies. The HR & CE Citizens Charter, linked to the agency's Web site (http://hrce.tn.nic.in) espoused the reformist rhetoric of efficiency and transparency, as well as the virtues of privatization—stating that it intended to secure at least 25 percent of the operating budget for these activities from private donations. Among the funds created by pooling public and private financing was the department's common good fund, its temple development fund, and temple renovation funds for villages and Dalit settlements, which together provided funds for reconsecrations, daily ritual performances, religious education, and other forms of maintenance. The department also served increasingly as a publicist for Hindu institutions with a listing of festival dates and contact information for temples on its Web site, by publication of a monthly magazine, and with its "e-pooja" service, which allowed devotees "to book poojas any time from any part of the world, online."

86. Meals distribution, carried out under the "Annadhanam" program inaugurated in 2001, has been one of the state's more heavily promoted welfare operations (http://www.tn.nic.in/annadhanam/). In its original outline, the program updated an earlier program crafted by MGR. That program, the Chief Minister's Nutritious Noon Meals Scheme, provided daily meals to public-school children and was later expanded to include meals for the elderly poor. That scheme yielded measurable nutritional and social benefits while redounding to MGR's reputation as a populist hero. Jayalalithaa's version sought similar outcomes, though her program was much more closely aligned with the Brahmanical Hinduism with which she is associated. It was framed as a self-sacrificing vow on the part of the chief minister, having been initiated (as in the temple maintenance program) with Jayalalithaa's donation of her monthly salary. She has made public her vow to continue such donations, and, following suit, other elected officials, business persons, and industrialists have made similar offerings.

87. Peter van der Veer and Hart Lehmann, eds., *Nation and Religion: Perspectives on Europe and Asia* (Princeton, N.J.: Princeton University Press, 1999), 3–12.

88. Chakrabarty, *Provincializing Europe*, 4.

89. Ibid.

90. Hayden White, *The Content of the Form* (Baltimore: Johns Hopkins University Press, 1987), 101–102.

91. Chakrabarty, *Provincializing Europe*, 15.

92. Ibid., 15–16.

93. See also Klein, "On the Emergence of Memory in Historical Discourse," 127–150.

5. Consuming the Past

1. The epigraph is excerpted from the text of an advertising flyer, produced by Deccan Tourism, the agency that owned and managed Kanchi Kudil.

2. Tourists' hardships are negligible compared to the daily challenges faced by more than a third of Chennai's residents—slum and pavement dwellers—who lack access to adequate (or any) sanitary facilities. The solutions are invariably demeaning and serve to further render them abject in the eyes of their more fortunate neighbors. Arjun Appadurai has discussed another kind of "toilet talk" in such contexts, in which the lack of toilets and basic sanitation is transformed from a matter of shame to a platform for activism ("The Capacity to Aspire: Culture and the Terms of Recognition," in *Culture and Public Action*, ed. Vijayendra Rao and Michael Walton, 59–84 [Stanford, Calif.: Stanford University Press, 2004]).

3. Predictably guidebooks catering to international visitors described sanitary facilities in hotels with bemusement, warnings, and occasionally moral panic; their inadequate plumbing and Indians' apparent acceptance were presented as signs of "fatalism," "other-worldliness," and "tradition." The stereotypes, besides the persistent Orientalism that they reveal, also support the small but growing industry of toilet "substitution" products (such as those found in the Magellan travel supplies catalog) that cater to tourists who are eager for international travel but queasy about intimate adjustments required by floor toilets and the absence of toilet paper.

4. See, for example, Tamil Nadu's Tenth Five-Year Plan, which reiterates the same concerns about hygiene that are found in the examples of toilet talk that I describe (Tamil Nadu State Planning Commission, *Tenth Five-Year Plan, 2002–2007* [Chennai: Government of Tamil Nadu, 2002], 777; http://www.tn.gov.in/spc/tenthplan/default.htm [accessed March 12, 2005]).

5. "Trichy" is the nickname for the temple town of Tiruchirappalli.

6. Herzfeld, *Cultural Intimacy*, 94.

7. Benedict Anderson, *Imagined Communities*, rev. ed. (London: Verso, 1991).

8. Herzfeld, *Cultural Intimacy*, 6.

9. As Linda Richter has demonstrated, India's interest in tourism did not arise in a vacuum (*The Politics of Tourism in Asia* [Honolulu: University of Hawai'i Press, 1989]). Under the British Raj, hill stations were developed as leisure travel destinations for Anglo-Indians, for princely rulers, and for affluent Indians. Through its archaeological survey agency (ASI), the colonial government also identified, cataloged, and maintained monuments and other antiquities; princely rulers similarly identified and sought to preserve antiquities lying in their territorial holdings. As discussed in chapter 2, visitation to these sites and to the museums that served as repositories for associated materials was encouraged for the didactic purposes of exposing Indians to the region's past glories and, by implication, its current degradation. A much deeper historical substrate lay in the pilgrimage- and festival-related travel undertaken for many centuries by all classes of the subcontinent's Hindus, Jains, Buddhists, Sikhs, Christians, and Muslims. The latter sites and routes, as well as sites of nationalist significance, were part of the tourism circuits promoted by the Indian government following independence.

Until the late 1960s domestic tourism attracted more official interest than did international tourism and was encouraged for purposes of "national integration." See Sargent Committee Report, cited in Richter, *The Politics of Tourism in Asia*, 114; Hindu Religious Endowments Commission, *Report of the Hindu Religious Endowments Commission;* and Committee on Emotional Integration, *Report of the Committee on Emotional Integration.* In 1949 the central government opened the Tourist Traffic Branch in the Ministry of Transport. Many of the sites that it deemed tourist destinations were, at that time, under the jurisdiction of other governmental and nongovernmental agencies. The Archaeological Survey of India maintained and controlled visitor access to sites designated as archaeological monuments and antiquities; a public agency, the Hindu Religious and Charitable Endowments Board, managed large Hindu temples in Tamil Nadu (then Madras State); private sectarian groups controlled access to other Hindu temples and to Muslim, Christian, Sikh, Buddhist, and Jain religious sites. Only in the past few years has the Indian government, recognizing a source of potential revenue, renewed its interest in promoting domestic tourism. See Government of India, Planning Commission, "Tourism Sector" (chapter 13), in *Midterm Appraisal of the Tenth Five-Year Plan* (2002–2007), (New Delhi: Planning Commission, 2004), http://planningcommission.gov.in/midterm/english-pdf/chapter-13.pdf (accessed April 12, 2007); National Council of Applied Economic Research, *Domestic Tourism Survey* (New Delhi: Ministry of Tourism, Government of India, 2003).

10. Richter, *The Politics of Tourism*, 115.

11. Though international tourist arrivals and tourism-generated revenues decreased in the late seventies and early eighties because of political instability and related shifts in policy, the years after 1985 saw a sharp growth, the result of more aggressive promotion of tourism, in the context of initiatives to promote economic liberalization. In 1986 international tourist arrivals exceeded one million for the first time and earnings were estimated at Rs.18 billion (at that time, the exchange rate was Rs.13 to U.S.$1), representing a 40 percent increase over 1985 earnings (Richter, *The Politics of Tourism*, 117). The central government established a Ministry of Tourism, invested more heavily in tourist services, and designated tourism as an industry. In development were resorts, three-star hotels for the domestic market, and simplified immigration procedures; funds were earmarked to

provide training in tourism management and for research and compilation of statistics on tourism (ibid., 117).

12. In the late 1980s, the number of jobs thought to be related, directly or indirectly, to tourism ranged from 4.5 to 10.5 million; 75 percent of these were in domestic tourism sectors (ibid., 112).

13. Fluency in other languages, especially French, German, Russian, and Japanese, was also valued. Persons fluent in non-Indic languages, other than English, are known as "Language Guides."

14. All the professional guides whom I interviewed criticized New Delhi–based Regional Guides who, they claimed, merely acted as agents for shopkeepers and vendors by directing tourists to their establishments and receiving commissions for that service. One private Chennai-based agent, who conducts tours throughout India, stated that he refused to use the services of any New Delhi guide.

15. Department of Culture, *Report of the Working Group on Art and Culture for the Sixth Five-Year Plan.*

16. Department of Culture, *Performance Budget 1985/86;* Kurin, "Cultural Conservation through Representation."

17. Kalakshetra, although now managed by the state government, was founded originally by affiliates of the Theosophical Society, headquartered in Madras. The land it now occupies was first owned by the Society. It was founded to train students in southern Indian styles of music, dance, and art, though its mission was not simply conservation and training but the classicization of art and performance traditions. The latter involved relocating those traditions from the low-caste contexts of performance and transmission (associated with courtesan culture) into the domains of Brahmanical religiosity and aesthetics. For further discussion of the history and gendered cultural politics of southern Indian musical forms, see Amanda Weidman, *Singing the Classical, Voicing the Modern* (Durham, N.C.: Duke University Press, 2006).

18. I discuss this in *Womanhood in the Making,* 39–45.

19. Following the adoption of structural adjustment policies in 1991, the role of tourism as a foreign-exchange earner (India's third largest after textiles and software) and domestic-employment generator has been more strongly emphasized though earnings have been less than anticipated. India's Ninth Five-Year Plan (1995/96–2000/2001) reported earnings in 1991–92 of Rs. 4,892 crores, and in 1996–97 Rs. 10,417 crores, which fell far below that which industry advocates predicted (Government of India, Planning Commission, "Tourism" [Section 7.6], *Ninth Five-Year Plan* [New Delhi: Planning Commission, 1995], http://planningcommission.gov.in/plans/planrel/fivehr/default.html (accessed June 20, 2006).

Tourist arrivals declined following the 9/11 attacks in the United States, the subsequent attacks on India's Parliament House, and renewed fears of an Indo-Pakistani conflict, although international arrivals have since increased (see note 20, below). Direct employment in tourism during 1995–96 was estimated at 8.5 million, or 2.4 percent of the labor force; in 2003–2004, direct and indirect employment in tourism sectors was estimated at 41.8 million, or 8.8 percent of the national labor force (Government of India, Planning Commission, *Report of the Special Group on Targeting Ten Million Employment Opportunities per Year* [New Delhi: Government of India, 2002]; Government of India, Planning Commission, *Report of the Working Group on Tourism,* Eleventh Five-Year Plan, 2007–2012 [New Delhi: Ministry of Tourism, 2007], http://planningcommission.gov.in/aboutus/committee/wrkgrp11/wg11-tourism.pdf [accessed April 12, 2007]).

20. According to Tamil Nadu's Tenth Five-Year Plan (2002–2007), domestic tourists during 2000 numbered 229 lakhs; international arrivals were estimated at 7.9 lakhs (1 lakh = 100,000). More recent figures for the state were not available at the time of this writing (December 2007). For India as a whole, however, the Working Group on Tourism has compiled data that indicate a 65 percent increase in foreign arrivals from 2002 to 2005, an increase, that is, from 2.38 million to 3.92 million in that period; 4.51 million arrivals were projected for 2006. That same group estimated that, for India generally, there were 269.6 million domestic tourist visits in 2002; in 2005, domestic tourist visits were estimated at 382.1 million (Government of India, *Report of the Working Group on Tourism,* 19–20).

21. Under provisions introduced during the period of the Eighth Five-Year Plan (1989/90–1994/95), individual states may recruit, certify, and regulate guides; state programs operate in addition to the

central government's training and certification program, which remains in operation (Government of India, Planning Commission, "Tourism," *Eighth Five-Year Plan* [New Delhi: Planning Commission, 1989]; http://planningcommission.gov.in/plans/planrel/fiveyr/default.html [accessed June 20, 2006]).

22. Other transportation-hub cities (Salem, Coimbatore, and Madurai) have also seen this sort of growth but not to the extent of Chennai.

23. Chitra refers here to Sathya Sai Baba, a renowned teacher and saint regarded as the reincarnation of Shirdi Sai Baba, an ascetic and teacher who died in 1918. Sathya Sai Baba preaches a universalist Hinduism and has an international following. He is reputed to perform miracles, such as materializing sacred ash, precious metals, and other substances. See Lawrence Babb, *Redemptive Encounters: Three Modern Styles in the Hindu Tradition* (Berkeley: University of California Press, 1986); Smriti Srinivas, *In the Presence of Sai Baba: Body, City and Memory in a Global Religious Movement* (Leiden: Brill, 2008).

24. The program was subsequently scaled down. In 2005 TTDC offered only four charter-tour packages, each for groups of thirty or more. It is described on TTDC's Web site: http://www.tamilnadutourism.org/ltc.htm.

25. http://www.tourismindia.com/indiainfo/states/tamilnadu/index.htm (accessed May 10, 2005).

26. The latter provisions were part of India's Eighth Five-Year Plan's "Equity Scheme"; this direction continued in the Ninth Five-Year Plan, which identified certain attractions that could be developed for domestic and international tourists, including indigenous and natural health ventures; rural areas, pilgrimage sites, and villages; and adventure and heritage-focused activities. India's Ninth Five-Year Plan further facilitated privatization by easing import restrictions for private tourism concerns, allowing them to import equipment and cars without bank guarantees. Similar, albeit more aggressively presented, recommendations appear in the Tenth Five-Year Plan. Central to these recommendations were higher levels of private-sector investment to court international and elite segments of the tourist market by developing cultural, spiritual, health-oriented, and eco/adventure tourism (Government of India, Planning Commission, *Tenth Five-Year Plan,* vol. 2, chap. 7, sec. 5 [New Delhi: Government of India, 2002], http://planningcommission.gov.in/plans/planrel/fiveyr/10th/volume2/v2_ch7_5.pdf [accessed May 20, 2006]).

27. http://www.tourismindia.com/ (accessed May 10, 2005).

28. http://64.239.149.251/atithidevobhava.htm (accessed May 20, 2005).

29. Tamil Nadu State Planning Commission, *Tenth Five-Year Plan, 2002–2007,* 785.

30. Government of India, Planning Commission, *Ninth Five-Year Plan,* vol. 7, chap. 6, sec. 2 (New Delhi: Government of India, 1995); http://planningcommission.gov.in/plans/planrel/fiveyr/9th/volume7/v2_ch6_2.pdf (accessed May 20, 2006).

31. Tamil Nadu State Planning Commission, *Tenth Five-Year Plan, 2002–2007,* 772, 774, 785. Because of several excellent allopathic medical centers, as well as Ayurvedic and homeopathic practitioners, the state (like Kerala) has been singled out more recently as a destination for medical and health tourism.

32. Government of Tamil Nadu, "Policy Note 2005–2006, Demand No. 28, Information and Tourism Department," (Chennai: Government of Tamil Nadu, 2005), 5; http://www.tn.gov.in/policynotes/tourism-1.htm (accessed March 4, 2006).

33. Nambiar and Krishnamurthy, "The Temples of Madras."

34. India's Tourism Ministry estimates that half its domestic tourists are involved in pilgrimage-focused travel. Domestic and international tourist streams are differentiated seasonally as well. The high season for international arrivals coincides with the cooler months that follow the northwest monsoon, which, in Tamil Nadu, falls between November and February. Domestic tourism is highest during school vacation periods (April–July) but may also spike during certain festival periods at other times of the year (S. M. Naqvi, Regional Director, Government of India Tourism Office, Chennai, interview with author, November 30, 1999).

35. Government of India, *Report of the Working Group on Tourism,* 19–20. In 2002 the number of domestic tourists was 549.4 million (National Council of Applied Economic Research, *Domestic Tourism Survey.* See also Ministry of Tourism, "Incredible India: Figures 2003," http://www.tourismindia.com (accessed May 20, 2005).

36. Tamil Nadu's Tenth Five-Year Plan describes the U.K. as the biggest source of tourists to India but that East and Southeast Asia are more important tourist-generating markets for southern India. The "products" thought to appeal to foreign tourists were listed as cultural and architectural heritage, temples and historic monuments, arts, performing arts, handicrafts, festivals, and wildlife (*Tenth Five-Year Plan*, 775).

37. India's Tourism Ministry approved additional pilgrimage tourism circuits in Tamil Nadu, including the Shankaracharya Circuit (2003–2004), the Murugan and Adi Shankara Circuits (2005–2006), and a Jain circuit, the Jain Teerthakshetras (2005–2006) (Government of India, *Report of the Working Group on Tourism*, 65).

38. What state and private tourism operations do *not* provide are leisure travel opportunities for the poor who constitute the majority of the state's urban population. The present emphasis on revenue generation vastly outweighs the national development and integration goals asserted by the government. The attractions that poor and working-class people consume, often without the mediation of tourist services, overlap with the sites marketed for the domestic middle class. Like those circuits, these networks of leisure and education are means by which poor traverse and come to know the urban landscape and its past.

39. http://www.tamilnadutourism.org

40. Government of Tamil Nadu, "Policy Note 2005–2006." Although Tamil Nadu has a large Christian minority (in 2001, they constituted 5.69 percent of the state's total population), the few Christian sites included on these circuits were dropped. Many Christians are poor or from Dalit communities or both; since the late 1990s they have been frequent victims of attacks initiated by Hindu nationalist groups. Interest in pilgrimage also exists among Muslims and Jains, though there are far fewer regional pilgrimage circuits in the south and less tourist industry attention; it was only in the 2005–2006 fiscal year that one Jain pilgrimage tourism circuit in southern India was authorized by the central government.

41. See "MGR Film City to give way to Knowledge Park," *Business Line* (Internet edition), August 3, 2002, http://www.thehindubusinessline.com/2002/08/03/stories/2002080309131700.htm (accessed March 12, 2005).

42. Among the cultural offerings of high-end heritage tourism are the services geared to "spiritual tourists"—international disciples of Sathya Sai Baba, Swami Satchidananda, Amma-ji, and others—whose stays at ashrams and consultations with astrologers and mediums are often combined with luxury accommodation and travel, boutique visits, and so forth. The demand is such that several private agencies in Chennai specialize in such arrangements.

43. K. Kalpana and Frank Schiffer, *Madras: The Architectural Heritage* (Chennai: INTACH, 2002).

44. The reviews are well deserved. Although legitimate questions about the site's claims to authenticity have been raised and the cultural politics of its representations criticized (see chapter 6), the museum is ably run by its founder-director, Deborah Thiagarajan. She developed the museum's exhibitions and programming, and, through the Madras Craft Foundation (DakshinaChitra's parent organization), assembled a talented staff to carry out the museum's design and operations, which include scholarly conferences as well as public programming.

45. Another such resort, managed by India's Sterling Corporation, is located in the temple town of Swamimalai, near Tanjavur in east-central Tamil Nadu, and it aims at achieving an even more encompassing heritage experience. The site, a renovated nineteenth-century estate, received a Global EcoTourism Award. One of the project's consulting architects whom I interviewed in 2000 described it as a "heritage hotel," with rooms, public spaces, cuisine, and entertainment designed to replicate a Brahman village and so enable visitors to experience, in a complete way, a very selective account of the region's past. Its recently mounted Web site provides a visual and acoustic entrée to the site: http://www.sterlingswamimalai.net. The town is considered an ancestral place (*cont ūr*) by many Brahmans whose parents and grandparents moved to Chennai earlier in the twentieth century and so occupies a place of familial memory for urban elites, including those who have participated in the resort's design and marketing.

46. The welding of heritage conservation and tourism was initiated in the 1980s, and the converted palaces and forts in Rajasthan, marketed as heritage hotels by (often) down-at-the-heels owners, were among the first models for this enterprise. The Neemrana "non-hotels," initiated in Rajasthan and now found throughout the country, are examples of this approach. Each is

prominently advertised as a heritage property, wrapped in nostalgia: "Even though history is a record of the past, it lives in the present and waits in the future. Come enact your private history in real life settings.... Travel, give value to the time you are spending on planet Earth" (http://www.neemranahotels.com). For example, Villa Pottipati, a twentieth-century "garden house" is described as located in a section of Bangalore that was its "once vegetarian-Brahmin stronghold." The Web page text promises that "when you stay at Villa Pottipati, you join Bangalore's fight to retain its magnificent heritage structures by making restoration a viable, self-sustainable tourism activity" (http://www.neemranahotels.com/villapottipati/index.html) (accessed May 12, 2005).

47. *Vaṇakkam* is a Tamil word meaning "welcome." It tends to be used on formal occasions, to greet or take leave of others.

48. He later clarified this comment, explaining: "I do make a decent living out of my tours as they cater to the niche market of those who are looking for ... something different, having done their share of mass tourism all over the world.... I offer it ... as access to the India and Indians that the tourism industry cannot quite accommodate as yet" (personal communication with author, September 30, 2006).

49. Kancha Ilaiah, *Why I Am Not a Hindu* (Calcutta: Samya, 1996); *Tirukkural,* trans. S. Subramuniyaswami (New Delhi: Abhinav, 2000).

50. Other examples of this sort of tourism are described on the Web site for Traidcraft, based in England: http://www.traidcraft.co.uk.

6. Recollecting the Rural in Suburban Chennai

1. MGM Dizzee World is part of the MGM Group of service companies, named after the founder and chair M. G. Muthu. The group includes distilleries, hotels and resorts, shipping, and export-import services, in addition to its theme park. See http://www.mgm-india.com

2. *A Vision of the South* is the English translation of the museum's name.

3. See http://www.dakshinachitra.net. This Web site was mounted in 2005, replacing a previous site, http://www.dakshinachitra.org.

4. In India these include Veega Land, MGM Dizzee World, Essel World, Kishkinta, Tikuji-Ni-Wadi, Black Thunder Water Theme Park, and Kovai Kondattam Water Theme Park. Recent work on such sites in India includes Paul Greenough, "Nation, Economy, and Tradition Displayed," in *Consuming Modernity,* ed. Carol Breckenridge, 216–248 (Minneapolis: University of Minnesota Press, 1995); Barbara Ramusack, "The Indian Princes as Fantasy: Palace Hotels, Palace Museums, and the Palace on Wheels," in Breckenridge, *Consuming Modernity*, 66–89; and Ann Hardgrove, "Merchant Houses as Spectacles of Modernity in Rajasthan and Tamil Nadu," in *Beyond Appearances? Visual Practices and Ideologies in Modern India,* ed. Sumathi Ramaswamy, 323–364 (New Delhi: Sage, 2003). Comparative and theoretical work includes Edward Bruner, *Culture on Tour: Ethnographies of Travel* (Chicago: University of Chicago Press, 2005); Joy Hendry, *The Orient Strikes Back: A Global View of Cultural Display* (Oxford: Berg, 2000); Ivan Karp, Corine Kratz, Lynn Szwaja, and Tomas Ybarra-Frausto, eds., *Museum Frictions: Public Cultures/Global Transformations* (Durham, N.C.: Duke University Press, 2006); Barbara Kirshenblatt-Gimblett, *Destination Culture* (Berkeley: University of California Press, 1998); Aviad Raz, *Riding the Black Ship: Japan and Tokyo Disneyland* (Cambridge, Mass.: Harvard University Asia Center, 1999); Hai Ren, "Economies of Culture: Theme Parks, Museums, and Capital Accumulation in China, Hong Kong, and Taiwan," Ph.D. diss., University of Washington, Seattle, 1998; Michael Sorkin, ed., *Variations on a Theme Park* (New York: Farrar, Straus, Giroux, 1992); Nick Stanley, *Being Ourselves for You: The Global Display of Cultures* (London: Middlesex, 1998); Rachel Teo and Brenda Yeoh, "Remaking Local Heritage for Tourism," *Annals of Tourism Research* 24 (1997): 192–213; Susan Willis, ed., *The World According to Disney,* Special Issue of *South Atlantic Quarterly* 92, no. 1 (winter 1993); Brenda Yeoh, "From Colonial Neglect to Post-Independence Heritage: The Housing Landscape in the Central Area of Singapore," *City and Society* 12 (2000): 103–124; and Zukin, *Landscapes of Power.*

5. Tony Bennett, "The Exhibitionary Complex," in *Culture/Power/History,* ed. Nicholas Dirks, Geoff Eley, and Sherry Ortner, 123–154 (Princeton, N.J.: Princeton University Press, 1995). See also Tony Bennett, *The Birth of the Museum* (London: Routledge, 1995).

6. This chapter is a substantially revised version of my article, "Subjects of Heritage in Urban South India," which appeared in *Environment and Planning D: Society and Space* 20, no. 6 (2001): 693–718 (Pion Limited, London).

7. In a 2000 interview with me, the center's director, Deborah Thiagarajan, estimated that DakshinaChitra received about 30,000 visitors between 1997 and 2000. At that time visitation figures were not systematically tabulated. In later conversations (October 2006 and June 2007), she reported that visitation had sharply increased. Since 2005, monthly visitation figures have been tabulated; in fiscal year 2005–2006, the center received 94,000 visitors and in fiscal year 2006–2007, visitor numbers increased to 104,000. Those figures included at least 24,000 children who arrived with school groups, as well as visitors who came for seminars, special events, and sales. She attributed the increases to growing interest among Chennai's middle-income groups and pointed out that foreign visitation ranges between 8 and 12 percent of the total. She noted, however, that NRI visitation may be underestimated in these figures as the counts are tabulated on entry ticket sales; if NRI visitors purchase less expensive domestic entry tickets (see note 13, below), as frequently occurs, they will be counted as domestic rather than foreign visitors.

8. In 2000 DakshinaChitra received an International Partnership among Museums Award from the American Association of Museums. Its U.S. partner was the Peabody Essex Museum in Salem, Massachusetts ("Around the City," *Hindu*, April 20, 2000). It has partnered with the Sastri Indo-Canadian Institute to produce an animated folk epic using materials from its collection. It has also mounted touring exhibitions and hosted a series of biennial seminars for scholars, artists, and preservationists, including a joint exhibition and workshop on contemporary art, with the Boras Museum of Modern Art in Lund, Sweden. See "DakshinaChitra: About Us—What We Do?" (http://www.dakshinachitra.net/scripts/whatwedo.asp [accessed March 30, 2006]).

9. Thiagarajan was the founder and first convenor of INTACH's Tamil Nadu chapter. Work on DakshinaChitra began in the mid-1980s under the auspices of the Madras Craft Foundation and in close association with INTACH. Thiagarajan and two associates provided seed money and launched an energetic program of documentation, planning, and fund-raising, targeting international foundations as well as state and national agencies. By the time the center opened in early 1997 Thiagarajan had resigned from INTACH, and the center no longer maintained any formal or informal connection with the association.

10. For a comparative discussion, see Linda Hoffman, Susan Fainstein, and Dennis Judd, eds., *Cities and Visitors: Regulating People, Markets, and City-Space* (Malden, Mass.: Blackwell, 2003).

11. Dennis Judd coined the term "tourist bubble" to refer to protected circuits of touristic consumption and movement that comprise hotels, stores, leisure and heritage sites, and the transportation arteries and services that connect them. See Dennis Judd, "Constructing the 'Tourist Bubble,'" in *The Tourist City*, ed. Dennis Judd and Susan Fainstein, 35–53 (New Haven, Conn.: Yale University Press, 1999).

12. Many of the cases under scrutiny that day were typical of the urban revitalization and gentrification efforts that have gained popularity since the 1970s. Conservation architects with INTACH described that group's efforts to identify and list the city's heritage structures. The efforts of commercial developers and arts marketing groups to designate an art and shopping district near Mumbai's commercial center were described by one presenter. Another speaker suggested that Chennai's annual festival of Carnatic music and dance, held since the late 1920s when it was inaugurated by upper-caste supporters of Gandhian nationalism, might serve as the anchor for a comparable urban arts district. Still others insisted that Chennai was in need of an Urban Arts Commission, like those in New Delhi and Bangalore, to ensure that the cultural and financial values of heritage ventures were recognized within the frameworks of municipal planning and governance.

13. Entry fees in 2007 were Rs.50 for adults, Rs.15 for children, and Rs.25 for students. The entry charge for foreigners was Rs.175. The exchange rate in 2007 was approximately Rs.41 to U.S.$1.

14. In early 2000 the American Express Corporation donated Rs.10 lakhs (1 million rupees—about $20,000), and Konica and other corporations have contributed by furnishing signage and advertising. A large textile gallery was set up with support from India's Co-Optex Handloom Corporation. DakshinaChitra has taken advantage of the Ford Foundation's funding initiatives

in its Media, Culture, and Arts Program; over the past decade it has secured U.S.$50,000 in seed money and U.S.$250,000 in stabilization funds.

15. DakshinaChitra is given top billing in upper-end tourism magazines and brochures such as *Namaste,* the in-room magazine published by the Welcomgroup, the hotel and resort corporation that manages the five-star Chola Sheraton and Park Sheraton in Chennai, as well as scores of other, similar properties across India. See Geeta Doctor, "DakshinaChitra: Living Museum of the South," and S. Muthiah, "Enjoying a Vision of the South," both in *Namaste* 19, no. 2 (1999): 15–19, 20–23. For a full immersion in heritage, a stay at one of DakshinaChitra's own guest rooms might be included. The Web site advertises standard overnight lodging for daily rates that range from Rs.500 to Rs.800. There are also special, themed packages that can be arranged, featuring lecture demonstrations and folk performances. In 2000, for example, a special overnight stay, "Introduction to South Indian Culture," was introduced and offered at a cost of Rs.1,000 per person. Other packages could be arranged on request.

16. Thiagarajan transformed DakshinaChitra from an idea to a ten-acre reality. Her role, however, has been a subject of comment and debate, with some critics intimating that she had stamped it with "American" consumerism. Others have questioned the authenticity of the site's representation of pre-industrial rural life, noting the various compromises with modern technology that the site's construction involved. Detailed disclosures about buildings' composition and techniques posted on the Web site and in printed material have sought to respond to the latter criticisms and to underscore the period accuracy that the site strives to achieve.

17. That family's affiliation with the Nattukottai Chettiar merchant and banking community is sometimes seen by critics of DakshinaChitra as the underlying reason for the particular type of cosmopolitanism that the museum embraces and for the prominence of exhibitions dedicated to Chettiar themes. This ad personam argument is both simple-minded and reductive. It bears noting, however, that the Nattukottai Chettiar community has a long, well-documented history of activities focused on the retention and reinvention of tradition, in the form of the conservation and restoration of public institutions such as Hindu temples and choultries, the erection of ancestral houses, and the creation of archives and libraries. For further discussion, see chapter 2.

18. She expressed this in conversations with me and in the text of an unpublished talk: Deborah Thiagarajan, n.d., "DakshinaChitra, a Living Heritage Centre for South India," the text of which she shared with me.

19. http://www.dakshinachitra.net/scripts/howdiditall.asp (accessed May 20, 2007).

20. This facility is the nation's second largest complex of this sort.

21. The Madras Atomic Power Station (MAPS) is a comprehensive nuclear power production, fuel reprocessing, and waste treatment facility that includes plutonium fuel fabrication for fast breeder reactors. Commercial operations at MAPS started in 1983. Background and further references are available at http://www.igcar.ernet.in and http://www.dae.gov.in/ar2002/igcar.pdf (accessed February 10, 2006).

22. Madras Metropolitan Development Authority, *Master Plan for Madras Metropolitan Area—2011;* Government of Tamil Nadu, *Tamil Nadu—An Economic Appraisal, 1999–2000*, 58–73; Government of Tamil Nadu, "Urban Development" (Section 6.2), in *Annual Plan 2004–05* (Chennai: Government of Tamil Nadu, State Planning Commission, 2004), http://www.tn.gov.in/spc/annualplan/default.htm (accessed January 20, 2005).

23. The development of DakshinaChitra and the IT corridor in Chennai's southwestern outskirts can be tied to the Indian state's recognition of the NRI as a type of offshore citizen and potential investor. This recognition has been institutionalized with those specific policies, such as tax holidays, concession packages, and relaxation of foreign investment rules, by which the Indian state has sought to engage NRIs as political and economic actors. Especially cementing the link between NRI capital, consumer-citizenship, and new geographies of neoliberalism has been the real estate boom that followed the deregulation of the early 1990s. Notable in this context have been the condominium developments, bearing names like NRI Nest and NRI First City, that have multiplied in ex-urbs, including the corridor on which DakshinaChitra is located. See "Gated Communities Carnival," *Hindu* (online edition), January 13, 2007, http://www.thehindu.com/thehindu/pp/2007/01/13/stories/2007011300180200.htm (accessed April 24, 2007). As Kim Dovey has observed in other contexts, these sorts of new residential developments invite NRI investors to bask in the nostalgia

of "home" without sacrificing the status or mobility that they have acquired while living abroad. Dovey (*Framing Places*, 149–151; see also King, *Spaces of Global Culture*, 97–110, 132–136. Amenities, like pools and tennis courts, lend "international" cachet to these residences, while nearby boutiques and restaurants offer up locality and the pastness that underwrites it, in the form of foodstuffs and crafts. See, for example, Ajita Shashidhar, "Craze for Condominiums," *Hindu* (Property Plus Section), January 14, 2005, http://www.thehindu.com/pp/2005/01/14/stories/2005011400040100.htm (accessed April 24, 2007).

24. King, *Spaces of Global Culture*, 103; A. Hopkins, ed. *Globalization in World History* (London: Pimlico, 2002).

25. On the ideologies of "globalism" and "localism" in social science, see Anna Tsing, "The Global Situation," in *The Anthropology of Globalization: A Reader*, ed. Jonathan Inda and Renato Rosaldo, 453–485 (Oxford: Blackwell, 2002).

26. Peter Taylor, *Modernities: A Geopolitical Intepretation* (Cambridge: Polity, 1999), 58.

27. Cognizant was founded in 1994 by Lakshmi Narayanan, a North American NRI, and in 2006 ranked thirty-second on *Business Week*'s list of top IT firms, with a 2005 revenue of U.S.$648.6 million garnered through "IT infrastructure services for business process outsourcing" (http://www.businessweek.com/it100/2005/company/CTSH.htm). Among the area's growing cadre of back-office service providers, Cognizant is one of the largest, fastest growing, and most technologically sophisticated. See also S. Long, "Now for the Hard Part: A Survey of Business in India," *The Economist* 379, no. 8480 (2006): 50A–50R.

28. Greenough, "Nation, Economy, and Tradition Displayed."

29. It allowed the museum to lease the government-held land on which its building complex sits but has offered little else in support of museum activities.

30. Mohandas Gandhi, *Hind Swaraj* (Ahmedabad: Navjivan Prakashan, 1997 [1909]).

31. DakshinaChitra was ceremonially inaugurated on December 14, 1996, just before the start of the Tamil month of *Mārkaḻi*, a month that, because of its association with religious austerities, is considered inauspicious for embarking on new projects. It opened to visitors in early January 1997.

32. Baker, an Indian citizen who died in 2007, was born in England. He had resided in India since the mid-1940s, when, as a Quaker conscientious objector to military service, he arrived to work in medical services. It was then that he became acquainted with Gandhi and, profoundly affected by his notions of self-sufficiency, turned to architecture. Baker's work was inspired by the vernacular housing of the regions in India in which he resided for extended periods. He has been compared to Hassan Fathy of Egypt and to John Turner of Latin America because of his popularization of the use of low-cost, local materials. Baker's principles are encoded in a distinctive style featuring exposed brick exteriors, central courtyards, and tiled roofs, and he has long been associated with the pro-poor community architecture movement (Gautam Bhatia, *Laurie Baker: Life, Works and Writings* [New Delhi: Penguin, 1991], 3–17; Jon Lang, M. Desai, and M. Desai, *Architecture and Independence* [Delhi: Oxford University Press, 1997]). I owe my understanding of Baker to the texts just cited and to extensive interviews with several of his students and associates. See chapter 7 for a more extended discussion of Baker's work and influence.

33. Ramanujan, *Poems of Love and War*, 236–246.

34. http://www.dakshinachitra.net/scripts/heritagehelp.asp (accessed May 20, 2007). In 1999 Deborah Thiagarajan had told me that generalized scouting expeditions were not effective in locating structures for acquisition. She found, instead, that it was more productive to consult industrialists who owned or managed sites in the region; they had proven to be helpful in identifying specific structures and assisting in negotiation with their owners. This strategy was formalized and incorporated into DakshinaChitra's endowment campaign.

35. Sorkin, *Variations on a Theme Park*, 226.

36. On "in-context" and "in-situ" strategies, see Kirshenblatt-Gimblett, *Destination Culture*, 18–23.

37. On the history of the Nattukottai community, see David Rudner, *Caste and Capitalism in Colonial India: The Nattukottai Chettiars* (Berkeley: University of California Press, 1994).

38. See also Hardgrove, "Merchant Houses as Spectacles of Modernity in Rajasthan and Tamil Nadu."

39. Kirshenblatt-Gimblett wrote: "The art of mimesis, whether in the form of period rooms, ethnographic villages, re-created environments, reenacted rituals, or photomurals, places objects (or replicas of them) in situ. In situ approaches to installations enlarge the ethnographic object by expanding its boundaries to include more of what was left behind, even if only in replica, after the object was excised from its physical, social and cultural settings. . . . At their most mimetic, in situ installations include live persons, preferably actual representatives of the cultures on display" (*Destination Culture*, 20).

40. Pierre Rivière, "The Ecomuseum: An Evolutive Definition." *Museum* 148 (1985): 182–183; see also Peter Davis, *Ecomuseums: A Sense of Place* (Leicester: Leicester University Press, 1999).

41. Walter Benjamin, "The Work of Art in the Age of Mechanical Reproduction," In *Illuminations*, 217–242, ed. H. Arendt (New York: Schocken, 1985 [1969]).

42. Walter Benjamin, "A Short History of Photography," in *One-Way Street and Other Writings*, trans. and ed. E. Jephcott and K. Shorter (London: Verso, 1997). See Michael Taussig's discussion of this article in "Physiognomic Aspects of Visual Worlds," in *Visualizing Theory*, ed. Lucien Taylor, 205–213 (New York: Routledge, 1997).

43. In "Paris, the capital of the Nineteenth Century (Expose of 1935)," Benjamin describes the Parisian arcades as "residues of a dream world" and continues: "The realization of dream elements, in the course of waking up, is the paradigm of dialectical thinking. Thus, dialectical thinking is the organ of historical awakening. Every epoch, in fact, not only dreams the one to follow but, in dreaming, precipitates its awakening. It bears its end within itself and unfolds it . . . by cunning. With the destabilizing of the market economy, we begin to recognize the monuments of the bourgeoisie as ruins even before they have crumbled" (Walter Benjamin, *The Arcades Project*, trans. H. Eiland and K. McLaughlin [Cambridge, Mass.: Belknap Press of Harvard University Press, 1999], 13). Susan Buck-Morss cites another version of the 1935 exposé in her 1989 study of the Arcades project, *The Dialectics of Seeing* (Cambridge, Mass.: MIT Press, 1989), "To the form of the new means of production which in the beginning is still dominated by the old one (Marx), there correspond in the collective consciousness images in which the new is intermingled with the old. These images are wish images, and in them the collective attempts to transcend as well as to illumine the incompletedness of the social order of production. . . . These tendencies turn the image fantasy, that maintains its impulse from the new, back to the ur-past" (Buck-Morss, *The Dialectics of Seeing*, 114, 409 n.).

44. These include the merchant, potter, and Brahman houses in Tamil Nadu, the granary and the Calicut, Trivandrum and Syrian Christian houses in Kerala, and Karnataka's weaver's house compound.

45. The five structures that had been reassembled on-site, albeit with some omissions, were Tamil Nadu's Brahman house and Kerala's Syrian Christian, Calicut, and Trivandrum houses, and its granary.

46. These included the Chuttillu house cluster (Andhra Pradesh), the agriculturalist house, mud houses, and weaver's house (Tamil Nadu).

47. http://www.dakshinachitra.net/scripts/tn-ayyanar.asp (accessed May 20, 2007).

48. Bhatia, *Laurie Baker: Life, Works, and Writings*, 25–29.

49. *A Vision of the South* (Chennai: Rajeswari Communications, 1997), videorecording.

50. The video's subtle assertion that environmentalism was a hallmark of premodern southern Indian culture bespeaks the desire, evident among some NGOs and environmental historians, to uncover an indigenous (often Hindu) genealogy for modern environmentalist concerns. See M. Chandrakanth, J. Gilless, V. Gowramma, and M. Nagaraja, "Temple Forests in India's Forest Development," *Agroforestry Systems* 11 (1990): 199–211; Madhav Gadgil and Ramachandra Guha, *This Fissured Land: An Ecological History of India* (Berkeley: University of California Press, 1992); M. Kalam, *Sacred Groves in Kodagu District of Karnataka (South India): A Socio-historical Study* (Pondicherry: Institut Francais de Pondichery, 1996); N. Venugopal Rao, "Learning from a Legacy: How and What?" *Economic and Political Weekly* 29 (1994): 288–289; and S. Sitaraman, "Society and Science," *Economic and Political Weekly* 29 (1994): 290.

51. I thank A. Srivathsan for this observation.

52. See also Thiagarajan, *DakshinaChitra: From Village to Centre*, 3.

53. http://www.dakshinachitra.net/scripts/support.asp (accessed May 20, 2007).

54. Salwar-kameez or churidar sets are three-piece outfits comprising loose trousers, a long overshirt, and a matching shawl worn across the top of the body.

55. Fisherman's Cove, owned by the Taj Group, is an international corporation and part of the Tata conglomerate of industrial, manufacturing, and service companies. Founded in 1903, the Taj Group is India's largest hotel chain and features business, luxury, and leisure properties, as well as three luxury residential properties. In Chennai, there are three Taj properties (Taj Coromandel and Taj Connemara, in the city's center, in addition to Fisherman's Cove).

56. Another corporation, the Arusuvai Arasu Group, was later tapped to operate the site's small restaurant and to provide catering services for special events.

57. Lacking the full-service dining and entertainment facilities of most resorts, its accommodation costs (in 2006) were comparatively modest, totaling Rs.800 per night for an air-conditioned room.

58. *Swadeshi,* a Sanskritic term meaning "one's own land," was used by anticolonial nationalists to refer to their goal of economic self-sufficiency.

59. A different, more romanticized objection came from advocates of alternative cultural tourism who criticized the objectification and commodification of craft production. Sanjeev, the alternative tourism provider discussed in chapter 5, compared DakshinaChitra to the Body Shop, charging that both removed craft production out of networks of use-value production and inserted it into exchange transactions in which efficiency, time discipline, and quality control were paramount. Though rightly critical of feudal overtones of elite patronage, such objections, predicated on the misrecognition of the market relations in which craft production existed, were no less infused by neoliberal nostalgia than was the center itself.

60. See Claire Wilkinson-Weber, "Women, Work, and the Imagination of Craft in South Asia," *Contemporary South Asia* 13, no. 3 (2004): 287–306.

61. I included this information in Hancock, "Subjects of Heritage." A similar comment, attributed to him, has been posted on DakshinaChitra's new (2005) Web site.

62. The Secondary School Leaving Certificate is comparable to a high school diploma in the U.S. educational system.

63. Anonymous, "The Changing Complexion of a Coastal Village: Muttukadu, Some Key Observations," unpublished manuscript on file, Madras Craft Foundation.

64. *Kōlam* are geometric designs, made by women using rice powder or chalk, and are applied daily to house thresholds and sometimes at the entry of *pūja* rooms. They are drawn after the space is swept and washed, and connote auspiciousness—marking a home as a hospitable and welcoming site. *Kōlam* exist within Hindu systems of meaning and practice, though non-Hindus often adopt the practice for both aesthetic and social reasons (See Hancock, *Womanhood in the Making,* 83–86).

65. Christopher Pinney, "The Indian Work of Art in the Age of Mechanical Reproduction," in *Media Worlds,* ed. Fay Ginsburg, Lila Abu-Lughod, and Brian Larkin, 355–369 (Berkeley: University of California Press, 2002).

66. See also Taussig, "Physiognomic Aspects of Visual Worlds," 208. Christopher Pinney relied on a similar reading of Benjamin in his examination of the way that the logic of *darśan* imbues a wide range of popular visual practice in India ("The Indian Work of Art in the Age of Mechanical Reproduction").

67. Huyssen, *Present Pasts.*

7. The Village as Vernacular Cosmopolis

1. These were the links deemed most relevant during a search conducted on April 24, 2007. Unless noted otherwise, all Web sites cited below were accessed between April 20 and 30, 2007.

2. "*Samathuvapuram*" is the transliteration ordinarily used in English-language government reports and newspapers. If transliterated according to the Tamil Lexicon's system, it would be rendered "*camattuvapuram.*"

3. Elango is spelled "Ilango" in some sources. In Tamil Nadu, the terms used to designate groups formerly known as "untouchable" include "Adi-Dravida" ("first Dravidians"), "Harijan" (a term coined by Gandhi, meaning children of god), and "Dalit," a Marathi word meaning

"oppressed" or "downtrodden." As the political visibility of these groups and their mobilization has increased, the term "Dalit" has become more common to signal both social position and oppositional consciousness.

4. These organizations include Aid India, Asha, One World, India Together, and Infochange India.

5. "Ethical Economics, Endless Enthusiasm: An India Together Conversation with Rangaswamy Elango," http://www.indiatogether.org/goft/local/interviews/elango.htm (accessed September 15, 2005).

6. The benefits (and actual reach) of neoliberalism for India's rural majority continue to be contested. The 2004 parliamentary elections, which removed the BJP-led coalition from power and installed a Congress-led ruling coalition, were broadly understood as a referendum on the failure of the country's leadership to deliver on liberalization's promises of prosperity and governance reform.

7. Ramanujan, "Towards an Anthropology of City Images," 242.

8. See also CMDA's 2007 *Draft Master Plan II for Chennai,* which proposes the development of Tiruvallur town, the district seat, as a satellite town (64).

9. Kuthambakkam's designation as "model village" (informally and for the purpose of participating in a special development program) reflected the relative absence of violent confrontation in the wake of panchayat elections. Elango, himself, attributes his ability to mediate between different interests to class privilege. Despite the stigma of his family's low-caste identity, their class status earned acceptance of his leadership by dominant communities.

10. India's Census reported Scheduled Castes (SC) as accounting for almost 11 million people in Tamil Nadu (19 percent of the state's population), with higher SC proportions of up to 25 percent in some districts. Nearly half of the state's SC population is rural, and, overall, SC make up 23 percent of the state's rural population. Their socioeconomic status remains low, with most making their livings as landless agricultural laborers, and high illiteracy and infant mortality rates prevail. As noted by Jean-Luc Racine and Josiane Racine, however, "these figures . . . give no indication of the extent to which untouchability is still practiced," including in physical violence (much of it unreported), "traditional patterns of contempt and submission," segregation, and persistent stereotypes of ritual impurity, coarseness, and quarrelsomeness ("Dalit Identities and the Dialectics of Oppression and Emancipation in a Changing India: The Tamil Case and Beyond," *Comparative Studies of South Asia, Africa, and the Middle East* 18, no. 1 [1998]: 5–19, 7). Hugh Gorringe points out that "the position of rural Dalits is particularly vulnerable and the assertion of their rights can lead to them to being ostracized or subjected to violence." He continues, however, by observing that recent economic and political restructuring has opened spaces for Dalit activism: "in both [urban and rural settings] the correlation between caste and class has increasingly been subjected to challenge by the liberalisation and modernisation of the economy and the provision of affirmative action programmes. Whilst Dalit activists contest the efficacy of government programmes, the emergence of an educated, professional and relatively wealthy Dalit middle class constitutes a resource base for social action" (*Untouchable Citizens: Dalit Movements and Democratization in Tamil Nadu* [New Delhi: Sage, 2005], 26).

11. The power of commemoration as the focus of Dalit mobilization was tragically illustrated during the Karanai Panchami Land Struggle, launched in Chengalpattu, a town in Chennai's western outskirts. The struggle began in 1989, in the wake of the declaration of 1987 as the International Year of Shelter for the Homeless, with an effort to reclaim land that had been designated (originally in 1890) for Dalits but reappropriated in the 1950s by caste Hindus. In October 1994, following the enactment of the constitutional amendment providing for panchayati raj, a statue of B. R. Ambedkar, the anticolonial nationalist and Dalit leader, was erected as a symbolic reclamation of the land but was pulled down and defaced. The demonstrations by Dalits that followed were met with police violence, resulting in the deaths of two and the wounding of fourteen others; scores more were beaten and over a dozen arrests were made. Shortly thereafter, a march of one hundred thousand representing 127 Dalit organizations, claimed land rights in an unprecedented show of Dalit militancy. Although this struggle, alone, did not initiate the commemorative fervor that rose over the 1990s, it ensured its prominence as a catalyst for Dalit mobilization, with its attention to the memorialization of Dalits killed or injured and its renewed focus on the commemoration of Ambedkar.

12. This has extended to the streets of Chennai itself, where statues, busts, and portraits of Ambedkar mark Dalit settlements. In 2000 a large memorial, known as a *mani mantapam*, was built as a remembrance of Ambedkar in an affluent residential area. As part of its ongoing effort to court Dalit votes, Tamil Nadu's ruling party had allocated space for such a memorial in Chennai, in a residential area south of the Marina. Despite challenges from consumer and environmentalist groups, who objected to the *mani mantapam*'s location in an estuarine zone, the memorial was completed in 2000 (*Consumer Action Group v. The Union of India*, 186 *Madras Law Journal Reports* 481 [1994]). It has since been the venue for conferences, classes, and the annual commemorative observances that, by celebrating the anniversary of Ambedkar's conversion to Buddhism, recognize and sustain a distinctive Dalit ethos. Styled after a Buddhist stupa, as has become conventional throughout India, it has enabled Tamil Dalits to connect with a powerful national movement.

13. Racine and Racine, "Dalit Identities."

14. B. R. Ambedkar, *Annihilation of Caste* (Bombay: Bharat Bhushan Press, 1945).

15. For further discussion of Ambedkar's representation, see Gary Tartakov, "Art and Identity: The Rise of a New Buddhist Imagery," *Art Journal* 49, no. 4 (winter 1990): 409–416.

16. Mohandas Gandhi emerged as a leader in India's anti-colonial nationalist movement in the second decade of the twentieth century. Though born and raised in India, Gandhi received his law degree in England and, following that, lived for twenty-three years in South Africa. It was in South Africa where he developed his philosophy of nationalism and the techniques of nonviolent resistance for which he is best known today. After his return to India in 1914, he initiated nationalist campaigns modeled on the South African programs. These campaigns employed symbolic politics and collective action, and culminated in a mass movement of resistance to colonial rule.

17. See Gandhi, *Hind Swaraj* and *Ashram Observances in Action*. For excellent overviews of Gandhian thought, see Bhikhu Parekh, *Gandhi's Political Philosophy: A Critical Examination* (Notre Dame, Ind.: University of Notre Dame Press, 1989); and Richard G. Fox, *Gandhian Utopia: Experiments with Culture* (Boston: Beacon, 1989).

18. This program had several precursors. In 1973, under the state's DMK government, the Task Force on Human Resources and Social Change for Economic Development envisioned a Tamil cultural renaissance in which clubs, radio broadcasts, domestic tourism, and circulation of Tamil literature and expressive culture could be used to publicize Tiruvalluvar's message of social equality (Task Force on Human Resources and Social Change for Economic Development, "Human Resources for Prosperity in Tamil Nadu," *Report of the Task Force on Human Resources and Social Change for Economic Development* 1 [Madras: State Planning Commission, 1973]). A little more than a decade later, under AIA-DMK rule, caste equality was sought through the construction and upgrading of rural housing in the "Three Million Houses" program.

19. Dominant caste groups, usually landholders, often control rural political and economic institutions and, allied with police and local party workers, exert forceful, often violent control over Dalits. Following the inauguration of panchayati raj provisions, including the reservation of some panchayats for Dalit officials, Dalit panchayat presidents have been murdered and intimidated; dominant castes have denied employment to Dalits; and caste Hindus have refused to cooperate with elected Dalit panchayat heads. Complaints to police and elected officials lodged by Dalits are rarely acted on. Practices that maintain "untouchability" persist: Dalits have been banned from using shops and wells; they are assaulted when they attempt to participate in temple festivals; and individuals who question the authority of upper castes are routinely humiliated. See, for example, S. Viswanathan, "Hampering Empowerment," *Frontline* (online edition), September 16–29, 2000, 17, 19, http://www.flonnet.com/f11719/17191150.htm; and S. Nambath, "Fear is the Key," *Hindu* (online edition), December 29, 2002, http://www.thehindu.com/2002/12/29/stories/2002122900081700.htm. For a well-researched account of violence against Dalits in the 1990s, see Human Rights Watch, "The Pattern of Abuse: Southern District Clashes in Tamil Nadu and the State Response," in *Broken People: Caste Violence against India's "Untouchables"* (New York and Washington, D.C.: Human Rights Watch, 1999); and "Hidden Apartheid," HRW Index No. C1903 (New York and Washington, D.C.: Human Rights Watch, 2007).

20. District authorities and panchayat leaders were charged with devising a method for selecting program beneficiaries so as to obtain a group of residents, representative of the range of caste communities in the area, who were willing to participate in the experiment.

21. "Camattuvapurattil cāti piraccinai illai" (There are no problems of caste in Samathuvapurams), *Tiṉatanti,* March 9, 2000; "Camattuvapurankaḷil entamata kōvilkaḷum kaṭṭkkuṭātu" (No temples should be built in Samathuvapurams), *Tiṉatanti,* March 29, 2000.

22. Since regaining control of Tamil Nadu's government in 2006, the DMK leadership has given no indication that it intends to resume the samathuvapuram program.

23. P. Sudhakar, "When Usurers Take Over Samathuvapuram," *Hindu* (online edition), November 4, 2002, http://www.thehindu.com/2002/11/04/stories/2002110403420500.htm (accessed September 10, 2005).

24. "The Samathuvapuram housing project, launched with great fanfare by the DMK government as a colony for people of all caste, flopped merely because the upper castes were in no mood for any 'artificial integration' even if it came at Government expense" (Nambath, "Fear is the Key").

25. E. Karuppaiyan, "Executive Summary" (Volume 1), *Rural Development Programmes and Externalities: A Study of Seven Villages in Tamil Nadu,* Final Report Submitted to Planning Commission, Government of India, July 2002 (Ref. no. O-15012/57/2000–SER), 37.

26. Karuppaiyan observed that the "lack of employment opportunities in proximity to the settlement clusters discouraged them from occupying the houses" (ibid., 37).

27. See V. Geetha and S. Rajadurai, *Towards a Non-Brahmin Millennium* (Calcutta: Seagull Books, 1998).

28. See, for example, E. V. Ramasami Periyar, *The Ramayana (A True Reading),* 3rd ed. (Madras: Periyar Self Respect Propaganda Institute, 1980).

29. The DMK leader Karunanidhi also pays homage to B. R. Ambedkar in his speeches and writings, composing works such as this biography: Kalaiñar, *Ṭākṭar Ampētkar,* [Dr. Ambedkar] (Tirāviṭa Muṉṉēṟṟak Kaḻkam, 1995). Kalaiñar, meaning "artist," is a title used by M. Karunanidhi.

30. Anna Marumalarchi Thittam is a rural development program meant to support village panchayat empowerment; Namakku Naame Thittam is a participatory rural development program. The former was criticized as a machine for dispensing party patronage (Karuppaiyan, *Rural Development Programs,* 8–10, 38–39).

31. Panchayat officers do not run as party candidates, and panchayats, nominally, are unaffiliated. However, party strength can be gauged by state assembly election returns and Kuthambakkam's elections exemplify this, suggesting that its voters have remained outside the Dravidianist parties' machinery since the early 1990s. The state assembly district of which Kuthambakkam is a part, Poonamallee, in 2001, returned Shanmugam of the PMK, the recently organized "people's party" set up in opposition to the ruling Dravidianist parties to be an umbrella for "backward" and scheduled castes and tribes. Previous assembly elections, in 1991 and 1996, returned Sudarshanam, a candidate who stood initially as a representative of the national Congress party and later of the offshoot state-level Congress party.

32. Two samathuvapurams, both in the outskirts of Chennai, were built according to Baker's principles. Kuthambakkam's, discussed here, was built by a firm with a long involvement in India's community architecture movement; the other project, in Padappai, was carried out by the state's construction agency.

33. Though slated to be the hundredth samathuvapuram, it was actually the seventy-sixth.

34. "District Profile," http://www.tiruvallur.tn.nic.in/profile.htm (accessed September 20, 2005).

35. Land use in the district was 33 percent industrial/nonagricultural and sixteen industrial estates, government and private, were in operation, although 47 percent of its workforce was employed in the agricultural sector (http://www.tiruvallur.tn.nic.in/profile.htm).

36. Tiruvallur's Collector, knowing of the firm's long-standing commitment to cost-effective architecture and its partners' antipathy to the conventional contracting system, considered PAC a natural choice for the project and had lobbied on their behalf.

37. The flushing mechanism troubled many villagers, because water returned to the bowl after waste was flushed. In their view, it seemed that the bowl was repeatedly refilled with the same water that carried waste away; in addition, they, like many in South and Southeast Asia, find squat toilets, which do not use a water-filled bowl, more hygienic and comfortable.

38. For some of the villagers, vernacular design and local materials were initially disappointing. Early on, a few had voiced a preference for more "modern" accommodations represented by poured concrete houses and city tenements. These sentiments changed in the course of construction, as they learned of the benefits, financial and functional, of the vernacular style.

39. John Turner, "Tools for Building Community: An Examination of 13 Hypotheses," *HABITAT International* 20 (1996): 339–347; John Turner and R. Fichter, eds., *Freedom to Build* (New York: Macmillan, 1972).

40. In 1987 Baker won India's National Habitat Award.

41. Sudhir characterized their aspirations:

> One of the things that we wanted was to work in a cooperative. . . . It's basically an identification with what we thought cooperativism meant—basically that everybody had equal rights in the business of the organization and also equal responsibilities. . . . We were looking at involving workers as part of the thing. We had always had this feeling that the workers in the construction sector were getting a very raw deal. . . . There was no real advancement in terms of education prospects, only in raw economic terms. . . . They are the second largest unorganized workforce in the country after agricultural laborers. That was a very serious lack, in the sense that the construction industry itself involves a lot of money.

42. See Lang et al., *Architecture and Independence,* 246–248.

43. In that project, the architects conducted extensive surveys among the residents and held community meetings to ascertain the nature of housing needs. During these meetings, they also developed, in consultation with the community, a means of selecting who, among the villagers, would receive the new homes. The result of this consultation was that the architects decided that they themselves would not build the houses but that they would work with the villagers as advisers. They informed villagers about building techniques and materials, helped with the construction, and assisted villagers in obtaining lower-cost materials. Thus they helped villagers re-create the kinds of homes that were familiar and desirable to them.

44. This conversation, which took place among the partners during an interview, serves to illustrate. Sudhir began:

> For the past two and a half years, we have been doing mostly residences in the city, for middle and upper income group families. In a sense that has been a success, because we have gotten slotted into the kind of group who does work that goes by the name of "Laurie Baker" work. It goes by the name of "low cost" work. But it is neither of these. We can spend from nine months to a year and half on the home of a single family. This seems absolutely unreasonable and unnecessary, but it's the only source of work. . . . We have to be thankful for the few people who opt for this kind of work.

Vishnupriya interjected: "If not for them, what kind of work would we be doing?" Nyas followed:

> There is a contradiction formed here. We're doing work in real terms. The fact is that we are working with families, with clients, who don't have this kind of thinking. A few of them have some commitment or interest in the kinds of issues that are important for us. . . . They also understand the environmental implications of building in conventional manners, they understand the problems of inequities in the construction sector. They sympathize. They happen to be much better off, and they have a choice. . . . It's not arrogance stemming from the fact that they have money. It is more the kind of reluctance to exercise their will, to give up certain luxuries. There are others who are extremely arrogant about their choices. They are not the sort that we usually deal with.

45. Elango has attributed his ability to act on his political aspirations to his wife, because she supported his quitting the CISR and agreed to support the family with her earnings, as a professional chemist with the Oil and Natural Gas Commission.

46. "Ethical Economics, Endless Enthusiasm: An India Together Conversation with Rangaswamy Elango."

47. http://www.ashoka.org/fellows/veiwprofile3.cfm?reid=996796.

48. Ironically the district Web site, mounted by the Tamil Nadu state government, includes little information about Kuthambakkam; nearly all online references to Kuthambakkam appear on news media sites geared to Indians living outside the country or NRI-based NGOs.

49. His talks and interviews are posted on the Web sites of Indian American NGOs: "An Experiment in Self-Governance (Swaraj), Self-Reliance, and Eco-Friendly Development: The Story of Kuthambakkam Village," http://www.aidportland.org/archives/talks/elango2002.htm; "Elango's Kuthambakkam: A Model Village," http://www.thesouthasian.org/archives/000022.html. A visit to Kuthambakkam by Ram Krishnan, an NRI and member of the NGO Agency for India's Development, following Elango's return is reported on a page linked to the AID site (http://akash-ganga-rwh.com/village/TripReportKuthambakkam.html). All Web sites accessed September 15, 2005.

50. Although community architecture is preferred, for political reasons, Baker-trained architects also work in the private housing market, as the conversation recounted in note 40 demonstrates. Baker-style housing has become very popular among a segment of the urban elite, and Baker-trained architects, as well as those with conventional training, have found work in this market. These houses are distinguished by stylistic features that are emblematic of Baker's work, such as exposed brick exteriors and *jali.* However, they are not necessarily constructed according to the methods that Baker advocates. There is, of course, design consultation between architects and client, though that is standard practice in the relation between architects and their affluent clients, and not specifically introduced by Baker. More telling is the degree of interaction between architect and construction workers. That is the more distinctive feature in Baker's work, and in the private housing arena it is rarely, if ever, present. More often, the conventional system is followed in which the architect supplies the design and the project is then contracted out with construction labor working under the supervision of a contractor. The use of materials, like brick and recycled design elements, may occur, but these are often adopted for aesthetic reasons rather than for cost-effectiveness. The adoption of a Laurie Baker style by urban elites thus may signal a generalized sympathy with or nostalgia for Gandhian nationalism, without specific commitments to Gandhian practice.

51. Men and women were meant to co-reside in ashrams as siblings, religious and caste boundaries were to be eliminated by inclusive membership, and work was to be shared in an egalitarian way. The ashrams were to be models and catalysts for the economic self-sufficiency and local self-governance advocated by Gandhi; key to this was agriculture and craft production as the bases for community livelihood. In practice, Gandhi's ashrams were complex social spaces, fraught with struggle and controlled violence, played out in Gandhi's efforts to control the actions and sentiments of those who shared space with the ashram, often in conjunction with his own ascetic practices, including the various tests to which he subjected himself and others (e.g., the well-known incident in which he tested his celibacy by sleeping in the nude with young women).

52. See J. C. Kumarappa, *The Gandhian Economy and Other Essays,* (Warda: Maganwadi, 1949); idem, *Gandhian Economic Thought* (Varanasi: Sarva Seva Sangh Prakashan, 1962); idem, *Swaraj for the Masses* (Bombay: Hind Kitab, 1948).

53. Most of the community architecture projects were intended initially to provide housing that would serve as an alternative to the multistoried tenements that had become standard government issue during the 1960s and 1970s. Later, as evictions became more frequent, community architecture projects were launched for resettlement housing, usually in peri-urban zones surrounding municipalities.

54. Baker's participation in such projects was initially an experiment to demonstrate that cost-effective housing could be produced on a large scale. In the mid-eighties he sought to regularize the process and, with some associates, set up a training, research, and building center for cost-effective work. Baker's influence expanded with the founding of the TVB School of Habitat Studies, in 1990, by A. G. Krishna Menon, one of Baker's students and a founding member of INTACH. The aim of the school was to train architecture students in methods of cost-effective work but, more important, to reorient training by linking design and building, and by emphasizing consultative and community work. Baker's efforts were also oppositional insofar as he bypassed the conventional contracting system and tried to rework the sociopolitical and economic fields in which housing construction and ownership negotiated.

55. See also Gandhi, *Hind Swaraj* and *Ashram Observances in Action.*

56. Gandhi, *Hind Swaraj*, 57.

57. David Harvey, *Spaces of Hope* (Berkeley: University of California Press, 2000), 189–196; Fox, *Gandhian Utopia*.

58. Ajay Skaria, "Gandhi's Politics: Liberalism and the Question of the Ashram," *South Atlantic Quarterly* 101, no. 4 (2002): 955–986, 956–957.

59. Ibid., 957.

60. Ibid., 983.

61. The idea that architectural references to the past anchor cultural memory and revivify collective life is one that is held by many conservation architects affiliated with INTACH. Several have trained with Baker or his associates, and Baker himself has contributed to INTACH projects—including drafting the original design for DakshinaChitra. One of INTACH's founding members, A. G. Krishna Menon, worked closely with Baker, has incorporated tenets of cost-effective architecture into INTACH's mission statements, and directs an architecture training institute, TVB School of Habitat Studies, founded in 1990 on cost-effective principles (see note 54). Another architect, a partner in a private Chennai firm, described his earlier involvement in cost-effective work:

> The techniques and material that were used in old buildings, we were also trying to experiment with in our work—the use of brick, lime mortar, not plastering the exterior of the buildings, working directly with the masons as we converted the drawing we do in the studio to the field, developing an understanding of the techniques of workmanship. . . . What was taught in the conservation course was how to use and apply the same techniques that we were using for contemporary buildings. . . . Conservation need not be about keeping old buildings intact or preserving monuments, it's not just about keeping the end product buildings, but it could also be trying to conserve the process, the method of constructing the building.

62. Irwin Altman and Setha Low, *Place Attachment* (New York: Plenum, 1992), 1–12.

63. These included the Tamil Nadu—based Dalit Media Network, publisher of the bimonthly *Dalit Murasu* (1996). In 2002 another journal, *The Dalit*, was launched.

64. These organizations were part of a wider network advocating for the rights of the poor, Dalit, and working classes and included the National Campaign for Dalit Human Rights, the International Dalit Solidarity Network, as well as the Tamil Nadu—based International Dr. Ambedkar Centenary Movement, the Tamilar Human Rights Organization, the Dalit Liberation and Educational Trust, and People's Watch.

65. Among their goals was the inclusion of caste- and descent-based discrimination and violence as a form of racism. They also recognized the integral role of commemorative practice in creating a community of interest and pressing for recognition. See, for example, "United Nations Interventions," posted online by the National Campaign for Dalit Human Rights, http://www.dalits.org/uninterventions.htm; "Caste and Descent-Based Discrimination: Statement by the International Dalit Solidarity Network," posted online by Human Rights Watch (http://www.hrw.org/campaigns/caste/idsn_prepcom1.htm; "Final Declaration of the Global Conference against Racism and Caste-Based Discrimination," posted online by Human Rights Watch, http://www.hrw.org/campaigns/caste/final_declaration.htm. All sites accessed September 20, 2005.

66. Appadurai, "The Capacity to Aspire."

67. Amartya Sen, *Commodities and Capabilities* (New York: Oxford University Press, 1999). See also idem, "How Does Culture Matter?" in Rao and Walton, *Culture and Public Action*, 37–58.

68. Appadurai, "The Capacity to Aspire."

8. Conclusion

1. Kim Fortun and Mike Fortun, "The Work of Markets: Filming within Indian Mediascapes, 1997," in *Para-Sites: A Casebook against Cynical Reason*, ed. George Marcus, 287–347 (Chicago: University of Chicago Press, 2000).

2. Fortun and Fortun, "The Work of Markets," 289.

3. Khilnani, *The Idea of India*, 11–12.

4. Chennai Metropolitan Development Authority, *Draft Master Plan II for Chennai Metropolitan Area*, 1, http://www.cmdachennai.org/SMP_short/html (accessed June 19, 2007).

5. Srinivas, *Landscapes of Urban Memory: The Sacred and the Civic in India's High-Tech City.* Environmental psychologists understand place attachment to be a fundamental part of human psychological development, especially within the identification processes by which "self" is constituted with and against "other" (Altman and Low, *Place Attachment*).

6. Concerns with place attachment and its mnemonic encoding are prominent in phenomenological interpretations of space which are concerned centrally with the ways that space is made meaningful, as a named, value-laden "place" through human action and ideation. I have argued that phenomenological concerns with place-bound meaning cannot be divorced from questions about the political and economic constitution of "space" and the spatiality of power. For reviews of these debates, see Edward Casey, "How to Get from Space to Place in a Fairly Short Stretch of Time: Phenomenological Prologomena," in *Senses of Place,* ed. Steven Feld and Keith Basso, 13–52 (Santa Fe, N.Mex.: School of American Research, 1996); and David Harvey, "From Space to Place and Back Again," in *Justice, Nature and the Geography of Difference* (Oxford: Blackwell, 1996), 291–328.

7. A. Srivathsan, personal communication with author, August 12, 2006.

8. Bharath Rathna, *Dr. B. R. Ambedkar Educational Trust v. The Union of India*, 2002 *Madras Writ Law Reporter,* 578.

9. S. Chumkat, *Pilgrim's Guide to St. Thomas Monuments in Madras* (Madras: Disciples of St. Thomas, n.d.); Pereira de Andrade, Albert (Msgr), *Our Lady of Mylapore and St. Thomas the Apostle* (Madras: Diocese of Madras, n.d.).

10. I could not find evidence to corroborate that date.

11. I could not find evidence to corroborate his figures. Seven, an important number in Hindu praxis, may have signalled the symmetry among different styles of religiosity in Mylapore and its general auspiciousness. See Waghorne, *Diaspora of the Gods,* for a knowledgeable discussion of Mylapore's Hindu religious sites.

12. Huyssen, *Present Pasts,* 27.

13. Ibid.

14. The phrase, "India Shining," made in reference to India's ascension in the global capitalist economy, was a campaign slogan of the Hindu nationalist Bharatiya Janata Party (BJP). Although the slogan came to represent an ironic commentary on globalization rather than a rallying cry, following the BJP's heavy losses in the 2004 elections, it captures the aspirations that privileged and upwardly mobile classes shared during the 1990s and continue to endorse.

15. On "traveling culture," see James Clifford, *Routes* (Cambridge, Mass.: Harvard University Press, 1997).

Bibliography

Abrams, Philip. "Notes on the Difficulty of Studying the State (1977)." *Journal of Historical Sociology* 1, no. 1 (1988): 58–89.

Achyuta Menon, C. "Dravidic Studies in Madras." In *Madras Tercentenary Commemoration Volume*, 393–406. Madras: Humphrey Milford/Oxford University Press, 1939.

Agamben, Giorgio. *State of Exception*. Translated by K. Attell. Chicago: University of Chicago Press, 2005.

Agarwal, Arun, and Sunita Narain, eds. *Dying Wisdom*. Bangalore: Center for Science and Environment, 1993.

Alley, Kelly. *On the Banks of the Ganga*. Ann Arbor: University of Michigan Press, 2002.

Ali, Daud, ed. *Invoking the Past*. New Delhi: Oxford University Press, 1999.

Altman, Irwin, and Setha Low, eds. *Place Attachment*. New York: Plenum, 1992.

Ambedkar, B. R. *Annihilation of Caste*. Bombay: Bharat Bhushan, 1945.

Amirthalingam, M. "Temple Tanks of Chennai: A Survey." *CPR Environmental Education Centre Newsletter* (October–March, 2003). http://cpreec.org/pubperiodicals-ecoheritage.htm.

______. "Status Survey of Temple Tanks of Chennai." *Indian Journal of Environmental Education* 4 (April 2004). http://cpreec.org/pubperiodicals-indjournal.htm.

Anandhi S. *Contending Identities: Dalits and Secular Politics in Madras Slums*. New Delhi: Indian Social Institute, 1995.

Anderson, Benedict. *Imagined Communities*. Rev. ed. London: Verso, 1991.

Anonymous. "The Changing Complexion of a Coastal Village: Muttukadu, Some Key Observations." Unpublished manuscript on file, Madras Craft Foundation, n.d.

Appadurai, Arjun. *Worship and Conflict under Colonial Rule*. Cambridge: Cambridge University Press, 1981.

______. "The Capacity to Aspire: Culture and the Terms of Recognition." In *Culture and Public Action*, ed. Vijayendra Rao and Michael Walton, 59–84. Stanford, Calif.: Stanford University Press, 2004.

Archaeological Survey of India. *Annual Progress Report of the Archaeological Survey of Madras and Coorg for the Year 1904–05* (Alexander Rea, Director). Madras: Government Press, 1905.

______. *Annual Progress Report of the Archaeological Survey Department, Southern Circle, for the Year 1905–06* (Alexander Rea, Director). Madras: Government Press, 1906.

______. *Annual Report of the Archaeological Department, Southern Circle, Madras, for the Year 1912–1913*. Madras, Government Press, 1913.

______. *Annual Report of the Archaeological Department, Southern Circle, Madras for the Years 1912–1915*. Madras, Government Press, 1915.

______. *Annual Report of the Archaeological Department, Southern Circle, Madras, for the Year 1915–1916*. Madras: Government Press, 1916.

______. *Annual Report of the Archaeological Department, Southern Circle, Madras, for the Year 1917–1918*. Madras: Government Press, 1918.

Archaeological Survey of Southern India. *List of Ancient Monuments Selected for Conservation in the Madras Presidency in 1891*. Compiled by Alexander Rea. Madras: Government Press, 1891.

_____. *Lists of Antiquarian Remains in the Presidency of Madras*, Vol. 1. Compiled by Robert Sewell. Madras: Government Press, 1882.

Archer, Mildred. *Early Views of India: The Picturesque Journeys of Thomas and William Daniell, 1786–1794*. London: Thames and Hudson, 1980.

Aretxaga, Begoña. "Maddening States." *Annual Review of Anthropology* 32 (2003): 393–410.

Asad, Talal. *Formations of the Secular: Christianity, Islam, Modernity*. Stanford, Calif.: Stanford University Press, 2003.

Babb, Lawrence. *Redemptive Encounters: Three Modern Styles in the Hindu Tradition*. Berkeley: University of California Press, 1986.

Babu, Hari, ed. *Dossier on Tourism: Issues in Tamil Nadu*. Bangalore: Equations, 1997.

Bajpai, N., and N. Radjou. *Raising the Global Competitiveness of Tamil Nadu's Information Technology Industry*. Development Discussion Paper no. 728, Harvard Institute for International Development. Cambridge, Mass.: Harvard University Press, 1999.

_____. "IT Industry: Great Prospects Ahead, II." *Hindu*, March 30, 2000, 12.

Bann, Stephen. *Romanticism and the Rise of History*. New York: Maxwell Macmillan International, 1995.

Barlow, Glyn. *The Story of Madras*. London: Humphrey Milford, 1921.

Baskaran, S. Theodore. "Cinema Houses of Chennai." In *The Unhurried City: Writings on Chennai*, ed. C. S. Lakshmi, 75–86. Harmondsworth, U.K.: Penguin, 2004.

Bate, John Bernard. "*Mēṭaiṭṭamiḻ* Oratory and Democratic Practice in Tamil Nadu." Ph.D. diss., University of Chicago, 2000.

Bavadam, Lyla. "To Save the Coast." *Frontline* (online edition), vol. 22, February 11, 2005. http://www.flonnet.com/fl2203/stories/20050211006513300.htm.

Benjamin, Walter. "The Work of Art in the Age of Mechanical Reproduction." In *Illuminations*, ed. Hannah Arendt, 217–242. New York: Schocken, 1985 [1969].

_____. "A Short History of Photography." In *One-Way Street and Other Writings*. Translated and edited by E. Jephcott and K. Shorter. London: Verso, 1997.

_____. "Paris, the Capital of the Nineteenth Century (Exposé of 1935)." In *The Arcades Project*, trans. H. Eiland and K. McLaughlin, 3–13. Cambridge, Mass.: Belknap Press of Harvard University Press, 1999.

Bennett, Tony. "The Exhibitionary Complex." In *Culture/Power/History*, ed. Nicholas Dirks, Geoff Eley, and Sherry Ortner, 123–154. Princeton, N.J.: Princeton University Press, 1995.

_____. *The Birth of the Museum*. London: Routledge, 1995.

Bharath Rathna, *Dr. B. R. Ambedkar Educational Trust v. The Union of India*, 2002 *Madras Writ Law Reporter*, 578 (2002).

Bhatia, Gautam. *Laurie Baker: Life, Works, and Writings*. New Delhi: Penguin, 1991.

Boym, Svetlana. *The Future of Nostalgia*. New York: Basic Books, 2001.

Breckenridge, Carol, ed. *Consuming Modernity: Public Culture in Contemporary India*. Minneapolis: University of Minnesota Press, 1995.

Brown, Wendy. *States of Injury: Power and Freedom in Late Modernity*. Princeton, N.J.: Princeton University Press, 1995.

Bruner, Edward. *Culture on Tour: Ethnographies of Travel*. Chicago: University of Chicago, 2005.

Buck-Morss, Susan. *The Dialectics of Seeing*. Cambridge, Mass.: MIT Press, 1989.

"Budget Speech 2007–2008." Chennai: Government of Tamil Nadu, 2007. http://www.tn.gov.in/budget/dubsp07_08.htm.

Butler, Thomas, ed. *Memory: History, Culture, and the Mind*. Oxford: Blackwell, 1989.

Casey, Edward. "How to Get from Space to Place in a Fairly Short Stretch of Time: Phenomenological Prologomena" In *Senses of Place*, ed. Steven Feld and Keith Basso, 13–52. Santa Fe, N.Mex.: School of American Research, 1996.

Cassirer, Ernst. *The Myth of the State*. New Haven, Conn.: Yale, 1961 [1946].

Chakrabarti, Vibhuti. *Indian Architectural Theory: Contemporary Uses of Vastu Vidya*. Delhi: Oxford University Press, 1999.

Chakrabarty, Dipesh. *Provincializing Europe*. Princeton, N.J.: Princeton University Press, 2000.

Chakravarthy, Pradeep. "In Precincts Serene and Green." *Hindu* (online edition), June 4, 2004. http://www.thehindu.com/2004/06/04/stories/2004060402030600.htm.

Chandrakanth, M., J. Gilless, V. Gowramma, and M. Nagaraja. "Temple Forests in India's Forest Development." *Agroforestry Systems* 11 (1990): 199–211.

Chatterjee, Partha. *A Possible India: Essays in Political Criticism*. New Delhi: Oxford University Press, 1997.

Chennai Metropolitan Development Authority. *Draft Master Plan II for Chennai Metropolitan Area*. Chennai: Chennai Metropolitan Development Authority, 2007. http://www.cmdachennai.org/SMP.html.

_____. *Draft Master Plan II for Chennai Metropolitan Area—Short Version*. Chennai: Chennai Metropolitan Development Authority, 2007. http://www.cmdachennai.org/SMP_short/html.

Chidambaram, G. *Madras 2011: Policy Imperatives—An Agenda for Action*. 11 vols. Madras: Madras Metropolitan Development Authority, 1991.

Chumkat, S. *Pilgrim's Guide to St. Thomas Monuments in Madras*. Madras: Disciples of St. Thomas, n.d.

Clifford, James. *Routes*. Cambridge, Mass.: Harvard University Press, 1997.

"CM Promises to Make Chennai Asia's Premier City." *New Indian Express*, September 26, 2003.

Cohn, Bernard. *An Anthropologist among the Historians and Other Essays*. Oxford: Oxford University Press, 1987.

_____. *Colonialism and Its Forms of Knowledge*. Princeton, N.J.: Princeton University Press, 1996.

Cole, Henry. *Preservation of National Monuments, Madras Presidency*. Simla: Government Central Branch Press, 1881.

Committee on Emotional Integration. *Report of the Committee on Emotional Integration*. New Delhi: Ministry of Education, 1962.

Committee on Religious and Moral Hygiene. *Report of the Committee on Religious and Moral Hygiene*. New Delhi: Ministry of Education, 1959.

Connerton, Paul. *How Societies Remember*. Cambridge: Cambridge University Press, 1989.

Consumer Action Group v. The Union of India. 186 *Madras Law Journal Reports* 481 (1994).

Coronil, Fernando. *The Magical State: Nature, Money, and Modernity in Venezuela*. Chicago: University of Chicago Press, 1997.

Corrigan, Philip, and Derek Sayer. *The Great Arch: English State Formation as Cultural Revolution*. Oxford: Blackwell, 1985.

"Court Offers Hope for Adyar Creek." *Madras Musings*, August 16–31, 2001, 1, 7.

Crowther, Geoff, Prakash Raj, Tony Wheeler, Hugh Finlay, and Bryn Thomas. *India: A Travel Survival Kit*. 5th ed. Singapore: Lonely Planet, 1993.

Daniell, Thomas. *Oriental Scenery: Twenty-four Views in Hindoostan*. Drawn and engraved by T. Daniell. London: William Daniell, 1795–1801.

Daniell, Thomas, and William Daniell, *A Picturesque Voyage to India, by Way of China*. London: Longman, Hurst, Rees, and Orme [etc.], 1810.

_____. "Government House, Fort St. George." London: British Library (P Series, P 944), 1798. Aquatint.

_____. "Western Entrance to Fort St. George." London: British Library (P Series, P 947), 1798. Aquatint.

Davis, Peter. *Ecomuseums: A Sense of Place*. Leicester, U.K.: Leicester University Press, 1999.

Department of Culture. *Report of the Working Group on Art and Culture for the Sixth Five-Year Plan*. New Delhi: Ministry of Education, Social Welfare, and Culture, 1978.

_____. *Performance Budget 1985/86*. New Delhi: Ministry of Education, Social Welfare, and Culture, 1986.

Dickey, Sara. *Cinema of the Urban Poor in South India*. Cambridge: Cambridge University Press, 1993.

_____. "Permeable Homes: Domestic Service, Household Space, and the Vulnerability of Class Boundaries in Urban India." *American Ethnologist* 27, no. 2 (2000): 462–489.

_____. "The Politics of Adulation: Cinema and the Production of Politicians in South India." *Journal of Asian Studies* 52 (1993): 340–372.

Directorate of Town Planning. *Interim Development Plan for Madras*. Madras: Government of Tamil Nadu, 1967.

_____. *Metropolitan Plan for Madras*. Madras: Government of Tamil Nadu, 1968.

_____. *Urban Development of Greater Madras*. Madras: Government of Tamil Nadu, 1970.

Dirks, Nicholas. *The Hollow Crown: Ethnohistory of an Indian Kingdom.* Ann Arbor: University of Michigan Press, 1993.

Dirks, Nicholas, Geoff Eley, and Sherry Ortner, eds. *Culture/Power/History.* Princeton, N.J.: Princeton University Press, 1995.

Doctor, Geeta. "DakshinaChitra: Living Museum of the South." *Namaste,* 19, no. 2 (1999): 15–19.

Douglas, Mary. "Secular Defilement." In idem, *Purity and Danger,* 29–40. London: Routledge and Kegan Paul, 1966.

Dovey, Kim. *Framing Places: Mediating Power in Built Form.* London: Routledge, 1999.

Dwyer, Rachel, and Christopher Pinney, eds. *Pleasure and the Nation: The History, Politics, and Consumption of Popular Culture in India.* New Delhi: Oxford University Press, 2002.

Echeverri-Gent, John. "Politics in India's Decentered Polity." In *India Briefing: Quickening the Pace of Change,* ed. A. Ayres and P. Oldenburg, 19–53. Armonk, N.Y.: M. E. Sharpe, 2002.

Eck, Diana. *Darsan: Seeing the Divine Image in India.* New York: Columbia University Press, 1998.

Elango, Rangaswamy. "Ethical Economics, Endless Enthusiasm: An India Together Conversation with Rangaswamy Elango" (2002). http://www.indiatogether.org/govt/local/interviews/elango.htm.

_____. "An Experiment in Self-Governance (Swaraj), Self-Reliance, and Eco-Friendly Development: The Story of Kuthambakkam Village." Lecture Presented by Rangaswamy Elango, Portland, 2002. http://www.aidportland.org/archives/talks/elango2002.htm.

_____. "Elango's Kuthambakkam: A Model Village." Lecture Presented by Rangaswamy Elango, 2002, Minneapolis. http://www.thesouthasian.org/archives/2002/elangos_Kuthambakkam_a_model_v.htm.

Feld, Steven, and Keith Basso, eds. *Senses of Place.* Santa Fe, N.Mex.: School of American Research, 1996.

Ferguson, James, and Akhil Gupta. "Spatializing States." *American Ethnologist* 29, no. 4 (2002): 981–1002.

Fernandes, Leela. *India's New Middle Class.* Minneapolis: University of Minnesota Press, 2006.

Fortun, Kim, and Mike Fortun. "The Work of Markets: Filming within Indian Mediascapes, 1997." In *Para-Sites: A Casebook against Cynical Reason,* ed. George Marcus, 287–347. Chicago: University of Chicago Press, 2000.

Foster, William. *Founding of Fort St. George.* London: Eyre and Spottiswoode, 1902.

Fox, Richard G. *Gandhian Utopia: Experiments with Culture.* Boston: Beacon, 1989.

Freitag, Sandria, ed. *Collective Action and Community.* Berkeley: University of California Press, 1989.

Freitag, Sandria. 2003. "The Realm of the Visual: Agency and Modern Civil Society." In *Beyond Appearances? Visual Practices and Ideologies in Modern India,* ed. Sumathi Ramaswamy, 365–397. New Delhi: Sage, 2003.

Freud, Sigmund. "Family Romances." In *The Freud Reader,* ed. Peter Gay, 297–300. New York: Norton, 1989.

Fuller, Christopher. *The Camphor Flame: Popular Hinduism and Society in India.* Princeton, N.J.: Princeton University Press, 1992.

_____. *The Renewal of the Priesthood: Modernity and Traditionalism in a South Indian Temple.* Princeton, N.J. : Princeton University Press, 2003.

_____. "The Vinayaka Chaturthi Festival and Hindutva in Tamil Nadu." *Economic and Political Weekly* 34 (2001): 1607–1616.

Gadgil, Madhav, and Ramachandra Guha. *This Fissured Land: An Ecological History of India.* Berkeley: University of California Press, 1992.

Gandhi, Mohandas. *Ashram Observances in Action.* Translated by V. G. Desai. Ahmedabad: Navjivan Prakashan, 1997 [1955].

_____. *Hind Swaraj, or Indian Home Rule.* Ahmedabad: Navjivan Prakashan, 1997 [1909].

Gay, Peter. "Introduction" to "Family Romances." *The Freud Reader,* ed. Peter Gay, 297. New York: Norton, 1989.

Geertz, Clifford. "Deep Play: Notes on the Balinese Cockfight." In idem, *The Interpretation of Cultures,* 412–453. New York: Basic Books, 1973.

Geetha, V., and S. Rajadurai, *Towards a Non-Brahmin Millennium.* Calcutta: Seagull Books, 1998.

Glassberg, David. *Sense of History: The Place of the Past in American Life*. Amherst: University of Massachusetts Press, 2001.
Gopakumar, S. "'A Good Occasion for Change': Interview with Prof. John Kurien, fisheries economy expert." *Frontline* (online edition), 22, February 11, 2005. http://www.flonnet.com/fl2203/stories/20050211005601800.htm.
Gorringe, Hugh. *Untouchable Citizens: Dalit Movements and Democratization in Tamil Nadu*. New Delhi: Sage, 2005.
Government of India. *The Conference of Orientalists, including Museums and Archaeology Conference*. Simla: Government Press, 1911.
Government of India, Planning Commission. *Ninth Five-Year Plan*. New Delhi: Government of India, 1995.
_____. *Report of the Special Group on Targeting Ten Million Employment Opportunities per Year*. New Delhi: Government of India, 2002.
_____. *Report of the Working Group on Tourism, Eleventh Five-Year Plan, 2007–2012*. New Delhi: Ministry of Tourism, 2007. http://planningcommission.gov.in/aboutus/committee/wrkgrp11/wg11-tourism.pdf.
_____. *Tenth Five-Year Plan*. New Delhi: Government of India, 2002. http://planningcommission.gov.in/plans/planrel/fiveyr/10th/volume2/v2_ch7_5.pdf.
_____. "Tourism" In *Eighth Five-Year Plan*. New Delhi: Planning Commission, 1989. http://planningcommission.gov.in/plans/planrel/fiveyr/default.html.
_____. "Tourism." In *Ninth Five-Year Plan*. New Delhi: Planning Commission, 1995. http://planningcommission.gov.in/plans/planrel/fiveyr/default.html.
_____. "Tourism Sector." In *Midterm Appraisal of the Tenth Five-Year Plan* (2002–2007). New Delhi: Planning Commission, 2004. http://planningcommission.gov.in/midterm/english-pdf/chapter-13.pdf.
Government of Tamil Nadu. "Policy Note 2005–2006, Demand No. 28, Information and Tourism Department." Chennai: Government of Tamil Nadu, 2005. http://www.tn.gov.in/policynotes/tourism-1.htm. Accessed March 4, 2006.
_____. "Policy Note 2006–2007, Demand No. 31, Information Technology Department." Chennai: Government of Tamil Nadu, 2006. http://www.tn.gov.in/policynotes/information_technology.htm.
_____. *Tamil Nadu—An Economic Appraisal, 1999–2000*. Chennai: Government of Tamil Nadu. http://www.tn.gov.in/dear/archive/index.htm.
_____. *Tamil Nadu Human Development Report*. Delhi: Social Science Press, 2003.
_____. "Urban Development." In *Annual Plan 2004–05*. Chennai: State Planning Commission, 2004. http://www.tn.gov.in/spc/annualplan/default.htm.
"Governor's Address in the Legislative Assembly on 24th May 2006." Chennai: Government of Tamil Nadu, 2006. http://www.tn.gov.in/tnassembly/Governors_address_May2006_2.htm.
Grant, Bruce. "New Moscow Monuments, or States of Innocence." *American Ethnologist* 28, 2 (2001): 332–362.
Greenough, Paul. "Nation, Economy and Tradition Displayed." In *Consuming Modernity: Public Culture in Contemporary India*, edited by Carol Breckenridge, 216–248. Minneapolis: University of Minnesota Press, 1995.
Guha, Ranajit and Gayatri Spivak, eds. *Selected Subaltern Studies*. New York: Oxford University Press, 1988.
Halbwachs, Maurice. *The Collective Memory*, edited and translated by Lewis Coser. Chicago: University of Chicago Press, 1992.
Hancock, Mary. *Womanhood in the Making*. Boulder, Colo.: Westview Press, 1999.
_____. "Subjects of Heritage in Urban South India." *Environment and Planning D: Society and Space* 20, 6 (2001): 693–718.
_____. "Modernities Remade: Hindu Temples and their Publics in Southern India." *City and Society* 14, 1 (2002): 5–35.
Hardgrove, Ann. 2003. "Merchant Houses as Spectacles of Modernity in Rajasthan and Tamil Nadu." In *Beyond Appearances? Visual Practices and Ideologies in Modern India*, edited by Sumathi Ramaswamy, 323–364. New Delhi: Sage, 2003.

Hardt, Michael and Antonio Negri. *Empire.* Cambridge, Mass.: Harvard University Press, 2001.
Harriss, John. "Middle-Class Activism and the Politics of the Informal Working Class." *Critical Asian Studies* 38, 4 (2006): 445–465.
_____. *Power Matters: Essays on Institutions, Politics and Society in India.* New Delhi: Oxford University Press, 2006.
Harvey, David. "From Space to Place and Back Again." In *Justice, Nature and the Geography of Difference,* 291–328. Oxford: Blackwell, 1996.
_____. *Spaces of Global Capitalism.* New York: Verso, 2006.
_____. *Spaces of Hope.* Berkeley: University of California Press, 2000.
Hendry, Joy. *The Orient Strikes Back: A Global View of Cultural Display.* Oxford: Berg, 2000.
Herzfeld, Michael. *Cultural Intimacy: Social Poetics in the Nation-State.* New York: Routledge, 1997.
Hillier, B.; A. Leaman; P. Stansall; and M. Bedford. "Space Syntax." *Environment and Planning B* 3 (1976): 147–185.
Hiltebeitel, Alf. 1994. "The Folklore of Draupadi: Saris and Hair." In *Gender, Genre and Power in South Asian Expressive Traditions* edited by A. Appadurai, F. Korom and M. Mills, 395–427. Philadelphia: University of Pennsylvania Press, 1994.
Hindu (Chennai), 1992–2007

"New Design for MGR Camati," August 24, 1992, 3.
"Rathas Carrying Rama Padukas Start Journey," October 3, 1992, 3.
"Why 'Chennai'?" (Metro Section), July 9, 1996, I.
"Chennai versus Madras" (Metro Section), July 29, 1996, I.
"Assembly Nod for Name Change," September 1, 1996, 4.
"Pavement Hawkers Removed from NSC Bose Road," November 28, 1996, 3.
"Hawkers on Poonamallee High Road Evicted," December 4, 1996, 3.
"Traffic Moves Faster after Clearance," December 5, 1996, 3.
"Squatters to be Rehabilitated Outside the City," December 5, 1996, 3.
"Garbage, Garbage Everywhere" (Metro Section), January 6, 1997, I.
"Around the City," April 20, 2000, 3.
"HC Order on 'Girivalam Scheme' in Tiruvannamalai Stayed" (online edition), August 7, 2001. http://www.thehindu.com/ 2001/08/07/stories/0207000c.htm.
"'Girivalam' Cleanliness Needs Greater Attention" (online edition), March 31, 2002. http://www.thehindu.com/2002/03/31/stories/2002033102340300.htm.
"ASI Move to Take Over Tiruvannamalai Temple Opposed" (online edition), November 4, 2002. http://www.thehindu.com/2002/11/04/stories/2002110405560700.htm.
"Tiruvannamalai Society Takes Up Greening Project" (online edition), August 1, 2003. http://www.thehindu.com/2003/08/01/stories/2003080106050300.htm.
"Declare Girivalam Path Part of Heritage Town: Centre" (online edition), April 7, 2005. http://www.thehindu.com/2005/04/07/stories/2005040709660100.htm.
"Statue Symbolizes Culture, says Chief Minister," (online edition), June 4, 2006. http://www.thehindu.com/2006/06/04/stories/2006060408060600.htm.
"Gated Communities Carnival" (online edition), January 13, 2007. http://www.thehindu.com/thehindu/pp/2007/01/13/stories/2007011300180200.htm.

Hindu Religious Endowments Commission. *Report of the Hindu Religious Endowments Commission.* New Delhi: Government of India, Ministry of Law, 1962.
Hoffman, Linda, Susan Fainstein, and Dennis Judd, eds. 2003. *Cities and Visitors: Regulating People, Markets and City-Space.* Malden, Mass.: Blackwell Press, 2003.
Hopkins, Anthony, ed. *Globalization in World History.* London: Pimlico, 2002.
Human Rights Watch. "Final Declaration of the Global Conference Against Racism and Caste-Based Discrimination." Posted online by Human Rights Watch, 2000. http://www.hrw.org/campaigns/caste/final_declaration.htm.
_____. "Hidden Apartheid." HRW Index No. C1903. New York, Washington, D.C.: Human Rights Watch, 2007.

_____. "The Pattern of Abuse: Southern District Clashes in Tamil Nadu and the State Response" in *Broken People: Caste Violence Against India's "Untouchables."* New York, Washington, D.C.: Human Rights Watch, 1999.

Hunt, Lynn. *The Family Romance of the French Revolution.* Berkeley: University of California Press, 1992.

Huyssen, Andreas. *Twilight Memories: Marking Time in a Culture of Amnesia.* New York: Routledge, 1995.

_____. *Present Pasts: Urban Palimpsests and the Politics of Memory.* Stanford, Calif.: Stanford University Press, 2003.

Ilaiah, Kancha. *Why I am not a Hindu.* Calcutta: Samya, 1996.

Imperial Gazetteer of India [new edition], Vol. 16. Oxford: Clarendon, 1908.

"India: Country Framework Report for Private Participation in Infrastructure," *Country Brief: India.* Washington, D.C.: The World Bank, 1998.

"India-Tamil Nadu Urban Development Project II," Project Information Document (Report No. PID 6850). Washington, D.C.: The World Bank, 1998.

"India-Tamil Nadu Urban Development Project II," Project Appraisal Document (Report No. 18400-IN). Washington, D.C.: The World Bank, 1999.

INTACH, *INTACH Charter.* (New Delhi: INTACH, 2006). http://www.intach.org/pdf/charter.pdf.

INTACH, *Mylapore: An Approach to its Conservation.* Final Report. (Madras, July 1993) Project Coordinators, N. Devi Prasad, A. Srivathsan.

International Dalit Solidarity Network. "Caste and Descent-Based Discrimination: Statement by the International Dalit Solidarity Network." Posted online by Human Rights Watch, 2000. http://www.hrw.org/campaigns/caste/idsn_prepcom1.htm.

Irschick, Eugene. *Tamil Revivalism in the 1930s.* Madras: Cre-A, 1986.

_____. *Dialogue and History: Constructing South India, 1795–1895.* Berkeley: California, 1994.

Jacob, Preminda. "From Co-Star to Deity: Popular Representations of Jayalalitha Jayaram." In *Representing the Body: Gender Issues in Indian Art* edited by V. Dehejia, 140–165. Delhi: Kali for Women, 1997.

Jairaj, Bharat, and K. Mehta. "One Five Star or One Fifty Villages: Tourism on the East Coast Road." *CAG Reports,* October-December 1999, 8–9.

Jameson, Fredric, and Masao Miyoshi, eds. *The Cultures of Globalization.* Durham, N.C.: Duke University Press, 1998.

Jawarhalal Nehru National Urban Renewal Mission. *City Development Plan.* New Delhi: Government of India, 2006. http://jnnurm.nic.in/cd_apprep_pdf/CDP_Appraisals_ASCI/CHENNAI/May_2006.pdf.

Judd, Dennis. "Constructing the 'Tourist Bubble.'" In *The Tourist City* edited by Dennis Judd and Susan Fainstein, 35–53. New Haven, Conn.: Yale University Press, 1999.

Kalaiñar, *Ṭākṭar Ampētkar,* [Dr. Ambedkar]. Tirāviṭa Muṉṉēṟṟa Kaḻkam, 1995.

Kalam, M. *Sacred Groves in Kodagu District of Karnataka (South India): A Socio-historical Study.* Pondicherry: Institut Francais de Pondichery, 1996.

Kalpana, K., and Frank Schiffer. *Madras: The Architectural Heritage.* INTACH: Chennai, 2002.

Karp, Ivan, Corine Kratz, Lynn Szwaja, and Tomas Ybarra-Frausto, eds., *Museum Frictions: Public Cultures/Global Transformations.* Durham, N.C.: Duke University Press, 2006.

Karuppaiyan, E. *Rural Development Programmes and Externalities: A Study of Seven Villages in Tamil Nadu.* Final Report Submitted to Planning Commission, Government of India, July 2002 (Ref. no. O-15012/57/2000–SER).

Kaviraj, Sudipta. "Filth and the Public Sphere: Concepts and Practices about Space in Calcutta." *Public Culture* 10, 1 (1997): 83–113.

Kennedy, Lorraine. 2004. "The Political Determinants of Reform Packaging." In *Regional Reflections: Comparing Politics Across India's States,* edited by Rob Jenkins, 29–65. New York: Oxford University Press, 2004.

Khilnani, Sunil. *The Idea of India.* New York: Farrar, Straus, Giroux, 1997.

King, Anthony. *The Bungalow: The Production of a Global Culture.* Revised edition. New York: Oxford University Press, 1995 [1976].

_____. *Spaces of Global Cultures: Architecture Urbanism Identity.* London: Routledge, 2004.

Kirshenblatt-Gimblett, Barbara. *Destination Culture.* Berkeley: University of California Press, 1998.
Klein, Kerwin. "On the Emergence of Memory in Historical Discourse." *Representations* 69 (Winter 2000): 127–150.
Koselleck, Reinhard. *Futures Past.* New York: Columbia, 2004 [1985].
Krishnakumar, B.; S. Murthy, and V. D'Souza. "Playing it Dirty." *The Week,* February 10, 1991, 29–31.
Krishna Menon, A. G. "Towards an Indian Charter." *Seminar* 467 (1998): 21–26.
Krishna Menon, A. G., and B. Thapar. *Historic Towns and Heritage Zones.* New Delhi: INTACH, 1988.
Krishnan, P., M. Ramesh Kumar, A. Azeez, and M. Rajkumar. *Heritage Conservation Plan for Pulicat.* Chennai: INTACH, 2000.
Krishnaswami Aiyangar, S. "The Character and Significance of the Foundation of Madras." In *Madras Tercentenary Commemoration Volume,* 39–50. Madras: Humphrey Milford/Oxford University Press, 1939.
Kumar, Sanjay and Yogendra Yadav. "Tamil Nadu's Changing Political Landscape." *Hindu* (online edition), May 10, 2006. http://www.thehindu.com/2006/05/10/stories/2006051008901200.htm
Kumarappa, J. C. *The Gandhian Economy and Other Essays.* Warda: Maganwadi, 1949.
_____. *Gandhian Economic Thought.* Varanasi: Sarva Seva Sangh Prakashan, 1962.
_____. *Swaraj for the Masses.* Bombay Hind Kitab Ltd, 1948.
Kurin, Richard. "Cultural Conservation through Representation: Festival of India Folklife Exhibitions at the Smithsonian Institution." In *Exhibiting Cultures: The Poetics and Politics of Museum Display* edited by I. Karp and S. Lavine, 315–343. Washington, D.C.: Smithsonian, 1991.
Lakshmi, C. S., ed. *The Unhurried City: Writings on Chennai.* Harmondsworth, U.K.: Penguin, 2004.
Lakshmi, K. "River Conservation Project nearing Completion." *Hindu* (online edition), April 1, 2004. http://www.thehindu.com/2004/0401/stories/2004040113320300.htm
Lanchester, Henry. *Town Planning in Madras.* London: Constable, 1918.
Lang, Jon, M. Desai, and M. Desai, *Architecture and Independence.* Delhi: Oxford University Press, 1997.
LeFebvre, Henri. *The Production of Space.* Trans. D. Nicholson-Smith. Cambridge: Blackwell Press, 1991.
LeGoff, Jacques. *History and Memory.* Trans. S. Rendall and E. Claman. New York: Columbia University Press, 1993.
Lewandowski, Susan. "The Built Environment and Cultural Symbolism in Post-Colonial Madras." In *The City in Cultural Context,* edited by John Agnew, John Mercer and David Sopher, 237–254. Boston: Allen and Unwin, 1984.
Linenthal, Edward. *Preserving Memory: The Struggle to Create America's Holocaust Museum.* New York: Viking, 2001.
List of Statues, Monuments, and Busts Erected in Madras. Madras: Government Press, 1898.
Long, S. "Now for the Hard Part: A Survey of Business in India." *The Economist* 379, 8480 (2006): 50A–50R.
Longhurst, A. H. *Annual Report of the Superintendent, Archaeological Survey, for 1916–17.* Madras: Government of Madras, Home Department (Education), 1917.
Love, Henry Davidson. *Vestiges of Old Madras, 1640–1800.* 4 Volumes. London: John Murray, 1913.
Lowenthal, David. The *Past is a Foreign Country.* Cambridge: Cambridge University Press, 1985.
_____. *Possessed by the Past.* Cambridge: Cambridge University Press, 1998.
Ludden, David, ed. *Making India Hindu.* New Delhi: Oxford University Press, 1996.
Madras Metropolitan Development Authority. *Madras Metropolitan Plan, 1971–1991.* Madras: Government of Tamil Nadu, 1973.
_____. *Structure Plan for Madras Metropolitan Area.* 2 Volumes. Madras: Madras Metropolitan Development Authority, 1980.
_____. *Master Plan for Madras Metropolitan Area—2011,* Draft. Madras: Madras Metropolitan Development Authority, 1995.
Madras Tercentenary Commemoration Committee. *Madras Tercentenary Commemoration Volume.* Madras: Humphrey Milford/Oxford University Press, 1939.
Maitra, S. "Financing Urban Development." *Economic and Political Weekly,* 35 (2000), 4647–4655.

Malliah, Santosh. "It Rains Ideas" *Business Line* (internet edition), September 24, 2001. http://www.thehindbusinessline.com/2001/09/24/stories/102425az.htm.

Mankekar, Purnima. *Screening Culture, Viewing Politics: An Ethnography of Television, Womanhood and Nation in Postcolonial India.* Durham, N.C.: Duke University Press, 1999.

Markham, Sydney and Harold Hargreaves. *The Museums of India.* London: The Museum Association, 1936.

Markus, Thomas and Deborah Cameron. *The Words Between the Spaces: Buildings and Language.* London: Routledge, 2002.

Menon, C. Achutya. "Dravidic Studies in Madras," In *Madras Tercentenary Commemoration Volume*, 393–406. Madras: Humphrey Milford/Oxford University Press, 1939.

Metcalf, Thomas. *An Imperial Vision.* Berkeley: University of California Press, 1989.

"MGR Film City to give way to Knowledge Park." *Business Line* (internet edition), August 3, 2002. http://www.thehindubusinessline.com/2002/08/03/stories/2002080309131700.htm.

Michell, George. *Architecture and Art of Southern India.* The New Cambridge History of India, I:6. Cambridge: Cambridge University Press, 1995.

Ministry of Tourism. "Incredible India: Figures 2003." New Delhi: Ministry of Tourism, 2003. http://www.tourismindia.com.

Mitchell, Timothy. "The Limits of the State: Beyond Statist Approaches and Their Critics." *American Political Science Review* 85 (1991): 77–96.

_____. "Society, Economy and the State Effect." In *State/Culture: State Formation after the Cultural Turn,* edited by George Steinmetz, 76–97. Ithaca, NY: Cornell University Press, 1999.

Morgan, David. *The Sacred Gaze: Religious Visual Culture in Theory and Practice.* Berkeley: University of California Press, 2005.

Murray, John. *A Handbook for Travelers in India, Pakistan, Burma and Ceylon.* London: Murray, 1892.

Muthiah, S. *Madras Rediscovered.* 4th Revised Edition. Chennai: East West Books, 1999.

_____. "Enjoying a Vision of the South." *Namaste*, 19, 2 (1999): 20–23.

Muthukumaraswamy, M.D. "From the Director." In *NFSC Folk Festival 2002 Souvenir.* (March 2002): 1–4.

Nair, Janaki. *The Promise of the Metropolis: Bangalore's Twentieth Century.* New Delhi: Oxford University Press, 2005.

Nambath, S. "Fear is the Key." *Hindu* (online edition), December 29, 2002. http://www.thehindu.com/2002/12/29/stories/2002122900081700.htm.

Nambiar, P. and N. Krishnamurthy. "Report on the Temples of Madras." *Census of India, 1961,* 9, 11–D, xv.

National Campaign for Dalit Human Rights. "United Nations Interventions." Statement posted online, 2000. http://www.dalits.org/uninterventions.htm.

National Council of Applied Economic Research. *Domestic Tourism Survey.* New Delhi: Ministry of Tourism, 2003.

Negt, Oskar, and Alexander Kluge. *Public Sphere and Experience.* Trans P. Labanyi, J. Daniel, A. Oksiloff. Minneapolis: University of Minnesota Press, 1993 [1972].

Neild, Susan. "Madras: The Growth of a Colonial City in India, 1780–1840." Ph.D. diss., University of Chicago, 1977.

Noble, W. "Houses with Centered Courtyards in Kerala and Elsewhere in India." In *Dimensions of Social Life: Essays in Honor of David Mandelbaum,* 215–262, edited by Paul Hockings. Berlin: Mouton de Gruyter, 1987.

Nora, Pierre. 1989. "Between Memory and History: Les Lieux de Memoire." *Memory and Counter-Memory.* Special Issue of *Representations* 26 (winter 1989): 7–24.

The Oriental Annual or Scenes in India, Comprising Twenty-two Engravings from Original Drawings by Wm Daniell, R.A. and a Descriptive Account by the Rev.J. Hobart Caunter, B.D. London, Edw. Bull, 1834.

Pakavati, K. *Ceṉṉai. Ceṉṉai*: Ulakattamiḻaraycci Niruvanam, 1995.

Palani Hills Conservation Council etc. v. The State of Tamil Nadu, etc. and others, 1995-2–*Writ Law Reporter* 737.

Pandian, M.S.S. *The Image Trap: M.G. Ramachandran in Film and Politics.* Newbury Park: Sage, 1992.

Parekh, Bhikhu. *Gandhi's Political Philosophy: A Critical Examination.* Notre Dame, Ind.: University of Notre Dame Press, 1989.
Parker, Samuel. "The Matter of Value Inside and Out: Aesthetic Categories in Contemporary Hindu Temple Arts." *Ars Orientalis* 22 (1992), 97–110.
Penny, Frank. *The Church in Madras.* London: Elder, 1904.
Pereira de Andrade, Albert (Msgr). *Our Lady of Mylapore and St. Thomas the Apostle.* Madras: Diocese of Madras, n.d.
Periyar, E.V. Ramasami. *The Ramayana (A True Reading).* 3rd edition. Madras: Periyar Self Respect Propaganda Institute, 1980.
Peterson, Indira. "Eighteenth-century Madras through Indian Eyes: Urban Space, Patronage, and Power in the Sanskrit text *Sarva-deva-vilasa.*" Paper presented at Annual Meeting of the Association for Asian Studies, Chicago, March 25, 2001.
Pinney, Christopher. "The Indian Work of Art in the Age of Mechanical Reproduction." In *Media Worlds,* edited by Fay Ginsburg, Lila Abu-Lughod, and Brian Larkin, 355–369. Berkeley: University of California Press, 2002.
_____. *Camera Indica.* Berkeley: University of California Press, 1997.
Pithavadian, F.B. "An Architect's View." *Madras on the Move.* Special Issue of *Civic Affairs* (December 1977): 32–33.
Prakash, Gyan. "Writing Post-Orientalist histories of the Third World: Perspectives from Indian Historiography." *Comparative Studies in Society and History* 32, 2 (1990): 383–408.
Presler, Franklin. *Religion Under Bureaucracy.* Cambridge: Cambridge University Press, 1987.
Price, Pamela. *Kingship and Political Practice in Colonial India.* New York: Cambridge University Press, 1996.
Racine, Jean-Luc and Josiane Racine. "Dalit Identities and the Dialectics of Oppression and Emancipation in a Changing India: The Tamil Case and Beyond." *Comparative Studies of South Asia, Africa and the Middle East,* 18, 1, (1998): 5–19.
Raghavan, V. "Notices of Madras in Two Sanskrit Works." In *Madras Tercentenary Commemoration Volume,* 107–112. Madras: Humphrey Milford/Oxford University Press, 1939.
Rajagopal, Arvind. *Politics After Television: Hindu Nationalism and the Reshaping of the Public in India.* Cambridge: Cambridge University Press, 2000.
Ramanujan, A.K. "Towards an Anthropology of City Images." In *Urban India: Society, Space and Image* edited by Richard G. Fox, 224–244. Durham: Monograph and Occasional Papers Series, Monograph 10, Duke University Program in Comparative Studies on Southern Asia, 1970.
_____. *Poems of Love and War.* New Delhi: Oxford University Press, 1988.
Ramaswamy, Sumathi. *Passions of the Tongue.* Berkeley: University of California Press, 1997.
_____. *The Lost Land of Lemuria.* Berkeley: University of California Press, 2004.
Ramusack, Barbara. "The Indian Princes as Fantasy: Palace Hotels, Palace Museums, and the Palace on Wheels." In *Consuming Modernity: Public Culture in Contemporary India,* ed. Carol Breckenridge, 66–89. Minneapolis: University of Minnesota Press, 1995.
Ranson, Charles W. *A City in Transition: Studies in the Social Life of Madras.* Madras: Christian Literature Society for India, 1938.
Rao, Vijayendra, and Michael Walton, eds. *Culture and Public Action.* Stanford, Calif.: Stanford University Press, 2004.
Rapoport, Amos. "A Framework for Studying Vernacular Design." *Journal of Architectural and Planning Research* 16, no. 1 (1999): 52–64.
Raz, Aviad. *Riding the Black Ship: Japan and Tokyo Disneyland.* Cambridge, Mass.: Harvard University Asia Center, 1999.
"Real Estate Rush," *Frontline* (online edition), August 25, 2006. http://www.flonnet.com/fl2316/stories/20060925003310600.htm.
Ren, Hai. "Economies of Culture: Theme Parks, Museums, and Capital Accumulation in China, Hong Kong, and Taiwan." Ph.D. diss., University of Washington, Seattle, 1998.
Richter, Linda. *The Politics of Tourism in Asia.* Honolulu: University of Hawai'i Press, 1989.
Rivière, Pierre. "The Ecomuseum: An Evolutive Definition." *Museum* 148 (1985): 182–183.
Robertson, Roland. "Globalisation or Glocalisation?" *Journal of International Communication* 1, no. 1 (1994): 33–52.

Rosaldo, Renato. "Imperialist Nostalgia." In idem, *Culture and Truth: The Remaking of Social Analysis*, 66–87. Boston: Beacon, 1991.

Rosenzweig, Roy, and David Thelen. *The Presence of the Past: Popular Uses of History in American Life*. New York: Columbia University Press, 1998.

Rudner, David. *Caste and Capitalism in Colonial India: The Nattukottai Chettiars*. Berkeley: University of California Press, 1994.

Rukmani, R. "Urbanisation and Socio-Economic Change in Tamil Nadu, 1901–91." *Economic and Political Weekly* 29 (1994): 3263–3272.

Runganadhan, S. E. Introduction to *Madras Tercentenary Commemoration Volume*, xiii. Madras: Humphrey Milford/Oxford University Press, 1939.

Sadasivan, D. *The Growth of Public Opinion in Madras Presidency*. Madras: University of Madras, 1974.

Samuel, Raphael. *Theatres of Memory*. London: Verso, 1994.

Schacter, Daniel. *Searching for Memory*. New York: Basic Books, 1996.

Schmitt, Carl. *Political Theology*. Translated by G. Schwab. Cambridge, Mass.: MIT Press, 1985 [1922].

Schulman, David. *Tamil Temple Myths: Sacrifice and Divine Marriage in the South Indian Saiva Tradition*. Princeton, N.J.: Princeton University Press, 1980.

Schumpter, Joseph. *Capitalism, Socialism, and Democracy*. New York: Harper and Row, 1962 [1942].

Sen, Amartya. *Commodities and Capabilities*. New York: Oxford University Press, 1999.

_____. "How Does Culture Matter?" In *Culture and Public Action*, ed. Vijayendra Rao and Michael Walton, 37–58. Stanford, Calif.: Stanford University Press, 2004.

Sen, S. P., ed. *Historians and Historiography in Modern India*. Calcutta: Institute of Historical Studies, 1973.

Shashidhar, Ajita. "Craze for Condominiums." *Hindu* (online edition), Property Plus Section, January 14, 2005. http://www.thehindu.com/pp/2005/01/14/stories/2005011400040100.htm.

Shaw, Annapurna. "Emerging Patterns of Urban Growth in India." *Economic and Political Weekly* 34 (1999): 969–978.

Singh, B. P. *India's Culture*. New Delhi: Oxford University Press, 1998.

Sitaraman, S. "Society and Science." *Economic and Political Weekly* 29 (1994): 290.

Skaria, Ajay. "Gandhi's Politics: Liberalism and the Question of the Ashram." *South Atlantic Quarterly* 101, no. 4 (2002): 955–986.

Sorkin, Michael, ed. *Variations on a Theme Park*. New York: Farrar, Straus and Giroux, 1992.

Special Housing Committee. *Report of the Special Housing Committee*. Madras: Corporation of Madras, 1933.

Srinivas, Smriti. *Landscapes of Urban Memory*. Minneapolis: University of Minnesota Press, 2001.

_____. *In the Presence of Sai Baba: Body, City and Memory in a Global Religious Movement*. Leiden: Brill, 2008.

Srivathsan, A. "Government tells CMDA to Prepare Fresh Draft Second Master Plan." *Hindu* (online edition), January 12, 2007. http://www.thehindu.com/2007/01/12/stories/2007011207940100.htm.

_____. "Chennai's Long Wait for a Master Plan." *Hindu* (online edition), January 13, 2007. http://www.thehindu.com/2007/01/13/stories/2007011300201000.htm.

_____. "Chennai Master Plan Is Ready." *Hindu* (online edition), March 6, 2007. http://www.thehindu.com/2007/03/06/stories/2007030617180300.htm.

_____. *Temple Tanks in Chennai: An Inventory*. Chennai: INTACH, 2001.

_____. "Politics of Tamil Monuments: 1968–1975." *South Indian Studies* 5 (1998): 59–82.

Stanley, Nick. *Being Ourselves for You: The Global Display of Cultures*. London: Middlesex, 1998.

Stapati, Kanapati. "Alai . . . Kalai . . . Tiruvaḷḷuvar cilai" (Waves . . . Art . . . Tiruvalluvar's Statue). *Tiṉatanti*, January 15, 2000.

Stein, Burton. *Peasant, State, and Society in Medieval South India*. Delhi: Oxford University Press, 1980.

Sturken, Marita. *Tangled Memories: The Vietnam War, the AIDS Epidemic, and the Politics of Remembering*. Berkeley: University of California Press, 1997.

Sturken, Marita, and Lisa Cartwright. *Practices of Looking*. Berkeley: University of California Press, 2003.

Subrahmanyam, Sanjay. *The Political Economy of Commerce: Southern India, 1500–1650*. Cambridge: Cambridge University Press, 2002.

_____. *Penumbral Visions: Making Polities in Early Modern South India*. Ann Arbor: University of Michigan Press, 2001.

Subrahmanyam, Sanjay, Velcheru Rao, and David Schulman, eds. *Textures of Time*. Oxford: Oxford University Press, 2001.

Subramaniam, Arundhati. "Madras." In *The Unhurried City: Writings on Chennai*, ed. C. S. Lakshmi, 134–135. Harmondsworth, U.K.: Penguin, 2004.

Subramanian, Narendra. *Ethnicity and Populist Mobilization*. New Delhi: Oxford University Press, 1999.

Subramanian, T. S. "The Conviction of Jayalalitha." *Frontline* (online edition), 17, February 19–March 3, 2000). http://www.flonnet.com/f11704/17040380.htm.

_____. "Promises to Keep," *Frontline* (online edition), vol. 23, June 2, 2006. http://www.flonnet.com/f12310/stories/20060602002002600.htm.

Subramuniyaswami, S., trans. *Tirukkural*. New Delhi: Abhinav, 2000.

Sudhakar, P. "When Usurers Take Over Samathuvapuram." *Hindu* (online edition), November 4, 2002. http://www.thehindu.com/2002/11/04/stories/2002110403420500.htm.

Tamil Nadu Slum Clearance Board. *Socio-economic Survey of Madras Slums*. Madras: TNSCB, 1975.

Tamil Nadu State Planning Commission. *Tenth Five-Year Plan, 2002–2007*. Chennai: Government of Tamil Nadu, 2002. http://www.tn.gov.in/spc/tenthplan/default.htm.

_____. *Tamil Nadu Human Development Report*. Chennai: Government of Tamil Nadu, 2003.

"Tamil Nadu Urban Development Project III." Project Information Document (Report No. AB734). Washington, D.C.: The World Bank, 2004.

Tartakov, Gary. "Art and Identity: The Rise of a New Buddhist Imagery." *Art Journal* 49, no. 4 (winter 1990): 409–416.

Task Force on Human Resources and Social Change for Economic Development. "Human Resources for Prosperity in Tamil Nadu." In *Report of the Task Force on Human Resources and Social Change for Economic Development* 1. Madras: State Planning Commission, 1973.

Taussig, Michael. "Physiognomic Aspects of Visual Worlds." In *Visualizing Theory*, ed. Lucien Taylor, 205–213. New York: Routledge, 1997.

_____. *The Magic of the State*. New York: Routledge, 1997.

Taylor, Peter. *Modernities: A Geopolitical Intepretation*. Cambridge: Polity, 1999.

Teo, Rachel, and Brenda Yeoh. "Remaking Local Heritage for Tourism." *Annals of Tourism Research* 24 (1997): 192–213.

Thapar, B. *Our Cultural Heritage*. New Delhi: INTACH, 1989.

Thiagarajan, Deborah. "DakshinaChitra, a Living Heritage Centre for South India." Unpublished manuscript, n.d.

_____. *DakshinaChitra: From Village to Centre*. Chennai: Madras Craft Foundation, 1999.

"Third Tamil Nadu Urban Development Project" (Project ID: PO83780). Washington, D.C.: The World Bank, 2003. http://go.worldbank.org/L67WLT8H3.

"Thiruvanmiyur." Wikipedia. http://en.wikipedia.org/wiki/Thiruvanmiyur/.

Thurston, Edgar and K. Rangachari. *The Tribes and Castes of South India*. Madras: Government Press, 1909.

Tillotson, Geoffrey. *The Tradition of Indian Architecture*. New Haven, Conn.: Yale University Press, 1989.

Tiṉatanti (Chennai)

"Eṉṉa naṭantālum cilai tiṟappatu uṟuti: Karuṇāniti pēccu" (Whatever happens, the statue will be unveiled: Karunanidhi's speech), December 22, 1999.

"Kaṉṉiyākumariyil Amaikkappaṭṭa 133 aṭiuyara Tiruvaḷḷuvar cilai: Karuṇāniti, nāḷai tiṟantu vaikkiṟār" (Karunanidhi to unveil the 133-foot-tall statue installed at Kanyakumari tomorrow), December 31, 1999.

"Em. Ji. Ar. Peyarai Maṟaikkavillai" (MGR's name is not hidden), January 6, 2000.

"Putiya Vaḷḷuvar cakāptattai uruvākkavēṇṭum: Karuṇāniti pēccu" (We must usher in a new "Valluvar" epoch: Karunanidhi's speech), January 17, 2000.

"Camattuvapurattil cāti piraccinai illai" (There are no problems of caste in Samathuvapurams), March 9, 2000.

"Camattuvapurankaḷil entamata kōvilkaḷum kaṭṭkkuṭātu" (No temples should be built in Samathuvapurams), March 29, 2000.

Trouillot, Michel-Rolphe. "The Anthropology of the State in the Age of Globalization." *Current Anthropology* 42 (2001): 125–138.

Tsing, Anna. "The Global Situation." In *The Anthropology of Globalization: A Reader*, ed. Jonathan Inda and Renato Rosaldo, 453–485. Oxford: Blackwell, 2002.

Turner, John. "Tools for Building Community: An Examination of 13 Hypotheses." *HABITAT International* 20 (1996): 339–347.

Turner, John, and R. Fichter, eds. *Freedom to Build.* New York: Macmillan, 1972.

Van der Veer, Peter, and Hart Lehmann, eds. *Nation and Religion: Perspectives on Europe and Asia.* Princeton, N.J.: Princeton University Press, 1999.

Varacharajan, D. *A Survey of Mamallapuram: Study Conducted for INTACH.* Madras: Madras School of Social Work, August 1986.

Varshney, Ashutosh. *Ethnic Conflict and Civic Life.* New Haven, Conn.: Yale University Press, 2002.

Venkatachalapathy, R., ed. *Chennai Not Madras: Perspectives on the City.* New Delhi: Marg, 2006.

Venkatakrishnan, P. V. "Madras City in Its Regional Setting." *Madras on the Move.* Special Issue of *Civic Affairs* 25, no. 5 (December 1977): 25–28.

Venugopal Rao, N. 1994. "Learning from a Legacy: How and What?" *Economic and Political Weekly* 29 (1994): 288–289.

Vijay, Hema. "Housing Board Flats Make Way for Gentrification." *Hindu* (online edition), July 29, 2006. http://www.thehindu.com/thehindu/pp/w006/07/29/stories/2006072900050100.htm.

Viramma, Josiane Racine, and Jean-Luc Racine. *Viramma: Life of an Untouchable.* Translated by W. Hobson. New York: Verso, 1997.

A Vision of the South. Chennai: Rajeswari Communications, 1997. Videorecording.

Viswanathan, S. "Hampering Empowerment." *Frontline* (online edition), 17, 19, September 16–29, 2000. http://www.flonnet.com/f11719/17191150.htm.

Waghorne, Joanne. *The Raja's Magic Clothes: Re-visioning Kingship and Divinity in England's India.* University Park: Pennsylvania State University Press, 1994.

_____. *Diaspora of the Gods: Hindu Temples in an Urban Middle Class World.* New York: Oxford University Press, 2004.

_____. "The Diaspora of the Gods: Hindu Temples in the New World System, 1640–1800." *Journal of Asian Studies* 58, no. 3 (1999): 648–686.

Walkowitz, Daniel, and Lisa Knauer, eds. *Memory and the Impact of Political Transformation in Public Space.* Durham: Duke University Press, 2004.

Washbrook, David. *The Emergence of Provincial Politics.* Cambridge: Cambridge University Press, 1976.

Weibe, Paul. *Tenants and Trustees: A Study of the Poor in Madras.* Delhi: Macmillan, 1977.

Weidman, Amanda. *Singing the Classical, Voicing the Modern.* Durham, N.C.: Duke University Press, 2006.

Wheeler, J. Talboys. *Madras in the Olden Times.* Madras: Graves, 1861–62.

White, Geoffrey. "Emotive Institutions." In *A Companion to Psychological Anthropology: Modernity and Psychocultural Change*, ed. C. Casey and R. Edgerton, 241–254. London: Blackwell, 2004.

White, Hayden. *The Content of the Form.* Baltimore: Johns Hopkins University Press, 1987.

Wilkinson-Weber, Claire. 2004 "Women, Work, and the Imagination of Craft in South Asia." *Contemporary South Asia* 13, no. 3 (2004): 287–306.

Willis, Susan, ed. *The World According to Disney.* Special Issue of *South Atlantic Quarterly* 92, no. 1 (winter 1993).

Wilson, James Q., and George Kelling. "Broken Windows." *Atlantic Monthly Online,* March 1982. http://www.theatlantic.com/politics/crime/windows.htm.

Yeoh, Brenda. "From Colonial Neglect to Post-Independence Heritage: The Housing Landscape in the Central Area of Singapore." *City and Society* 12 (2000): 103–124.

Zelizer, Barbie. "Reading the Past against the Grain: The Shape of Memory Studies." *Critical Studies in Mass Communication* 12, no. 2 (1995): 214–239.

Zukin, Sharon. *Landscapes of Power.* Berkeley: University of California Press, 1991.

Website URL Addresses

AIA-DMK Political Party: http://www.aiadmkindia.org/ (no longer active)

Annai Vailankanni: http://www.annaivailankanni.org/annaivailankanni/default.html

Business Line (weekly, English): http://www.thehindubusinessline.com

Business Week (weekly, English): http://www.businessweek.com/

C. P. Ramaswamy Environmental Education Center: http://cpreec.org/

Chennai Metropolitan Development Authority: http://www.cmdachennai.org/

Corporation of Chennai: http://www.chennaicorporation.com/

DakshinaChitra: http://www.dakshinachitra.net/

EPrarthana: http://www.eprarthana.com/

Frontline (biweekly, English): http://www.flonnet.com/

Government of India Planning Commission: http://planningcommission.gov.in/

Government of Tamil Nadu: http://www.tn.gov.in/

Hindu (daily, English): http://www.thehindu.com/

Human Rights Watch: http://www.hrw.org/

India Together: http://www.indiatogether.org/

Indira Gandhi Centre for Atomic Research: http://www.igcar.ernet.in/

INTACH: http://www.intach.org/

Jawarhalal Nehru National Urban Renewal Mission: http://jnnurm.nic.in/

MGM Dizzee World: http://www.mgm-india.com/

Ministry of Hindu Religious and Charitable Endowments, Tamil Nadu: http://www.hrce.tn.nic.in/

Ministry of Tourism, Government of India: http://www.tourismindia.com/

National Campaign for Dalit Human Rights: http://www.dalits.org/

Neemrana Heritage Hotels and Resorts: http://www.neemranahotels.com/

Planning Commission, Government of India: http://planningcommission.gov.in/

Swamimalai Heritage Hotel: http://www.sterlingswamimalai.net/

Tamil Nadu State Planning Commission: http://www.tn.gov.in/spc/

Tamil Nadu Tourism Development Corporation: http://www.tamilnadutourism.org/

Templenet: http://www.indiantemples.com/

The World Bank (pages on India): http://www.worldbank.org/in/

Tiruvallur District (Tamil Nadu): http://www.tiruvallur.tn.nic.in/

Traidcraft: http://www.traidcraft.co.uk/

Index

Italicized page numbers indicate illustrations.

MARY E. HANCOCK is Professor of Anthropology and History at the University of California, Santa Barbara.